D1238372

Official Catholic Teachings

social justice

Rev. Vincent P. Mainelli

Manufactured in the United States of America

Library of Congress Card Catalog Number: 78-53833
ISBN: 0-8434-0712-3
ISBN: 0-8434-0718-2 paper

The publisher gratefully acknowledges permission to quote from the following copyrighted publications.

MISSIONARY SOCIETY OF ST. PAUL THE APOSTLE IN THE STATE OF NEW YORK
MATER ET MAGISTRA, National Catholic Welfare Conference, ©1961.

NATIONAL CATHOLIC NEWS SERVICE
MESSAGE OF POPE PAUL VI ISSUED IN UNION WITH THE SYNOD OF BISHOPS, ©1974.

NATIONAL CONFERENCE OF CATHOLIC BISHOPS
JUSTICE IN THE WORLD, 1971.

OUR SUNDAY VISITOR
ADDRESS OF POPE PAUL VI TO THE CONGREGATION OF THE ITALIAN WOMEN'S CENTER; ADDRESS OF POPE PAUL VI FOR THE WORLD DAY OF PEACE, The Pope Speaks, Volume 22, Number 1, ©1977.

PONTIFICAL COMMISSION "JUSTITIA ET PAX"
THE CHURCH AND HUMAN RIGHTS, ©1975.

SODEPAX
MESSAGE OF POPE PAUL VI FOR THE WORLD DAY OF THE ENVIRONMENT, as reprinted in "Church Alert", Number 16, September-October, 1977.

UNITED STATES CATHOLIC CONFERENCE
ADDRESS OF POPE PAUL TO THE UNITED NATIONS GENERAL ASSEMBLY, 1965; *A CALL TO ACTION*, 1971; *EVANGELII NUNTIANDI*, 1975; *GAUDIUM ET SPES*, 1965; *HUMANAE VITAE*, 1968; *PACEM IN TERRIS*, 1963; *POPULORUM PROGRESSIO*, 1967.

WORKING FOR JUSTICE; ADDRESS OF POPE PAUL TO THE DIPLOMATIC CORPS; MESSAGE OF POPE PAUL VI CELEBRATING THE WORLD DAY OF PEACE, "Teachings of Paul VI", 1972.

MESSAGE OF POPE PAUL VI TO LEOPOLDO BENITES, "Teachings of Paul VI", 1973.

Table of Contents

Introduction

The documents of Catholic social teaching presented in this reference work begin with the encyclical *Mater et Magistra* of Pope John XXIII. The decision to begin here was based on the new spirit conveyed by this document and not to slight the earlier tradition dating back to Pope Leo XIII and his encyclical *Rerum Novarum* (1891).

"From Pope John XXIII onwards, previous teaching is certainly taken up and integrated, but the traditional pattern of problems nevertheless falls apart. The church adopts a different attitude to the world: that of a 'servant', it will soon be said, of the human community. An organized synthesis takes shape. It comprises a wider and more complex field than that of the earlier documents. The political sphere is given greater prominence, for on it largely depends the solution of economic, social, cultural, educational, food and other problems. There is even a tendency to proceed from international to national, from communal to individual, from world-wide to regional. And this approach brings up again in new form problems such as the right of association, wages and before long, that of natural resources."[1]

The "revolution" of Pope John included a range of new departures in Catholic social thought. Pope John looked at social, economic, and political problems through the other end of the telescope, that is to say, from the point of view of the Third World. Pope John presented The Church as forming part of the human community; the Church is at the service of human beings and their society. Pope John put his finger on the multiple new forms of human solidarity, and in this light examines in particular the problems of workers' participation, agriculture and underdevelopment. Pope John addresses not Christians alone, but all men of good will. Finally, Pope John studies the "signs of the times" and introduces a methodology which shows its fruitfulness in subsequent Church teaching.[2]

The documents included since Pope John XXIII include an amazing outpouring of new work from Pope Paul VI, the Second Vatican Council, International Synods of Bishops, and The Pontifical Commission on Justice and Peace.

Since this collection was first published in 1975, several other similar collections have been published. This new edition is warranted by new material, such as "On Evangelization in the Modern World" by Pope Paul VI, in which he clearly integrates Catholic social teaching with the overall mission of the Church, and the working paper," The Church and Human Rights," of the Pontifical Commission on Justice and Peace. The topic of human rights has become too important not to have this work available in the broader collection of teaching. The primary purpose of this edition remains the same, namely to be a handy reference work. Editorial changes have been made to enhance that end.

The recent publishing activity focused on Catholic social teaching is really a response to the new importance this teaching has achieved in the life of the Church. This new importance was strongly noted by the International Synod of Bishops in 1971, when they wrote what has become an often quoted and sometimes controversial paragraph.

"The uncertainty of history and the painful convergences in the ascending path of the human community direct us to sacred history; there God has revealed himself to and made known to us, as it is brought progressively to realization, his plan of liberation and salvation which is once and for all fulfilled in the Paschal Mystery of Christ. Action on behalf of justice and participation in the transformation of the world fully appear to us as a constitutive dimension of the preaching of the Gospel, or, in other words, of the Church's mission for the redemption of the human race and its liberation from every oppressive situation."[3]

The meaning of "as a constitutive dimension of the preaching of the gospel" is controversial, as The International Theological Commission notes.[4] "It seems to require a more exact interpretation according to which, limiting ourselves to the strict meaning of the words, it refers to an integral but non-essential part." The commission cites The Synod of 1974 for this interpretation.

Pope Paul VI in his Apostolic Exhortation of December 8, 1975, "On Evangelization in the Modern World," returns to this fundamental concept of the integral relationship of action on behalf of justice to the preaching of the Gospel.

"But evangelization would not be complete if it did not take account of the unceasing interplay of the Gospel and of man's concrete life, both personal and social. This is why evangelization involves an explicit message, adapted to the different situations constantly being realized, about the rights and duties of every human being, about family life without which personal growth and development is hardly possible, about life in society, about international life, peace, justice and development—a message especially energetic today about liberation."

"It is well known in what terms Bishops from all the continents spoke of this at the last Synod, especially the Bishops from the Third World, with a pastoral accent resonant with the voice of the millions of sons and daughters of the church who make up those peoples. Peoples, as we know, engaged with all their energy in the effort and struggle to overcome everything which condemns them to remain on the margin of life: famine, chronic disease, illiteracy, poverty, injustices in international relations and especially in commercial exchanges, situations of economic and cultural neo-colonialism sometimes as cruel as the old political colonialism. The Church, as the Bishops repeated, has the duty to proclaim the liberation of millions of human beings, many of whom are her own children—the duty of assisting the birth of this liberation, of giving witness to it, of ensuring that it is complete. This is not foreign to evangelization."[5]

Pope Paul VI makes clear the importance of action on behalf of justice to the mission of the Church, but he reaffirms, as does the International Theological Commission, that this must not obscure "the primacy of her spiritual vocation and refuses to replace the proclamation of the Kingdom by the proclamation of forms of human liberation; she even states that her contribution to liberation is incomplete if she neglects to proclaim salvation in Jesus Christ."[6]

The significance of this fundamental relationship is also stressed by the International Theological Commission," one compromises the fundamental relationships we have recalled above, if one stresses action for social and political liberation to such an extent as to push into the background the worship of God, prayer, the Eucharist and other sacraments, individual morality, the problem of the last things (death and eternal life), the harsh struggle against the powers of darkness. But, on the other hand, in situations of sin and injustice, it is necessary to proclaim and practice the truths of faith we have just stated."[7]

The Church is involved then and should be involved in action on behalf of justice, but using her own "evangelical means." What are these? They include encouraging large numbers of Christians to devote themselves to the liberation of others, providing these Christians with the inspiration of faith, motivation of fraternal love, and of a social teaching which "the true Christian cannot ignore and which he must make the foundation of his wisdom and of his experience in order to translate it concretely into forms of action, participation and commitment."[8]

We will not find all the practical solutions to social issues in these documents. Catholic social teaching does not pretend to give such short cuts to complex concrete issues. We will find the expression of faith to form our consciences and principles of justice to help us develop the wisdom to understand our own experience, so that we might act to create a more just society.

The Second Vatican Council clearly summarized the Christian attitude toward transforming the social order. "It is clear that men are not deterred by the Christian message from building up the world or impelled to neglect the welfare of their fellows, but that they are the more stringently bound to do these very things."[9]

There is an ongoing development in this Catholic social teaching and concepts such as dignity of the human person, the common good, workers' rights, and private property. These concepts will be used for illustrative purposes because of their timeliness.

Human Dignity

"There is a growing awareness of the exalted dignity proper to the human person, since he stands above all things, and his rights and duties are universal and inviolable."[10]

This statement of the Second Vatican Council had been preceded by the encyclical *Pacem in Terris,* of Pope John XXIII, where he extensively taught the dignity of the human person and expanded our awareness of a person's rights to education, to information, and to more political participation. In his writings Pope Paul VI places confidence in the United Nations to safeguard these rights. And most recently, the Pontifical Commission on Justice and Peace has published an extensive summary of teaching on this important subject, "The Church and Human Rights," which is contained in this text.

The Church is aware also that human dignity is under grave threat in many parts of the globe, and, while denouncing such sins against persons as racism and sexism, has strongly championed the equality of all persons.

"Since all men possess a rational soul and are created in God's likeness, since they have the same nature and origin, have been redeemed by Christ, and enjoy the same divine calling and destiny, the basic equality of all must receive increasingly greater recognition."

"True all men are not alike from the point of view of varying physical power and the diversity of intellectual and moral resources. Nevertheless, with respect to the fundamental rights of the person, every type of discrimination, whether social or cultural, whether based on sex, race, color, social conditions, language, or religion, is to be overcome and eradicated as contrary to God's intent."[11]

Common Good

With its emphasis on the dignity of the human person and human rights, Catholic social teaching does not present an individualistic ethic. "Man's social nature makes it evident that the progress of the human person and the advance of society itself hinge on each other. For the beginning, the subject and the goal of all social institutions is and must be the human person, which for its part and by its very nature stands completely in need of social life. This social life is not something added on to man. Hence, through his dealing with others, through reciprocal duties, and through fraternal dialogue, he develops all his gifts and is able to rise to his destiny."[12]

This emphasis on the dignity and rights of the human person is balanced in Catholic social thought by emphasis on human interdependence, which is growing all over the world and has taken on in our day an international dimension. This human interdependence is classically expressed by the concept of the common good.

"The common good, that is, the sum of those conditions of social life which allow social groups and their individual members relatively thorough and ready access to their own fulfillment."[13]

The common good is presented as a task to accomplish rather than a static order. The social conditions of the common good must work to the benefit of the human person. This social order requires constant improvement. Widespread changes in society will have to take place. Finally, this dynamic process must be directed by God's Spirit, Who renews the face of the earth, and by the Gospel, which raises the consciousness of believers to their God-given dignity.

The common good is given as a call to responsibility and active participation. Every social group must consider the needs and legitimate aspirations of other groups, and even of the general welfare of the entire human family. We are called to establish social institutions better able to respect the dignity of every human person.[14]

We can see the importance of these fundamental concepts of the dignity of the human person and the common good on the development of Catholic social teaching, if we study the economy, and workers' rights, and private property.

Workers' Rights

Pope John saw that one of the goals of economic enterprises was to build "a true human fellowship."

"Pope John XXIII re-emphasized this broader view of work relations, when in *Mater et Magistra,* he reaffirmed what Pius XI had said, namely, 'that work agreements [should] be tempered in certain respects with partnership arrangements, so that workers and officials become participants in ownership, or management, or share in some manner in profits.' Pope John developed this theme more fully in the same encyclical: 'Furthermore, as did our predecessors, we regard as justifiable the desire of employees to be partners in enterprises with which they are associated and wherein they work.' He admits this will vary from situation, but states emphatically: 'We do not doubt that employees should have an active part in the affairs of the enterprise wherein they work, whether these be private or public. But it is of the most importance that productive enterprises assume the character of a true human fellowship whose spirit suffuses the dealings, activities and standing of all its members.'

"This is no isolated theme in Catholic social teaching. Vatican II reemphasized it in its Pastoral Constitution on the Church in the Modern World: 'Therefore, taking account of the prerogatives of each—owner or employee, management or labor—and without doing harm to the necessary unity of management, the active sharing of all in the administration and profits of these enterprises in ways to be properly determined should be promoted.'

"Pope Paul VI broadened and contined the evolution of this view of economic development in his encyclical, *On the Development of Peoples.* He laid great stress on integral development, the good of every man and the whole man, as opposed to a narrow view that limits development to mere economic growth.

"Four years later, in the letter of 1971 to Cardinal Maurice Roy, that it popularly known as "A Call to Action," Pope Paul VI acknowledged that great progress had been made in the area of labor relations, especially the rights of labor unions, but he also felt that in this immense field much needs to be done. Further reflection, research, and experimentation must be actively pursued, unless one is to be late in meeting the legitimate aspirations of the workers—aspirations which are increasingly asserted according to their education and their consciousness of their dignity, and as the strength of their organizations increases."[15]

Property

The Church has defended since the earliest centuries the right of everyone to have a share of earthly goods. But in recent times she has fought to maintain this right against totalitarian states of the left and of the right.

More recent attention in view of the excesses of capitalism and of state ownership has focused on the common purpose of created things. The Second Vatican Council teaches that "God intended the earth and all that it contains for the use of every human being and people. Thus, as all men follow justice and unite in charity, created goods should abound for them on a reasonable basis. Whatever the forms of ownership may be, as adapted to the legitimate institutions of people according to diverse and changeable circumstances, attention must always be paid to the universal purpose for which created goods are meant. In using them, therefore, a man should regard his lawful possessions not merely as his own but also as common property in the sense that they should accrue to the benefit of not only himself but of others."[16]

The Council takes note of the situation in many parts of the world, where huge estates are owned by a few people, who often let vast acreages remain idle. Meanwhile, countless others are without land, adequate food, or work. In light of this situation, the Council states forcefully that "by its very nature, private property has a social quality deriving from the law of the communal purpose of earthly goods. If this social quality is overlooked, property often becomes an occasion of greed and of serious disturbances."[17]

In their analysis of property, the Fathers of the Council show the interplay of the themes of the rights of the person and the common good.

These examples of themes from the body of the Church's social teaching are used to illustrate the relatedness of the various documents and yet also point out the development of basic themes over the span of time since Pope John XXIII in particular. The documents must be treated as a whole and not as a repository of quotations with which to prove a point. The documents are presented here in their entirety and with substantial cross-indexing to further such a thoughtful process of study.

1 Schooyans, Rev. Michel, "Catholic Social Thought to 1966: An Historical Outline, *Church Alert*, November-December, 1977, p. 4.

2 Schooyans, *op. cit.*, p. 3.

3 Synod of Bishops, "Justice in The World," *U.S.C.C. Publications*, 1312 Mass. Ave., N.W., Washington, D.C., 1972, p. 34.

4 "Declaration on Human Development and Christian Salvation," International Theological Commission, *U.S.C.C. Publications*, 1312 Mass. Ave., N.W., Washington, D.C., 1977, p. 11.

5 Pope Paul VI, "On Evangelization in the Modern World," *U.S.C.C. Publications*, 1312 Mass. Ave., N.W., Washington, D.C., 1976, n. 29-30.

6 Pope Paul VI, *op. cit.*, n. 34.

7 International Theological Commission, *op. cit.*, pp. 12-13.

8 Pope Paul VI, *op. cit.*, n. 38.

9 "Pastoral Constitution on the Church in the Modern World," n. 34.

10 *Ibid.*, n. 26.

11 *Ibid.*, n. 29.

12 *Ibid.*, n. 25.

13 *Ibid.*, n. 26.

14 Aspects de doctrine sociale du magistere catholique: bien commun, muvements sociaux et syndicalisme selon Vatican II. Pro Manuscripto. Prospective, Brussels, December, 1976, GRO 116/77.

15 Mainelli, Rev. Vincent P., "Democracy in the Workplace," *America*, January 15, 1977, pp. 29-30.

16 "Pastoral Constitution on the Church in the Modern World," n. 69.

17 *Ibid.*, n. 71.

Subject Index

MATER ET MAGISTRA

Encyclical Letter of
Pope John XXIII
on Christianity and Social Progress
May 15, 1961

The Catholic Church has been established by Jesus Christ as MOTHER AND TEACHER of nations, so that all who in the course of centuries come to her loving embrace, may find salvation as well as the fullness of a more excellent life. To this Church, "the pillar and mainstay of the truth,"[1] her most holy Founder has entrusted the double task of begetting those whom she begets, guiding with maternal providence the life both of individuals and of peoples. The lofty dignity of this life, she has always held in the highest respect and guarded with watchful care.

2. For the teaching of Christ joins, as it were, earth with heaven, in that it embraces the whole man, namely, his soul and body, intellect and will, and bids him to lift up his mind from the changing conditions of human existence to that heavenly country where he will one day enjoy unending happiness and peace. 2

3. Hence, although Holy Church has the special task of sanctifying souls and of making them sharers of heavenly blessings, she is also solicitious for the requirements of men in their daily lives, not merely those relating to food and sustenance, but also to their comfort and advancement in various kinds of goods and in varying circumstances of time. 3

4. Realizing all this, Holy Church implements the commands of her Founder, Christ, who refers primarily to man's eternal salvation when He says, "I am the Way, and 4

the Truth, and the Life"[2] and elsewhere "I am the Light of the World."[3] On other occasions, however, seeing the hungry crowd, He was moved to exclaim sorrowfully, "I have compassion on the crowd,"[4] thereby indicating that He was also concerned about the earthly needs of mankind. The divine Redeemer shows this care not only by His words but also by the actions of His life, as when, to alleviate the hunger of the crowds, He more than once miraculously multiplied bread.

5 5. By this bread, given for the nourishment of the body, He wished to foreshadow that heavenly food of the soul which He was to give to men on *the day before He suffered.*

6 6. It is no wonder, then, that the Catholic Church, instructed by Christ and fulfilling His commands, has for two thousand years, from the ministry of the early deacons to the present time, tenaciously held aloft the torch of charity not only by her teaching but also by her widespread example—the charity which, by combining in a fitting manner the precepts and the practice of mutual love, puts into effect in a wonderful way this twofold commandment of *giving,* wherein is contained the full social teaching and action of the Church.

7 7. By far the most notable evidence of this social teaching and action, which the Church has set forth through the centuries, undoubtedly is the very distinguished Encyclical Letter *Rerum Novarum,*[5] issued seventy years ago by our predecessor of immortal memory, Leo XIII. Therein he put forward teachings whereby the question of the workers' condition would be resolved in conformity with Christian principles.

8 8. Seldom have the admonitions of a Pontiff been received with such universal approbation, as was that Encyclical of Leo XIII, rivaled by few in the depth and scope of its reasoning and in the forcefulness of its expression. Indeed, the norms and recommendations contained therein were so momentous that their memory will never fall into oblivion. As a result, the action of the Catholic Church became more widely known. For its Supreme Pastor, making his own the

problems of weak and harassed men, their complaints and aspirations, had devoted himself especially to the defense and restoration of their rights.

9. Even today, in spite of the long lapse of time since the Letter was published, much of its effectiveness is still evident. It is indeed evident in the documents of the Popes who succeeded Leo XIII, and who, when they discussed economic and social affairs, have always borrowed something from it, either to clarify its application or to stimulate further activity on the part of Catholics. The efficacy of the document also is evident in the laws and institutions of many nations. Thus does it become abundantly clear that the solidly grounded principles, the norms of action, and the paternal admonitions found in the masterly Letter of our predecessor, even today retain their original worth. Moreover, from it can be drawn new and vital criteria, whereby men may judge the nature and extent of the social question, and determine what their responsibilities are in this regard. 9

10. The teachings addressed to mankind by this most wise Pontiff undoubtedly shone with greater brilliance because they were published when innumerable difficulties obscured the issue. On the one hand, the economic and political situation was in process of radical change; on the other, numerous clashes were flaring up and civil strife had been provoked. 10

11. As is generally known, in those days an opinion widely prevailed and was commonly put into practice, according to which, in economic matters, everything was to be attributed to inescapable, natural forces. Hence, it was held that no connection existed between economic and moral laws. Wherefore, those engaged in economic activity need look no further than their own gain. Consequently, mutual relations between economic agents could be left to the play of free and unregulated competition. Interest on capital, prices of goods and services, profits and wages, were to be determined purely mechanically by the laws of the marketplace. Every precaution was to be taken lest the civil authority intervene in any way in economic affairs. During that era, trade unions, according to circumstances in different countries, 11

were sometimes forbidden, sometimes tolerated, sometimes recognized in private law.

12 12. Thus, at that time, not only was the proud rule of the stronger regarded as legitimate, so far as economic affairs were concerned, but it also prevailed in concrete relations between men. Accordingly, the order of economic affiars was, in general, radically disturbed.

13 13. While a few accumulated excessive riches, large masses of workingmen daily labored in very acute need. Indeed, wages were insufficient for the necessities of life, and sometimes were at starvation level. For the most part, workers had to find employment under conditions wherein there were dangers to health, moral integrity, and religious faith. Especially inhuman were the working conditions to which children and women wre subjected. The spectre of unemployment was ever present, and the family was exposed to a process of disorganization.

14 14. As a natural consequence, workers, indignant at their lot, decided that this state of affairs must be publicly protested. This explains why, among the working classes, extremist theories that propounded remedies worse than the evil to be cured, found widespread favor.

15 15. Such being the trend of the times, Leo XIII, in his Encyclical Letter *Rerum Novarum,* proclaimed a social message based on the requirements of human nature itself and conforming to the precepts of the Gospel and reason. We recall it as a message which, despite some expected opposition, evoked response on all sides and aroused widespread enthusiasm. However, this was not the first time the Apostolic See, in regard to the affairs of this life, undertook the defense of the needy, since that same predecessor of happy memory, Leo XIII, published other documents which to some extent paved the way for the document mentioned above. But this Letter so effected for the first time an organization of principles, and, as it were, set forth singlemindedly a future course of action, that we may regard it as a summary of Catholic teaching, so far as economic and social matters are concerned.

16. It can be said with considerable assurance that such proved to be the situation. For while some, confronted with the social question, unashamedly attacked the Church as if she did nothing except preach resignation to the poor and exhort the rich to generosity, Leo XIII did not hesitate to proclaim and defend quite openly the sacred rights of workers. In beginning his exposition of the principles and norms of the Church in social matters, he frankly stated: "We approach the subject with confidence and in the exercise of the rights that belong to us. For no satisfactory solution of this question will ever be found without the assistance of religion and the Church."[6] 16

17. Venerable Brothers, you are quite familiar with those basic principles expounded both clearly and authoritatively by the illustrious Pontiff, according to which human society should be renewed in so far as economic and social matters are concerned. 17

18. He first and foremost stated that work, inasmuch as it is an expression of the human person, can by no means be regarded as a mere commodity. For the great majority of mankind, work is the only source from which the means of livelihood are drawn. Hence, its remuneration is not to be thought of in terms of merchandise, but rather according to the laws of justice and equity. Unless this is done, justice is violated in labor agreements, even though they are entered into freely on both sides. 18

19. Private property, including that of productive goods, is a natural right possessed by all, which the State may by no means suppress. However, as there is from nature a social aspect to private property, he who uses his right in this regard must take into account not merely his own welfare but that of others as well. 19

20. The State, whose purpose is the realization of the common good in the temporal order, can by no means disregard the economic activity of its citizens. Indeed, it should be present to promote in a suitable manner the production of a sufficient supply of material goods, "the use of which is necessary for the practice of virtue."[7] Moreover, it should 20

safeguard the rights of all citizens, but especially the weaker, such as workers, women, and children. Nor may the State ever neglect its duty to contribute actively to the betterment of the living conditions of workers.

21 21. In addition, the State should see to it that labor agreements are entered into according to the norms of justice and equity, and that in the environment of work the dignity of the human being is not violated either in body or spirit. On this point, Leo XIII's Letter delineated the broad principles regarding a just and proper human existence. These principles, modern States have adopted in one way or another in their social legislation, and they have—as our predecessor of immortal memory, Pius XI declared, in his Encyclical Letter, *Quadragesimo Anno*[8]—contributed much to the establishment and promotion of that new section of legal science known as *labor law.*

22 22. In the same Letter, moreover, there is affirmed the natural right to enter corporately into associations, whether these be composed of workers only or of workers and management; and also the right to adopt that organizational structure judged more suitable to meet their professional needs. And workers themselves have the right to act freely and on their own initiative within the above-mentioned associations, without hindrance and as their needs dictate.

23 23. Workers and employers should regulate their mutual relations in a spirit of human solidarity and in accordance with the bond of Christian brotherhood. For the unregulated competition which so-called *liberals* espouse, or the class struggle in the *Marxist sense*, are utterly opposed to Christian teaching and also in the very nature of man.

24 24. These, Venerable Brothers, are the fundamental principles on which a healthy socio-economic order can be built.

25 25. It is not surprising, therefore, that outstanding Catholic men inspired by these appeals began many activities in order to put these principles to action. Nor were there lacking other men of good will in various parts of the world who, impelled by the needs of human nature, followed a similar course.

26. For these reasons the Encyclical is known even to the present day as the *Magna Charta*[9] for the reconstruction of the economic and social order. 26

27. Furthermore, after a lapse of forty years since publication of that outstanding corpus, as it were, of directives, our predecessor of happy memory, Pius XI, in his turn decided to publish the Encyclical Letter *Quadragesimo Anno.*[10] 27

28. In it the Supreme Pontiff first of all confirmed the right and duty of the Catholic Church to make its special contribution in resolving the more serious problems of society which call for the full cooperation of all. Then he reaffirmed those principles and directives of Leo XIII's Letter related to the conditions of the times. Finally, he took this occasion not only to clarify certain points of doctrine on which even Catholics were in doubt, but he also showed how the principles and directives themselves regarding social affairs should be adapted to the changing times. 28

29. For at that time, some were in doubt as to what should be the judgment of Catholics regarding private property, the wage system, and more especially, a type of moderate socialism. 29

30. Concerning private property, our predecessor reaffirmed its natural-law character. Furthermore, he set forth clearly and emphasized the social character and function of private ownership. 30

31. Turning to the wage system, after having rejected the view that would declare it unjust by its very nature, the Pontiff criticized the inhuman and unjust forms under which it was sometimes found. Moreover, he carefully indicated what norms and conditions were to be observed, lest the wage system stray from justice and equity. 31

32. In this connection, it is today advisable as our predecessor clearly pointed out, that work agreements be tempered in certain respects with partnership arrangements, so that "workers and officials become participants in ownership, or management, or share in some manner in profits."[11] 32

33. Of great theoretical and practical importance is the affirmation of Pius XI that "if the social and individual char- 33

acter of labor be overlooked, the efficiency of men can neither be justly appraised nor equitably recompensed."[12] Accordingly, in determining wages, justice definitely requires that, in addition to the needs of the individual worker and his family, regard be had on the one hand for conditions within the productive enterprises wherein the workers labor; on the other hand, for the "public economic good"[13] in general.

34 34. Furthermore, the Supreme Bishop emphasized that the views of *communists,* as they are called, and of Christians are radically opposed. Nor may Catholics, in any way, give approbation to the teachings of *socialists* who seemingly profess more moderate views. From their basic outlook it follows that, inasmuch as the order of social life is confined to time, it is directed solely to temporal welfare; that since the social relationships of men pertain merely to the production of goods, human liberty is excessively restricted and the true concept of social authority is overlooked.

35 35. Pius XI was not unaware that, in the forty years that had elapsed since the appearance of Leo XIII's Letter, historical conditions had profoundly altered. In fact, unrestricted competition, because of its own inherent tendencies, had ended by almost destroying itself. It had caused a great accumulation of wealth and a corresponding concentration of power in the hands of a few who "are frequently not the owners, but only the trustees and directors of invested funds, who administer them at their good pleasure."[14]

36 36. Therefore, as the Supreme Pontiff noted, "economic power has been substituted for the free marketplace. Unbridled ambition for domination has replaced desire for gain; the whole economy has become harsh, cruel, and relentless in frightful measure."[15] Thus it happened that even public authorities were serving the interests of more wealthy men and that concentrations of wealth, to some extent, achieved power over all peoples.

37 37. In opposition to this trend, the Supreme Pontiff laid down the following fundamental principles: the organization of economic affairs must be conformable to practical morality; the interests of individuals or of societies especially must

be harmonized with the requirements of the common good. This evidently requires, as the teaching of our predecessor indicated, the orderly reorganization of society with smaller professional and economic groups existing in their own right, and not prescribed by public authority. In the next place, civil authority should reassume its function and not overlook any of the community's interests. Finally, on a world-wide scale, governments should seek the economic good of all peoples.

38. The two fundamental points that especially characterize the Encyclical of Pius XI are these: First, one may not take as the ultimate criteria in economic life the interests of individuals or organized groups, nor unregulated competition, nor excessive power on the part of the wealthy, nor the vain honor of the nation or its desire for domination, nor anything of this sort. 38

39. Rather, it is necessary that economic undertakings be governed by justice and charity as the principal laws of social life. 39

40. The second point that we consider to be basic to the Letter of Pius XI is that both within individual countries and among nations there be established a juridical order, with appropriate public and private institutions, inspired by social justice, so that those who are involved in economic activities are enabled to carry out their tasks in conformity with the common good. 40

41. In specifying social rights and obligations, our predecessor of immortal memory, Pius XII, made a significant contribution, when on the feast of Pentecost, June 1, 1941, he broadcast to the world community a message: "in order to call to the attention of the Catholic world the memory of an event worthy of being written in letters of gold on the Calendar of the Church: namely, the fiftieth anniversary of the publication of the epoch-making Encyclical of Leo XIII, *Rerum Navarum*."[16] He broadcast this message, moreover, "to render special thanks to Almighty God that His Vicar on earth, in a Letter such as this, gave to the Church so great a gift, and also to render praise to the eternal Spirit that 41

through this same Letter, He enkindled a fire calculated to rouse the whole human race to new and better effort."[17]

42 42. In the message, the great Pontiff claimed for the Church "the indisputable competence" to "decide whether the bases of a given social system are in accord with the unchangeable order which God our Creator and Redeemer has fixed both in the natural law and revelation."[18] He noted that the Letter of Leo XIII is of permanent value and has rich and abiding usefulness. He takes the occasion "to explain in greater detail what the Catholic Church teaches regarding the three principal issues of social life in economic affairs, which are mutually related and connected one with the other, and thus interdependent: namely, the use of material goods, labor, and the family."[19]

43 43. Concerning the use of material goods, our predecessor declared that the right of every man to use them for his own sustenance is prior to all other rights in economic life, and hence is prior even to the right of private ownership. It is certain, however, as our predecessor noted, that the right of private property is from the natural law itself. Nevertheless, it is the will of God the Creator that this right to own property should in no wise obstruct the flow of "material goods created by God to meet the needs of all men, to all equitably, as justice and charity require."[20]

44 44. As regards labor, Pius XII repeating what appeared in Leo XIII's Letter, declared it to be both a duty and a right of every human being. Consequently, it is in the first place the responsibility of men themselves to regulate mutual labor relations. Only in the event that the interested parties are unwilling or unable to fulfill their functions, does it "devolve upon the State to intervene and to assign labor equitably, safeguarding the standards and aims that the good properly understood demands."[21]

45 45. Turning to the family, the Supreme Pontiff stresses that private ownership of material goods helps to safeguard and develop family life. Such goods are an apt means "to secure for the father of a family the healthy liberty he needs in order to fulfill the duties assigned him by the Creator, regarding the physical, spiritual, and religious wel-

fare of the family."[22] From this arises the right of the family to migrate. Accordingly, our predecessor reminds governments, both those permitting emigration and those accepting immigrants, that "they never permit anything whereby mutual and sincere understanding between States is diminished or destroyed."[23] If this be mutually accomplished, it will come to pass that benefits are equalized and diffused widely among peoples, as the supply of goods and the arts and crafts are increased and fostered.

46. But just as contemporary circumstances seemed to Pius XII quite dissimilar from those of the earlier period, so they have changed greatly over the past twenty years. This can be seen not only in the internal situation of each individual country, but also in the mutual relations of countries. 46

47. In the fields of science, technology, and economics, these developments are especially worthy of note: the discovery of atomic energy, employed first for military purposes and later increasingly for peaceful ends; the almost limitless possibilities opened up by chemistry in synthetic products; the growth of automation in the sectors of industry and services; the modernization of agriculture; the nearly complete conquest, especially through radio and television, of the distance separating peoples; the greatly increased speed of all manner of transportation; the initial conquests of outer space. 47

48. Turning to the social field, the following contemporary trends are evident: development of systems for social insurance; the introduction of social security systems in some more affluent countries; greater awareness among workers, as members of unions, of the principal issues in economic and social life; a progressive improvement of basic education; wider diffusion among the classes; greater interest than heretofore in world affairs on the part of those with average education. Meanwhile, if one considers the social and economic advances made in a growing number of countries, he will quickly discern increasingly pronounced imbalances: first, between agriculture on the one hand and industry and the services on the other; be- 48

tween the more and the less developed regions within countries; and, finally, on a world-wide scale, between countries with differing economic resources and development.

49 49. Turning now to political affairs, it is evident that there, too, a number of innovations have occurred. Today, in many communities, citizens from almost all social strata participate in public life. Public authorities intervene more and more in economic and soical affairs. The peoples of Asia and Africa, having set aside colonial systems, now govern themselves according to their own laws and institutions. As the mutual relationships of peoples increase, they become daily more dependent one upon the other. Throughout the world, assemblies and councils have become more common, which, being supranational in character, take into account the interests of all peoples. Such bodies are concerned with economic life, or with social affairs, or with culture and education, or, finally, with the mutual relationships of peoples.

50 50. Now, reflecting on all these things, we feel it our duty to keep alive the torch lighted by our great predecessors and to exhort all to draw from their writings light and inspiration, if they wish to resolve the social question in ways more in accord with the needs of the present time. Therefore, we are issuing this present Letter not merely to commemorate appropriately the Encyclical Letter of Leo XIII, but also, in the light of changed conditions, both to confirm and explain more fully what our predecessors taught, and to set forth the Church's teaching regarding the new and serious problems of our day.

51 51. At the outset it should be affirmed that in economic affairs first place is to be given to the private initiative of individual men who, either working by themselves, or with others in one fashion or another, pursue their common interests.

52 52. But in this matter, for reasons pointed out by our predecessors, it is necessary that public authorities take active interest, the better to increase output of goods and to further social progress for the benefit of all citizens.

53. This intervention of public authorities that encourages, stimulates, regulates, supplements, and complements, is based on the *principle of subsidiarity*[24] as set forth by Pius XI in his Encyclical *Quadragesimo Anno:* "It is a fundamental principle of social philosophy, fixed and unchangeable, that one should not withdraw from individuals and commit to the community what they can accomplish by their own enterprise and industry. So, too, it is an injustice and at the same time a grave evil and a disturbance of right order, to transfer to the larger and higher collectivity functions which can be performed and provided for by lesser and subordinate bodies. Inasmuch as every social activity should, by its very nature, prove a help to members of the body social, it should, by its very nature, prove a help to members of the body social, it should never destroy or absorb them."[25] 53

54. Indeed, as is easily perceived, recent developments of science and technology provide additional reasons why, to a greater extent than heretofore, it is within the power of public authorities to reduce imbalances, whether these be between various sectors of economic life, or between different regions of the same nation, or even between different peoples of the world as a whole. These same developments make it possible to keep fluctuations in the economy within bounds, and to provide effective measures for avoiding mass unemployment. Consequently, it is requested again and again of public authorities responsible for the common good, that they intervene in a wide variety of economic affairs, and that, in a more extensive and organized way than heretofore, they adapt institutions, tasks, means, and procedures to this end. 54

55. Nevertheless, it remains true that precautionary activities of public authorities in the economic field, although widespread and penetrating, should be such that they not only avoid restricting the freedom of private citizens, but also increase it, so long as the basic rights of each individual person are preserved inviolate. Included among these is the right and duty of each individual normally to provide the necessities of life for himself and his dependents. This implies that whatever be the economic system, it allow and 55

facilitate for every individual the opportunity to engage in productive activity.

56 56. Furthermore, the course of events thus far makes it clear that there cannot be a prosperous and well-ordered society unless both private citizens and public authorities work together in economic affairs. Their activity should be characterized by mutual and amicable efforts, so that the roles assigned to each fit in with requirements of the common good, as changing times and customs suggest.

57 57. Experience, in fact, shows that where private initiative of individuals is lacking, political tyranny prevails. Moreover, much stagnation occurs in various sectors of the economy, and hence all sorts of consumer goods and services, closely connected with needs of the body and more especially of the spirit, are in short supply. Beyond doubt, the attainment of each goods and services provides remarkable opportunity and stimulus for individuals to exercise initiative and industry.

58 58. Where, on the other hand, appropriate activity of the State is lacking or defective, commonwealths are apt to experience incurable disorders, and there occurs exploitation of the weak by the unscrupulous strong, who flourish, unfortunately, like cockle among the wheat, in all times and places.

59 59. One of the principal characteristics of our time is the multiplication of social relationships, that is, a daily more complex interdependence of citizens, introducing into their lives and activities many and varied forms of association, recognized for the most part in private and even in public law. This tendency seemingly stems from a number of factors operative in the present era, among which are technical and scientific progress, greater productive efficiency, and a higher standard of living among citizens.

60 60. These developments in social living are at once both a symptom and a cause of the growing intervention of public authorities in matters which, since they pertain to the more intimate aspects of personal life, are of serious moment and not without danger. Such, for example, are the care of health, the instruction and education of youth, the choice of

a personal career, the ways and means of rehabilitating or assisting those handicapped mentally or physically. But this trend also indicates and in part follows from that human and natural inclination, scarcely resistible, whereby men are impelled voluntarily to enter into association in order to attain objectives which each one desires, but which exceed the capacity of single individuals. This tendency has given rise, especially in recent years, to organizations and institutes on both national and international levels, which relate to economic and social goals, to cultural and recreational activities, to athletics, to various professions, and to political affairs.

61. Such an advance in social relationships definitely brings numerous services and advantages. It makes possible, in fact, the satisfaction of many personal rights, especially those of economic and social life; these relate, for example, to the minimum necessities of human life, to health services, to the broadening and deepening of elementary education, to a more fitting training in skills, to housing, to labor, to suitable leisure and recreation. In addition, through the ever more perfect organization of modern means for the diffusion of thought—press, cinema, radio, television—individuals are enabled to take part in human events on a world-wide scale. 61

62. But as these various forms of association are multiplied and daily extended, it also happens that in many areas of activity, rules and laws controlling and determining relationships of citizens are multiplied. As a consequence, opportunity for free action by individuals is restricted within narrower limits. Methods are often used, procedures are adopted, and such an atmosphere develops wherein it becomes difficult for one to make decisions independently of outside influences, to do anything on his own initiative, to carry out in a fitting way his rights and duties, and to fully develop and perfect his personality. Will men perhaps, then become automatons, and cease to be personally responsible, as these social relationships multiply more and more? It is a question which must be answered negatively. 62

63. Actually, increased complexity of social life by no means results from a blind drive of natural forces. Indeed, 63

as stated above, it is the creation of free men who are so disposed to act by nature as to be responsible for what they do. They must, of course, recognize the laws of human progress and the development of economic life and take these into account. Furthermore, men are not altogether free of their milieu.

64 64. Accordingly, advances in social organization can and should be so brought about that maximum advantages accrue to citizens while at the same time disadvantages are averted or at least minimized.

65 65. That these desired objectives be more readily obtained, it is necessary that public authorities have a correct understanding of the common good. This embraces the sum total of those conditions of social living, whereby men are enabled more fully and more readily to achieve their own perfection. Hence, we regard it as necessary that the various intermediary bodies and the numerous social undertakings wherein an expanded social structure primarily finds expression, be ruled by their own laws, and as the common good itself progresses, pursue this objective in a spirit of sincere concord among themselves. Nor is it less necessary that the above mentioned groups present the form and substance of a true community. This they will do, only if individual members are considered and treated as persons, and are encouraged to participate in the affairs of the group.

66 66. Accordingly, as relationships multiply between men, binding them more closely together, commonwealths will more readily and appropriately order their affairs to the extent these two factors are kept in balance: (1) the freedom of individual citizens and groups of citizens to act autonomously, while cooperating one with the other; (2) the activity of the State whereby the undertakings of private individuals and groups are suitably regulated and fostered.

67 67. Now if social systems are organized in accordance with the above norms and moral laws, their extension does not necessarily mean that individual citizens will be gravely discriminated against or excessively burdened. Rather, we can hope that this will enable man not only to develop and perfect his natural talents, but also will lead to an appro-

priate structuring of the human community. Such a structure, as our predecessor of happy memory, Pius XI, warned in his Encyclical Letter *Quadragessimo Anno,*[26] is absolutely necessary for the adequate fulfillment of the rights and duties of social life.

68. Our heart is filled with profound sadness when we observe, as it were, with our own eyes a wretched spectacle indeed—great masses of workers who, in not a few nations, and even in whole continents, receive too small a return from their labor. Hence, they and their families must live in conditions completely out of accord with human dignity. This can be traced, for example, to the fact that in these regions, modern industrial techniques either have only recently been introduced or have made less than satisfactory progress. 68

69. It happens in some of these nations that, as compared with the extreme need of the majority, the wealth and conspicuous consumption of a few stand out, and are in open and bold contrast with the lot of the needy. It happens in other places that excessive burdens are placed upon men in order that the commonwealth may achieve within a brief span, an increase of wealth such as can by no means be achieved without violating the laws of justice and equity. Finally, it happens elsewhere that a disproportionate share of the revenue goes toward the building up of national prestige, and that large sums of money are devoted to armaments. 69

70. Moreover, in the economically developed countries, it frequently happens that great, or sometimes very great, remuneration is had for the performance of some task of lesser importance or doubtful utility. Meanwhile, the diligent and profitable work that whole classes of decent and hard-working citizens perform, receives too low a payment and one insufficient for the necessities of life, or else, one that does not correspond to the contribution made to the community, or to the revenues of the undertakings in which they are engaged, or to the national income. 70

71. Wherefore, we judge it to be our duty to reaffirm once again that just as remuneration for work cannot be left en- 71

tirely to unregulated competition, neither may it be decided arbitrarily at the will of the more powerful. Rather, in this matter, the norms of justice and equity should be strictly observed. This requires that workers receive a wage sufficient to lead a life worthy of man and to fulfill family responsibilities properly. But in determining what constitutes an appropriate wage, the following must necessarily be taken into account: first of all, the contribution of individuals to the economic effort; the economic state of the enterprises within which they work; the requirements of each community, especially as regards over-all employment; finally, what concerns the common good of all peoples, namely, of the various States associated among themselves, but differing in character and extent.

72 72. It is clear that the standards of judgment set forth above are binding always and everywhere. However, the measure in which they are to be applied in concrete cases cannot be established unless account is taken of the resources at hand. These resources can and in fact do vary in quantity and quality among different peoples, and may even change within the same country with the passing of time.

73 73. Whereas in our era the economics of various countries are evolving very rapidly, more especially since the last great war, we take this opportunity to draw the attention of all to a strict demand of social justice, which explicitly requires that, with the growth of the economy, there occur a corresponding social development. Thus, all classes of citizens will benefit equitably from an increase in national wealth. Toward this end vigilance should be exercised and effective steps taken that class differences arising from disparity of wealth not be increased, but lessened so far as possible.

74 74. "National wealth"—as our predecessor of happy memory, Pius XII, rightfully observed—"inasmuch as it is produced by the common efforts of the citizenry, has no other purpose than to secure without interruption those material conditions in which individuals are enabled to lead a full and perfect life. Where this is consistently the case,

then such a people is to be judged truly rich. For the system whereby both the common prosperity is achieved and individuals exercise their right to use material goods, conforms fully to norms laid down by God the Creator."[27] From this it follows that the economic prosperity of any people is to be assessed not so much from the sum total of goods and wealth possessed as from the distribution of goods according to norms of justice, so that everyone in the community can develop and perfect himself. For this, after all, is the end toward which all economic activity of a community is by nature ordered.

75. We must here call attention to the fact that in many countries today, the economic system is such that large and medium size productive enterprises achieve rapid growth precisely because they finance replacement and plant expansion from their own revenues. Where this is the case, we believe that such companies should grant to workers some share in the enterprise, especially where they are paid no more than the minimum wage. 75

76. In this matter, the principle laid down by our predecessor of happy memory, Pius XI, in the Encyclical Letter *Quadragesimo Anno,* should be borne in mind: "It is totally false to ascribe to a single factor of production what is in fact produced by joint activity; and it is completely unjust for one factor to arrogate to itself what is produced, ignoring what has been contributed by other factors."[28] 76

77. The demands of justice referred to, can be met in various ways, as experience shows. Not to mention other ways, it is very desirable that workers gradually acquire some share in the enterprise by such methods as seem more appropriate. For today, more than in the times of our predecessor, "every effort should be made that at least in the future, only an equitable share of the fruits of production accumulate in the hands of the wealthy, and a sufficient and ample portion go to the workingmen."[29] 77

78. But we should remember that adjustments between remuneration for work and revenues are to be brought about in conformity with the requirements of the common good, both of one's own community and of the entire human family. 78

79 79. Considering the common good on the national level, the following points are relevant and should not be overlooked: to provide employment for as many workers as possible; to take care lest privileged groups arise even among the workers themselves; to maintain a balance between wages and prices; to make accessible the goods and services for a better life to as many persons as possible; either to eliminate or to keep within bounds the inequalities that exist between different sectors of the economy—that is, between agriculture, industry and services; to balance properly any increases in output with advances in services provided to citizens, especially by public authority; to adjust, as far as possible, the means of production to the progress of science and technology; finally, to ensure that the advantages of a more humane way of existence not merely subserve the present generation but have regard for future generations as well.

80 80. As regards the common good of human society as a whole, the following conditions, should be fulfilled: that the competitive striving of peoples to increase output be free of bad faith; that harmony in economic affairs and a friendly and beneficial cooperation be fostered; and, finally, that effective aid be given in developing the economically underdeveloped nations.

81 81. It is evident from what has been said that these demands of the common good, on both the national and world levels, should be borne in mind, when there is question of determining the share of earnings assigned to those responsible for directing the productive enterprise, or as interest and dividends to those who have invested capital.

82 82. Justice is to be observed not merely in the distribution of wealth, but also in regard to the conditions under which men engage in productive activity. There is, in fact, an innate need of human nature requiring that men engaged in productive activity have an opportunity to assume responsibility and to perfect themselves by their efforts.

83 83. Consequently, if the organization and structure of economic life be such that the human dignity of workers is com-

promised, or their sense of responsibility is weakened, or their freedom of action is removed, then we judge such an economic order to be unjust, even though it produces a vast amount of goods, whose distribution conforms to the norms of justice and equity.

84. Nor is it possible in economic affairs to determine in one formula all the measures that are more conformable to the dignity of man, or are more suitable in developing in him a sense of responsibility. Nevertheless, our predecessor of happy memory, Pius XII, appropriately laid down certain norms of action: "Small and medium-sized holdings in agriculture, in the arts and crafts, in commerce and industry, should be safeguarded and fostered. Such enterprises should join together in mutual-aid societies in order that the services and benefits of large-scale enterprises will be available to them. So far as these larger enterprises are concerned, work agreements should in some way be modified by partnership arrangements."[30] 84

85. Wherefore, conformably to requirements of the common good and the state of technology, artisan and farm enterprises of family type should be safeguarded and fostered, as should also cooperatives that aim to complement and perfect such enterprises. 85

86. We shall return shortly to the subject of farm enterprises. Here, we think it appropriate to say something about artisan enterprises and cooperative associations. 86

87. Above all, it must be emphasized that enterprises and bodies of this sort, in order that they may survive and flourish, should be continuously adapted—both in their productive structure and in their operating methods—to new conditions of the times. These new conditions constantly arise from advances in science and technology, or from changing consumer needs and preferences. It is especially appropriate that all this be done by the craftsmen themselves and by the associates in the cooperatives. 87

88. Hence, it is most fitting not only that both these groups be suitably formed in technical and in spiritual and intellectual matters, but also that they be joined together professionally. Nor is it less fitting tht the State make spe- 88

cial provision for them in regard to instruction, taxes, credit facilities, social security and insurance.

89 89. Moreover, the measures taken by the State on behalf of the craftsmen and members of cooperatives are also justified by the fact that these two categories of citizens are producers of genuine wealth, and contribute to the advance of civilization.

90 90. Accordingly, we paternally exhort our beloved sons, craftsmen and members of cooperatives throughout the world, that they fully realize the dignity of their role in society, since, by their work, the senses of responsibility and spirit of mutual aid can be daily more intensified among the citizenry, and the desire to work with dedication and originality be kept alive.

91 91. Furthermore, as did our predecessors, we regard as justifiable the desire of employees to be partners in enterprises with which they are assoicated and wherein they work. We do not think it possible, however, to decide with certain and explicit norms the manner and degree of such partnership, since this must be determined according to the state of the individual productive enterprises. For the situation is not everywhere the same, and, in fact, it can change suddenly within one and the same enterprise. Nevertheless, we do not doubt that employees should have an active part in the affairs of the enterprise wherein they work, whether these be private or public. But it is of the utmost importance that productive enterprises assume the character of a true human fellowhsip whose spirit suffuses the dealings, activities, and standing of all its members.

92 92. This requires that mutual relations between employers and directors on the one hand and the employees of the enterprise on the other, be marked by mutual respect, esteem, and good will. It also demands that all collaborate sincerely and harmoniously in their joint undertaking, and that they perform their work not merely with the objective of deriving an income, but also of carrying out the role assigned them and of performing a service that results in benefit to others. This means that the workers may have a say in, and may make a contribution toward, the efficient

running and development of the enterprise. Thus, our predecessor of happy memory, Pius XII, clearly indicated: "The economic and social functions which everyone aspires to fulfill, require that efforts of individuals be not wholly subjected to the will of others."[31] Beyond doubt, an enterprise truly in accord with human dignity should safeguard the necessary and efficient unity of administration. But it by no means follows that those who work daily in such an enterprise are to be considered merely as servants, whose sole function is to execute orders silently, and who are not allowed to interject their desires and interests, but must conduct themselves as idle standbys when it comes to assignment and direction of their tasks.

93. Finally, attention is drawn to the fact that the greater amount of responsibility desired today by workers in productive enterprises, not merely accords with the nature of man, but also is in conformity with historical developments in the economic, social, and political fields. 93

94. Unfortunately, in our day, there occur in economic and social affairs many imbalances that militate against justice and humanity. Meanwhile, throughout all of economic life, errors are spread that seriously impair its operation, purposes, organization, and the fulfillment of responsibilities. Nevertheless, it is an undeniable fact that the more recent productive systems, thanks to the impulse deriving from advances in technology and science, are becoming more modern and efficient, and are expanding at a faster rate than in the past. This demands of workers greater abilities and professional qualifications. Accordingly, workers should be provided with additional aids and time to achieve a suitable and more rounded formation, and to carry out more fittingly their duties as regards studies, morals, and religion. 94

95. Thus it happens that in our day youths can be alloted additional years to acquire a basic education and necessary skills. 95

96. Now if these things be done, a situation will emerge wherein workers are enabled to assume greater responsibilities even within their own enterprises. As regards the commonwealth as such, it is of great importance that all ranks 96

of citizens feel themselves daily more obligated to safeguard the common good.

97 97. Now, as is evident to all, in our day associations of workers have become widespread, and for the most part have been given legal status within individual countries and even across national boundaries. These bodies no longer recruit workers for purposes of strife, but rather for pursuing a common aim. And this is achieved especially by collective bargaining between associations of workers and those of management. But it should be emphasized how necessary, or at least very appropriate, it is to give workers an opportunity to exert influence outside the limits of the individual productive unit, and indeed within all ranks of the commonwealth.

98 98. The reason is that individual productive units, whatever their size, efficiency, or importance within the commonwealth, are closely connected with the over-all economic and social situation in each country, whereon their own prosperity ultimately depends.

99 99. Nevertheless, to decide what is more helpful to the over-all economic situation is not the prerogative of individual productive enterprises, but pertains to the public authorities and to those institutions which, established either nationally or among a number of countries, function in various sectors of economic life. From this is evident the propriety or necessity of ensuring that not only managers or agents of management are represented before such authorities and institutions, but also workers or those who have the responsibility of safeguarding the rights, needs, and aspirations of workers.

100 100. It is fitting, therefore, that our thoughts and paternal affection be directed toward the various professional groups and associations of workers which, in accord with principles of Christian teaching, carry on their activities on several continents. We are aware of the many and great difficulties experienced by these beloved sons of ours, as they effectively worked in the past and continue to strive, both within their national boundaries and throughout the

world, to vindicate the rights of workingmen and to improve their lot and conduct.

101. Furthermore, we wish to give deserved praise to the work of these our sons. Their accomplishments are not always immediately evident, but nevertheless permeate practically the entire field of labor, spreading correct norms of action and thought, and the beneficial influence of the Christian religion. 101

102. And we wish also to praise paternally those dear sons of ours who, imbued with Christian principles, give their special attention to other labor associations and those groups of workingmen that follow the laws of nature and respect the religious and moral liberty of individuals. 102

103. Nor can we at this point neglect to congratulate and to express our esteem for the International Labor Organization--variously signified popularly by the letters O.I.L. or I.L.O. or O.I.T.—which, for many years, has done effective and valuable work in adapting the economic and social order everywhere to the norms of justice and humanity. In such an order, the legitimate rights of workers are recognized and preserved. 103

104. In recent years, as we are well aware, the role played by the owners of capital in very large productive enterprises has been separated more and more from the role of management. This has occasioned great difficulties for governments whose duty it is to make certain that directors of the principal enterprises, especially those of greatest influence in the economic life of the entire country, do not depart from the requirements of the common good. These difficulties, as we know from experience, are by no means less, whether it be private citizens or public bodies that make the capital investments requisite for large-scale enterprises. 104

105. It is also quite clear that today the number of persons is increasing who, because of recent advances in insurance programs and various systems of social security, are able to look to the future with tranquillity. This sort of tranquillity once was rooted in the ownership of property, albeit modest. 105

106 106. It sometimes happens in our day that men are more inclined to seek some professional skill than possession of goods. Moreover, such men have greater esteem for income from labor or rights arising from labor, than for that deriving from capital investment or rights associated therewith.

107 107. This clearly accords with the inherent characteristics of labor, inasmuch as this proceeds directly from the human person, and hence is to be thought more of than wealth in external goods. These latter, by their very nature, must be regarded as instruments. This trend indicates an advance in civilization.

108 108. Economic conditions of this kind have occasioned popular doubt as to whether, under present circumstances, a principle of economic and social life, firmly enunciated and defended by our predecessors, has lost its force or is to be regarded as of lesser moment; namely, the principle whereby it is established that men have from nature a right of privately owning goods, including those of a productive kind.

109 109. Such a doubt has no foundation. For the right of private property, including that pertaining to goods devoted to productive enterprises, is permanently valid. Indeed, it is rooted in the very nature of things, whereby we learn that individual men are prior to civil society, and hence, that civil society is to be directed toward man as its end. Indeed, the right of private individuals to act freely in economic affairs is recognized in vain, unless they are at the same time given an opportunity of freely selecting and using things necessary for the exercise of this right. Moreover, experience and history testify that where political regimes do not allow to private individuals the possession also of productive goods, the exercise of human liberty is violated or completely destroyed in matters of primary importance. Thus it becomes clear that in the right of property, the exercise of liberty finds both a safeguard and a stimulus.

110 110. This explains the fact that socio-political groups and associations which endeavor to reconcile freedom with justice within society, and which until recently did not uphold the right of private property in productive goods, have now, en-

lightened by the course of social events, modified their views and are disposed actually to approve this right.

111. Accordingly, we make our own the insistence of our predecessor of happy memory, Pius XII: "In defending the right of private property, the Church has in mind a very important ethical aim in social matters. She does not, of course, strive to uphold the present state of affairs as if it were an expression of the divine will. And even less does she accept the patronage of the affluent and wealthy, while neglecting the rights of the poor and needy. . . .The Church rather does intend that the institution of private property be such as is required by the plan of divine wisdom and the law of nature."[32] Private ownership should safeguard the rights of the human person, and at the same time make its necessary contribution to the establishment of right order in society. 111

112. While recent developments in economic life progress rapidly in a number of countries, as we have noted, and produce goods ever more efficiently, justice and equity require that remuneration for work also be increased within limits allowed by the common good. This enables workers to save more readily and hence to achieve some property status of their own. Wherefore, it is indeed surprising that some reject the natural role of private ownership. For it is a right which continually draws its force and vigor from the fruitfulness of labor, and which, accordingly, is an effective aid in safeguarding the dignity of the human person and the free exercise of responsibility in all fields of endeavor. Finally, it strengthens the stability and tranquillity of family life, thus contributing to the peace and prosperity of the commonwealth. 112

113. It is not enough, then, to assert that man has from nature the right of privately possessing goods as his own, including those of productive character, unless, at the same time, a continuing effort is made to spread the use of this right through all ranks of the citizenry. 113

114. Our predecessor of happy memory, Pius XII, clearly reminded us that on the one hand the dignity of the human person necessarily "requires the right of using external goods 114

in order to live according to the right norm of nature. And to this right corresponds a most serious obligation, which requires that, so far as possible, there be given to all an opportunity of possessing private property."[33] On the other hand, the nobility inherent in work, besides other requirements, demands "the conservation and perfection of a social order that makes possible a secure, although modest property to all classes of the people."[34]

115 115. It is especially appropriate that today, more than heretofore, widespread private ownership should prevail, since as noted above, the number of nations increases wherein the economic systems experience daily growth. Therefore, by prudent use of various devices already proven effective, it will not be difficult for the body politic to modify economic and social life so that the way is made easier for widespread private possession of such things as durable goods, homes, gardens, tools requisite for artisan enterprises and family-type forms, investments in enterprises of medium or large size. All of this has occurred satisfactorily in some nations with developed social and economic systems.

116 116. Obviously, what we have said above does not preclude ownership of goods pertaining to production of wealth by States and public agencies, especially "if these carry with them power too great to be left in private hands, without injury to the community at large."[35]

117 117. It seems characteristic of our times to vest more ownership of goods in the State and in other public bodies. This is partially explained by the fact that the common good requires public authorities to exercise ever greater responsibilities. However, in this matter, the *principle of subsidiarity,* already mentioned above, is to be strictly observed. For it is lawful for States and public corporation to expand their doman of ownership only when manifest and genuine requirements of the common good so require, and then with safeguards, lest the possession of private citizens be diminished beyond measure, or, what is worse, destroyed.

118 118. Finally, we cannot pass over in silence the fact that economic enterprises undertaken by the State or by public

corporations should be entrusted to citizens outstanding in skill and integrity, who will carry out their responsibilities to the commonwealth with a deep sense of devotion. Moreover, the activity of these men should be subjected to careful and continuing supervision, lest, in the administration of the State itself, there develop an economic imperialism in the hands of a few. For such a development is in conflict with the highest good of the commonwealth.

119. Our predecessors have always taught that in the right of private property there is rooted a social responsibility. Indeed, in the wisdom of God the Creator, the overall supply of goods is assigned, first of all, that all men may lead a decent life. As our predecessor of happy memory, Leo XIII, clearly reminded us in the Encyclical Letter *Rerum Novarum,* "This is the heart of the matter: whoever has received from the divine bounty a larger share of blessings, whether these be corporal or external or gifts of the mind, has received them to use for his own perfection, and, at the same time, as the minister of God's providence, for the benefit of others. 'He who has a talent' [says St. Gregory the Great], 'let him take care that he hides it not; he who has abundance, let him arouse himself to mercy and generosity; he who has skill in managing affairs, let him make special effort to share the use and utility thereof with his neighbor.' "[36] 119

120. Although in our day, the role assigned the State and public bodies has increased more and more, it by no means follows that the social function of private ownership is obsolescent, as some seem to think. For social responsibility in this matter derives its force from the very right of private property. Furthermore, it is quite clear that there always will be a wide range of difficult situations, as well as hidden and grave needs, which the manifold providence of the State leaves untouched, and of which it can in no way take account. Wherefore, there is always wide scope for humane action by private citizens and for Christian charity. Finally, it is evident that in stimulating efforts relating to spiritual welfare, the work done by individual men or by private civic groups has more value than what is done by public authorities. 120

121 121. Moreover, it is well to recall here that the right of private ownership is clearly evident in the Gospels, which reveal Jesus Christ ordering the rich to share their goods with the poor so as to turn them into spiritual possessions: "Do not lay up for yourselves treasures on earth, where rust and moth consume, and where thieves break in and steal; but lay up for yourselves treasures in heaven, where neither rust nor moth consumes nor thieves break in and steal."[37] And the divine Master states that whatever is done for the poor is done for Him: "Amen I say to you, as long as you did it for one of these, the least of My brethren, you did it for Me."[38]

122 122. The progress of events and of time have made it increasingly evident that the relationships between workers and management in productive enterprises must be readjusted according to norms of justice and charity. But the same is also true of the systems whereby various types of economic activity and the differently endowed regions within a country ought to be linked together. Meanwhile, within the over-all human community, many nations with varied endowments have not made identical progress in their economic and social affairs.

123 123. First of all, to lay down some norms in regard to agriculture, we would note that the over-all number of rural dwellers seemingly has not diminished. Beyond doubt, however, many farmers have abandoned their rural birthplace, and seek out either the more populous centers or the cities themselves. Now since this is the case in almost all countries, and since it affects large numbers of human beings, problems concerning life and dignity of citizens arise, which are indeed difficult to overcome.

124 124. Thus, as economic life progresses and expands, the percentage of rural dwellers diminishes, while the great number of industrial and service workers increases. Yet, we feel that those who transfer from rural activities to other productive enterprises often are motivated by reasons arising from the very evolution of economic affairs. Very often, however, they are caught up by various enticements of which the following are noteworthy: a desire to escape from a con-

fined environment offering no prospect of a more comfortable life; the wish, so common in our age, to undertake new activities and to acquire new experiences; the attraction of quickly acquired goods and fortunes; a longing after a freer life, with the advantages that larger towns and cities usually provide. But there is no doubt about this point: rural dwellers leave the fields because nearly everywhere they see their affairs in a state of depression, both as regards labor productivity and the level of living of farm populations.

125. Accordingly, in this grave matter, about which enquiries are made in nearly all countries, we should first of all ask what is to be done to prevent so great imbalances between agriculture, industry, and the services in the matter of productive efficiency? Likewise, what can be done to minimize differences between the rural standard of living and that of city dwellers whose money income is derived from industry or some service or other? Finally, how can it be brought about that those engaged in agricultural pursuits no longer regard themselves as inferior to others? Indeed, rural dwellers should be convinced not only that they can strengthen and develop their personalities by their toil, but also that they can look forward to the future vicissitudes with confidence. 125

126. Accordingly, we judge it opportune in this connection to lay down some norms of permanent validity; although, as is evident, these must be adapted as various circumstances of time and place permit, or suggest, or absolutely require. 126

127. First, it is necessary that everyone, and especially public authorities, strive to effect improvements in rural areas as regards the principal services needed by all. Such are, for example: highway construction; transport services; marketing facilities; pure drinking water; housing; medical services; elementary, trade, and professional schools; things requisite for religion and for recreation; finally, furnishings and equipment needed in the modern farm home. Where these requirements for a dignified farm life are lacking to rural dwellers, economic and social progress does not 127

occur at all, or else very slowly. Under such conditions, nothing can be done to keep men from deserting the fields, nor can anyone readily estimate their number.

128 128. It is desirable, moreover, that economic development of commonwealths proceed in orderly fashion, meanwhile preserving appropriate balance between the various sectors of the economy. In particular, care must be had that within the agricultural sector innovations are introduced as regards productive technology, whether these relate to productive methods, or to cultivation of the fields, or to equipment for the rural enterprise, as far as the overall economy allows or requires. And all this should be done as far as possible, in accordance with technical advances in industry and in the various services.

129 129. In this way, agriculture not only absorbs a larger share of industrial output, but also demands a higher quality of services. In its turn, agriculture offers to the industrial and service sectors of the economy, as well as to the community as a whole, those products which in kind and in quantity better meet consumer needs. Thus, agriculture contributes to stability of the purchasing power of money, a very positive factor for the orderly development of the entire economic system.

130 130. By proceeding in this manner, the following advantages, among others arise: first of all, it is easier to know the origins and destinations of rural dwellers displaced by modernization of agriculture. Thereupon, they can be instructed in skills needed for other types of work. Finally, economic aids and helps will not be lacking for their intellectual and cultural development, so that they can fit into a new social groups.

131 131. To achieve orderly progress in various sectors of economic life, it is absolutely necessary that as regards agriculture, public authorities give heed and take action in the following matters: taxes and duties, credit, insurance, prices, the fostering of requisite skills, and, finally, improved equipment for rural enterprises.

132 132. As regards taxation, assessment according to ability to pay is fundamental to a just and equitable system.

133. But in determining taxes for rural dwellers, the general welfare requires public authorities to bear in mind that income in a rural economy is both delayed and subject to greater risk. Moreover, there is difficulty in finding capital so as to increase returns. 133

134. Accordingly, those with money to invest are more inclined to invest it in enterprises other than in the rural economy. And for the same reason, rural dwellers cannot pay prevailing market rates for capital wherewith to carry on and expand their operations. Wherefore, the general welfare requires that public authorities not merely make special provision for agricultural financing, but also for establishment of banks that provide capital to farmers at reasonable rates of interest. 134

135. It also seems necessary to make provision for a twofold insurance, one covering agricultural output, the other covering farmers and their families. Because, as experience shows, the income of individual farmers is, on the average, less than that of workers in industry and the services, it does not seem to be fully in accord with the norms of social justice and equity to provide farmers with insurance or social security benefits that are inferior to those of other classes of citizens. For those insurance plans or provisions that are established generally should not differ markedly one from the other, whatever be the economic sector wherein the citizens work, or from which they derive their income. 135

136. Moreover, since social security and insurance can help appreciably in distributing national income among the citizens according to justice and equity, these systems can be regarded as means whereby imbalances among various classes of citizens are reduced. 136

137. Since agricultural products have special characteristics, it is fitting that their price be protected by methods worked out by economic experts. In this matter, although it is quite helpful that those whose interests are involved take steps to safeguard themselves, setting up, as it were, appropriate goals, public authorities cannot stand entirely aloof from the stabilization procedure. 137

138 138. Nor should this be overlooked, that, generally speaking, the price of rural products is more a recompense for farmers labor than for capital investment.

139 139. Thus, our predecessor of happy memory, Pius XI, touching on the welfare of the human community, appropriately notes in his Encyclical Letter *Quadragesimo Anno,* that "a reasonable relationship between different wages here enters into consideration." But he immediately adds, "Intimately connected with this is a reasonable relationship between the prices obtained for the products of the various economic groups: agrarian, industrial, and so forth."[39]

140 140. Inasmuch as agricultural products are destined especially to satisfy the basic needs of men, it is necessary that their price be such that all can afford to buy them. Nevertheless, there is manifest injustice in placing a whole group of citizens, namely, the farmers, in an inferior economic and social status, with less purchasing power than required for a decent livelihood. This, indeed, is clearly contrary to the common good of the country.

141 141. In rural areas it is fitting that industries be fostered and common services be developed that are useful in preserving, processing, and finally, in transporting farms products. There is need, moreover, to establish councils and activities relating to various sectors of economic and professional affairs. By such means, suitable opportunity is given farm families to supplement their incomes, and that within the milieu wherein they live and work.

142 142. Finally, no one person can lay down a universal rule regarding the way in which rural affairs should be definitely organized, since in these matters there exists considerable variation within each country, and the difference is even greater when we consider the various regions of the world. However, those who hold man and the family in proper esteem, whether this be based upon nature alone, or also upon Christian principles, surely look toward some form of agricultural enterprise, and particularly of the family type, which is modeled upon the community of men wherein mutual relationships of members and the

organization of the enterprise itself are conformed to norms of justice and Christian teaching. And these men strive mightily that such organization of rural life be realized as far as circumstances permit.

143. The family farm will be firm and stable only when it yields money income sufficient for decent and humane family living. To bring this about, it is very necessary that farmers generally receive instruction, be kept informed of new developments, and be technically assisted by trained men. It is also necessary that farmers form among themselves mutual aid societies; that they establish professional associations; that they function efficiently in public life, that is, in various administrative bodies and in political affairs. 143

144. We are of the opinion that in rural affairs, the principal agents and protagonists of economic improvement of cultural betterment, or of social advance, should be the men personally involved, namely, the farmers themselves. To them it should be quite evident that their work is most noble, because it is undertaken, as it were, in the majestic temple of creation; because it often concerns the life of plants and animals, a life inexhaustible in its expression, inflexible in its laws, rich in allusions to God, Creator and Provider. Moreover, labor in the fields not only produces various foodstuffs wherewith humankind is nourished, but also furnishes an increasing supply of raw materials for industry. 144

145. Furthermore, this is a work endowed with a dignity of its own, for it bears a manifold relationship to the mechanical arts, chemistry, and biology: these must be continually adapted to the requirements of emerging situations because scientific and technological advance is of great importance in rural life. Work of this kind, moreover, possesses a special nobility because it requires farmers to understand well the course of the seasons and to adapt themselves to the same; that they await patiently what the future will bring; that they appreciate the importance and seriousness of their duties; that they constantly remain alert and ready for new developments. 145

146. Nor may it be overlooked that in rural areas, as indeed in every productive sector, farmers should join to- 146

gether in fellowships, especially when the family itself works the farm. Indeed, it is proper for rural workers to have a sense of solidarity. They should strive jointly to set up mutual-aid societies and professional associations. All these are very necessary either to keep rural dwellers abreast of scientific and technical progress, or to protect the prices of goods produced by their labor. Besides, acting in this manner, farmers are put on the same footing as other classes of workers who, for the most part, join together in such fellowships. Finally, by acting thus, farmers will achieve an importance and influence in public affairs proportionate to their own role. For today it is unquestionably true that the solitary voice speaks, as they say, to the winds.

147 147. But when rural dwellers, just as other classes of workers, wish to make their influence and importance felt, they should never disregard moral duties or civil law. Rather they should strive to bring their rights and interests into line with the rights and needs of other classes, and to refer the same to the common good. In this connection, farmers who strive vigorously to improve the yield of their farm may rightly demand that their efforts be aided and complemented by public authorities, provided they themselves keep in mind the common needs of all and also relate their own efforts to the fulfillment of these needs.

148 148. Wherefore, we wish to honor appropriately those sons of ours who everywhere in the world, either by founding and fostering mutual-aid societies or some other type of association, watchfully strive that in all civic affairs farmers enjoy not merely economic prosperity but also a status in keeping with justice.

149 149. Since everything that makes for man's dignity, perfection, and development seems to be invoked in agricultural labor, it is proper that man regard such work as an assignment from God with a sublime purpose. It is fitting, therefore, that man dedicate work of this kind to the most provident God who directs all events for the salvation of men. Finally, the farmer should take upon himself, in some measure, the task of educating himself and others for the advancement of civilization.

150. It often happens that in one and the same country citizens enjoy different degrees of wealth and social advancement. This especially happens because they dwell in areas which, economically speaking, have grown at different rates. Where such is the case, justice and equity demand that the government make efforts either to remove or to minimize imbalances of this sort. Toward this end, efforts should be made, in areas where there has been less economic progress, to supply the principal public services, as indicated by circumstances of time and place and in accord with the general level of living. But in bringing this about, it is necessary to have very competent administration and organization to take careful account of the following: labor supply, internal migration, wages, taxes, interest rates, and investments in industries that foster other skills and developments—all of which will further not merely the useful employment of workers and the stimulation of initiative, but also the exploitation of resources locally available. 150

151. But it is precisely the measures for advancement of the general welfare which civil authorities must undertake. Hence, they should take steps, having regard for the needs of the whole community, that progress in agriculture, industry, and services be made at the same time and in a balanced manner so far as possible. They should have this goal in mind, that citizens in less developed countries—in giving attention to economic and social affairs, as well as to cultural matters—feel themselves to be the ones chiefly responsible for their own progress. For a citizen has a sense of his own dignity when he contributes the major share to progress in his own affairs. 151

152. Hence, those also who rely on their own resources and initiative should contribute as best they can to the equitable adjustment of economic life in their own community. Nay, more, those in authority should favor and help private enterprise in accordance with the *principle of subsidiarity,* in order to allow private citizens themselves to accomplish as much as is feasible. 152

153. It is appropriate to recall at this point that in a number of nations there exists a discrepancy between 153

available agricultural land and the number of rural dwellers. Some nations experience a shortage of citizens, but have rich land resources; others have many citizens but an insufficiency of agricultural land.

154 154. Nor are there lacking nations wherein, despite their great resource potential, farmers use such primitive and obsolete methods of cultivation that they are unable to produce what is needed for the entire population. On the other hand, in certain countries, agriculture has so adapted itself to recent advances that farmers produce surpluses which to some extent harm the economy of the entire nation.

155 155. It is evident that both the solidarity of the human race and the sense of brotherhood which accords with Christian principles, require that some peoples lend other energetic help in many ways. Not merely would this result in a freer movement of goods, of capital, and of men, but it also would lessen imbalances between nations. We shall treat of this point in more detail below.

156 156. Here, however, we cannot fail to express our approval of the efforts of the Institute known as F.A.O. which concerns itself with the feeding of peoples and the improvement of agriculture. This Institute has the special goal of promoting mutual accord among peoples, of bringing it about that rural life is modernized in less developed nations, and finally, that help is brought to people experiencing food shortages.

157 157. Perhaps the most pressing question of our day concerns the relationship between economically advanced commonwealths and those that are in process of development. The former enjoy the conveniences of life; the latter experience dire poverty. Yet, today men are so intimately associated in all parts of the world that they feel, as it were, as if they are members of one and the same household. Therefore, the nations that enjoy a sufficiency and abundance of everything may not overlook the plight of other nations whose citizens experience such domestic problems that they are all but overcome by poverty and hunger, and are not able to enjoy basic human rights. This is all the more so, inasmuch as countries each day seem to become

more dependent on each other. Consequently, it is not easy for them to keep the peace advantageously if excessive imbalances exist in their economic and social conditions.

158. Mindful of our role of universal father, we think it opportune to stress here what we have stated in another connection: "We all share responsibility for the fact that populations are undernourished.[40] [Therefore], it is necessary to arouse a sense of responsibility in individuals and generally, especially among those more blessed with this world's goods."[41] 158

159. As can be readily deduced, and as the Church has always seriously warned, it is proper that the duty of helping the poor and unfortunate should especially stir Catholics, since they are members of the Mystical Body of Christ. "In this we have come to know the love of God," said John the Apostle, "that He laid down His life for us; and we likewise ought to lay down our life for the brethren. He who has the goods of this world and sees his brother in need and closes his heart to him, how does the love of God abide in him?"[42] 159

160. Wherefore, we note with pleasure that countries with advanced productive systems are lending aid to less privileged countries, so that these latter may the more readily improve their condition. 160

161. It is clear to everyone that some nations have surpluses in foodstuffs, particularly of farm products, while elsewhere large masses of people experience want and hunger. Now justice and humanity require that the richer countries come to the aid of those in need. Accordingly, to destroy entirely or to waste goods necessary for the lives of men, runs counter to our obligations in justice and humanity. 161

162. We are quite well aware that to produce surpluses, especially of farm products, in excess of the needs of a country, can occasion harm to various classes of citizens. Nevertheless, it does not herefore follow that nations with surpluses have no obligation to aid the poor and hungry where some particular emergency arises. Rather, diligent efforts should be made that inconveniences arising from 162

surplus goods be minimized and borne by every citizen on a fair basis.

163 163. However, the underlying causes of poverty and hunger will not be removed in a number of countries by these means alone. For the most part, the causes are to be found in the primitive state of the economy. To effect a remedy, all available avenues should be explored with a view, on the one hand, to instruct citizens fully in necessary skills and in carrying out their responsibilities, and, on the other hand, to enable them to acquire the capital wherewith to promote economic growth by ways and means adapted to our times.

164 164. It has not escaped our attention that in recent years there has grown in many minds a deep awareness of their duty to aid poorer countries still lacking suitable economic development, in order that these may more readily make economic and social progress.

165 165. Toward this end, we look to councils, either of a number of nations, or within individual nations; we look to private enterprises and societies to exert daily more generous efforts on behalf of such countries, transmitting to them requisite productive skills. For the same reason help is given to as many youths as possible that they may study in the great universities of more developed countries, thus acquiring a knowledge of the arts and sciences in line with the standards of our time. Moreover, international banks, single nations, or private citizens often make loans to these countries that they may initiate various programs calculated to increase production. We gladly take this opportunity to give due praise to such generous activity. It is hoped that in the future the richer countries will make greater and greater efforts to provide developing countries with aid designed to promote sciences, technology, and economic life.

166 166. In this matter we consider it our duty to offer some warnings.

167 167. First of all, it seems only prudent for nations which thus far have made little or no progress, to weigh

well the principal factor in the advance of nations that enjoy abundance.

168. Prudent foresight and common need demand that not only more goods be produced, but that this be done more efficiently. Likewise, necessity and justice require that wealth produced be distributed equitably among all citizens of the commonwealth. Accordingly, efforts should be made to ensure that improved social conditions accompany economic advancement. And it is very important that such advances occur simultaneously in the agricultural, industrial, and various service sectors. 168

169. It is indeed clear to all that countries in process of development often have their own individual characteristics, and that these arise from the nature of the locale, or from cultural tradition, or from some special trait of the citizens. 169

170. Now when economically developed countries assist the poorer ones they not only should have regard for these characteristics and respect them, but also should take special care lest, in aiding these nations, they seek to impose their own way of life upon them. 170

171. Moreover, economically developed countries should take particular care lest, in giving aid to poorer countries, they endeavor to turn the prevailing political situation to their own advantage, and seek to dominate them. 171

172. Should perchance such attempts be made, this clearly would be but another form of colonialism, which, although disguised in name, merely reflects their earlier but outdated dominion, now abandoned by many countries. When international relations are thus obstructed, the orderly progress of all peoples is endangered. 172

173. Genuine necessity, as well as justice, require that whenever countries give attention to the fostering of skills or commerce, they should aid the less developed nations without thought of domination, so that these latter eventually will be in a position to progress economically and socially on their own intitiative. 173

174 174. If this be done, it will help much toward shaping a community of all nations, wherein each one, aware of its rights and duties, will have regard for the prosperity of all.

175 175. There is no doubt that when a nation makes progress in science, technology, economic life, and the prosperity of its citizens, a great contribution is made to civilization. But all should realize that these things are not the highest goods, but only instruments for pursuing such goods.

176 176. Accordingly, we note with sorrow that in some nations economic life indeed progresses, but that not a few men are there to be found, who have no concern at all for the just ordering of goods. No doubt, these men either completely ignore spiritual values, or put these out of their minds, or else deny they exist. Nevertheless, while they pursue progress in science, technology, and economic life, they make so much of external benefits that for the most part they regard these as the highest goods of life. Accordingly, there are not lacking grave dangers in the help provided by more affluent nations for development of the poorer ones. For among the citizens of these latter nations, there is operative a general awareness of the higher values on which moral teaching rests—an awareness derived from ancient traditional custom which provides them with motivation.

177 177. Thus, those who seek to undermine in some measure the right instincts of these peoples, assuredly do something immoral. Rather, those attitudes, besides being held in honor, should be perfected and refined, since upon them true civilization depends.

178 178. Moreover, the Church by divine right pertains to all nations. This is confirmed by the fact that she already is everywhere on earth and strives to embrace all peoples.

179 179. Now, those peoples whom the Church has joined to Christ have always reaped some benefits, whether in economic affairs or in social organization, as history and contemporary events clearly record. For everyone who professes Christianity promises and gives assurance that he will contribute as far as he can to the advancement of civil institutions. He must also strive with all his might not only that human dignity suffer no dishonor, but also, by the removal

of every kind of obstacle, that all those forces be promoted which are conducive to moral living and contribute to it.

180. Moreover, when the Church infuses her energy into the life of a people, she neither is, nor feels herself to be, an alien institution imposed upon that people from without. This follows from the fact that wherever the Church is present, there individual men are reborn or resurrected in Christ. Those who are thus reborn or who have risen again in Christ feel themselves oppressed by no external force. Rather, realizing they have achieved perfect liberty, they freely move toward God. Hence, whatever is seen by them as good and morally right, that they approve and put into effect. 180

181. "The Church of Jesus Christ," as our predecessor Pius XII clearly stated, "is the faithful guardian of God's gracious wisdom. Hence, she makes no effort to discourage or belittle those characteristics and traits which are proper to particular nations, and which peoples religiously and tenaciously guard, quite justly, as a sacred heritage. She aims indeed at a unity which is profound and in conformity with that heavenly love whereby all are moved in their innermost being. She does not seek a uniformity with that heavenly love whereby all are moved in their innermost being. She does not seek a uniformity which is merely external in its effects and calculated to weaken the fibre of the peoples concerned. And all within bounds of these capacities and forces, which indeed have their deeply rooted ethnic traits, have the Church's approval and maternal prayers, provided they are not in opposition to those duties which spring from the common origin and destiny of all mortal men."[43] 181

182. We note with deep satisfaction that Catholic men, citizens of the less developed nations, are for the most part second to no other citizens in furthering efforts of their countries to make progress economically and socially according to their capacity. 182

183. Furthermore, we note that Catholic citizens of the richer nations are making extensive efforts to ensure that aid given by their own countries to needy countries is di- 183

rected increasingly toward economic and social progress. In this connection, it seems specially praiseworthy that appreciable aid in various forms is provided increasingly each year to young people from Africa and Asia, so that they may pursue literary and professional studies in the great universities of Europe and America. The same applies to the great care that has been taken in training for every responsibility of their office men prepared to go to less developed areas, there to carry out their profession and duties.

184 184. To those sons of ours who, by promoting solicitously the progress of peoples and by spreading, as it were, a wholesome civilizing influence, everywhere demonstrate the perennial vitality of Holy Church and her effectiveness, we wish to express our paternal praise and gratitude.

185 185. More recently, the question often is raised how economic organization and the means of subsistence can be balanced with population increase, whether in the world as a whole or within the needy nations.

186 186. As regards the world as a whole, some, consequent to statistical reasoning, observe that within a matter of decades mankind will become very numerous, whereas economic growth will proceed much more slowly. From this some conclude that unless procreation is kept within limits, there subsequently will develop an even greater imbalance between the number of inhabitants and the necessities of life.

187 187. It is clearly evident from statistical records of less developed countries that, because recent advances in public health and in medicine are there widely diffused, the citizens have a longer life expectancy consequent to lowered rates of infant mortality. The birth rate, where it has traditionally been high, tends to remain at such levels, at least for the immediate future. Thus the birth rate in a given year exceeds the death rate. Meanwhile the productive systems in such countries do not expand as rapidly as the number of inhabitants. Hence, in poorer countries of this sort, the standard of living does not advance and may even deteriorate. Wherefore, lest a serious crisis occur, some

are of the opinion that the conception or birth of human should be avoided or curbed by every possible means.

188. Now to tell the truth, the interrelationships on a global scale between the number of births and available resources are such that we can infer grave difficulties in this matter do not arise at present, nor will in the immediate future. The arguments advanced in this connection are so inconclusive and controversial that nothing certain can be drawn from them. 188

189. Besides, God in His goodness and wisdom has, on the one hand, provided nature with almost inexhaustible productive capacity; and, on the other hand, has endowed man with such ingenuity that, by using suitable means, he can apply nature's resources to the needs and requirements of existence. Accordingly, that the question posed may be clearly resolved, a course of action is not indeed to be followed whereby, contrary to the moral law laid down by God, procreative function also is violated. Rather, man should, by the use of his skills and science of every kind, acquire an intimate knowledge of the forces of nature and control them ever more extensively. Moreover, the advances hitherto made in science and technology give almost limitless promise for the future in this matter. 189

190. When it comes to questions of this kind, we are not unaware that in certain locales and also in poorer countries, it is often argued that in such an economic and social order, difficulties arise because citizens, each year more numerous, are unable to acquire sufficient food or sustenance where they live, and peoples do not show amicable cooperation to the extent they should. 190

191. But whatever be the situation, we clearly affirm these problems should be posed and resolved in such a way that man does not have recourse to methods and means contrary to his dignity, which are proposed by those persons who think of man and his life solely in material terms. 191

192. We judge that this question can be resolved only if economic and social advances preserve and augment the genuine welfare of individual citizens and of human society as a whole. Indeed, in a matter of this kind, first place 192

must be accorded everything that pertains to the dignity of man as such, or to the life of individual men, than which nothing can be more precious. Moreover, in this matter, international cooperation is necessary, so that, conformably with the welfare of all, information, capital, and men themselves may move about among the peoples in orderly fashion.

193 193. In this connection, we strongly affirm that human life is transmitted and propagated through the instrumentality of the family which rests on marriage, one and indissoluble, and, so far as Christians are concerned, elevated to the dignity of a sacrament. Because the life of man is passed on to other men deliverately and knowingly, it therefore follows that this should be done in accord with the most sacred, permanent, inviolate prescriptions of God. Everyone without exception is bound to recognize and observe these laws. Wherefore, in this matter, no one is permitted to use methods and procedures which may indeed be permissible to check the life of plants and animals.

194 194. Indeed, all must regard the life of man as sacred, since from its inception, it requires the action of God the Creator. Those who depart from this plan of God not only offend His divine majesty and dishonor themselves and the human race, but they also weaken the inner fibre of the commonwealth.

195 195. In these matters it is of great importance that new offspring, in addition to being very carefully educated in human culture and in religion—which indeed is the right and duty of parents—should also show themselves very conscious of their duties in every action of life. This is especially true when it is a question of establishing a family and of procreating and educating children. Such children should be imbued not only with a firm confidence in the providence of God, but also with a strong and ready will to bear the labors and inconveniences which cannot be lawfully avoided by anyone who undertakes the worthy and serious obligation of associating his own activity with God in transmitting life and in educating offspring. In this most important matter certainly nothing is more relevant

than the teachings an supernatural aids provided by the Church. We refer to the Church whose right of freely carrying out her function must be recognized also in ths connection.

196. When God, as we read in the book of Genesis, imparted human nature to our first parents, He assigned them two tasks, one of which complements the other. For He first directed: "Be fruitful and multiply,"[44] and then immediately added: "Fill the earth and subdue it."[45] 196

197. The second of these tasks, far from anticipating a destruction of goods, rather assigns them to the service of human life. 197

198. Accordingly, with great sadness we note two conflicting trends: on the one hand, the scarcity of goods is vaguely described as such that the life of men reportedly is in danger of perishing from misery and hunger; on the other hand, the recent discoveries of science, technical advances, and economic productivity are transformed into means whereby the human race is led toward ruin and a horrible death. 198

199. Now the provident God has bestowed upon humanity sufficient goods wherewith to bear with dignity the burdens associated with procreation of children. But this task will be difficult or even impossble if men, straying from the right road and with a perverse outlook, use the means mentioned above in a manner contrary to human reason or to their social nature, and hence, contrary to the directives of God Himself. 199

200. Since the relationships between countries today are closer in every region of the world, by reason of science and technology, it is proper that peoples become more and more interdependent. 200

201. Accordingly, contemporary problems of moment—whether in the fields of science and technology, or of economic and social affairs, or of public administration, or of cultural advancement—these, because they may exceed the capacities of individual States, very often affect a number of nations and at times all the nations of the earth. 201

202 202. As a result, individual countries, although advanced in culture and civilization, in number and industry of citizens, in wealth, in geographical extent, are not able by themselves to resolve satisfactorily their basic problems. Accordingly, because States must on occasion complement or perfect one another, they really consult their own interests only when they take into account at the same time the interests of others. Hence, dire necessity warns commonwealths to cooperate among themselves and provide mutual assistance.

203 203. Although this becomes more and more evident each day to individuals and even to all peoples, men, and especially those with high responsibility in public life, for the most part seem unable to accomplish the two things toward which peoples aspire. This does not happen because peoples lack scientific, technical, or economic means, but rather because they distrust one another. Indeed, men, and hence States, stand in fear of one another. One country fears lest another is contemplating aggression and lest the other seize an opportunity to put such plans into effect. Accordingly, countries customarily prepare defenses for their cities and homeland, namely, armaments designed to deter other countries from aggression.

204 204. Consequently, the energies of man and the resources of nature are very widely directed by peoples to destruction rather than to the advantage of the human family, and both individual men and entire peoples become so deeply solicitous that they are prevented from undertaking more important works.

205 205. The cause of this state of affairs seems to be that men, more especially leaders of States, have differing philosophies of life. Some even dare to assert that there exists no law of truth and right which transcends external affairs and man himself, which of necessity pertains to everyone, and, finally, which is equitable for all men. Hence, men can agree fully and surely about nothing, since one and the same law of justice is not accepted by all.

206 206. Although the word *justice* and the related term *demands of justice* are on everyone's lips, such verbaliza-

tions do not have the same meaning for all. Indeed, the opposite frequently is the case. Hence, when leaders invoke *justice* or the *demands of justice*, not only do they disagree as to the meaning of the words, but frequently find in them an occasion of serious contention. And so they conclude that there is no way of achieving their rights or advantages, unless they resort to force, the root of very serious evils.

207. That mutual faith may develop among rulers and nations and may abide more deeply in their minds, the laws of truth and justice first must be acknowledged and preserved on all sides. 207

208. However, the guiding principles of morality and virtue can be based only on God; apart from Him, they necessarily collapse. For man is composed not merely of body, but of soul as well, and is endowed with reason and freedom. Now such a composite being absolutely requires a moral law rooted in religion, which, far better than any external force or advantage, can contribute to the resolution of problems affecting the lives of individual citizens or groups of citizens, or with a bearing upon single States or all States together. 208

209. Yet, there are today those who assert that, in view of the flourishing state of science and technology, men can achieve the highest civilization even apart from God and by their own unaided powers. Nevertheless, it is because of this very progress in science and technology that men often find themselves involved in difficulties which affect all peoples, and which can be overcome only if they duly recognize the authority of God, author and ruler of man and of all nature. 209

210. That this is true, the advances of science seem to indicate, opening up, as they do, almost limitless horizons. Thus, an opinion is implanted in many minds that inasmuch as mathematical sciences are unable to discern the innermost nature of things and their changes, or express them in suitable terms, they can scarcely draw inferences about them. And when terrified men see with their own eyes that the vast forces deriving from technology and machines can be used 210

for destruction as well as for the advantage of peoples, they rightly conclude that things pertaining to the spirit and to moral life are to be preferred to all else, so that progress in science and technology do not result in destruction of the human race, but prove useful as instruments of civilization.

211 211. Meanwhile it comes to pass that in more affluent countries men, less and less satisfied with external goods, put out of their minds the deceptive image of a happy life to be lived here forever. Likewise, not only do men grow daily more conscious that they are fully endowed with all the rights of the human person, but they also strive mightily that relations among themselves become more equitable and more conformed to human dignity. Consequently, men are beginning to recognize that their own capacities are limited, and they seek spiritual things more intensively than heretofore. All of which seems to give some promise that not only individuals, but even peoples may come to an understanding for extensive and extremely useful collaboration.

212 212. As in the past, so too in our day, advances in science and technology have greatly multiplied relationships between citizens; it seems necessary, therefore, that the relationships themselves, whether within a single country or between all countries, be brought into more humane balance.

213 213. In this connection many systems of thought have been developed and committed to writing: some of these already have been dissipated as mist by the sun; others remain basically unchanged today; still others now elicit less and less response from men. The reason for this is that these popularized fancies neither encompass man, whole and entire, nor do they affect his inner being. Moreover, they fail to take into account the weaknesses of human nature, such as sickness and suffering: weaknesses that no economic or social system, no matter how advanced, can completely eliminate. Besides, men everywhere are moved by a profound and unconquerable sense of religion, which no force can ever destroy nor shrewdness suppress.

214. In our day, a very false opinion is popularized which holds that the sense of religion implanted in men by nature is to be regarded as something adventitious or imaginary, and hence, is to be rooted completely from the mind as altogether inconsistent with the spirit of our age and the progress of civilization. Yet, this inward proclivity of man to religion confirms the fact that man himself was created by God, and irrevocably tends to Him. Thus we read in Augustine: "Thou hast made us for Thyself, O Lord, and our hearts are restless until they rest in Thee."[46] 214

215. Wherefore, whatever the progress in technology and economic life, there can be neither justice nor peace in the world, so long as men fail to realize how great is their dignity; for they have been created by God and are His children. We speak of God, who must be regarded as the first and final cause of all things He has created. Separated from God, man becomes monstrous to himself and others. Consequently, mutual relationships between men absolutely require a right ordering of the human conscience in relation to God, the source of all truth, justice, and love. 215

216. It is well known and recognized by everyone that in a number of countries, some of ancient Christian culture, many of our very dear brothers and sons have been savagely persecuted for a number of years. Now this situation, since it reveals the great dignity of the persecuted, and the refined cruelty of their persecutors, leads many to reflect on the matter, though it has not yet healed the wounds of the persecuted. 216

217. However, no folly seems more characteristic of our time than the desire to establish a firm and meaningful temporal order, but without God, its necessary foundation. Likewise, some wish to proclaim the greatness of man, but with the source dried up from which such greatness flows and receives nourishment: that is, by impeding and, if it were possible, stopping the yearning of souls for God. But the turn of events in our times, whereby the hopes of many are shattered and not a few have come to grief, unquestionably confirm the words of Scripture: "Unless the Lord build the house, they labor in vain who built it."[47] 217

218 218. What the Catholic Church teaches and declares regarding the social life and relationships of men is beyond question for all time valid.

219 219. The cardinal point of this teaching is that individual men are necessarily the foundation, cause, and end of all social institutions. We are referring to human beings, insofar as they are social by nature, and raised to an order of existence that transcends and subdues nature.

220 220. Beginning with this very basic principle whereby the dignity of the human person is affirmed and defended, Holy Church—especially during the last century and with the assistance of learned priests and laymen, specialists in the field—has arrived at clear social teachings whereby the mutual relationships of men are ordered. Taking general norms into account, these principles are in accord with the nature of things and the changed conditions of man's social life, or with the special genius of our day. Moreover, these norms can be approved by all.

221 221. But today, more than ever, principles of this kind must not only be known and understood, but also applied to those systems and methods, which the various situations of time or place either suggest or require. This is indeed a difficult, though lofty, task. Toward its fulfillment we exhort not only our brothers and sons everywhere, but all men of good will.

222 222. Above all, we affirm that the social teaching proclaimed by the Catholic Church cannot be separated from her traditional teaching regarding man's life.

223 223. Wherefore, it is our earnest wish that more and more attention be given to this branch of learning. First of all, we urge that attention be given to such studies in Catholic schools on all levels, and especially in seminaries, although we are not unaware that in some of these latter institutions this is already being done admirably. Moreover, we desire that social study of this sort be included among the religious materials used to instruct and inspire the lay apostolate, either in parishes or in associations. Let this diffusion of knowledge be accomplished by every modern means: that is, in journals, whether

daily or periodical; in doctrinal books, both for the learned and the general reader; and finally, by means of radio and television.

224. We judge that our sons among the laity have much to contribute through their work and effort, that this teaching of the Catholic Church regarding the social question be more and more widely diffused. This they can do, not merely by learning it themselves and governing their actions accordingly, but also by taking special care that others also come to know its relevance. 224

225. Let them be fully persuaded that in no better way can they show this teaching to be correct and effective, than by demonstrating that present day social difficulties will yield to its application. In this way they will win minds today antagonistic to the teaching because they do not know it. Perhaps it will also happen that such men will find some enlightenment in the teaching. 225

226. But social norms of whatever kind are not only to be explained but also applied. This is especially true of the Church's teaching on social matters, which has truth as its guide, justice as its end, and love as its driving force. 226

227. We consider it, therefore, of the greatest importance that our sons, in addition to knowing these social norms, be reared according to them. 227

228. To be complete, the education of Christians must relate to the duties of every class. It is therefore necessary that Christians thus inspired, conform their behavior in economic and social affairs to the teachings of the Church. 228

229. If it is indeed difficult to apply teaching of any sort to concrete situations, it is even more so when one tries to put into practice the teaching of the Catholic Church regarding social affairs. This is especially true for the following reasons: there is deeply rooted in each man an instinctive and immoderate love of his own interests; today there is widely diffused in society a materialistic philosophy of life; it is difficult at times to discern the demands of justice in a given situation. 229

230. Consequently, it is not enough for men to be instructed, according to the teachings of the Church, on 230

their obligation to act in a Christian manner in economic and social affairs. They must also be shown ways in which they can properly fulfill their duty in this regard.

231 231. We do not regard such instructions as sufficient, unless there be added to the work of instruction that of the formation of man, and unless some action follow upon the teaching, by way of experience.

232 232. Just as, proverbially, no one really enjoys liberty unless he uses it, so no one really knows how to act according to Catholic teaching in the economic and social fields, unless he acts according to this teaching in the same area.

233 233. Accordingly, in popular instruction of this kind, it seems proper that considerable attention be paid to groups promoting the lay apostolate, especially those whose aim is to ensure that efforts in our present concern draw their inspiration wholly from Christian law. Seeing that members of such groups can first train themselves by daily practice in these matters, they subsequently will be able the better to instruct young people in fulfilling obligations of this kind.

234 234. It is not inappropriate in this connection to remind all, the great no less than the lowly, that the will to preserve moderation and to bear difficulties, by God's grace, can in no wise be separated from the meaning of life handed down to us by Christian wisdom.

235 235. But today, unfortunately, very many souls are preoccupied with an inordinate desire for pleasure. Such persons see nothing more important in the whole of life than to seek pleasure, to quench the thirst for pleasure. Beyond doubt, grave ills to both soul and body proceed therefrom. Now in this matter, it must be admitted that one who judges even with the aid of human nature alone, concludes that it is the part of the wise and prudent man to preserve balance and moderation in everything, and to restrain the lower appetities. He who judges matters in the light of divine revelation, assuredly will not overlook the fact that the Gospel of Christ and the Catholic Church, as well as the ascetical tradition handed down to us, all demand that Christians steadfastly mortify themselves and bear the inconveniences of life with singu-

lar patience. These virtues, in addition to fostering a firm and moderate rule of mind over body, also present an opportunity of satisfying the punishment due to sin, from which, except for Jesus Christ and His Immaculate Mother, no one is exempt.

236. The teachings in regard to social matters for the most part are put into effect in the following three stages: first, the actual situation is examined; then, the situation is evaluated carefully in relation to these teachings; then only is it decided what can and should be done in order that the traditional norms may be adapted to circumstances of time and place. These three steps are at times expressed by the three words: *observe, judge, act.* 236

237. Hence, it seems particularly fitting that youth not merely reflect upon this order of procedure, but also, in the present connection, follow it to the extent feasible, lest what they have learned be regarded merely as something to be thought about but not acted upon. 237

238. However, when it comes to reducing these teachings to action, it sometimes happens that even sincere Catholic men have differing views. When this occurs they should take care to have and to show mutual esteem and regard, and to explore the extent to which they can work in cooperation among themselves. Thus they can in good time accomplish what necessity requires. Let them also take great care not to weaken their efforts in constant controversies. Nor should they, under pretext of seeking what they think best, meanwhile, fail to do what they can and hence should do. 238

239. But in the exercise of economic and social functions, Catholics often come in contact with men who do not share their view of life. On such occasions, those who profess Catholicism must take special care to be consistent and not compromise in matters wherein the integrity of religion or morals would suffer harm. Likewise, in their conduct they should weigh the opinions of others with fitting courtesy and not measure everything in the light of their own interests. They should be prepared to join sincerely in doing whatever is naturally good or conducive to good. If, indeed, it happens that in these matters sacred authorities have prescribed or decreed anything, it is evident that this judgment is to be 239

observed promptly by Catholics. For it is the Church's right and duty not only to safeguard principles relating to the integrity of religion and morals, but also to pronounce authoritatively when it is a matter of putting these principles into effect.

240 240. But what we have said about the norms of instruction should indeed be put into practice. This has special relevance for those beloved sons of ours who are in the ranks of the laity inasmuch as their activity ordinarily centers around temporal affairs and making plans for the same.

241 241. To carry out this noble task, it is necessary that laymen not only should be qualified, each in his own profession, and direct their energies in accordance with rules suited to the objective aimed at, but also should conform their activity to the teachings and norms of the Church in social matters. Let them put sincere trust in her wisdom; let them accept her admonitions as sons. Let them reflect that, when in the conduct of life they do not carefully observe principles and norms laid down by the Church in social matters, and which we ourselves reaffirm, then they are negligent in their duty and often injure the rights of others. At times, matters can come to a point where confidence in this teaching is diminished, as if it were indeed excellent but really lacks the force which the conduct of life requires.

242 242. As we have already noted, in this present age men have searched widely and deeply into the laws of nature. Then they invented instruments whereby they can control the forces of nature; they have perfected and continue to perfect remarkable works worthy of deep admiration. Nevertheless, while they endeavor to master and transform the external world, they are also in danger, lest they become neglectful and weaken the powers of body and mind. This is what our predecessor of happy memory, Pius XI, noted with sorrow of spirit in his Encyclical Letter *Quadragesimo Anno:* "And so bodily labor, which was decreed by divine providence for the good of man's body and soul even after original sin, has too often been changed into an instrument

of perversion: for dead matter leaves the factory ennobled and transformed whereas men are there corrupted and degraded."[48]

243. And our predecessor of happy memory, Pius XII, rightly asserted that our age is distinguished from others precisely by the fact that science and technology have made incalculable progress, while men themselves have departed correspondingly from a sense of dignity. It is a "monstrous masterpiece" of this age "to have transformed man, as it were, into a giant as regards the order of nature, yet in the order of the supernatural and the eternal, to have changed him into a pygmy."[49] 243

244. Too often in our day is verified the testimony of the Psalmist concerning worshipers of false gods, namely, human beings in their captivity very frequently neglect themselves, but admire their own works as if these were gods: "These idols are silver and gold; the handiwork of men."[50] 244

245. Wherefore, aroused by the pastoral zeal wherewith we embrace all men, we strongly urge our sons that, in fulfilling their duties and in pursuing their goals, they do not allow their consciousness of responsibilities to grow cool, nor neglect the order of the more improtant goods. 245

246. For it is indeed clear that the Church has always taught and continues to teach that advances in science and technology and the prosperity resulting therefrom, are truly to be counted as good things and regarded as signs of the progress of civilization. But the Church likewise teaches that goods of this kind are to be judged properly in accordance with their natures: they are always to be considered as instruments for man's use, the better to achieve his highest end: that he can the more easily improve himself in both the natural and supernatural orders. 246

247. Wherefore, we ardently desire that our sons should at all times heed the words of the divine Master: "For what does it profit a man, if he gain the whole world, but suffer the loss of his own soul? Or what will a man give in exchange for his soul?"[51] 247

248. Not unrelated to the above admonitions is the one having to do with rest to be taken on feast days. 248

249 249. In order that the Church may defend the dignity with which man is endowed, because he is created by God and because God has breathed into him a soul to His own image, she has never failed to insist that the third commandment: "Remember to keep holy the Sabbath day,"[52] be carefully observed by all. It is the right of God, and within His power, to order that man put aside a day each week for proper and due worship of the divinity. He should direct his mind to heavenly things, setting aside daily business. He should explore the depths of his conscience in oder to know how necessary and inviolable are his relations with God.

250 250. In addition, it is right and necessary for man to cease for a time from labor, not merely to relax his body from daily hard work and likewise to refresh himself with decent recreation, but also to foster family unity, for this requires that all its members preserve a community of life and peaceful harmony.

251 251. Accordingly, religion, moral teaching, and care of health in turn require that relaxation be had at regular times. The Catholic Church has decreed for many centuries that Christians observe this day of rest on Sunday, and that they be present on the same day at the Eucharistic Sacrifice because it renews the memory of the divine Redemption and at the same time imparts its fruits to the souls of men.

252 252. But we note with deep sorrow, and we cannot but reprove the many who, though they perhaps do not deliberately despise this holy law, yet more and more frequently disregard it. Whence it is that our very dear workingmen almost necessarily suffer harm, both as to the salvation of their souls and to the health of their bodies.

253 253. And so, taking into account the needs of soul and body, we exhort, as it were, with the words of God Himself, all men, whether public officials or representatives of management and labor, that they observe this command of God Himself and of the Catholic Church, and judge in their souls that they have a responsibility to God and society in this regard.

254. From what we have briefly touched upon above, let none of our sons conclude, and especially the laity, that they act prudently if, in regard to the transitory affairs of this life, they become quite remiss in their specific Christian contributions. On the contrary, we reaffirm that they should be daily more zealous in carrying out this role. 254

255. Indeed, when Christ our Lord made that solemn prayer for the unity of His Church, He asked this from the Father on behalf of His disciples: "I do not pray that Thou take them out of the world, but that Thou keep them from evil."[53] Let no one imagine that there is any opposition between these two things so that they cannot be properly reconciled: namely, the perfection of one's own soul and the business of this life, as if one had no chance but to abandon the activities of this world in order to strive for Christian perfection, or as if one could not attend to these pursuits without endangering his own dignity as a man and as a Christian. 255

256. However, it is in full accord with the designs of God's providence that men develop and perfect themselves by exercise of their daily tasks, for this is the lot of practically everyone in the affairs of this mortal life. Accordingly, the role of the Church in our day is very difficult: to reconcile man's modern respect for progress with the norms of humanity and of the Gospel teaching. Yet, the times call the Church to this role; indeed, we may say, earnestly beseech her, not merely to pursue the higher goals, but also to safeguard her accomplishments without harm to herself. To achieve this, as we have already said, the Church especially asks the cooperation of the laity. For this reason, in their dealings with men, they are bound to exert effort in such a way that while fulfilling their duties to others, they do so in union with God through Christ, for the increase of God's glory. Thus the Apostle Paul asserts: "Whether you eat or drink, or do anything else, do all for the glory of God."[54] And elsewhere: "Whatever you do in word or in work do all in the name of the Lord Jesus Christ, giving thanks to God the Father through Him."[55] 256

257 257. As often, therefore, as human activity and institutions having to do with the affairs of this life, help toward spiritual perfection and everlasting beatitude, the more they are to be regarded as an efficacious way of obtaining the immediate end to which they are directed by their very nature. Thus, valid for all times is that noteworthy sentence of the divine Master: "Seek first the kingdom of God and His justice, and all these things shall be given you besides."[56] For he who is, as it were, a light in the Lord,[57] and walks as a son of light,[58] he perceives more clearly what the requirements of justice are, in the various sectors of human zeal, even in those that involve greater difficulties because of the excessive love which many have for their own interests, or those of their country, or race. It must be added that when one is motivated by Christian charity, he cannot but love others, and regard the needs, sufferings and joys of others as his own. His work, wherever it be, is constant, adaptable, humane, and has concern for the needs of others: For "Charity is patient, is kind; charity does not envy, is not pretentious, is not puffed up, is not ambitious, is not self seeking, is not provoked; thinks no evil, does not rejoice over wickedness, but rejoices with the truth; bears with all things, believes all things, hopes all things, endures all things."[59]

258 258. But we do not wish to bring this letter of ours to a close, Venerable Brothers, without recalling to your minds that most fundamental and true element of Catholic teaching, whereby we learn that we are living members of His Mystical Body, which is the Church: "For as the body is one and has many members, and all the members of the body, many as they are, form one body, so also is it with Christ."[60]

259 259. Wherefore, we urgently exhort all our sons in every part of the world, whether clergy or laity, that they fully understand how great is the nobility and dignity they derive from being joined to Christ, as branches to the vine, as He Himself said: "I am the vine, you are the branches,"[61] and that they are sharers of His divine life. Whence it is, that if Christians are also joined in mind and heart with the most Holy Redeemer, when they apply themselves to temporal

affairs, their work in a way is a continuation of the labor of Jesus Christ Himself, drawing from it strength and redemptive power: "He who abides in Me, and I in him, he bears much fruit."[62] Human labor of this kind is so exalted and ennobled that it leads men engaged in it to spiritual perfection, and can likewise contribute to the diffusion and propagation of the fruits of the Redemption to others. So also it results in the flow of that Gospel leaven, as it were, through the veins of civil society wherein we live and work.

260. Although it must be admitted that the times in which we live are torn by increasingly serious errors, and are troubled by violent disturbances, yet, it happens that the Church's laborers in this age of ours have access to enormous fields of apostolic endeavor. This inspires us with uncommon hope. 260

261. Venerable Brothers and beloved sons, beginning with that marvelous letter of Leo, we have thus far considered with you the varied and serious issues which pertain to the social conditions of our time. From them we have drawn norms and teachings, upon which we especially exhort you not merely to meditate deeply, but also to do what you can to put them into effect. If each one of you does his best courageously, it will necessarily help in no small measure to establish the kingdom of Christ on earth. This is indeed: "A kingdom of truth and of life; a kingdom of holiness and grace; a kingdom of justice, of love and of peace."[63] And this we shall some day leave to go to that heavenly beatitude, for which we were made by God, and which we ask for with most ardent prayers. 261

262. For it is a question here of the teaching of the Catholic and Apostolic Church, mother and teacher of all nations, whose light illumines, sets on fire, inflames. Her warning voice, filled with heavenly wisdom, reaches out to every age. Her power always provides efficacious and appropriate remedies for the growing needs of men, for the cares and solicitudes of this mortal life. With this voice, the age-old song of the Psalmist is in marvelous accord, to strengthen at all times and to uplift our souls: "I will bear what God pro- 262

claims; the Lord—for He proclaims peace to His people, and to His faithful ones, and to those who put in Him their hope. Near indeed is His salvation to those who fear Him, glory dwelling in our land. Kindness and truth shall meet; justice and peace shall kiss. Truth shall spring out of the earth, and justice shall look down from heaven. The Lord Himself will give His benefits; our land shall yield its increase. Justice shall walk before Him, and salvation, along the way of His steps."[64]

263 263. This is the plea, Venerable Brothers, we make at the close of this Letter, to which we have for a considerable time directed our concern about the Universal Church. We desire that the divine Redeemer of mankind, "who has become for us God-given wisdom, and justice, and sanctification, and redemption"[65] may reign and triumph gloriously in all things and over all things, for centuries on end. We desire that, in a properly organized order of social affairs, all nations will at last enjoy prosperity, and happiness, and peace.

264 264. As an evidence of these wishes, and a pledge of our paternal good will, we affectionately bestow in the Lord our apostolic blessing upon you, Venerable Brothers, and upon all the faithful committed to your care, and especially upon those who will reply with generosity to our appeals.

265 265. Given at Rome, at Saint Peter's, the fifteenth day of May, in the year 1961, the third year of our Pontificate.

PACEM IN TERRIS
Encyclical Letter of Pope John XXIII
on Establishing Universal Peace
in Truth, Justice, Charity and Liberty
April 11, 1963

Peace on earth, which all men of every era have most eagerly yearned for, can be firmly established only if the order laid down by God be dutifully observed.

2. The progress of learning and the inventions of technology clearly show that, both in living things and in the forces of nature, an astonishing order reigns, and they also bear witness to the greatness of man, who can understand that order and create suitable instruments to harness those forces of nature and use them to his benefit. 267

3. But the progress of science and the inventions of technology show above all the infinite greatness of God, Who created the universe and man himself. He created all things out of nothing, pouring into them the abundance of His wisdom and goodness, so that the holy psalmist praises God in these words: O Lord our master, the majesty of thy name fills all the earth.[1] Elsewhere he says: *What diversity, Lord, in thy creatures! What wisdom has designed them all!*[2] God also created man in His own *image and likeness,*[3] endowed him with intelligence and freedom, and made him lord of creation, as the same psalmist declares in the words: *Thou hast placed him only a little below the angels, crowning him with glory and honor and bidding him rule over the works of thy hands. Thou hast put all under his dominion.*[4] 268

4. How strongly does the turmoil of individual men and peoples contrast with the perfect order of the universe! 269

It is as if the relationships which bind them together could be controlled only by force.

270 5. But the Creator of the world has imprinted in man's heart an order which his conscience reveals to him and enjoins him to obey: *This shows that the obligations of the law are written in their hearts: their conscience utters its own testimony.*[5] And how could it be otherwise? For whatever God has made shows forth His infinite wisdom, and it is manifested more clearly in the things which have greater perfection.[6]

271 6. But fickleness of opinion often produces this error, that many think that the relationships between men and States can be governed by the same laws as the forces and irrational elements of the universe, whereas the laws governing them are of quite a different kind and are to be sought elsewhere, namely, where the Father of all things wrote them, that is, in the nature of man.

272 7. By these laws men are most admirably taught, first of all how they should conduct their mutual dealings among themselves, then how the relationships between the citizens and the public authorities of each State should be regulated, then how States should deal with one another, and finally how, on the one hand individual men and States, and on the other hand the community of all peoples, should act towards each other, the establishment of such a community being urgently demanded today by the requirements of universal common goods.

273 8. First of all, it is necessary to speak of the order which should exist between men.

274 9. Any human society, if it is to be well-ordered an productive, must lay down as a foundation this principle, namely, that every human being is a person, that is, his nature is endowed with intelligence and free will. Indeed, precisely because he is a person he has rights and obligations flowing directly and simultaneously from his very nature,[7] and as these rights and obligations are universal and inviolable so they cannot in any way be surrendered.

275 10. If we look upon the dignity of the human person in the light of divinely revealed truth, we cannot help but

esteem it far more highly; for men are redeemed by the blood of Jesus Christ, they are by grace the children and friends of God and heirs of eternal glory.

11. Beginning our discussion of the rights of man, we see that every man has the right to life, to bodily integrity, and to the means which are suitable for the proper development of life; these are primarily food, clothing, shelter, rest, medical care, and finally the necessary social services. Therefore a human being also has the right to security in cases of sickness, inability to work, widowhood, old age, unemployment, or in any other case in which he is deprived of the means of subsistence through no fault of his own.[8] 276

12. By the natural law every human being has the right to respect for his person, to his good reputation; the right to freedom in searching for truth and in expressing and communicating his opinions, and in pursuit of art, within the limits laid down by the moral order and the common good; and he has the right to be informed truthfully about public events. 277

13. The natural law also gives man the right to share in the benefits of culture, and therefore the right to a basic education and to technical and professional training in keeping with the stage of educational development in the country to which he belongs. Every effort should be made to ensure that persons be enabled, on the basis of merit, to go on to higher studies, so that, as far as possible, they may occupy posts and take on responsibilities in human society in accordance with their natural gifts and the skills they have acquired.[9] 278

14. This too must be listed among the rights of a human being, to honor God according to the sincere dictates of his own conscience, and therefore the right to practice his religion privately and publicly. For as Lactantius so clearly taught: *We were created for the purpose of showing to the God Who bore us the submission we owe Him, of recognizing Him alone, and of serving Him. We are obliged and bound by this duty to God; from this religion itself receives its name.*[10] And on this point Our Predeces- 279

sor of immortal memory, Leo XIII, declared: *This genuine, this honorable freedom of the sons of God, which most nobly protects the dignity of the human person, is greater than any violence or injustice; it has always been sought by the Church, and always most dear to her. This was the freedom which the Apostles claimed with intrepid constancy, which the apologists defended with their writings, and which the martyrs in such numbers consecrated with their blood.*[11]

280 15. Human beings have the right to choose freely the state of life which they prefer, and therefore the right to set up a family, with equal rights and duties for man and woman, and also the right to follow a vocation to the priesthood or the religious life.[12]

281 16. The family, grounded on marriage freely contracted, monogamous and indissoluble, is and must be considered the first and essential cell of human society. From this it follows that most careful provision must be made for the family both in economic and social matters as well as in those which are of a cultural and moral nature, all of which look to the strengthening of the family and helping it carry out its function.

282 17. Parents, however, have a prior right in the support and education of their children.[13]

283 18. If we turn our attention to the economic sphere it is clear that man has a right by the natural law not only to an opportunity to work, but also to go about his work without coercion.[14]

284 19. To these rights is certainly joined the right to demand working conditions in which physical health is not endangered, morals are safeguarded, and young people's normal development is not impaired. Women have the right to working conditions in accordance with their requirements and their duties as wives and mothers.[15]

285 20. From the dignity of the human person, there also arises the right to carry on economic activities according to the degree of responsibility of which one is capable.[16] Furthermore—and this must be specially emphasized—the worker has a right to a wage determined according to criteri-

ons of justice, and sufficient, therefore, in proportion to the available resources, to give the worker, and his family a standard of living in keeping with the dignity of the human person. In this regard, Our Predecessor Pius XII said: *To the personal duty to work imposed by nature, there corresponds and follows the natural right of each individual to make of his work the means to provide for his own life and the lives of his children; so fundamental is the law of nature which commands man to preserve his life.*[17]

21. The right to private property, even of productive goods, also derives from the nature of man. This right, as We have elsewhere declared, *is an effective means for safeguarding the dignity of the human person and for the exercise of responsibility in all fields; it strengthens and gives serenity to family life, thereby increasing the peace and prosperity of the state.*[18] 286

22. However, it is opportune to point out that there is a social duty essentially inherent in the right of private property.[19] 287

23. From the fact that human beings are by nature social, there arises the right of assembly and association. They have also the right to give the societies of which they are members the form they consider most suitable for the aim they have in view, and to act within such societies on their own initiative and on their own responsibility in order to achieve their desired objectives.[20] 288

24. And, as We Ourselves in the encyclical *Mater et Magistra* have strongly urged, it is by all means necessary that a great variety of organizations and intermediate groups be established which are capable of achieving a goal which an individual cannot effectively attain by himself. These societies and organizations must be considered the indispensable means to safeguard the dignity of the human person and freedom while leaving intact a sense of responsibility.[21] 289

25. Every human being has the right to freedom of movement and of residence within the confines of his own country; and, when there are just reasons for it, the right to emigrate to other countries and take up residence there.[22] 290

The fact that one is a citizen of a particular state does not detract in any way from his membership in the human family as a whole, nor from his citizenship in the world community.

291 26. The dignity of the human person involves the right to take an active part in public affairs and to contribute one's part to the common good of the citizens. For, as Our Predecessor of happy memory, Pius XII, pointed out: *The human individual, far from being an object and, as it were, a merely passive element in the social order, is in fact, must be and must continue to be, its subject, its foundation and its end.*[23]

292 27. The human person is also entitled to a jurdical protection of his rights, a protection that should be efficacious, impartial and inspired by the true norms of justice. As Our Predecessor Pius XII teaches: *That perpetual privilege proper to man, by which every individual has a claim to the protection of his rights, and by which there is assigned to each a definite and particular sphere of rights, immune from all arbitrary attacks, is the logical consequence of the order of justice willed by God.*[24]

293 28. The natural rights with which We have been dealing however, inseparably connected, in the very person who is their subject, with just as many respective duties; and rights well as duties find their source, their sustenance and their inviolability in the natural law which grants or enjoins them.

294 29. Therefore, to cite a few examples, the right of every man to life is correlative with the duty to preseve it; his right to a decent standard of living with the duty of living it becomingly; and his right to investigate the truth freely, with the duty of seeking it ever more completely and profoundly.

295 30. Once this is admitted, it also follows that in human society to one man's right there corresponds a duty in all other persons: the duty, namely, of acknowledging and respecting the right in question. For every fundamental human right draws its indestructible moral force from the natural law, which in granting it imposes a corresponding obligation. Those, therefore, who claim their own rights, yet altogether forget or neglect to carry out their respective

duties, are people who build with one hand and destroy with the other.

31. Since men are social by nature they are meant to live with others and to work for one another's welfare. A well-ordered human society requires that men recognize and observe their mutual rights and duties. It also demands that each contribute generously to the establishment of a civic order in which rights and duties are more sincerely and effectively acknowledged and fulfilled. 296

32. It is not enough, for example, to acknowledge and respect every man's right to the means of subsistence if we do not strive to the best of our ability for a sufficient supply of what is necessary for his sustenance. 297

33. The society of men must not only be organized but must also provide them with abundant resources. This certainly requires that they observe and recognize their mutual rights and duties; it also requires that they collaborate in the many enterprises that modern civilization either allows or encourages or even demands. 298

34. The dignity of the human person also requires that every man enjoy the right to act freely and responsibly. For this reason, therefore, in social relations man should exercise his rights, fulfill his obligations and, in the countless forms of collaboration with others, act chiefly on his own responsibility and initiative. This is to be done in such a way that each one acts on his own decision, of set purpose and from a consciousness of his obligation, without being moved by force or pressure brought to bear on him externally. For any human society that is established on relations of force must be regarded as inhuman, inasmuch as the personality of its members is repressed or restricted, when in fact they should be provided with appropriate incentives and means for developing and perfecting themselves. 299

35. A civic society is to be considered well-ordered, beneficial and in keeping with human dignity if it is grounded on truth. As the Apostle Paul exhorts us: *Away with falsehood then; let everyone speak out the truth to his neighbor; membership of the body binds us to one another.*[25] This will be accomplished when each one duly recog- 300

nizes both his rights and his obligations towards others. Furthermore, human society will be such as We have just described it, if the citizens, guided by justice, apply themselves seriously to respecting the rights of others and discharging their own duties; if they are moved by such fervor of charity as to make their own the needs of others and share with others their own goods: if finally, they work for a closer fellowship in the world of spiritual values. Yet this is not sufficient; for human society is bound together by freedom, that is to say, in ways and means in keeping with the dignity of its citizens, who accept the responsibility of their actions, precisely because they are by nature rational beings.

301 36. Therefore, venerable brothers and beloved children, human society must primarily be considered something pertaining to the spiritual. Through it, in the bright light of truth men should share their knowledge, be able to exercise their rights and fulfill their obligations, be inspired to seek spiritual values, mutually derive genuine pleasure from the beautiful of whatever order it be, always be readily disposed to pass on to others the best of their own cultural heritage and eagerly strive to make their own the spiritual achievements of others. These benefits not only influence, but at the same time give aim and scope to all that has bearing on cultural expressions, economic and social institutions, political movements and forms, laws, and all other structures by which society is outwardly established and constantly developed.

302 37. The order which prevails in society is by nature moral. Grounded as it is in truth, it must function according to the norms of justice, it should be inspired and perfected by mutual love, and finally it should be brought to an ever more refined and human balance in freedom.

303 38. Now an order of this kind, whose principles are universal, absolute and unchangeable, has its ultimate source in the one true God, Who is personal and transcends human nature. Inasmuch as God is the first Truth and the highest Good, He alone is that deepest source from which human society can draw its vitality, if that society is to be well or-

dered, beneficial, and in keeping with human dignity.[26] As St. Thomas Aquinas says: *Human reason is the norm of the human will, according to which its goodness is measured, because reason derives from the eternal law which is the divine reason itself. It is evident then that the goodness of the human will depends much more on the eternal law than on human reason.*[27]

39. Our age has three distinctive characteristics. 304

40. First of all, the working classes have gradually gained ground in economic and public affairs. They began by claiming their rights in the socio-economic sphere; they extended their action then to claims on the political level, and finally applied themselves to the acquisition of the benefits of a more refined culture. Today, therefore, workers all over the world refuse to be treated as if they were irrational objects without freedom, to be used at the arbitrary disposition of others. They insist that they be always regarded as men with a share in every sector of human society: in the social and economic sphere, in the fields of learning and culture, and in public life. 305

41. Secondly, it is obvious to everyone that women are now taking a part in public life. This is happening more rapidly perhaps in nations of Christian civilization, and, more slowly but broadly, among peoples who have inherited other traditions or cultures. Since women are becoming ever more conscious of their human dignity, they will not tolerate being treated as mere material instruments, but demand rights befitting a human person both in domestic and in public life. 306

42. Finally, in the modern world human society has taken on an entirely new appearance in the field of social and political life. For since all nations have either achieved or are on the way to achieving independence, there will soon no longer exist a world divided into nations that rule others and nations that are subject to others. 307

43. Men all over the world have today—or will soon have—the rank of citizens in independent nations. No one wants to feel subject to political powers located outside his own country or ethnical group. Thus in very many human 308

beings the inferiority complex which endured for hundreds and thousands of years is disappearing, while in others there in an attenuation and gradual fading of the corresponding superiority complex which had its roots in social-economic privileges, sex or political standing.

309 44. On the contrary, the conviction that all men are equal by reason of their natural dignity has been generally accepted. Hence racial discrimination can in no way be justified, at least doctrinally or in theory. And this is of fundamental importance and significance for the formation of human society according to those principles which We have outlined above. For, if a man becomes conscious of his rights, he must become equally aware of his duties. Thus he who possesses certain rights has likewise the duty to claim those rights as marks of his dignity, while all others have the obligation to acknowledge those rights and respect them.

310 45. When the relations of human society are expressed in terms of rights and duties, men become conscious of spiritual values, understand the meaning and significance of truth, justice, charity and freedom, and become deeply aware that they belong to this world of values. Moreover, when moved by such concerns, they are brought to a better knowledge of the true God Who is personal and transcendent, and thus they make the ties that bind them to God the solid foundation and supreme criterion of their lives, both of that life which they live interiorly in the depths of their own souls and of that in which they are united to other men in society.

311 46. Human society can be neither well-ordered nor prosperous unless it has some people invested with legitimate authority to preserve its institutions and to devote themselves as far as is necessary to work and care for the good of all. These however derive their authority from God, as St. Paul teaches in the words, *Authority comes from God alone.*[28] These words of St. Paul are explained thus by St. John Chrysostom: *What are you saying? Is every ruler appointed by God? I do not say that, he replies, for I am not dealing now with individual rulers, but with authority itself. What I say is, that it is the divine wisdom and not mere chance,*

that has ordained that there should be government, that some should command and others obey.[29] Moreover, since God made men social by nature, and since no society *can hold together unless some one be over all, directing all to strive earnestly for the common good, every civilized community must have a ruling authority, and this authority, no less than society itself, has its source in nature, and has, consequently, God for its author.*[30]

47. But authority is not to be thought of as a force lacking all control. Indeed, since it is the power to command according to right reason, authority must derive its obligatory force from the moral order, which in turn has God for its first source and final end. Wherefore Our Predecessor of happy memory, Pius XII, said: *The absolute order of living beings and man's very destiny (We are speaking of man who is free, bound by obligations and endowed with inalienable rights, and at once the basis of society and the purpose for which it exits) also includes the state as a necessary society invested with the authority without which it could not come into being or live. . . And since this absolute order, as we learn from sound reason, and especially from the Christian faith can have no origin save in God Who is our Creator, it follows that the dignity of the state's authority is due to its sharing to some extent in the authority of God Himself.*[31] 312

48. Wherefore, a civil authority which uses as its only or its chief means either threats and fear of punishment or promises of rewards cannot effectively move men to promote the common good of all. Even if it did so move them, this would be altogether opposed to their dignity as men, endowed with reason and free will. As authority rests chiefly on moral force, it follows that civil authority must appeal primarily to the conscience of individual citizens, that is, to each one's duty to collaborate readily for the common good of all. But since by nature all men are equal in human dignity, it follows that no one may be coerced to perform interior acts. That is in the power of God alone, Who sees and judges the hidden designs of men's hearts. 313

49. Those therefore who have authority in the State may oblige men in conscience only if their authority is intrin- 314

sically related with the authority of God and shares in it.[32]

315 50. By this principle the dignity of the citizens is protected. When in fact, men obey their rulers it is not at all as men that they obey them, but through their obedience it is God, the provident creator of all things, Whom they reverence, since He has decreed that men's dealings with one another should be regulated by an order which He Himself has established. Moreover, in showing this due reverence to God, men not only do not debase themselves but rather perfect and ennoble themselves. *For to serve God is to rule.*[33]

316 51. Since the right to command is required by the moral order and has its source in God, it follows that, if civil authorities pass laws or command anything opposed to the moral order and consequently contrary to the will of God, neither the laws made nor the authorizations granted can be binding on the consciences of the citizens, since *God has more right to be obeyed than men.*[34] Otherwise, authority breaks down completely and results in shameful abuse. As St. Thomas Aquinas teaches: *Human law has the true nature of law only in so far as it corresponds to right reason, and in this respect it is evident that it is derived from the eternal law. In so far as it falls short of right reason, a law is said to be a wicked law; and so, lacking the true nature of law, it is rather a kind of violence.*[35]

317 52. It must not be concluded, however, because authority comes from God, that therefore men have no right to choose those who are to rule the state, to decide the form of government, and to determine both the way in which authority is to be exercised and its limits. It is thus clear that the doctrine which We have set forth can be fully consonant with any truly democratic regime.[36]

318 53. Individual citizens and intermediate groups are obliged to make their specific contributions to the common welfare. One of the chief consequences of this is that they must bring their own interests into harmony with the needs of the community, and must contribute their goods and their services as civil authorities have prescribed, in accord with the norms of justice and within the limits of

their competence. Clearly then those who wield power in the state must do this by such acts which not only have been justly carried out, but which also either have the common welfare primarily in view or which can lead to it.

54. Indeed since the whole reason for the existence of civil authorities is the realization of the common good, it is clearly necessary that, in pursuing this objective, they should respect its essential elements, and at the same time conform their laws to the circumstances of the day.[37] 319

55. Assuredly, the ethnic characteristics of the various human groups are to be respected as constituent elements of the common good,[38] but these values and characteristics by no means exhaust the content of the common good. For the common good since it is intimately bound up with human nature cannot therefore exist fully and completely unless the human person is taken into consideration and the essential nature and realization of the common good be kept in mind.[39] 320

56. In the second place, the very nature of the common good requires that all members of the state be entitled to share in it, although in different ways according to each one's tasks, merits and circumstances. For this reason, every civil authority must take pains to promote the common good of all, without preference for any single citizen or civic group. As Our Predecessor of immortal memory, Leo XIII, has said: *The civil power must not serve the advantage of any one individual, or of some few persons, inasmuch as it was established for the common good of all.*[40] Considerations of justice and equity, however, can at times demand that those involved in civil government give more attention to the less fortunate members of the community, since they are less able to defend their rights and to assert their legitimate claims.[41] 321

57. In this context, We judge that attention should be called to the fact that the common good touches the whole man, the needs both of his body and of his soul. Hence it follows that the civil authorities must undertake to effect the common good by ways and means that are proper to them; that is, while respecting the hierarchy of values, 322

they should promote simultaneously both the material and the spiritual welfare of the citizens.[42]

323 58. These principles are clearly contained in the doctrine stated in Our Encyclical, *Mater et Magistra,* where We emphasized that the common good of all *embraces the sum total of those conditions of social living whereby men are enabled to achieve their own integral perfection more fully and more easily.*[43]

324 59. Men, however, composed as they are of bodies and immortal souls, can never in this mortal life succeed in satisfying all their need or in attaining perfect happiness. Therefore the common good is to be procured by such ways and means which not only are not detrimental to man's eternal salvation but which positively contribute to it.[44]

325 60. It is agreed that in our time the common good is chiefly guaranteed when personal rights and duties are maintained. The chief concern of civil authorities must therefore be to ensure that these rights are acknowledged, respected, coordinated with other rights, defended and promoted, so that in this way each one may more easily carry out his duties. For *to safeguard the inviolable rights of the human person, and to facilitate the fulfillment of his duties, should be the chief duty of every public authority.*[45]

326 61. This means that, if any government does not acknowledge the rights of man or violates them, it not only fails in its duty, but its orders completely lack juridical force.[46]

327 62. One of the fundamental duties of civil authorities, therefore, is to coordinate social relations in such fashion that the exercise of one man's rights does not threaten others in the exercise of their own rights nor hinder them in the fulfillment of their duties. Finally, the rights of all should be effectively safeguarded and, if they have been violated, completely restored.[47]

328 63. It is also demanded by the common good that civil authorities should make earnest efforts to bring about a situation in which individual citizens can easily exercise their rights and fulfill their duties as well. For experience has taught us that, unless these authorities take suitable action with regard to economic, political and cultural

matters, inequalities between the citizens tend to become more and more widespread, especially in the modern world, and as a result human rights are rendered totally ineffective and the fulfillment of duties is compromised.

64. It is therefore necessary that the administration give wholehearted and careful attention to the social as well as to the economic progress of the citizens, and to the development, in keeping with the the development of the productive system, of such essential services as the building of roads, transportation, communications, water supply, housing, public health, education, facilitation of the practice of religion, and recreational facilities. It is necessary also that governments make efforts to see that insurance systems are made available to the citizens, so that, in case of misfortune or increased family responsibilities, no person will be without the necessary means to maintain a decent standard of living. The government should make similarly effective efforts to see that those who are able to work can find employment in keeping with their aptitudes, and that each worker receives a wage in keeping with the laws of justice and equity. It should be equally the concern of civil authorities to ensure that workers be allowed their proper responsibility in the work undertaken in industrial organization, and to facilitate the establishment of intermediate groups which will make social life richer and more effective. Finally, it should be possible for all the citizens to share as far as they are able in their country's cultural advantages. 329

65. The common good requires that civil authorities maintain a careful balance between coordinating and protecting the rights of the citizens, on the one hand, and promoting them, on the other. It should not happen that certain individuals or social groups derive special advantage from the fact that their rights have received preferential protection. Nor should it happen that governments in seeking to protect these rights, become obstacles to their full expression and free use. *For this principle must always be retained: that State activity in the economic field, no matter what its breadth or depth may be, ought not to be exercised in such a way as to curtail an individual's freedom of personal initia-* 330

tive. Rather it should work to expand that freedom as much as possible by the effective protection of the essential personal rights of each and every individual.[48]

331 66. The same principle should inspire the various steps which governments take in order to make it possible for the citizens more easily to exercise their rights and fulfill their duties in every sector of social life.

332 67. It is impossible to determine, in all cases, what is the most suitable form of government, or how civil authorities can most effectively fulfill their respective functions, i.e., the legislative, judicial and executive functions of the state.

333 68. In determining the structure and operation of government which a state is to have, great weight has to be given to the circumstances of a given people, circumstances which will vary at different times and in different places. We consider, however, that it is in keeping with the innate demands of human nature that the state should take a form which embodies the three-fold division of powers corresponding to the three principal functions of public authority. In that type of state, not only the official functions of government but also the mutual relations between citizens and public officials are set down according to law, which in itself affords protection to the citizens both in the enjoyment of their rights and in the fulfillment of their duties.

334 69. If, however, this political and juridical structure is to produce the advantages which may be expected of it, public officials must strive to meet the problems which arise in a way that conforms both to the complexities of the situation and the proper exercise of their function. This requires that, in constantly changing conditions, legislators never forget the norms of morality, or constitutional provisions, or the common good. Moreover, executive authorities must coordinate the activities of society with discretion, with a full knowledge of the law and after a careful consideration of circumstances, and the courts must administer justice impartially and without being influenced by favoritism or pressure. The good order of society also demands that individual citizens and intermediate organizations should be

effectively protected by law whenever they have rights to be exercised or obligations to be fulfilled. This protection should be granted to citizens both in their dealings with each other and in their relations with government agencies.[49]

70. It is unquestionable that a legal structure in conformity with the moral order and corresponding to the level of development of the state is of great advantage to achievement of the common good. 335

71. And yet, social life in the modern world is so varied, complex and dynamic that even a juridical structure which has been prudently and thoughtfully established often seems inadequate for the needs of society. 336

72. It is also true that the relations of the citizens with each other, of citizens and intermediate groups with public authorities, and finally of the public authorities with one another, are often so complex and so sensitive that they cannot be regulated by inflexible legal provisions. Such a situation therefore demands that the civil authorities have clear ideas about the nature and extent of their official duties if they wish to maintain the existing juridical structure in its basic elements and principles, and at the same time meet the exigencies of social life, adapting their legislation to the changing social scene and solving new problems. They must be men of great equilibrium and integrity, competent and courageous enough to see at once what the situation requires and to take necessary action quickly and effectively.[50] 337

73. It is in keeping with their dignity as persons that human beings should take an active part in government, although the manner in which they share in it will depend on the level of development of the country to which they belong. 338

74. Men will find new and extensive advantages in the fact that they are allowed to participate in government. In this situation, those who administer the government come into frequent contact with the citizens, and it is thus easier for them to learn what is really needed for the common good. And since public officials hold office only for a specified 339

period of time their authority, far from withering, rather takes on a new vigor in a measure proportionate to the development of human society.[51]

340 75. From these considerations it becomes clear that in the juridical organization of states in our times the first requisite is that a charter of fundamental human rights be drawn up in clear and precise terms and that it be incorporated in its entirety in the constitution.

341 76. The second requisite is that the constitution of each state be drawn up, phrased in correct juridical terminology, which prescribes the manner of designating the public officials along with their mutual relations, the spheres of their competence, the forms and systems they are obliged to follow in the performance of their office.

342 77. The last requisite is that the relations between the government and the governed are then set forth in terms of rights and duties; and it is clearly laid down that the paramount task assigned to government officials is that of recognizing, respecting, reconciling, protecting and promoting the rights and duties of citizens.

343 78. It is of course impossible to accept the theory which professes to find the original and single source of civil rights and duties, of the binding force of the constitution, and of a government's right to command, in the mere will of human beings, individually or collectively.[52]

344 79. The tendencies to which We have referred, however, do clearly show that the men of our time are becoming increasingly conscious of their dignity as human persons. This awareness prompts them to claim a share in the public administration of their country, while it also accounts for the demand that their own inalienable and inviolable rights be protected by law. It also requires, that government officials be chosen in conformity with constitutional procedures and perform their specific functions within the limits of law.

345 80. Our Predecessors have constantly maintained, and We join them in reasserting, that nations are reciprocally subjects of rights and duties. This means that their relationships also must be harmonized in truth, in justice, in a

working solidarity, in liberty. The same natural law, which governs relations between individual human beings, serves also to regulate the relations of nations with one another.

81. This is readily clear to anyone if he would consider that the heads of states can in no way put aside their natural dignity while they represent their country and provide for its welfare, and that they are never allowed to depart from the natural law by which they are bound and which is the norm of their conduct. 346

82. Moreover, it is inconceivable that men because they are heads of government are forced to put aside their human endowments. On the contrary, they occupy this place of eminence for the very reason that they have earned a reputation as outstanding members of the body politic in view of their excellent intellectual endowments and accomplishments. 347

83. Indeed it follows from the moral order itself that authority is necessary for civil society, for civil society is ruled by authority; and that authority cannot be used to thwart the moral order without instantly collapsing because its foundation has been destroyed. This is the warning of God Himself: *A word, then, for the kings, ears to hear, kings' hearts to heed: a message for you, rulers, wherever you be! Listen well, all you that have multitudes at your command, foreign hordes to do your bidding. Power is none but comes to you from the Lord, nor any royalty but from One who is above all. He it is that will call you to account for your doings with a scrutiny that reads your inmost thoughts.*[53] 348

84. Lastly it is to be borne in mind that also in the regulating of relations between states, authority is to be exercised for the achievement of the common good, which constitutes the reason for its existence. 349

85. But a fundamental factor of the common good is acknowledgment of the moral order and exact observance of its commands. *A well established order among nations must be built upon the unshakable and unchangeable rock of the moral law, made manifest in the order of nature by the Creator Himself and by Him engraved on the hearts of men with letters than can never be effaced. . . .Like the rays of a gleam-* 350

ing beacon, its principles must guide the plans and policies of men and nations. From its signals, which give warning and point out the safe and sure course, they must get their norms and guidance if they would not see all their laborious efforts to establish a new order condemned to tempest and shipwreck.[54]

351 86. First among the rules governing the relations between states is that of truth. This calls, above all, for the elimination of every trace of racism, and the consequent recognition of the principle that all states are by nature equal in dignity. Each of them accordingly is vested with the right to existence, to self-development, to the means fitting to its attainment, and to be the one primarily responsible for this self-development. Add to that the right of each to its good name, and to the respect which is its due.

352 87. Very often, experience has taught us, individuals will be found to differ enormously, in knowledge, power, talent and wealth. From this, however, no justification is ever found for those who surpass the rest to subject others to their control in any way. Rather they have a more serious obligation which binds each and everyone to lend mutual assistance to others in their efforts for improvement.

353 88. Likewise it can happen that one country surpasses another in scientific progress, culture and economic development. But this superiority, far from permitting it to rule others unjustly, imposes the obligation to make a greater contribution to the general development of the people.

354 89. In fact, men cannot by nature be superior to others since all enjoy an equal natural dignity. From this it follows that countries too do not differ at all from one another in the dignity which they derive from nature. Individual states are like a body whose members are human beings. Furthermore, we know from experience that nations are wont to be very sensitive in all matters which in any way concern their dignity and honor, and rightly so.

355 90. Truth further demands that the various media of social communications made available by modern progress, which enable the nations to know each other better, be used with serene objectivity. That need not, of course, rule

out any legitimate emphasis on the positive aspects of their way of life. But methods of information which fall short of the truth, and by the same token impair the reputation of this people or that, must be discarded.[55]

91. Relations between nations are to be further regulated by justice. This implies, over and above recognition of their mutual rights, the fulfillment of their respective duties. 356

92. Since nations have a right to exist, to develop themselves, to acquire a supply of the resources necessary for their development, to defend their good name and the honor due to them, it follows that they are likewise bound by the obligation of effectively guarding each of these rights and of avoiding those actions by which these rights can be jeopardized. As men in their private enterprises cannot pursue their own interests to the detriment of others, so too states cannot lawfully seek that development of their own resources which brings harm to other states and unjustly oppresses them. This statement of St. Augustine seems to be very apt in this regard: *What are kingdoms without justice but large bands of robbers.*[56] 357

93. Not only can it happen, but it actually does happen that the advantages and conveniences which nations strive to acquire for themselves become objects of contention; nevertheless, the resulting disagreements must be settled, not by force, nor by deceit or trickery, but rather in the only manner which is worthy of the dignity of man, i.e., by a mutual assessment of the reasons on both sides of the dispute, by a mature and objective investigation of the situation, and by an equitable reconciliation of differences of opinion. 358

94. Closely related to this point is the political trend which since the nineteenth century has gathered momentum and gained ground everywhere, namely, the striving of people of the same ethnic group to become independent and to form one nation. Since this cannot always be accomplished for various reasons, the result is that minorities often dwell within the territory of a people of another ethnic group, and this is the source of serious problems. 359

95. In the first place, it must be made clear that justice is seriously violated by whatever is done to limit the strength 360

and numerical increase of these lesser peoples; the injustice is even more serious if vicious attempts of this kind are aimed at the very extinction of these groups.

361 96. It is especially in keeping with the principles of justice that effective measures be taken by the civil authorities to improve the lot of the citizens of an ethnic minority, particularly when that betterment concerns their language, the development of their natural gifts, their ancestral customs, and their accomplishments and endeavors in the economic order.[57]

362 97. It should be noted, however, that these minority groups, either because of their present situation which they are forced to endure, or because of past experiences, are often inclined to exalt beyond due measure anything proper to their own people, and to such a degree as to look down on things common to all mankind as if the welfare of the human family must yield to the good of their own ethnic group. Reason rather demands that these very people recognize also the advantages that accrue to them from their peculiar circumstances; for instance, no small contribution is made toward the development of their particular talents and spirit by their daily dealings with people who have grown up in a different culture since from this association they can gradually make their own the excellence which belongs to the other ethnic group. But this will happen only if the minorities through association with the people who live around them make an effort to share in their customs and institutions. Such, however, will not be the case if they sow discord which causes great damage and hinders progress.

363 98. Since the mutual relations among nations must be regulated by the norm of truth and justice, they must also derive great advantage from an energetic union of mind, heart and resources. This can be effected at various levels by mutual cooperation in many ways, as is happening in our own time with beneficial results in the economic, social, political, educational, public health and sports spheres. We must remember that, of its very nature, civil authority exists, not to confine its people within the boundaries of their nation, but rather to protect, above all else, the common good of

that particular civil society, which certainly cannot be divorced from the common good of the entire human family.

99. So it happens that civil societies in pursuing their interests not only must not harm others, but must join their plans and forces whenever the efforts of an individual government cannot achieve its desired goals; but in the execution of such common efforts, great care must be taken lest what helps some nations should injure others. 364

100. Furthermore, the universal common good requires that in every nation friendly relations be fostered in all fields between the citizens and their intermediate societies. Since in many parts of the world there are groups of people of varying ethnic backgrounds, we must be on our guard against isolating one ethnic group from its fellow men. This is clearly inconsistent with modern conditions since distances which separate people from each other have been almost wiped out. Neither are we to overlook the fact that men of every ethnic group, in addition to their own characteristic endowments by which they are distinguished from the rest of men, have other important gifts of nature in common with their fellow men by which they can make more and more progress and perfect themselves, particularly in matters that pertain to the spirit. They have the right and duty therefore to live in communion with one another. 365

101. Everyone certainly knows that in some parts of the world there is an imbalance between the amount of arable land and the size of the population, and in other parts between the fertility of the soil and available farm implements. Consequently, necessity demands a cooperative effort on the part of the people to bring about a quicker exchange of goods, or of capital, or the migration of people themselves. 366

102. In this case We think it is most opportune that as far as possible employment should seek the worker, not vice versa. For then most citizens have an opportunity to increase their holdings without being forced to leave their native environment and seek a new home with many a 367

heartache, and adopt a new state of affairs and make new social contacts with other citizens.

368 103. The sentiment of universal fatherhood which the Lord has placed in Our heart makes Us feel profound sadness in considering the phenomenon of political refugees: a phenomenon which has assumed large proportions and which always hides numberless and acute sufferings.

369 104. Such expatriations show that there are some political regimes which do not guarantee for individual citizens a sufficient sphere of freedom within which their souls are allowed to breathe humanly; in fact, under those regimes even the lawful existence of such a sphere of freedom is either called into question or denied. This undoubtedly is a radical inversion of the order of human society, because the reason for the existence of public authority is to promote the common good, a fundamental element of which is the recognition of that sphere of freedom and the safeguarding of it.

370 105. At this point it will not be superfluous to recall that such exiles are persons, and that all their rights as persons must be recognized, since they do not lose those rights on losing the citizenship of the state of which they are former members.

371 106. Now among the rights of a human person there must be included that by which a man may enter a political community where he hopes he can more fittingly provide a future for himself and his dependents. Wherefore, as far as the common good rightly understood permits, it is the duty of that state to accept such immigrants and to help to integrate them into itself as new members.

372 107. Wherefore, on this occasion, We publicly approve and commend every undertaking, founded on the principles of human solidarity and Christian charity, which aims at making migration of persons from one country to another less painful.

373 108. And We will be permitted to signal for the attention and gratitude of all right-minded persons the manifold work which specialized international agencies are carrying out in this very delicate field.

109. On the other hand, it is with deep sorrow that We note the enormous stocks of armaments that have been and still are being made in more economically developed countries, with a vast outlay of intellectual and economic resources. And so it happens that, while the people of these countries are loaded with heavy burdens, other countries as a result are deprived of the collaboration they need in order to make economic and social progress. 374

110. The production of arms is allegedly justified on the grounds that in present-day conditions peace cannot be preserved without an equal balance of armaments. And so, if one country increases its armaments, others feel the need to do the same; and if one country is equipped with nuclear weapons, other countries must produce their own, equally destructive. 375

111. Consequently, people live in constant fear lest the storm that every moment threatens should break upon them with dreadful violence. And with good reason, for the arms of war are ready at hand. Even though it is difficult to believe that anyone would dare bring upon himself the appalling destruction and sorrow that war would bring in its train, it cannot be denied that the conflagration can be set off by some unexpected and unpremediated act. And one must bear in mind, that, even though the monstrous power of modern weapons acts as a deterrent, there is nevertheless reason to fear that the mere continuance of nuclear tests, undertaken with war in mind, can seriously jeopardize various kinds of life on earth. 376

112. Justice, then, right reason and consideration for human dignity and life urgently demand that the arms race should cease; that the stockpiles which exist in various countries should be reduced equally and simultaneously by the parties concerned; that nuclear weapons should be banned; and finally that all come to an agreement on a fitting program of disarmament, employing mutual and effective controls. In the words of Pius XII, Our Predecessor of happy memory: *The calamity of a world war, with the economic and social ruin and the moral excesses and dissolution that accompany it, must not be permitted to envelop the human race for a third time.*[59] 377

378 113. All must realize that there is no hope of putting an end to the building up of armaments, nor of reducing the present stocks, nor, still less—and this is the main point—of abolishing them altogether, unless the process is complete and thorough and unless it proceeds from inner conviction: unless, that is, everyone sincerely cooperates to banish the fear and anxious expectation of war with which men are oppressed. If this is to come about, the fundamental principle on which our present peace depends must be replaced by another, which declares that the true and solid peace of nations consists not in equality of arms but in mutual trust alone. We believe that this can be brought to pass, and we consider that, since it concerns a matter not only demanded by right reason but also eminently desirable in itself, it will prove to be the source of many benefits.

379 114. In the first place, it is an objective demanded by reason. There can be, or at least there should be no doubt that relations between states, as between individuals, should be regulated not by the force of arms but by the light of reason, by the rule, that is, of truth, of justice and of active and sincere cooperation.

380 115. Secondly, we say that it is an objective earnestly to be desired in itself. Is there anyone who does not ardently yearn to see dangers of war banished, to see peace preserved and daily more firmly established?

381 116. And finally, it is an objective which will be fruitful source of many benefits, for its advantages will be felt everywhere, by individuals, by families, by nations, by the whole human family. The warning of Pius XII still rings in our ears: *Nothing is lost by peace; everything may be lost by war.*[60]

382 117. Since this is so, We, the Vicar on earth of Jesus Christ, Savior of the World and Author of Peace, and as interpreter of the very profound longing of the entire human family, following the impulse of Our heart, seized by anxiety for the good of all, We feel it Our duty to beseech men, especially those who have the responsibility of public affairs, to spare no pain or effort until world events follow a course in keeping with man's destiny and dignity.

118. In the highest and most authoritative assemblies, let men give serious thought to the problem of a peaceful adjustment of relations between political communities on a world level: an adjustment founded on mutual trust, on sincerity in negotiations, on faithful fulfillment of obligations assumed. Let them study the problem until they find that point of agreement from which it will be possible to commence to go forward towards accords that will be sincere, lasting and fruitful. 383

119. We, for Our part, will not cease to pray God to bless these labors so that they may lead to fruitful results. 384

120. It has also to be borne in mind that relations between states should be based on freedom, that is to say, that no country may unjustly oppress others or unduly meddle in their affairs. On the contrary, all should help to develop in others a sense of responsibility, a spirit of enterprise, and an earnest desire to be the first to promote their own advancement in every field. 385

121. Because all men are joined together by reason of their common origin, their redemption by Christ, and their supernatural destiny, and are called to form one Christian family, We appealed in the Encyclical *Mater et Magistra* to economically developed nations to come to the aid of those which were in the process of development.[61] 386

122. We are greatly consoled to see how widely that appeal has been favorably received; and We are confident that even more so in the future it will contribute to the end that the poorer countries, in as short a time as possible, will arrive at that degree of economic development which will enable every citizen to live in conditions more in keeping with his human dignity. 387

123. But is never sufficiently repeated that the cooopera-tion, to which reference has been made, should be effected with the greatest respect for the liberty of the countries being developed, for these must realize that they are primarly responsible, and that they are the principal artisans in the promotion of their own economic development and social progress. 388

389 124. Our Predecessor Pius XII already proclaimed that *in the field of a new order founded on moral principles, there is no room for violation of freedom, integrity and security of other nations, no matter what may be their territorial extension or their capacity for defense. It is inevitable that the powerful states, by reason of their greater potential and their power, should pave the way in the establishment of economic groups comprising not only themselves but also smaller and weaker states as well. It is nevertheless indispensable that in the interests of the common good they, as all others, should respect the rights of those smaller states to political freedom, to economic development and to the adequate protection, in the case of conflicts between nations, of that neutrality which is theirs according to the natural, as well as international, law. In this way, and in this way only, will they be able to obtain a fitting share of the common good, and assure the material and spiritual welfare of their people.*[62]

390 125. It is vitally important, therefore, that the wealthier states, in providing varied forms of assistance to the poorer, should respect the moral values and ethnic characteristics peculiar to each, and also that they should avoid any intention of political domination. If this is done, *a precious contribution will be made towards the formation of a world community, a community in which each member, whilst conscious of its own individual rights and duties, will work in a relationship of equality towards the attainment of the universal common good.*[63]

391 126. Men are becoming more and more convinced that disputes which arise between states should not be resolved by recourse to arms, but rather by negotiation.

392 127. We grant indeed that this conviction is chiefly based on the terrible destructive force of modern weapons and a fear of the calamities and frightful destruction which such weapons would cause. Therefore, in an age such as ours which prides itself on its atomic energy it is contrary to reason to hold that war is now a suitable way to restore rights which have been violated.

128. Nevertheless, unfortunately, the law of fear still reigns among peoples, and it forces them to spend fabulous sums for armaments, not for aggression they affirm—and there is no reason for not believing them—but to dissuade others from aggression. 393

129. There is reason to hope, however, that by meeting and negotiating, men may come to discover better the bonds that unite them together, deriving from the human nature which they have in common; and that they may also come to discover that one of the most profound requirements of their common nature is this: that between them and their respective peoples it is not fear which should reign but love, a love which tends to express itself in a collaboration that is loyal, manifold in form and productive of many benefits. 394

130. The recent progress of science and technology, since it has profoundly influenced human conduct, is rousing men everywhere in the world to more and more cooperation and association with one another. Today the exchange of goods and ideas, travel from one country to another have greatly increased. Consequently, the close relations of individuals, families, intermediate associations belonging to different countries have become vastly more frequent and conferences between heads of states are held at shorter intervals. At the same time the interdependence of national economies has grown deeper, one becoming progressively more closely related to the other, so that they become, as it were, integral parts of the one world economy. Finally, the social progress, order, security and peace of each country are necessarily connected with the social progress, order, security and peace on all other countries. 395

131. Given these conditions, it is obvious that individual countries cannot rightly seek their own interests and develop themselves in isolation from the rest, for the prosperity and progress of all the rest and partly produces that prosperity and progress. 396

132. No era will destroy the unity of the human family since it is made up of human beings sharing with equal right their natural dignity. For this reason, necessity, root- 397

ed in man's very nature, will always demand that the common good be sought in sufficient measure because it concerns the entire human family.

398 133. In times past, it seemed that the leaders of nations might be in a position to provide for the universal common good, either through normal diplomatic channels, or through top-level meetings, or through conventions or treaties, by making use of methods and instruments suggested by natural law, the law of nations, or international law.

399 134. In our time, however, relationships between states have changed greatly. On the one hand, the universal common good poses very serious questions which are difficult and which demand immediate solution especially because they are concerned with safeguarding the security and peace of the whole world. On the other hand the heads of individual states, inasmuch as they are juridically equal, are not entirely successful no matter how often they meet or how hard they try to find more fitting juridical instruments. This is due not to lack of goodwill and initiative but to lack of adequate power to back up their authority.

400 135. Therefore, under the present circumstances of human society both the structure and form of governments as well as the power which public authority wields in all the nations of the world, must be considered inadequate to promote the universal common good.

401 136. Moreover, if we carefully consider the essential nature of the common good on the one hand, and the nature and function of public authority on the other, everyone sees that there is an intrinsic connection between the two. And, indeed, just as the moral order needs public authority to promote the common good in civil society, a likewise demands that public authority actually be able to attain it. From this it follows that the governmental institutions, on which public authority depends and through which it functions and pursues its end, should be provided with such structure and efficacy that they can lead to the common good by ways and methods which are suitably adapted to various contingencies.

137. Today the universal common good poses problems of worldwide dimensions, which cannot be adequately tackled or solved except by the efforts of public authority endowed with a wideness of powers, structure and means of the same proportions: that is, of public authority which is in a position to operate in an effective manner on a world-wide basis. The moral order itself, therefore, demands that such a form of public authority be established. 402

138. This public authority, having world-wide power and endowed with the proper means for the efficacious pursuit of its objective, which is the universal common good in concrete form, must be set up by common accord and not imposed by force. The reason is that such an authority must be in a position to operate effectively; yet, at the same time, its action must be inspired by sincere and real impartiality: it must be an action aimed at satisfying the universal common good. The difficulty is that there would be reason to fear that a supra-national or world-wide public authority, imposed by force by the more powerful nations might be an instrument of one-sided interests; and even should this not happen, it would be difficult for it to avoid all suspicion of partiality in its actions, and this would take from the force and effectiveness of its activity. Even though there may be pronounced differences between nations as regards the degree of their economic development and their military power, they are all very sensitive as regards their juridical equality and the excellence of their way of life. For that reason, they are right in not easily yielding obedience to an authority imposed by force, or to an authority in whose creation they had no part, or to which they themselves did not decide to submit by their own free choice. 403

139. Like the common good of individual states, so too the universal common good cannot be determined except by having regard for the human person. Therefore, the public and universal authority, too, must have as its fundamental objective the recognition, respect, safeguarding and promotion of the rights of the human person; this can be done by direct action when required, or by creating on a 404

world scale an environment in which leaders of the individual countries can suitably maintain their own functions.

405 140. Moreover, just as it is necessary in each state that relations which the public authority has with its citizens, families and intermediate associations be controlled and regulated by the principle of subsidiarity, it is equally necessary that the relationships which exist between the world-wide public authority and the public authorities of individual nations be governed by the same principle. This means that the world-wide public authority must tackle and solve problems of an economic, social, political or cultural character which are posed by the universal common good. For, because of the vastness, complexity and urgency of those problems, the public authorities of the individual states are not in a position to tackle them with any hope of a positive solution.

406 141. The world-wide public authority is not intended to limit the sphere of action of the public authority of the individual state, much less to take its place. On the contrary, its purpose is to create, on a world basis, an environment in which the public authorities of each state, its citizens and intermediate associations, can carry out their tasks, fulfill their duties and exercise their rights with greater security.[64]

407 142. As is known, the United Nations Organization (U.N.O.) was established on June 26, 1945, and to it there were subsequently added specialized agencies consisting of members designated by the public authority of the various countries with important international tasks in the economic, social, cultural, educational and health fields. The United Nations Organization had as its essential purpose the maintenance and consolidation of peace between peoples, fostering between them friendly relations, based on the principles of equality, mutual respect, and varied forms of cooperation in every sector of human endeavor.

408 143. An act of the highest importance performed by the United Nations Organization was the Universal Declaration of Human Rights, approved in the General Assembly of December 10, 1948. In the preamble of that Declaration, the recognition and respect of those rights and respective liber-

ties is proclaimed as a goal to be achieved by all peoples and all countries.

144. We are fully aware that some objections and reservations were raised regarding certain points in the Declaration, and rightly so. There is no doubt, however, that the document represents an important step on the path towards the juridical-political organization of all the peoples of the world. For in it, in most solemn form, the dignity of a human person is acknowledged to all human beings; and as a consequence there is proclaimed, as a fundamental right, the right of every man freely to investigate the truth and to follow the norms of moral good and justice, and also the right to a life worthy of man's dignity, while other rights connected with those mentioned are likewise proclaimed. 409

145. It is therefore our ardent desire that the United Nations Organization—in its structure and in its means—may become ever more equal to the magnitude and nobility of its tasks, and may the time come as quickly as possible when every human being will find therein an effective safeguard for the rights which derive directly from his dignity as a person, and which are therefore universal, inviolable and inalienable rights. This is all the more to be hoped for since all human beings, as they take an ever more active part in the public life of their own country, are showing an increasing interest in the affairs of all peoples, and are becoming more consciously aware that they are living members of the whole human family. 410

146. Once again We exhort Our children to take an active part in public life, and to contribute towards the attainment of the common good of the entire human family as well as to that of their own country. They should endeavor, therefore, in the light of the Faith and with the strength of love, to ensure that the various institutions—whether economic, social, cultural or political in purpose—should be such as not to create obstacles, but rather to facilitate or render less arduous man's perfecting of himself both in the natural order as well as in the supernatural. 411

147. Nevertheless, in order to imbue civilization with right norms and Christian principles, it is not enough to be illu- 412

mined with the gift of faith and enkindled with the desire of forwarding a good cause. For this end it is necessary to take an active part in the various organizations and influence them from within.

413 148. And since our present age is one of outstanding scientific and technical progress and excellence, one will not be able to enter these organizations and work effectively from within unless he is scientifically competent, technically capable and skilled in the practice of his own profession.

414 149. We desire to call attention to the fact that scientific competence, technical capacity and professional experience, although necessary, are not of themselves sufficient to elevate the relationships of society to an order that is genuinely human: that is, to an order whose foundation is truth, whose measure and objective is justice, whose driving force is love, and whose method of attainment is freedom.

415 150. For this end it is certainly necessary that human beings carry on their own temporal activities in accordance with the laws governing them and following the methods corresponding to their nature. But at the same time it is also necessary that they should carry on those activities as acts within the moral order: therefore, as the exercise or vindication of a right, as the fulfillment of a duty or the performance of a service, as a positive answer to the providential design of God directed to our salvation. In other words, it is necessary that human beings, in the intimacy of their own consciences, should so live and act in their temporal lives as to create a synthesis between scientific, technical and professional elements on the one hand, and spiritual values on the other.

416 151. It is no less clear that today, in traditionally Christian nations, secular institutions, although demonstrating a high degree of scientific and technical perfection, and efficiency in achieving their respective ends, not infrequently are but slightly affected by Christian motivation or inspiration.

417 152. It is beyond question that in the creation of those institutions many contributed and continue to contribute who were believed to be and who consider themselves Christians; and without doubt, in part at least, they were and are.

How does one explain this? It is Our opinion that the explanation is to be found in an inconsistency in their minds between religious belief and their action in the temporal sphere. It is necessary, therefore, that their interior unity be re-established, and that in their temporal activity faith should be present as a beacon to give light, and charity as a force to give life.

153. It is Our opinion, too, that the above-mentioned inconsistency between the religious faith in those who believe and their activities in the temporal sphere, results—in great part—from the lack of a solid Christian education. Indeed, it happens in many quarters and too often that there is no proportion between scientific training and religious instruction: the former continues and is extended until it reaches higher degrees, while the latter remains at elementary level. It is indispensable, therefore, that in the training of youth, education should be complete and without interruption, namely, that in the minds of the young religious values should be cultivated and the moral conscience refined in a manner to keep pace with the continuous and ever more abundant assimilation of scientific and technical knowledge. And it is indispensable, too, that they be instructed regarding the proper way to carry out their actual tasks.[65] 418

154. We deem it opportune to point out how difficult it is to understand clearly the relation between the objective requirements of justice and concrete situations, namely, to define the degrees and forms in which doctrinal principles and directives ought to be applied to reality. 419

155. And the definition of those degrees and forms is all the more difficult in our times, which are marked by a pronounced dynamism. For this reason, the problem of bringing social reality into line with the objective requirements of justice is a problem which will never admit of a definitive solution. Meanwhile, Our children must watch over themselves lest they relax and feel satisfied with objectives already achieved. 420

156. In fact, all human beings ought rather to reckon that what has been accomplished is but little in comparison with what remains to be done in regard to organs of production, 421

trade unions, associations, professional organizations, insurance systems, legal systems, political regimes, institutions for cultural, health, recreational or sporting purposes. These must all be adjusted to the era of the atom and of the conquest of space: an era which the human family has already entered, wherein it has commenced its new advance towards limitless horizons.

422 157. The doctrinal principles outlined in this document derive from both nature itself and the natural law. In putting these principles into practice it frequently happens that Catholics in many ways cooperate either with Christians separated from this Apostolic See, or with men of no Christian faith whatever, but who are endowed with reason and adorned with a natural uprightness of conduct. *In such relations let the faithful be careful to be always consistent in their actions, so that they may never come to any compromise in matters of religion and morals. At the same time, however, let them be, and show themselves to be, animated by a spirit of understanding and detachment, and disposed to work loyally in the pursuit of objectives which are of their nature good, or conducive to good.*[66]

423 158. However, one must never confuse error and the person who errs, not even when there is question of error or inadequate knowledge of truth in the moral or religious field. The person who errs is always and above all a human being, and he retains in every case his dignity as a human person; and he must be always regarded and treated in accordance with that lofty dignity. Besides, in every human being, there is a need that is congenital to this nature and never becomes extinguished, compelling him to break through the web of error and open his mind to the knowledge of truth. And God will never fail to act on his interior being, with the result that a person, who at a given moment of his life lacked the clarity of faith or even adheres to erroneous doctrines, can at a future date be enlightened and believe the truth. For Catholics, if for the sake of promoting the temporal welfare they cooperate with men who either do not believe in Christ or whose belief is faulty because they are involved in error, can pro-

vide them either the occasion or the inducement to turn to truth.

159. It is, therefore, especially to the point to make a clear distinction between false philosophical teachings regarding the nature, origin, and destiny of the universe and of man, and movements which have a direct bearing either on economic and social questions, or cultural matters or on the organization of the state, even if these movements owe their origin and inspiration to these false tenets. While the teaching once it has been clearly set forth is no longer subject to change, the movements, precisely because they take place in the midst of changing conditions, are readily susceptible of change. Besides, who can deny that those movements, in so far as they conform to the dictates of right reason and are interpreters of the lawful aspirations of the human person, contain elements that are positive and deserving of approval? 424

160. For these reasons it can at times happen that meetings for the attainment of some practical results which previously seemed completely useless now are either actually useful or may be looked upon as profitable for the future. But to decide whether this moment has arrived, and also to lay down the ways and degrees in which work in common might be possible for the achievement of economic, social, cultural, and political ends which are honorable and useful, these are the problems which can only be solved with the virtue of prudence, which is the guiding light of the virtues that regulate the moral life, both individual and social. Therefore, as far as Catholics are concerned, this decision rests primarily with those who live and work in the specific sectors of human society in which those problems arise, always, however, in accordance with the principles of the natural law, with the social doctrine of the church, and with the directives of ecclesiastical authorities. For it must not be forgotten that the Church has the right and the duty not only to safeguard the principles of ethics and religion, but also to intervene authoritatively with Her children in the temporal sphere, when there is a question of judging the application of those principles to concrete cases.[67] 425

426 161. There are some souls, particularly endowed with generosity, who, on finding situations where the requirements of justice are not satisfied or not satisfied in full, feel enkindled with the desire to change the state of things, as if they wished to have recourse to something like a revolution.

427 162. It must be borne in mind that to proceed gradually is the law of life in all its expressions; therefore in human institutions, too, it is not possible to renovate for the better except by working from within them, gradually. Pius XII proclaimed: *Salvation and justice are not to be found in revolution, but in evolution through concord. Violence has always achieved only destruction, not construction: the kindling of passions, not their pacification; the accumulation of hate and ruin, not the reconciliation of the contending parties. And it has reduced men and parties to the difficult task of rebuilding, after sad experience, on the ruins of discord.*[68]

428 163. We must therefore consider this point most closely joined to the great tasks of magnanimous men, namely, to establish with truth, justice, charity, and liberty new methods of relationships in human society: the relations among individual citizens, among citizens and their own countries, among nations themselves, among individuals, families, intermediate associations and individual states on the one hand, and with the community of all mankind on the other. This is a most exalted task, for it is the task of bringing about true peace in the order established by God.

429 164. These men, necessarily few in number, but deserving recognition for their contributions in the field of human relations, We publicly praise and at the same time We earnestly invite them to persevere in their work with ever greater zeal. And We are comforted by the hope that their number will increase, especially among those who believe. For it is an imperative of duty; it is a requirement of Love. Every believer in this world of ours must be a spark of light a center of love, a vivifying leaven amidst his fellowmen: and he will be this all the more perfectly the more closely

he lives in communion with God and in the intimacy of his own soul.

165. In fact, there can be no peace between men unless there is peace within each one of them, unless, that is, each one builds up within himself the order wished by God. Hence St. Augustine asks: *Does your soul desire to overcome your lower inclinations? Let it be subject to Him Who is on high and it will conquer the lower self: there will be peace in you; true, secure and well-ordered peace. In what does that order consist? God commands the soul; the soul commands the body; and there is nothing more orderly than this.*[69] 430

166. These words of Ours, which We have wished to dedicate to the problems that most beset the human family today and on the just solution of which the ordered progress of society depends, are dictated by a profound aspiration which We know is shared by all men of good will: the consolidation of peace in the world. 431

167. As the humble and unworthy Vicar of Him whom the Prophet announced as the *Prince of Peace,*[70] We have the duty to expend all Our energies in an effort to protect and strengthen this gift. However, Peace will be but an empty-sounding word unless it is founded on the order which this present document has outlined in confident hope: an order founded on truth, built according to justice, vivified and integrated by charity, and put into practice in freedom. 432

168. This is such a noble and elevated task that human resources, even though inspired by the most praiseworthy good will, cannot bring it to realization alone. In order that human society may reflect as faithfully as possible the Kingdom of God, help from on high is absolutely necessary. 433

169. For this reason, during these sacred days Our supplication is raised with greater fervor towards Him Who by His painful Passion and death overcame sin—the root of discord and the source of sorrows and inequalities—and by His Blood reconciled mankind to the Eternal Father: *For he himself is our peace, he it is that hath made both one . . . And coming he announced the good tidings of peace to you who were afar off, and of peace to those who were near.*[71] 434

435 170. And in the Liturgy of these days we hear the announcement: *Our Lord Jesus Christ, after His resurrection, stood in the midst of His disciples and said "Peace be to you," alleluia: the disciples rejoiced seeing the Lord.*[72] He leaves us peace, He brings us peace: *Peace I leave with you, my peace I give to you; not as the world gives do I give to you.*[73]

436 171. This is the peace which We implore of Him with the ardent yearning of Our prayer. May He banish from the hearts of men whatever might endanger peace, may He transform them into witnesses of truth, justice and brotherly love. May He enlighten the rulers of peoples so that in addition to their solicitude for the proper welfare of their citizens, they may guarantee and defend the great gift of peace; may He enkindle the wills of all, so that they may overcome the barriers that divide, cherish the bonds of mutual charity, understand others, and pardon those who have done them wrong; by virtue of His action, may all peoples of the earth become as brothers, and may the most longed for peace blossom forth and reign always among them.

437 172. As a pledge of this peace, and with the ardent wish that it may shine forth on the Christian communities entrusted to your care, especially for the benefit of those who are most lowly and in the greatest need of help and defense, We are glad to impart to you, venerable brothers, to the priests both secular and religious, to the religious men and women and to the faithful of your dioceses, particularly to those who make every effort to put these exhortations of Ours into practice, Our Apostolic Blessing. Finally, upon all men of good will, to whom this encyclical letter is also addressed. We implore from Almighty God health and prosperity.

438 173. Given at Rome at St. Peter's, on Holy Thursday, the eleventh day of April, in the year 1963, the fifth of Our Pontificate.

GAUDIUM ET SPES
Pastoral Constitution on the
Church in the Modern World
December 7, 1965

PREFACE

The joys and the hopes, the griefs and the anxieties of the men of this age, especially those who are poor or in any way afflicted, these are the joys and hopes, the griefs and anxieties of the followers of Christ. Indeed, nothing genuinely human fails to raise an echo in their hearts. For theirs is a community composed of men. United in Christ, they are led by the Holy Spirit in their journey to the Kingdom of their Father and they have welcomed the news of salvation which is meant for every man. That is why this community realizes that it is truly linked with mankind and its history by the deepest of bonds.

2. Hence this Second Vatican Council, having probed more profoundly into the mystery of the Church, now addresses itself without hesitation, not only to the sons of the Church and to all who invoke the name of Christ, but to the whole of humanity. For the Council yearns to explain to everyone how it conceives of the presence and activity of the Church in the world of today.

Therefore, the Council focuses its attention on the world of men, the whole human family along with the sum of those realities in the midst of which it lives; that world which is the theater of man's history, and the heir of his energies, his tragedies and his triumphs; that world which the Christian sees as created and sustained by its Maker's love, fallen indeed into the bondage of sin, yet emancipated now by

441

Christ, Who was crucified and rose again to break the stranglehold of personified evil, so that the world might be fashioned anew according to God's design and reach its fulfillment.

442 3. Though mankind is stricken with wonder at its own discoveries and its power, it often raises anxious questions about the current trend of the world, about the place and role of man in the universe, about the meaning of its individual and collective strivings, and about the ultimate destiny of reality and of humanity. Hence, giving witness and voice to the whole People of God gathered together by Christ, this Council can provide no more eloquent proof of its solidarity with, as well as its respect and love for the entire human family with which it is bound up, than by engaging with it in conversation about these various problems. The Council brings to mankind light kindled from the Gospel, and puts at its disposal those saving resources which the Church herself, under the guidance of the Holy Spirit, receives from her Founder. For the human person deserves to be preserved; human society deserves to be renewed. Hence the focal point of our total presentation will be man himself, whole and entire, body and soul, heart and conscience, mind and will.

443 Therefore, this Sacred Synod, proclaiming the noble destiny of man and championing the godlike seed which has been sown in him, offers to mankind the honest assistance of the Church in fostering that brotherhood of all men which corresponds to this destiny of theirs. Inspired by no earthly ambition, the Church seeks but a solitary goal: to carry forward the work of Christ under the lead of the befriending Spirit. And Christ entered this world to give witness to the truth, to rescue and not to sit in judgment, to serve and not to be served.[1]

INTRODUCTORY STATEMENT

444 *The Situation of Men in the Modern World*

4. To carry out such a task, the Church has always had the duty of scrutinizing the signs of the times and of interpreting them in the light of the Gospel. Thus, in language intelli-

gible to each generation, she can respond to the perennial questions which men ask about this present life and the life to come, and about the relationship of the one to the other. We must therefore recognize and understand the world in which we live, its expectations, its longings, and its often dramatic characteristics. Some of the main features of the modern world can be sketched as follows.

445 Today, the human face is involved in a new stage of history. Profound and rapid changes are spreading by degrees around the whole world. Triggered by the intelligence and creative energies of man, these changes recoil upon him, upon his decisions and desires, both individual and collective, and upon his manner of thinking and acting with respect to things and to people. Hence we can already speak of a true cultural and social transformation, one which has repercussions on man's religious life as well.

446 As happens in any crisis of growth, this transformation has brought serious difficulties in its wake. Thus while man extends his power in every direction, he does not always succeed in subjecting it to his own welfare. Striving to probe more profoundly into the deeper recesses of his own mind, he frequently appears more unsure of himself. Gradually and more precisely he lays bare the laws of society, only to be paralyzed by uncertainty about the direction to give it.

447 Never has the human race enjoyed such an abundance of wealth, resources and economic power, and yet a huge proportion of the world's citizens are still tormented by hunger and poverty, while countless numbers suffer from total illiteracy. Never before has man had so keen an understanding of freedom, yet at the same time, new forms of social and psychological slavery make their appearance. Although the world of today has a very vivid awareness of its unity and of how one man depends on another in needful solidarity, it is most grievously torn into opposing camps by conflicting forces. For political, social, economic, racial and ideological disputes still continue bitterly, and with them the peril of a war which would reduce everything to ashes. True, there is a growing exchange of ideas, but the very words by which key concepts are expressed take on quite different meanings in

diverse ideological systems. Finally, man painstakingly searches for a better world, without a corresponding spiritual advancement.

448 Influenced by such a variety of complexities, many of our contemporaries are kept from accurately identifying permanent values and adjusting them properly to fresh discoveries. As a result, buffeted between hope and anxiety and pressing one another with questions about the present course of events, they are burdened down with uneasiness. This same course of events leads men to look for answers; indeed, it forces them to do so.

449 5. Today's spiritual agitation and the changing conditions of life are part of a broader and deeper revolution. As a result of the latter, intellectual formation is ever increasingly based on the mathematical and natural sciences and on those dealing with man himself, while in the practical order the technology which stems from these sciences takes on mounting importance.

450 This scientific spirit has a new kind of impact on the cultural sphere and on modes of thought. Technology is now transforming the face of the earth, and is already trying to master outer space. To a certain extent, the human intellect is also broadening its dominion over time: over the past by means of historical knowledge; over the future, by the art of projecting and by planning.

451 Advances in biology, psychology, and the social sciences not only bring men hope of improved self-knowledge; in conjunction with technical methods, they are helping men exert direct influence on the life of social groups.

452 At the same time, the human race is giving steadily increasing thought to forecasting and regulating its own population growth. History itself speeds along on so rapid a course that an individual person can scarcely keep abreast of it. The destiny of the human community has become all of a piece, where once the various groups of men had a kind of private history of their own.

453 Thus, the human race has passed from a rather static concept of reality to a more dynamic, evolutionary one. In consequence there has arisen a new series of problems, a

series as numerous as can be, calling for new efforts of analysis and synthesis.

6. By this very circumstance, the traditional local communities such as families, clans, tribes, villages, various groups and associations stemming from social contacts, experience more thorough changes every day. 454

The industrial type of society is gradually being spread, leading some nations to economic affluence, and radically transforming ideas and social conditions established for centuries. 455

Likewise, the cult and pursuit of city living has grown, either because of a multiplication of cities and their inhabitants, or by a transplantation of city life to rural settings. 456

New and more efficient media of social communication are contributing to the knowledge of events; by setting off chain reactions they are giving the swiftest and widest possible circulation to styles of thought and feeling. 457

It is also noteworthy how many men are being induced to migrate on various counts, and are thereby changing their manner of life. Thus a man's ties with his fellows are constantly being multiplied, and at the same time "socialization" brings further ties, without, however, always promoting appropriate personal development and truly personal relationships. 458

This kind of evolution can be seen more clearly in those nations which already enjoy the conveniences of economic and technological progress, though it is also astir among peoples still striving for such progress and eager to secure for themselves the advantages of an industrialized and urbanized society. These peoples, especially those among them who are attached to older traditions, are simultaneously undergoing a movement toward more mature and personal exercise of liberty. 459

7. A change in attitudes and in human structures frequently calls accepted values into question, especially among young people, who have grown impatient on more than one occasion, and indeed become rebels in their distress. Aware of their own influence in the life of society, they want a part in it sooner. This frequently causes parents and educators to 460

experience greater difficulties day by day in discharging their tasks. The institutions, laws and modes of thinking and feeling as handed down from previous generations do not always seem to be well adapted to the contemporary state of affairs; hence arises an upheaval in the manner and even the norms of behavior.

461 Finally, these new conditions have their impact on religion. On the one hand, a more critical ability to distinguish religion from a magical view of the world and from the superstitions which still circulate purifies it and exacts day by day a more personal and explicit adherence to faith. As a result many persons are achieving a more vivid sense of God. On the other hand, growing numbers of people are abandoning religion in practice. Unlike former days, the denial of God or of religion, or the abandonment of them, are no longer unusual and individual occurrences. For today it is not rare for such things to be presented as requirements of scientific progress or of a certain new humanism. In numerous places these views are voiced not only in the teachings of philosophers, but on every side they influence literature, the arts, the interpretation of the humanities and of history and civil laws themselves. As a consequence, many people are shaken.

462 8. This development coming so rapidly and often in a disorderly fashion, combined with keener awareness itself of the inequalities in the world beget or intensify contradictions and imbalances.

463 Within the individual person there develops rather frequently an imbalance between an intellect which is modern in practical matters, and a theoretical system of thought which can neither master the sum total of its ideas, nor arrange them adequately into a synthesis. Likewise an imbalance arises between a concern for practicality and efficiency, and the demands of moral conscience; also very often between the conditions of collective existence and the requisites of personal thought, and even of contemplation. At length there develops an imbalance between specialized human activity and a comprehensive view of reality.

464 As for the family, discord results from population, economic and social pressures, or from difficulties which arise

between succeeding generations, or from new social relationships between men and women.

465 Differences crop up too between races and between various kinds of social orders; between wealthy nations and those which are less influential or are needy; finally, between international institutions born of the popular desire for peace, and the ambition to propagate one's own ideology, as well as collective greed existing in nations or other groups.

466 What results is mutual distrust, enmities, conflicts and hardships. Of such is man at once the cause and the victim.

467 9. Meanwhile the conviction grows not only that humanity can and should increasingly consolidate its control over creation, but even more, that it devolves on humanity to establish a political, social and economic order which will increasingly serve man and help individuals as well as groups to affirm and develop the dignity proper to them.

468 As a result many persons are quite aggressively demanding those benefits of which with vivid awareness they judge themselves to be deprived either through injustice or unequal distribution. Nations on the road to progress, like those recently made independent, desire to participate in the goods of modern civilization, not only in the political field but also economically, and to play their part freely on the world scene. Still they continually fall behind while very often their economic and other forms of dependence on wealthier nations increases more rapidly.

69 People hounded by hunger call upon those better off. Where they have not yet won it, women claim for themselves an equity with men before the law and in fact. Laborers and farmers seek not only to provide for the necessities of life, but to develop the gifts of their personality by their labors and indeed to take part in regulating economic, social, political and cultural life. Now, for the first time in human history all people are convinced that the benefits of culture ought to be and actually can be extended to everyone.

470 Still, beneath all these demands lies a deeper and more widespread longing: persons and societies thirst for a full and free life worthy of man; one in which they can subject to their own welfare all that the modern world can offer them

so abundantly. In addition, nations try harder every day to bring about a kind of universal community.

471 Since all these things are so, the modern world shows itself at once powerful and weak, capable of the noblest deeds or the foulest; before it lies the path to freedom or to slavery, to progress or retreat, to brotherhood or hatred. Moreover, man is becoming aware that it is his responsibility to guide aright the forces which he has unleashed and which can enslave him or minister to him. That is why he is putting questions to himself.

472 10. The truth is that the imbalances under which the modern world labors are linked with that more basic imbalance which is rooted in the heart of man. For in man himself many elements wrestle with one another. Thus, on the one hand, as a creature he experiences his limitations in a multitude of ways; on the other he feels himself to be boundless in his desires and summoned to a higher life. Pulled by manifold attractions he is constantly forced to choose among them and to renounce some. Indeed, as a weak and sinful being, he often does what he would not, and fails to do what he would.[2] Hence he suffers from internal divisions, and from these flow so many and such great discords in society. No doubt many whose lives are infected with a practical materialism are blinded against any sharp insight into this kind of dramatic situation; or else, weighed down by unhappiness they are prevented from giving the matter any thought. Thinking they have found serenity in an interpretation of reality everywhere proposed these days, many look forward to a genuine and total emancipation of humanity wrought solely by human effort; they are convinced that the future rule of man over the earth will satisfy every desire of his heart. Nor are there lacking men who despair of any meaning to life and praise the boldness of those who think that human existence is devoid of any inherent significance and strive to confer a total meaning on it by their own ingenuity alone.

473 Nevertheless, in the face of the modern development of the world, the number constantly swells of the people who raise the most basic questions or recognize them with a new sharpness: what is man? What is this sense of sorrow, of evil,

of death, which continues to exist despite so much progress? What purpose have these victories secured at so high a cost? What can man offer to society, what can he expect from it? What follows this earthly life?

The Church firmly believes that Christ, who died and was raised up for all,[3] can through His Spirit offer man the light and the strength to measure up to his supreme destiny. Nor has any other name under heaven been given to man by which it is fitting for him to be saved.[4] She likewise holds that in her most benign Lord and Master can be found the key, the focal point and the goal of man, as well as of all human history. The Church also maintains that beneath all changes there are many realities which do not change and which have their ultimate foundation in Christ, Who is the same yesterday and today, yes and forever.[5] Hence under the light of Christ, the image of the unseen God, the firstborn of every creature,[6] the Council wishes to speak to all men in order to shed light on the mystery of man and to cooperate in finding the solution to the outstanding problems of our time. 474

PART I

The Church and Man's Calling

11. The People of God believes that it is led by the Lord's Spirit, Who fills the earth. Motivated by this faith, it labors to decipher authentic signs of God's presence and purpose in the happenings, needs and desires in which this People has a part along with other men of our age. For faith throws a new light on everything, manifests God's design for man's total vocation, and thus directs the mind to solutions which are fully human. 475

This Council, first of all, wishes to assess in this light those values which are most highly prized today and to relate them to their divine source. Insofar as they stem from endowments conferred by God on man, these values are exceedingly good. Yet they are often wrenched from their rightful function by 476 the taint in man's heart, and hence stand in need of purification.

477 What does the Church think of man? What needs to be recommended for the upbuilding of contemporary society? What is the ultimate significance of human activity throughout the world? People are waiting for an answer to these questions. From the answers it will be increasingly clear that the People of God and the human race in whose midst it lives render service to each other. Thus the mission of the Church will show its religious, and by that very fact, its supremely human character.

CHAPTER I

The Dignity of the Human Person

478 12. According to the most unanimous opinion of believers and unbelievers alike, all things on earth should be related to man as their center and crown.

479 But what is man? About himself he has expressed, and continues to express, many divergent and even contradictory opinions. In these he often exalts himself as the absolute measure of all things or debases himself to the point of despair. The result is doubt and anxiety. The Church certainly understands these problems. Endowed with light from God, she can offer solutions to them, so that man's true situation can be portrayed and his defects explained, while at the same time his dignity and destiny are justly acknowledged.

480 For Sacred Scripture teaches that man was created "to the image of God," is capable of knowing and loving his Creator, and was appointed by Him as master of all earthly creatures[7] that he might subdue them and use them to God's glory.[8] "What is man that you should care for him? You have made him little less than the angels, and crowned him with glory and honor. You have given him rule over the works of your hands, putting all things under his feet."(*Ps*. 8:5-7).

481 But God did not create man to be alone, for from the beginning "male and female he created them" (*Gen*. 1:27). Their companionship produces the primary form of inter-

personal communion. For by his innermost nature man is a social being, and unless he relates himself to others he can neither live nor develop his potential.

482 Therefore, as we read elsewhere in Holy Scripture, God saw "all that he had made, and it was very good" (*Gen.* 1:31).

483 13. Although he was made by God in a state of holiness, from the very beginning of his history man abused his liberty, at the urging of the Evil One. Man set himself against God and sought to attain his goal apart from God. Although they knew God, they did not glorify Him as God, but their senseless minds were darkened and they served the creature rather than the Creator.[9] What divine revelation makes known to us conforms with experience. Examining his heart, man finds that he has inclinations toward evil too, and is engulfed by manifold ills which cannot come from his good Creator. Often refusing to acknowledge God as his beginning, man has disrupted also his proper relationship to his own ultimate goal as well as his whole relationship toward himself and others and all created things.

484 Therefore man is split within himself. As a result, all of human life, whether individual or collective, shows itself to be a dramatic struggle between good and evil, between light and darkness. Indeed, man finds that by himself he is incapable of battling the assaults of evil successfully, so that everyone feels as though he is bound by chains. But the Lord Himself came to free and strengthen man, renewing him inwardly and casting out that "prince of this world" (*John* 12:31) who held him in the bondage of sin.[10] For sin has diminished man, blocking his path to fulfillment.

485 The call to grandeur and the depths of misery, both of which are a part of human experience, find their ultimate and simultaneous explanation in the light of this revelation.

486 14. Though made of body and soul, man is one. Through his bodily composition he gathers to himself the elements of the material world; thus they reach their crown through him, and through him raise their voice in free praise of the Creator.[11] For this reason man is not allowed to despise his bodily life; rather he is obliged to regard his body as good and honorable since God has created it and will raise it up on

the last day. Nevertheless wounded by sin, man experiences rebellious stirrings in his body. But the very dignity of man postulates that man glorify God in his body[12] and forbids it to serve the evil inclinations of his heart.

487 Now, man is not wrong when he regards himself as superior to bodily concerns, and as more than a speck of nature or a nameless constituent of the city of man. For by his interior qualities he outstrips the whole sum of mere things. He plunges into the depths of reality whenever he enters into his own heart; God, Who probes the heart,[13] awaits him there; there he discerns his proper destiny beneath the eyes of God. Thus, when he recognizes in himself a spiritual and immortal soul, he is not being mocked by a fantasy born only of physical or social influences, but is rather laying hold of the proper truth of the matter.

488 15. Man judges rightly that by his intellect he surpasses the material universe, for he shares in the light of the divine mind. By relentlessly employing his talents through the ages he has indeed made progress in the practical sciences and in technology and the liberal arts. In our times he has won superlative victories, especially in his probing of the material world and in subjecting it to himself. Still he has always searched for more penetrating truths, and finds them. For his intelligence is not confined to observable data alone, but can with genuine certitude attain to reality itself as knowable, though in consequence of sin that certitude is partly obscured and weakened.

489 The intellectual nature of the human person is perfected by wisdom and needs to be, for wisdom gently attracts the mind of man to a quest and a love for what is true and good. Steeped in wisdom, man passes through visible realities to those which are unseen.

490 Our era needs such wisdom more than bygone ages if the discoveries made by man are to be further humanized. For the future of the world stands in peril unless wiser men are forthcoming. It should also be pointed out that many nations, poorer in economic goods, are quite rich in wisdom and can offer noteworthy advantages to others.

It is, finally, through the gift of the Holy Spirit that man comes by faith to the contemplation and appreciation of the divine plan.[14] 491

16. In the depths of his conscience, man detects a law which he does not impose upon himself, but which holds him to obedience. Always summoning him to love good and avoid evil, the voice of conscience when necessary speaks to his heart: do this, shun that. For man has in his heart a law written by God; to obey it is the very dignity of man; according to it he will be judged.[15] Conscience is the most secret core and sanctuary of a man. There he is alone with God, Whose voice echoes in his depths.[16] In a wonderful manner conscience reveals that law which is fulfilled by love of God and neighbor.[17] In fidelity to conscience, Christians are joined with the rest of men in the search for truth, and for the genuine solution to the numerous problems which arise in the life of individuals and from social relationships. Hence the more correct conscience holds sway, the more persons and groups turn aside from blind choice and strive to be guided by the objective norms of morality. Conscience frequently errs from invincible ignorance without losing its dignity. The same cannot be said for a man who cares but little for truth and goodness, or for a conscience which by degrees grown practically sightless as a result of habitual sin. 492

17. Only in freedom can man direct himself toward goodness. Our contemporaries make much of this freedom and pursue it eagerly; and rightly to be sure. Often, however, they foster it perversely as a license for doing whatever pleases them, even if it is evil. For its part, authentic freedom is an exceptional sign of the divine image within man. For God has willed that man remain "under the control of his own decisions,"[18] so that he can seek his Creator spontaneously, and come freely to utter and blissful perfection through loyalty to Him. Hence man's dignity demands that he act according to a knowing and free choice that is personally motivated and prompted from within, not under blind internal impulse nor by mere external pressure. Man achieves such dignity when, emancipating himself from all captivity to passion, he pursues 493

his goal in a spontaneous choice of what is good and procures for himself, through effective and skilful action, aids to that end. Since man's freedom has been damaged by sin, only by the aid of God's grace can he bring such a relationship with God into full flower. Before the judgment seat of God each man must render an account of his own life, whether he has done good or evil.[19]

494 18. It is in the face of death that the riddle of human existence grows most acute. Not only is man tormented by pain and by the advancing deterioration of his body, but even more so by a dread of perpetual extinction. He rightly follows the intuition of his heart when he abhors and repudiates the utter ruin and total disappearance of his own person. He rebels against death because he bears in himself an eternal seed which cannot be reduced to sheer matter. All the endeavors of technology, though useful in the extreme, cannot calm his anxiety; for a prolongation of biological life is unable to satisfy that desire for a higher life which is inescapably lodged in his breast.

495 Although the mystery of death utterly beggars the imagination, the Church has been taught by divine revelation and firmly teaches that man has been created by God for a blissful purpose beyond the reach of earthly misery. In addition, that bodily death from which man would have been immune had he not sinned[20] will be vanquished, according to the Christian faith, when man who was ruined by his own doing is restored to wholeness by an almighty and merciful Saviour. For God has called man and still calls him so that with his entire being he might be joined to Him in an endless sharing of a divine life beyond all corruption. Christ won this victory when He rose to life, for by His death He freed man from death.[21] Hence to every thoughtful man a solidly established faith provides the answer to his anxiety about what the future holds for him. At the same time faith gives him the power to be united in Christ with his loved ones who have already been snatched away by death; faith arouses the hope that they have found true life with God.

496 19. The basic source of human dignity lies in man's call to communion with God. From the very circumstance of his

origin man is already invited to converse with God. For man would not exist were he not created by God's love and constantly preserved by it; and he cannot live fully according to truth unless he freely acknowledges that love and devotes himself to his Creator. Still, many of our contemporaries have never recognized this intimate and vital link with God, or have explicitly rejected it. Thus atheism must be accounted among the most serious problems of this age, and is deserving of closer examination.

497 The word atheism is applied to phenomena which are quite distinct from one another. For while God is expressly denied by some, others believe that man can assert absolutely nothing about Him. Still others use such a method to scrutinize the question of God as to make it seem devoid of meaning. Many, unduly transgressing the limits of the positive sciences, contend that everything can be explained by this kind of scientific reasoning alone or, by contrast, they altogether disallow the fact that there is any absolute truth. Some laud man so extravagantly that their faith in God lapses into a kind of anemia, though they seem more inclined to affirm man than to deny God. Again some form for themselves such a fallacious idea of God that when they repudiate this figment they are by no means rejecting the God of the Gospel. Some never get to the point of raising questions about God, since they seem to experience no religious stirrings nor do they see why they should trouble themselves about religion. Moreover, atheism results not rarely from a violent protest against the evil in this world, or from the absolute character with which certain human values are unduly invested, and which thereby already accords them the stature of God. Modern civilization itself often complicates the approach to God not for any essential reason but because it is so heavily engrossed in earthly affairs.

498 Undeniably, those who willfully shut out God from their hearts and try to dodge religious questions are not following the dictates of their consciences, and hence are not free of blame; yet believers themselves frequently bear some responsibility for this situation. For, taken as a whole, atheism is not a spontaneous development but stems from a variety of

causes, including a critical reaction against religious beliefs, and in some places against the Christian religion in particular. Hence believers can have more than a little to do with the birth of atheism. To the extent that they neglect their own training in the faith, or teach erroneous doctrine, or are deficient in their religious, moral or social life, they must be said to conceal rather than reveal the authentic face of God and religion.

499 20. Modern atheism often takes on a systematic expression which, in addition to other causes, stretches the desire for human independence to such a point that it poses difficulties against any kind of dependence on God. Those who profess atheism of this sort maintain that it gives man freedom to be an end unto himself, the sole artisan and creator of his own history. They claim that this freedom cannot be reconciled with the affirmation of a Lord Who is author and purpose of all things, or at least that this freedom makes such an affirmation altogether superfluous. The sense of power which modern technical progress generates in man can nourish this belief.

500 Not to be overlooked among the forms of modern atheism is that which anticipates the liberation of man especially through his economic and social emancipation. This form argues that by its nature religion thwarts this liberation by arousing man's hope for a deceptive future life, thereby diverting him from the constructing of the earthly city. Consequently when the proponents of this doctrine gain governmental power they vigorously fight against religion, and promote atheism by using, especially in the education of youth, those means of pressure which public power has at its disposal.

501 21. In her loyal devotion to God and men, the Church has already repudiated[22] and cannot cease repudiating, sorrowfully but as firmly as possible, those poisonous doctrines and actions which contradict reason and the common experience of humanity, and dethrone man from his native excellence.

502 Still, she strives to detect in the atheistic mind the hidden causes for the denial of God; conscious of how weighty are the questions which atheism raises, and motivated by love for

all men, she believes these questions ought to be examined seriously and more profoundly.

503 The Church holds that the recognition of God is in no way hostile to man's dignity, since this dignity is rooted and perfected in God. For man was made an intelligent and free member of society by the God Who created him; but even more important, he is called as a son to commune with God and share in His happiness. She further teaches that a hope related to the end of time does not diminish the importance of intervening duties but rather undergirds the acquittal of them with fresh incentives. By contrast, when a divine substructure and the hope of life eternal are wanting, man's dignity is most grievously lacerated, as current events often attest; the riddles of life and death, of guilt and of grief go unsolved, with the frequent result that men succumb to despair.

504 Meanwhile every man remains to himself an unsolved puzzle, however obscurely he may perceive it. For on certain occasions no one can entirely escape the kind of self-questioning mentioned earlier, especially when life's major events take place. To this questioning only God fully and most certainly provides an answer as he summons man to higher knowledge and humbler probing.

505 The remedy which must be applied to atheism, however, is to be sought in a proper presentation of the Church's teaching as well as in the integral life of the Church and her members. For it is the function of the Church, led by the Holy Spirit Who renews and purifies her ceaselessly,[23] to make God the Father and His Incarnate Son present and in a sense visible. This result is achieved chiefly by the witness of a living and mature faith, namely, one trained to see difficulties clearly and to master them. Many martyrs have given luminous witness to this faith and continue to do so. This faith needs to prove its fruitfulness by penetrating the believer's entire life, including its worldly dimensions, and by activating him toward justice and love, especially regarding the needy. What does the most reveal God's presence, however, is the brotherly charity of the faithful who are united in spirit as they work

together for the faith of the Gospel[24] and who prove themselves a sign of unity.

506 While rejecting atheism, root and branch, the Church sincerely professes that all men, believers and unbelievers alike, ought to work for the rightful betterment of this world in which all alike live; such an ideal cannot be realized, however, apart from sincere and prudent dialogue. Hence the Church protests against the distinction which some state authorities make between believers and unbelievers, with prejudice to the fundamental rights of the human person. The Church calls for the active freedom of believers to build up in this world God's temple too. She courteously invites atheists to examine the Gospel of Christ with an open mind.

507 Above all the Church knows that her message is in harmony with the most secret desires of the human heart when she champions the dignity of the human vocation, restoring hope to those who have already despaired of anything higher than their present lot. Far from diminishing man, her message brings to his development light, life and freedom. Apart from this message nothing will avail to fill up the heart of man: "Thou hast made us for Thyself," O Lord, "and our hearts are restless till they rest in Thee."[25]

508 22. The truth is that only in the mystery of the Incarnate Word does the mystery of man take on light. For Adam, the first man, was a figure of Him Who was to come,[26] namely Christ the Lord. Christ, the final Adam, by the revelation of the mystery of the Father and His love, fully reveals man to man himself and makes his supreme calling clear. It is not surprising, then, that in Him all the aforementioned truths find their root and attain their crown.

509 He Who is "the image of the invisible God" (*Col.* 1:15),[27] is Himself the perfect man. To the sons of Adam He restores the divine likeness which had been disfigured from the first sin onward. Since human nature as He assumed it was not annulled,[28] by that very fact it has been raised up to a divine dignity in our respect too. For by His incarnation the Son of God has united Himself in some fashion with every man. He worked with human hands, He thought with a human mind, acted by human choice[29] and loved with a human heart.

Born of the Virgin Mary, He has truly been made one of us, like us in all things except sin.[30]

510 As an innocent lamb He merited for us life by the free shedding of His own blood. In Him God reconciled us[31] to Himself and among ourselves; from bondage to the devil and sin He delivered us, so that each one of us can say with the Apostle: The Son of God "loved me and gave Himself up for me" (*Gal.* 2:20). By suffering for us He not only provided us with an example for our imitation,[32] He blazed a trail, and if we follow it, life and death are made holy and take on a new meaning.

511 The Christian man, conformed to the likeness of that Son Who is the firstborn of many brothers,[33] received "the first-fruits of the Spirit" (*Rom.* 8:23) by which he becomes capable of discharging the new law of love.[34] Through this Spirit, who is "the pledge of our inheritance" (*Eph.* 1:14), the whole man is renewed from within, even to the achievement of "the redemption of the body" (*Rom.* 8:23): "If the Spirit of him who raised Jesus from the dead dwells in you, then he who raised Jesus Christ from the dead will also bring to life your mortal bodies because of his Spirit who dwells in you" (*Rom.* 8:23): "If the Spirit of him who raised Jesus Christ from the dead will also bring to life your mortal bodies because of his Spirit who dwells in you" (*Rom.* 8:11).[35] Pressing upon the Christian to be sure, are the need and the duty to battle against evil through manifold tribulations and even to suffer death. But, linked with the paschal mystery and patterned after the dying Christ, he will hasten forward to resurrection in the strength which comes from hope.[36]

512 All this holds true not only for Christians, but for all men of good will in whose hearts grace works in an unseen way.[37] For, since Christ died for all men,[38] and since the ultimate vocation of man is in fact one, and divine, we ought to believe that the Holy Spirit in a manner known only to God offers to every man the possibility of being associated with this paschal mystery.

513 Such is the mystery of man, and it is a great one, as seen by believers in the light of Christian revelation. Through Christ and in Christ, the riddles of sorrow and death grow

meaningful. Apart from His Gospel, they overwhelm us. Christ has risen, destroying death by His death; He has lavished life upon us[39] so that, as sons in the Son, we can cry out in the Spirit: Abba, Father![40]

CHAPTER II

The Community of Mankind

514 23. One of the salient features of the modern world is the growing interdependence of men one on the other, a development promoted chiefly by modern technical advances. Nevertheless brotherly dialogue among men does not reach its perfection on the level of technical progress, but on the deeper level of interpersonal relationships. These demand a mutual respect for the full spiritual dignity of the person. Christian revelation contributes greatly to the promotion of this communion between persons, and at the same time leads us to a deeper understanding of the laws of social life which the Creator has written into man's moral and spiritual nature.

515 Since rather recent documents of the Church's teaching authority have dealt at considerable length with Christian doctrine about human society,[41] this Council is merely going to call to mind some of the more basic truths, treating their foundations under the light of revelation. Then it will dwell more at length on certain of their implications having special significance for our day.

516 24. God, Who has fatherly concern for everyone, has willed that all men should constitute one family and treat one another in a spirit of brotherhood. For having been created in the image of God, Who "from one man has created the whole human race and made them live all over the face of the earth" (*Acts* 17:26), all men are called to one and the same goal, namely God Himself.

517 For this reason, love for God and neighbor is the first and greatest commandment. Sacred Scripture, however, teaches us that the love of God cannot be separated from love of neighbor: "If there is any other commandment, it is summed up in this saying: Thou shalt love thy neighbor as

thyself . . . Love therefore is the fulfillment of the Law" (*Rom.* 13:9, 10; cf. *I John* 4:20). To men growing daily more dependent on one another, and to a world becoming more unified every day, this truth proves to be of paramount importance.

518 Indeed, the Lord Jesus, when He prayed to the Father, "that all may be one . . . as we are one" (*John* 17:21, 22) opened up vistas closed to human reason, for He implied a certain likeness between the union of the divine Persons, and the unity of God's sons in truth and charity. This likeness reveals that man, who is the only creature on earth which God willed for itself, cannot fully find himself except through a sincere gift of himself.[34]

519 25. Man's social nature makes it evident that the progress of the human person and the advance of society itself hinge on one another. For the beginning, the subject and the goal of all social institutions is and must be the human person, which for its part and by its very nature stands completely in need of social life.[43] Since this social life is not something added on to man, through his dealings with others, through reciprocal duties, and through fraternal dialogue he develops all his gifts and is able to rise to his destiny.

520 Among those social ties which man needs for his development some, like the family and political community, relate with greater immediacy to his innermost nature; others originate rather from his free decision. In our era, for various reasons, reciprocal ties and mutual dependencies increase day by day and give rise to a variety of associations and organizations, both public and private. This development, which is called socialization, while certainly not without its dangers, brings with it many advantages with respect to consolidating and increasing the qualities of the human person, and safeguarding his rights.[44]

521 But if by this social life the human person is greatly aided in responding to his destiny, even in its religious dimensions, it cannot be denied that men are often diverted from doing good and spurred toward evil by the social circumstances in which they live and are immersed from their birth. To be sure the disturbances which so frequently occur in the social order

result in part from the natural tensions of economic, political and social forms. But at a deeper level they flow from man's pride and selfishness, which contaminate even the social sphere. When the structure of affairs is flawed by the consequences of sin, man, already born with a bent toward evil, finds there new inducements to sin, which cannot be overcome without strenuous efforts and the assistance of grace.

522 26. Every day human interdependence tightens and spreads by degrees over the whole world. As a result the common good, that is, the sum of those conditions of social life which allow social groups and their individual members relatively thorough and ready access to their own fulfillment, today takes on an increasingly universal complexion and consequently involves rights and duties with respect to the whole human race. Every social group must take account of the needs and legitimate aspirations of other groups, and even of the general welfare of the entire human family.[45]

523 At the same time, however, there is a growing awareness of the exalted dignity proper to the human person, since he stands above all things, and his rights and duties are universal and inviolable. Therefore, there must be made available to all men everything necessary for leading a life truly human, such as food, clothing, and shelter; the right to choose a state of life freely and to found a family, the right to education, to employment, to a good reputation, to respect, to appropriate information, to activity in accord with the upright norm of one's own conscience, to protection of privacy and to rightful freedom, even in matters religious.

524 Hence, the social order and its development must always work to the benefit of the human person if the disposition of affairs is to be subordinate to the personal realm and not contrariwise, as the Lord indicated when He said that the Sabbath was made for man, and not man for the Sabbath.[46]

525 This social order requires constant improvement. It must be founded on truth, built on justice and animated by love; in freedom it should grow every day toward a more humane balance.[47] An improvement in attitudes and numerous changes in society will have to take place if these objectives are to be gained.

God's Spirit, Who with a marvelous providence directs the unfolding of time and renews the face of the earth, is not absent from this development. The ferment of the Gospel too has aroused and continues to arouse in man's heart the irresistible requirements of his dignity. 526

27. Coming down to practical and particularly urgent consequences, this Council lays stress on reverence for man; everyone must consider his every neighbor without exception as another self, taking into account first of all his life and the means necessary to living it with dignity,[48] so as not to imitate the rich man who had no concern for the poor man Lazarus.[49] 527

In our times a special obligation binds us to make ourselves the neighbor of every person without exception, and of actively helping him when he comes across our path, whether he be an old person abandoned by all, a foreign laborer unjustly looked down upon, a refugee, a child born of an unlawful union and wrongly suffering for a sin he did not commit, or a hungry person who disturbs our conscience by recalling the voice of the Lord, "As long as you did it for one of these the least of my brethren, you did it for me" (*Matt.* 25:40). 528

Furthermore, whatever is opposed to life itself, such as any type of murder, genocide, abortion, euthanasia or wilful self-destruction, whatever violates the integrity of the human person, such as mutilation, torments inflicted on body or mind, attempts to coerce the will itself; whatever insults human dignity, such as subhuman living conditions, arbitrary imprisonment, deportation, slavery, prostitution, the selling of women and children; as well as disgraceful working conditions, where men are treated as mere tools for profit, rather than as free and responsible persons; all these things and others of their like are infamies indeed. They poison human society, but they do more harm to those who practice them than those who suffer from the injury. Moreover, they are a supreme dishonor to the Creator. 529

28. Respect and love ought to be extended also to those who think or act differently than we do in social, political and even religious matters. In fact, the more deeply we come to understand their ways of thinking through such courtesy 530

and love, the more easily will we be able to enter into dialogue with them.

531 This love and good will, to be sure, must in no way render us indifferent to truth and goodness. Indeed love itself impels the disciples of Christ to speak the saving truth to all men. But it is necessary to distinguish between error, which always merits repudiation, and the person in error, who never loses the dignity of being a person even when he is flawed by false or inadequate religious notions.[50] God alone is the judge and searcher of hearts; for that reason He forbids us to make judgments about the internal guilt of anyone.[51]

532 The teaching of Christ even requires that we forgive injuries[52] and extends the law of love to include every enemy, according to the command of the New Law: "You have heard that it was said: Thou shalt love thy neighbor and hate thy enemy. But I say to you: love your enemies, do good to those who hate you, and pray for those who persecute and calumniate you" (*Matt.* 5:43, 44).

533 29. Since all men possess a rational soul and are created in God's likeness, since they have the same nature and origin, have been redeemed by Christ and enjoy the same divine calling and destiny, the basic equality of all must receive increasingly greater recognition.

534 True, all men are not alike from the point of view of varying physical power and the diversity of intellectual and moral resources. Nevertheless, with respect to the fundamental rights of the person, every type of discrimination, whether social or cultural, whether based on sex, race, color, social condition, language or religion, is to be overcome and eradicated as contrary to God's intent. For in truth it must still be regretted that fundamental personal rights are not yet being universally honored. Such is the case of a woman who is denied the right to choose a husband freely, to embrace a state of life or to acquire an education or cultural benefits equal to those recognized for men.

535 Therefore, although rightful differences exist between men, the equal dignity of persons demands that a more humane and a just condition of life be brought about. For excessive economic and social differences between the members of the

one human family or population groups cause scandal, and militate against social justice, equity, the dignity of the human person, as well as social and international peace.

Human institutions, both private and public, must labor to minister to the dignity and purpose of man. At the same time let them put up a stubborn fight against any kind of slavery, whether social or political, and safeguard the basic rights of man under every political system. Indeed human institutions themselves must be accommodated by degrees to the highest of all realities, spiritual ones, even though meanwhile, a long enough time will be required before they arrive at the desired goal. 536

30. Profound and rapid changes make it more necessary that no one ignoring the trend of events or drugged by laziness, content himself with a merely individualistic morality. It becomes increasingly true that the obligations of justice and love are fulfilled only if each person, contributing to the common good, according to his own abilities and the needs of others, also promotes and assists the public and private institutions dedicated to bettering the conditions of human life. Yet there are those who, while professing grand and rather noble sentiments, nevertheless in reality live always as if they cared nothing for the needs of society. Many in various places even make light of social laws and precepts, and do not hesitate to resort to various frauds and deceptions in avoiding just taxes or other debts due to society. Others think little of certain norms of social life, for example those designed for the protection of health, or laws establishing speed limits; they do not even avert to the fact that by such indifference they imperil their own life and that of others. 537

Let everyone consider it his sacred obligation to esteem and observe social necessities as being among the primary duties of modern man. For the more unified the world becomes, the more plainly do the offices of men extend beyond particular groups and spread by degrees to the whole world. But this development cannot occur unless individual men and their associations cultivate in themselves the moral and social virtues, and promote them in society; thus, with the needed 538 help of divine grace men who are truly new and artisans of a new humanity can be forthcoming.

539 31. Individual men, in order to discharge with great exactness the obligations of their conscience toward themselves and the various groups to which they belong, must be carefully educated to a higher degree of culture through the use of the immense resources available today to the human race. Above all the education of youth from every social background has to be undertaken, so that there can be produced not only men and women of refined talents, but those great-souled persons who are so desperately required by our times.

540 Now a man can scarcely arrive at the needed sense of responsibility, unless his living conditions allow him to become conscious of his dignity, and to rise to his destiny by spending himself for God and for others. But human freedom is often crippled when a man encounters extreme poverty, just as it withers when he indulges in too many of life's comforts and imprisons himself in a kind of splendid isolation. Freedom acquires new strength, by contrast, when a man consents to the unavoidable requirements of social life, takes on the manifold demands of human partnership, and commits himself to the service of the human community.

541 Hence, the will to play one's role in common endeavors should be everywhere encouraged. Praise is due to those national processes which allow the largest possible number of citizens to participate in public affairs with genuine freedom. Account must be taken, to be sure, of the actual conditions of each people and the firmness required by public authority. If every citizen is to feel inclined to take part in the activities of the various groups which make up the social body, these must offer advantages which will attract members and dispose them to serve others. We can justly consider that the future of humanity lies in the hands of those who are strong enough to provide coming generations with reasons for living and hoping.

542 32. As God did not create man for life in isolation, but for the formation of social unity, so also "it has pleased God to make men holy and save them not merely as individuals, without bond or link between them, but by making them into

a single people, a people which acknowledges Him in truth and serves Him in holiness."[53] So from the beginning of salvation history He has chosen men not just as individuals but as members of a certain community. Revealing His mind to them, God called these chosen ones "His people" (*Ex.* 3:7, 12), and even made a covenant with them on Sinai.[54]

543 This communitarian character is developed and consummated in the work of Jesus Christ. For the very Word made flesh willed to share in the human fellowship. He was present at the wedding of Cana, visited the house of Zachaeus, ate with publicans and sinners. He revealed the love of the Father and the sublime vocation of man in terms of the most common of social realities and by making use of the speech and the imagery of plain everyday life. Willingly obeying the laws of His country, He sanctified those human ties, especially family ones, which are the foundation of social structures. He chose to lead the life proper to an artisan of His time and place.

544 In His preaching He clearly taught the sons of God to treat one another as brothers. In His prayers He pleaded that all His disciples might be "one." Indeed as the Redeemer of all, He offered Himself for all even to the point of death. "Greater love than this no one has, that one lay down his life for his friends" (*John* 15:13). He commanded His Apostles to preach to all peoples the Gospel's message that the human race was to become the Family of God, in which the fullness of the Law would be love.

545 As the firstborn of many brethren and by the giving of His Spirit, He founded after His death and resurrection a new brotherly community composed of all those who receive Him in faith and in love. This He did through His Body, which is the Church. There everyone, as members one of the other, would render mutual service according to the different gifts bestowed on each.

546 This solidarity must be constantly increased until that day on which it will be brought to perfection. Then, saved by grace, men will offer flawless glory to God as a family beloved of God and of Christ their Brother.

CHAPTER III

Man's Activity Throughout the World

547 33. Through his labors and his native endowments man has ceaselessly striven to better his life. Today, however, especially with the help of science and technology, he has extended his mastery over nearly the whole of nature and continues to do so. Thanks to increased opportunities for many kinds of social contact among nations, the human family is gradually recognizing that it comprises a single world community and is making itself so. Hence many benefits once looked for, especially from heavenly powers, man has now enterprisingly procured for himself.

548 In the face of these immense efforts which already preoccupy the whole human race, men raise numerous questions among themselves. What is the meaning and value of this feverish activity? How should all these things be used? To the achievement of what goal are the strivings of individuals and societies heading? The Church guards the heritage of God's Word and draws from it moral and religious principles without always having at hand the solution to particular problems. As such she desires to add the light of revealed truth to mankind's store of experience, so that the path which humanity has taken in recent times will not be a dark one.

549 34. Throughout the course of the centuries, men have labored to better the circumstances of their lives through a monumental amount of individual and collective effort. To believers, this point is settled: considered in itself, this human activity accords with God's will. For man, created to God's image, received a mandate to subject to himself the earth and all it contains, and to govern the world with justice and holiness;[55] a mandate to relate himself and the totality of things to Him Who was to be acknowledged as the Lord and Creator of all. Thus, by the subjection of all things to man, the name of God would be wonderful in all the earth.[56]

This mandate concerns the whole range of everyday activity as well. For while providing the substance of life for themselves and their families, men and women are performing their activities in a way which appropriately benefits society. They can justly consider that by their labor they are unfolding the Creator's work, consulting the advantages of their brother men, and are contributing by their personal industry to the realization in history of the divine plan.[59] 550

Thus, far from thinking that works produced by man's own talent and energy are in opposition to God's power, and that the rational creature exists as a kind of rival to the Creator, Christians are convinced that the triumphs of the human race are a sign of God's grace and the flowering of His own mysterious design. For the greater man's power becomes, the further his individual and community responsibility extends. Hence it is clear that men are not deterred by the Christian message from building up the world, or impelled to neglect the welfare of their fellows, but that they are rather more stringently bound to do these very things.[58] 551

35. Human activity, to be sure, takes its significance from its relationship to man. Just as it proceeds from man, so it is ordered toward man. For when a man works he not only alters things and society, he develops himself as well. He learns much, he cultivates his resources, he goes outside of himself and beyond himself. Rightly understood, this kind of growth is of greater value than any external riches which can be garnered. A man is more precious for what he is than for what he has.[59] Similarly, all that men do to obtain greater justice, wider brotherhood, a more humane ordering of social relationships has greater worth than technical advances. For these advances can supply the material for human progress, but of themselves alone they can never actually bring it about. 552

Hence, the norm of human activity is this: that in accord with the divine plan and will, it harmonize with the genuine good of the human race, and that it allow men as individuals and as members of society to pursue their total vocation and fulfil it. 553

36. Now many of our contemporaries seem to fear that a closer bond between human activity and religion will work 554

against the independence of men, of societies, or of the sciences.

555 If by the autonomy of earthly affairs we mean that created things and societies themselves enjoy their own laws and values which must be gradually deciphered, put to use, and regulated by men, then it is entirely right to demand that autonomy. This is not merely required by modern man, but harmonizes also with the will of the Creator. For by the very circumstance of their having been created, all things are endowed with their own stability, truth, goodness, proper laws and order. Man must respect these as he isolates them by the appropriate methods of the individual sciences or arts. Therefore if methodical investigation within every branch of learning is carried out in a genuinely scientific manner and in accord with moral norms, it never truly conflicts with faith, for earthly matters and the concerns of faith derive from the same God.[60] Indeed whoever labors to penetrate the secrets of reality with a humble and steady mind, even though he is unaware of the fact, is nevertheless being led by the hand of God, Who holds all things in existence, and gives them their identity. Consequently, we cannot but deplore certain habits of mind, which are sometimes found too among Christians, which do not sufficiently attend to the rightful independence of science and which, from the arguments and controversies they spark, lead many minds to conclude that faith and science are mutually opposed.[61]

556 But if the expression, the autonomy of temporal affairs, is taken to mean that created things do not depend on God, and that man can use them without any reference to their Creator, anyone who acknowledges God will see how false such a meaning is. For without the Creator the Creature would disappear. For their part, however, all believers of whatever religion always hear His revealing voice in the discourse of creatures. When God is forgotten, however, the creature itself grows unintelligible.

557 37. Sacred Scripture teaches the human family what the experience of the ages confirms: that while human progress is a great advantage to man, it brings with it a strong temptation. For when the order of values is jumbled and bad is mixed

with the good, individuals and groups pay heed solely to their own interests, and not to those of others. Thus it happens that the world ceases to be a place of true brotherhood. In our own day, the magnified power of humanity threatens to destroy the race itself.

558 For a monumental struggle against the powers of darkness pervades the whole history of man. The battle was joined from the very origins of the world and will continue until the last day, as the Lord has attested.[62] Caught in this conflict, man is obliged to wrestle constantly if he is to cling to what is good, nor can he achieve his own integrity without great efforts and the help of God's grace.

559 That is why Christ's Church, trusting in the design of the Creator, acknowledges that human progress can serve man's true happiness, yet she cannot help echoing the Apostle's warning: "Be not conformed to this world" (*Rom.* 12:2). Here by the world is meant that spirit of vanity and malice which transforms into an instrument of sin those human energies intended for the service of God and man.

560 Hence if anyone wants to know how this unhappy situation can be overcome, Christians will tell him that all human activity, constantly imperiled by man's pride and deranged self-love, must be purified and perfected by the power of Christ's Cross and resurrection. For redeemed by Christ and made a new creature in the Holy Spirit, man is able to love the things themselves created by God, and ought to do so. He can receive them from God and respect and reverence them as flowing constantly from the hand of God. Grateful to his Benefactor for these creatures, using and enjoying them in detachment and liberty of spirit, man is led forward into a true possession of them, as having nothing, yet possessing all things.[63] "All are yours, and you are Christ's, and Christ is God's" (*I Cor.* 3:22-23).

561 38. For God's Word, through Whom all things were made, was Himself made flesh and dwelt on man's earth.[64] Thus He entered the world's history as a perfect man, taking that history up into Himself and summarizing it.[65] He Himself revealed to us that "God is love" (I *John* 4:8) and at the same time taught us that the new command of love was the basic

law of human perfection and hence of the world's transformation.

562 To those, therefore, who believe in divine love, He gives assurance that the way of love lies open to men and that the effort to establish a universal brotherhood is not a hopeless one. He cautions them at the same time that this love is not something to be reserved for important matters, but must be pursued chiefly in the ordinary circumstances of life. Undergoing death itself for all of us sinners,[66] He taught us by example that we too must shoulder that cross which the world and the flesh inflict upon those who search after peace and justice. Appointed Lord by His resurrection and given all power in heaven and on earth,[67] Christ is now at work in the hearts of men through the energy of His Spirit, arousing not only a desire for the age to come, but by that very fact animating, purifying and strengthening those noble longings too by which the human family makes its life more human and strives to render the whole earth submissive to this goal.

563 Now, the gifts of the Spirit are diverse: while He calls some to give clear witness to the desire for a heavenly home and to keep that desire fresh among the human family, He summons others to dedicate themselves to the earthly service of men and to make ready the material of the celestial realm by this ministry of theirs. Yet He frees all of them so that by putting aside love of self and bringing all earthly resources into the service of human life they can devote themselves to that future when humanity itself will become an offering accepted by God.[68]

564 The Lord left behind a pledge of this hope and strength for life's journey in that sacrament of faith where natural elements refined by man are gloriously changed into His Body and Blood, providing a meal of brotherly solidarity and a foretaste of the heavenly banquet.

565 39. We do not know the time for the consummation of the earth and of humanity,[69] nor do we know how all things will be transformed. As deformed by sin, the shape of this world will pass away;[70] but we are taught that God is preparing a new dwelling place and a new earth where justice will abide,[71] and whose blessedness will answer and surpass all the longings for peace which spring up in the human heart.[72]

Then, with death overcome, the sons of God will be raised up in Christ, and what was sown in weakness and corruption will be clothed with incorruptibility.[73] Enduring with charity and its fruits,[74] all that creation[75] which God made on man's account will be unchained from the bondage of vanity.

566 Therefore, while we are warned that it profits a man nothing if he gain the whole world and lose himself,[76] the expectation of a new earth must not weaken but rather stimulate our concern for cultivating this one. For here grows the body of a new human family, a body which even now is able to give some kind of foreshadowing of the new age.

567 Hence, while earthly progress must be carefully distinguished from the growth of Christ's Kingdom, to the extent that the former can contribute to the better ordering of human society, it is of vital concern to the Kingdom of God.[77]

568 For after we have obeyed the Lord, and in His Spirit nurtured on earth the values of human dignity, brotherhood and freedom, and indeed all the good fruits of our nature and enterprise, we will find them again, but freed of stain, burnished and transfigured, when Christ hands over to the Father: "a kingdom eternal and universal, a kingdom of truth and life, of holiness and grace, of justice, love and peace."[78] On this earth that Kingdom is already present in mystery. When the Lord returns it will be brought into full flower.

CHAPTER IV

The Role of the Church in the Modern World

569 40. Everything we have said about the dignity of the human person, and about the human community and the profound meaning of human activity, lays the foundation for the relationship between the Church and the world, and provides the basis for dialogue between them.[79] In this chapter, presupposing everything which has already been said by this Council concerning the mystery of the Church, we must now consider this same Church inasmuch as she exists in the world, living and acting with it.

570 Coming forth from the eternal Father's love,[80] founded in time by Christ the Redeemer and made one in the Holy Spirit,[81] the Church has a saving and an eschatological purpose which can be fully attained only in the future world. But she is already present in this world, and is composed of men, that is, of members of the earthly city who have a call to form the family of God's children during the present history of the human race, and to keep increasing it until the Lord returns. United on behalf of heavenly values and enriched by them, this family has been "constituted and structured as a society in this world"[82] by Christ, and is equipped "by appropriate means for visible and social union."[83] Thus the Church, at once "a visible association and a spiritual community,"[84] goes forward together with humanity and experiences the same earthly lot which the world does. She serves as a leaven and as a kind of soul for human society[85] as it is to be renewed in Christ and transformed into God's family.

571 That the earthly and the heavenly city penetrate each other is a fact accessible to faith alone; it remains a mystery of human history, which sin will keep in great disarray until the splendor of God's sons is fully revealed. Pursuing the saving purpose which is proper to her, the Church does not only communicate divine life to men but in some way casts the reflected light of that life over the entire earth, most of all by its healing and elevating impact on the dignity of the person, by the way in which it strengthens the seams of human society and imbues the everyday activity of men with a deeper meaning and importance. Thus through her individual members and her whole community, the Church believes she can contribute greatly toward making the family of man and its history more human.

572 In addition, the Catholic Church gladly holds in high esteem the things which other Christian Churches and ecclesial communities have done or are doing cooperatively by way of achieving the same goal. At the same time, she is convinced that she can be abundantly and variously helped by the world in the matter of preparing the ground for the Gospel. This help she gains from the talents and industry of

individuals and from human society as a whole. The Council now sets forth certain general principles for the proper fostering of this mutual exchange and assistance in concerns which are in some way common to the world and the Church.

41. Modern man is on the road to a more thorough development of his own personality, and to a growing discovery and vindication of his own rights. Since it has been entrusted to the Church to reveal the mystery of God, Who is the ultimate goal of man, she opens up to man at the same time the meaning of his own existence, that is, the innermost truth about himself. The Church truly knows that only God, Whom she serves, meets the deepest longings of the human heart, which is never fully satisfied by what this world has to offer. 573

She also knows that man is constantly worked upon by God's Spirit, and hence can never be altogether indifferent to the problems of religion. The experience of past ages proves this, as do numerous indications in our own times. For man will always yearn to know, at least in an obscure way, what is the meaning of his life, of his activity, of his death. The very presence of the Church recalls these problems to his mind. But only God, Who created man to His own image and ransomed him from sin, provides a fully adequate answer to these questions, and this He does through what He has revealed in Christ His Son, Who became man. Whoever follows after Christ, the perfect man, becomes himself more of a man. For by His incarnation the Father's Word assumed, and sanctified through His cross and resurrection, the whole of man, body and soul, and through that totality the whole of nature created by God for man's use. 574

Thanks to this belief, the Church can anchor the dignity of human nature against all tides of opinion, for example those which undervalue the human body or idolize it. By no human law can the personal dignity and liberty of man be so aptly safeguarded as by the Gospel of Christ which has been entrusted to the Church. For this Gospel announces and proclaims the freedom of the sons of God, and repudiates all the bondage which ultimately results from sin (cf. *Rom.* 8:14- 575

17);[86] it has a sacred reverence for the dignity of conscience and its freedom of choice, constantly advises that all human talents be employed in God's service and men's and, finally, commends all to the charity of all (cf. *Matt.* 22:39).[87]

576 This agrees with the basic law of Christian dispensation. For though the same God is Saviour and Creator, Lord of human history as well as of salvation history, in the divine arrangement itself, the rightful autonomy of the creature, and particularly of man is not withdrawn, but is rather re-established in its own dignity and strengthened in it.

577 The Church, therefore, by virtue of the Gospel committed to her, proclaims the rights of man; she acknowledges and greatly esteems the dynamic movements of today by which these rights are everywhere fostered. Yet these movements must be penetrated by the spirit of the Gospel and protected against any kind of false autonomy. For we are tempted to think that our personal rights are fully ensured only when we are exempt from every requirement of divine law. But this way lies not the maintenance of the dignity of the human person, but its annihilation.

578 42. The union of the human family is greatly fortified and fulfilled by the unity, founded on Christ,[88] of the family of God's sons.

579 Christ, to be sure, gave His Church no proper mission in the political, economic or social order. The purpose which He set before her is a religious one.[89] But out of this religious mission itself come a function, a light and an energy which can serve to structure and consolidate the human community according to the divine law. As a matter of fact, when circumstances of time and place produce the need, she can and indeed should initiate activities on behalf of all men, especially those designed for the needy, such as the works of mercy and similar undertakings.

580 The Church recognizes that worthy elements are found in today's social movements, especially an evolution toward unity, a process of wholesome socialization and of association in civic and economic realms. The promotion of unity belongs to the innermost nature of the Church, for she is, "thanks to her relationship with Christ, a sacramental sign

and an instrument of intimate union with God, and of the unity of the whole human race."[90] Thus she shows the world that an authentic union, social and external, results from a union of minds and hearts, namely from that faith and charity by which her own unity is unbreakably rooted in the Holy Spirit. For the force which the Church can inject into the modern society of man consists in that faith and charity put into vital practice, not in any external dominion exercised by merely human means.

Moreover, since in virtue of her mission and nature she is bound to no particular form of human culture, nor to any political, economic or social system, the Church by her very universality can be a very close bond between diverse human communities and nations, provided these trust her and truly acknowledge her right to true freedom in fulfilling her mission. For this reason, the Church admonishes her own sons, but also humanity as a whole, to overcome all strife between nations and races in this family spirit of God's children, and in the same way, to give internal strength to human associations which are just. 581

Therefore, this Council regards with great respect all the true, good and just elements inherent in the very wide variety of institutions which the human race has established for itself and constantly continues to establish. The Council affirms, moreover, that the Church is willing to assist and promote all these institutions to the extent that such a service depends on her and can be associated with her mission. She has no fiercer desire than that in pursuit of the welfare of all she may be able to develop herself freely under any kind of government which grants recognition to the basic rights of person and family, to the demands of the common good and to the free exercise of her own mission. 582

43. This Council exhorts Christians, as citizens of two cities, to strive to discharge their earthly duties conscientiously and in response to the Gospel spirit. They are mistaken who, knowing that we have here no abiding city but seek one which is to come,[91] think that they may therefore shirk their earthly responsibilities. For they are forgetting that by the faith itself they are more obliged than ever to 583

measure up to these duties, each according to his proper vocation.[92] Nor, on the contrary, are they any less wide of the mark who think that religion consists in acts of worship alone and in the discharge of certain moral obligations, and who imagine they can plunge themselves into earthly affairs in such a way as to imply that these are altogether divorced from the religious life. This split between the faith which many profess and their daily lives deserves to be counted among the more serious errors of our age. Long since, the Prophets of the Old Testament fought vehemently against this scandal[93] and even more so did Jesus Christ Himself in the New Testament threaten it with grave punishments.[94] Therefore, let there be no false opposition between professional and social activities on the one part, and religious life on the other. The Christian who neglects his temporal duties, neglects his duties toward his neighbor and even God, and jeopardizes his eternal salvation. Christians should rather rejoice that, following the example of Christ Who worked as an artisan, they are free to exercise all their earthly activities by gathering their humane, domestic, professional, social and technical enterprises into one vital synthesis with religious values, under whose supreme direction all things are harmonized unto God's glory.

584 Secular duties and activities belong properly although not exclusively to laymen. Therefore acting as citizens in the world, whether individually or socially, they will observe the laws proper to each discipline, and labor to equip themselves with a genuine expertise in their various fields. They will gladly work with men seeking the same goals. Acknowledging the demands of faith and endowed with its force, they will unhesitatingly devise new enterprises, where they are appropriate, and put them into action. Laymen should also know that it is generally the function of their well-formed Christian conscience to see that the divine law is inscribed in the life of the earthly city; from priests they may look for spiritual light and nourishment. Let the layman not imagine that his pastors are always such experts, that to every problem which arises, however complicated, they can readily give him a concrete solution, or even that such is their mission. Rather enlight-

ened by Christian wisdom and giving close attention to the teaching authority of the Church,[95] let the layman take on his own distinctive role.

Often enough the Christian view of things will itself suggest some specific solution in certain circumstances. Yet it happens rather frequently, and legitimately so, that with equal sincerity some of the faithful will disagree with others on a given matter. Even against the intentions of their proponents, however, solutions proposed on one side or another may be easily confused by many people with the Gospel message. Hence it is necessary for people to remember that no one is allowed in the aforementioned situations to appropriate the Church's authority for his opinion. They should always try to enlighten one another through honest discussion, preserving mutual charity and caring above all for the common good. 585

Since they have an active role to play in the whole life of the Church, laymen are not only bound to penetrate the world with a Christian spirit, but are also called to be witnesses to Christ in all things in the midst of human society. 586

Bishops, to whom is assigned the task of ruling the Church of God, should, together with their priests, so preach the news of Christ that all the earthly activities of the faithful will be bathed in the light of the Gospel. All pastors should remember too that by their daily conduct and concern[96] they are revealing the face of the Church to the world, and men will judge the power and truth of the Christian message thereby. By their lives and speech, in union with Religious and their faithful, may they demonstrate that even now the Church, by her presence alone and by all the gifts which she contains, is an unspent fountain of those virtues which the modern world needs the most. 587

By unremitting study they should fit themselves to do their part in establishing dialogue with the world and with men of all shades of opinion. Above all let them take to heart the words which this Council has spoken: "Since humanity today increasingly moves toward civil, economic and social unity, it is more than ever necessary that priests, with joint concern and energy, and under the guidance of the bishops 588 and the supreme pontiff, erase every cause of division, so that the whole human race may be led to the unity of God's family."[97]

589 Although by the power of the Holy Spirit the Church will remain the faithful spouse of her Lord and will never cease to be the sign of salvation on earth, still she is very well aware that among her members,[98] both clerical and lay, some have been unfaithful to the Spirit of God during the course of many centuries; in the present age, too, it does not escape the Church how great a distance lies between the message she offers and the human failings of those to whom the Gospel is entrusted. Whatever be the judgment of history on these defects, we ought to be conscious of them, and struggle against them energetically, lest they inflict harm on spread of the Gospel. The Church also realizes that in working out her relationship with the world she always has great need of the ripening which comes with the experience of the centuries. Led by the Holy Spirit, Mother Church unceasingly exhorts her sons "to purify and renew themselves so that the sign of Christ can shine more brightly on the face of the Church."[99]

590 44. Just as it is in the world's interest to acknowledge the Church as a historical reality, and to recognize her good influence, so the Church herself knows how richly she has profited by the history and development of humanity.

591 The experience of past ages, the progress of the sciences, and the treasures hidden in the various forms of human culture, by all of which the nature of man himself is more clearly revealed and new roads to truth are opened, these profit the Church, too. For, from the beginning of her history she has learned to express the message of Christ with the help of the ideas and terminology of various philosophers, and has tried to clarify it with their wisdom, too. Her purpose has been to adapt the Gospel to the grasp of all as well as to the needs of the learned, insofar as such was appropriate. Indeed this accommodated preaching of the revealed Word ought to remain the law of all evangelization. For thus the ability to express Christ's message in its own way is developed in each nation, and at the same time there is fostered a living exchange between the Church and the diverse cultures

of people.[100] To promote such exchange, especially in our days, the Church requires the special help of those who live in the world, are versed in different institutions and specialties, and grasp their innermost significance in the eyes of both believers and unbelievers. With the help of the Holy Spirit, it is the task of the entire People of God, especially pastors and theologians, to hear, distinguish and interpret the many voices of our age, and to judge them in the light of the divine Word, so that revealed truth can always be more deeply penetrated, better understood and set forth to greater advantage.

592 Since the Church has a visible and social structure as a sign of her unity in Christ, she can and ought to be enriched by the development of human social life, not that there is any lack in the constitution given her by Christ, but that she can understand it more penetratingly, express it better, and adjust it more successfully to our times. Moreover, she gratefully understands that in her community life no less than in her individual sons, she receives a variety of helps from men of every rank and condition, for whoever promotes the human community at the family level, culturally, in its economic, social and political dimensions, both nationally and internationally, such a one, according to God's design, is contributing greatly to the Church as well, to the extent that she depends on things outside herself. Indeed, the Church admits that she has greatly profited and still profits from the antagonism of those who oppose or who persecute her.[101]

593 45. While helping the world and receiving many benefits from it, the Church has a single intention: that God's Kingdom may come, and that the salvation of the whole human race may come to pass. For every benefit which the People of God during its earthly pilgrimage can offer to the human family stems from the fact that the Church is "the universal sacrament of salvation",[102] simultaneously manifesting and exercising the mystery of God's love for man.

594 For God's Word, by Whom all things were made, was Himself made flesh so that as perfect man He might save all men and sum up all things in Himself. The Lord is the Goal of human history, the focal point of the longings of history and

of civilization, the center of the human race, the joy of every heart and the answer to all its yearnings.[103] He it is Whom the Father raised from the dead, lifted on high and stationed at His right hand, making Him judge of the living and the dead. Enlivened and united in His Spirit, we journey toward the consummation of human history, one which fully accords with the counsel of God's love: "To re-establish all things in Christ, both those in the heavens and those on the earth" (*Eph.* 11:10).

595 The Lord Himself speaks: "Behold I come quickly! And my reward is with me, to render to each one according to his works. I am the Alpha and the Omega, the first and the last, the beginning and the end"(*Apoc.* 22:12-13).

PART II

Some Problems of Special Urgency

596 46. This Council has set forth the dignity of the human person, and the work which men have been destined to undertake throughout the world both as individuals and as members of society. There are a number of particularly urgent needs characterizing the present age, needs which go to the roots of the human race. To a consideration of these in the light of the Gospel and of human experience, the Council would now direct the attention of all.

597 Of the many subjects arousing universal concern today, it may be helpful to concentrate on these: marriage and the family, human progress, life in its economic, social and political dimensions, the bonds between the family of nations, and peace. On each of these may there shine the radiant ideals proclaimed by Christ. By these ideals may Christians be led, and all mankind enlightened, as they search for answers to questions of such complexity.

CHAPTER I

Fostering the Nobility of Marriage and the Family

47. This well-being of the individual person and of human and Christian society is intimately linked with the healthy condition of that community produced by marriage and family. Hence Christians and all men who hold this community in high esteem sincerely rejoice in the various ways by which men today find help in fostering this community of love and perfecting its life, and by which parents are assisted in their lofty calling. Those who rejoice in such aids look for additional benefits from them and labor to bring them about. 598

Yet the excellence of this institution is not everywhere reflected with equal brilliance, since polygamy, the plague of divorce, so-called free love and other disfigurements have an obscuring effect. In addition, married love is too often profaned by excessive self-love, the worship of pleasure and illicit practices against human generation. Moreover, serious disturbances are caused in families by modern economic conditions, by influences at once social and psychological, and by the demands of civil society. Finally, in certain parts of the world problems resulting from population growth are generating concern. 599

All these situations have produced anxiety of conscience. Yet, the power and strength of the institution of marriage and family can also be seen in the fact that time and again, despite the difficulties produced, the profound changes in modern society reveal the true character of this institution in one way or another. 600

Therefore, by presenting certain key points of Church doctrine in a clearer light, this sacred Synod wishes to offer guidance and support to those Christians and other men who are trying to preserve the holiness and to foster the natural dignity of the married state and its superlative value. 601

48. The intimate partnership of married life and love has been established by the Creator and qualified by His laws, 602

and is rooted in the conjugal covenant of irrevocable personal consent. Hence by that human act whereby spouses mutually bestow and accept each other a relationship arises which by divine will and in the eyes of society too is a lasting one. For the good of the spouses and their offspring as well as of society, the existence of the sacred bond no longer depends on human decisions alone. For God Himself is the author of matrimony, endowed as it is with various benefits and purposes.[104] All of these have a very decisive bearing on the continuation of the human race, on the personal development and eternal destiny of the individual members of a family, and on the dignity, stability, peace and prosperity of the family itself and of human society as a whole. By their very nature, the institution of matrimony itself and conjugal love are ordained for the procreation and education of children, and find in them their ultimate crown. Thus a man and a woman, who by their compact of conjugal love "are no longer two, but one flesh" (*Matt.* 19:6), render mutual help and service to each other through an intimate union of their persons and of their actions. Through this union they experience the meaning of their oneness and attain to it with growing perfection day by day. As a mutual gift of two persons, this intimate union and the good of the children impose total fidelity on the spouses and argue for an unbreakable oneness between them.[105]

603 Christ the Lord abundantly blessed this many-faceted love, welling up as it does from the fountain of divine love and structured as it is on the model of His union with His Church. For as God of old made Himself present[106] to His people through a covenant of love and fidelity, so now the Saviour of men and the Spouse[107] of the Church comes into the lives of married Christians through the Sacrament of Matrimony. He abides with them thereafter so that, just as He loved the Church and handed Himself over on her behalf,[108] the spouses may love each other with perpetual fidelity through mutual self-bestowal.

604 Authentic married love is caught up into divine love and is governed and enriched by Christ's redeeming power and the saving activity of the Church, so that this love may lead the

spouses to God with powerful effect and may aid and strengthen them in the sublime office of being a father or a mother.[109] For this reason Christian spouses have a special sacrament by which they are fortified and receive a kind of consecration in the duties and dignity of their state.[110] By virtue of this sacrament, as spouses fulfill their conjugal and family obligations, they are penetrated with the spirit of Christ, which suffuses their whole lives with faith, hope and charity. Thus they increasingly advance the perfection of their own personalities, as well as their mutual sanctification, and hence contribute jointly to the glory of God.

605 As a result, with their parents leading the way by example and family prayer, children and indeed everyone gathered around the family hearth will find a readier path to human maturity, salvation and holiness. Graced with the dignity and office of fatherhood and motherhood, parents will energetically acquit themselves of a duty which devolves primarily on them, namely education and especially religious education.

606 As living members of the family, children contribute in their own way to making their parents holy. For they will respond to the kindness of their parents with sentiments of gratitude, with love and trust. They will stand by them as children should when hardships overtake their parents and old age brings its loneliness. Widowhood, accepted bravely as a continuation of the marriage vocation, should be esteemed by all.[111] Families too will share their spiritual riches generously with other families. Thus the Christian family, which springs from marriage as a reflection of the loving covenant uniting Christ with the Church,[112] and as a participation in that covenant, will manifest to all men Christ's living presence in the world, and the genuine nature of the Church. This the family will do by the mutual love of the spouses, by their generous fruitfulness, their solidarity and faithfulness, and by the loving way in which all members of the family assist one another.

607 49. The biblical Word of God several times urges the betrothed and the married to nourish and develop their wedlock by pure conjugal love and undivided affection.[113] Many men of our own age also highly regard true love between hus-

band and wife as it manifests itself in a variety of ways depending on the worthy customs of various peoples and times.

608 This love is an eminently human one since it is directed from one person to another through an affection of the will; it involves the good of the whole person, and therefore can enrich the expressions of the body and mind with a unique dignity, ennobling these expressions as special ingredients and signs of the friendship distinctive of marriage. This love God has judged worthy of special gifts, healing, perfecting and exalting gifts of grace and of charity. Such love, merging the human with the divine, leads the spouses to a free and mutual gift of themselves, a gift proving itself by gentle affection and by deed; such love pervades the whole of their lives:[114] indeed by its active generosity it grows better and grows greater. Therefore it far excels mere erotic inclination, which, selfishly pursued, soon enough fades wretchedly away.

609 This love is uniquely expressed and perfected in the special area of matrimony. The actions within marriage by which the couple are united intimately and chastely are noble and worthy ones. Expressed in a manner which is truly human, these actions promote that mutual self-giving by which spouses enrich each other with a joyful and a ready will. Sealed by mutual faithfulness and hallowed above all by Christ's sacrament, this love remains steadfastly true in body and in mind, in bright days or dark. It will never be profaned by adultery or divorce. Firmly established by the Lord, the unity of marriage will radiate from the equal personal dignity of wife and husband, a dignity acknowledged by mutual and total love. The constant fulfilment of the duties of this Christian vocation demands notable virtue. For this reason, strengthened by grace for holiness of life, the couple will painstakingly cultivate and pray for steadfastness of love, large-heartedness and the spirit of sacrifice.

610 Authentic conjugal love will be more highly prized, and wholesome public opinion created regarding it if Christian couples give outstanding witness to faithfulness and harmony in their love, and to their concern for educating their children; also, if they do their part in bringing about the needed cultural, psychological and social renewal on behalf of mar-

riage and the family. Especially in the heart of their own families, young people should be aptly and seasonably instructed in the dignity, duty and work of married love. Trained thus in the cultivation of chastity, they will be able at a suitable age to enter a marriage of their own after an honorable courtship.

50. Marriage and conjugal love are by their nature ordained toward the begetting and educating of children. Children are really the supreme gift of marriage and contribute very substantially to the welfare of their parents. The God Himself Who said, "it is not good for man to be alone" (*Gen.* 2:18) and "Who made man from the beginning male and female" (*Matt.* 19:4); wishing to share with man a certain special participation in His own creative work, blessed male and female, saying: "Increase and multiply" (*Gen.* 1:28). Hence, while not making the other purposes of matrimony of less account, the true practice of conjugal love, and the whole meaning of the family life which results from it, have this aim: that the couple be ready with stout hearts to cooperate with the love of the Creator and the Saviour, Who through them will enlarge and enrich His own family day by day. 611

Parents should regard as their proper mission the task of transmitting human life and educating those to whom it has been transmitted. They should realize that they are thereby cooperators with the love of God the Creator, and are, so to speak, the interpreters of that love. Thus they will fulfill their task with human and Christian responsibility, and, with docile reverence toward God, will make decisions by common counsel and effort. Let them thoughtfully take into account both their own welfare and that of their children, those already born and those which the future may bring. For this accounting they need to reckon with both the material and the spiritual conditions of the times as well as of their state in life. Finally, they should consult the interests of the family group, of temporal society, and of the Church herself. The parents themselves should ultimately make this judgment in the sight of God. But in their manner of acting, spouses should be aware that they cannot proceed arbitrarily, but must always be governed according to a conscience dutifully 612 conformed to the divine law itself, and should be submissive toward the Church's teaching office, which authentically interprets that law in the light of the Gospel. That divine law reveals and protects the integral meaning of conjugal love, and impels it toward a truly human fulfilment. Thus, trusting in divine Providence and refining the spirit of sacrifice,[115] married Christians glorify the Creator and strive toward fulfilment in Christ when with a generous human and Christian sense of responsibility they acquit themselves of the duty to procreate. Among the couples who fulfil their God-given task in this way, those merit special mention who with a gallant heart, and with wise and common deliberation, undertake to bring up suitably even a relatively large family.[116]

613 Marriage to be sure is not instituted solely for procreation; rather, its very nature as an unbreakable compact between persons, and the welfare of the children, both demand that the mutual love of the spouses be embodied in a rightly ordered manner, that it grow and ripen. Therefore, marriage persists as a whole manner and communion of life, and maintains its value and indissolubility, even when, despite the often intense desire of the couple, offspring are lacking.

614 51. This Council realizes that certain modern conditions often keep couples from arranging their married lives harmoniously, and that they find themselves in circumstances where at least temporarily the size of their families should not be increased. As a result, the faithful exercise of love and the full intimacy of their lives is hard to maintain. But where the intimacy of married life is broken off, its faithfulness can sometimes be imperiled and its quality of fruitfulness ruined, for then the upbringing of the children and the courage to accept new ones are both endangered.

615 To these problems there are those who presume to offer dishonorable solutions indeed; they do not recoil even from the taking of life. But the Church issues the reminder that a true contradiction cannot exist between the divine laws pertaining to the transmission of life and those pertaining to authentic conjugal love.

For God, the Lord of life, has conferred on men the surpassing ministry of safeguarding life in a manner which is worthy of man. Therefore from the moment of its conception life must be guarded with the greatest care. The sexual characteristics of man and the human faculty of reproduction wonderfully exceed the dispositions of lower forms of life. Hence the acts themselves which are proper to conjugal love and which are exercised in accord with genuine human dignity must be honored with great reverence. Hence when there is question of harmonizing conjugal love with the responsible transmission of life, the moral aspect of any procedure does not depend solely on sincere intentions or on an evaluation of motives, but must be determined by objective standards. These, based on the nature of the human person and his acts preserve the full sense of mutual self-giving and human procreation in the context of true love. Such a goal cannot be achieved unless the virtue of conjugal chastity is sincerely practiced. Relying on these principles, sons of the Church may not undertake methods of birth regulation which are found blameworthy by the teaching authority of the Church in its unfolding of the divine law.[117] 616

All should be persuaded that human life and the task of transmitting it are not realities bound up with this world alone. Hence they cannot be measured or perceived only in terms of it, but always have a bearing on the eternal destiny of men. 617

52. The family is a kind of school of deeper humanity. But if it is to achieve the full flowering of its life and mission, it needs the kindly communion of minds and the joint deliberation of spouses, as well as the painstaking cooperation of parents in the education of their children. The active presence of the father is highly beneficial to their formation. The children, especially the younger among them, need the care of their mother at home. This domestic role of hers must be safely preserved, though the legitimate social progress of women should not be underrated on that account. 618

Children should be so educated that as adults they can follow their vocation, including a religious one, with a mature 619 sense of responsibility and can choose their state of life; if they marry, they can thereby establish their family in favorable moral, social and economic conditions. Parents or guardians should by prudent advice provide guidance to their young with respect to founding a family, and the young ought to listen gladly. At the same time no pressure, direct or indirect, should be put on the young to make them enter marriage or choose a specific partner.

620 Thus the family, in which the various generations come together and help one another grow wiser and harmonize personal rights with the other requirements of social life, is the foundation of society. All those, therefore, who exercise influence over communities and social groups should work effectively for the welfare of marriage and the family. Public authority should regard it as a sacred duty to recognize, protect and promote their authentic nature, to shield public morality and to favor the prosperity of home life. The right of parents to beget and educate their children in the bosom of the family must be safeguarded. Children too who unhappily lack the blessing of a family should be protected by prudent legislation and various undertakings and assisted by the help they need.

621 Christians, redeeming the present time[118] and distinguishing eternal realities from their changing expressions, should actively promote the values of marriage and the family, both by the example of their own lives and by cooperation with other men of good will. Thus when difficulties arise, Christians will provide on behalf of family life those necessities and helps which are suitably modern. To this end the Christian instincts of the faithful, the upright moral consciences of men, and the wisdom and experience of persons versed in the sacred sciences will have much to contribute.

622 Those too who are skilled in other sciences, notably the medical, biological, social and psychological, can considerably advance the welfare of marriage and the family along with peace of conscience if by pooling their efforts they labor to explain more thoroughly the various conditions favoring a proper regulation of births.

It devolves on priests duly trained about family matters to nurture the vocation of spouses by a variety of pastoral means, by preaching God's Word, by liturgical worship, and by other spiritual aids to conjugal and family life; to sustain them sympathetically and patiently in difficulties, and to make them courageous through love, so that families which are truly illustrious can be formed. 623

Various organizations, especially family associations, should try by their programs of instruction and action to strengthen young people and spouses themselves, particularly those recently wed, and to train them for family, social and apostolic life. 624

Finally, let the spouses themselves, made to the image of the living God and enjoying the authentic dignity of persons, be joined to one another[119] in equal affection, harmony of mind and the work of mutual sanctification. Thus, following Christ who is the principle of life,[120] by the sacrifices and joys of their vocation and through their faithful love, married people can become witnesses of the mystery of love which the Lord revealed to the world by His dying and His rising up to life again.[121] 625

CHAPTER II

The Proper Development of Culture

53. Man comes to a true and full humanity only through culture, that is through the cultivation of the goods and values of nature. Wherever human life is involved, therefore, nature and culture are quite intimately connected one with the other. 626

The word "culture" in its general sense indicates everything whereby man develops and perfects his many bodily and spiritual qualities; and strives by his knowledge and his labor, to bring the world itself under his control. He renders social life more human both in the family and the civic community, through improvement of customs and institutions. Throughout the course of time he expresses, communicates and con- 627 serves in his works, great spiritual experiences and desires, that they might be of advantage to the progress of many, even of the whole human family.

628 Thence it follows that human culture has necessarily a historical and social aspect and the world "culture" also often assumes a sociological and ethnological sense. According to this sense we speak of a plurality of cultures. Different styles of life and multiple scales of values arise from the diverse manner of using things, of laboring, of expressing oneself, of practicing religion, of forming customs, of establishing laws and juridical institutions, of cultivating the sciences, the arts and beauty. Thus the customs handed down to it form the patrimony proper to each human community. It is also in this way that there is formed the definite, historical milieu which enfolds the man of every nation and age and from which he draws the values which permit him to promote civilization.

Section 1: The circumstances of culture in the world today.

629 54. The circumstances of the life of modern man have been so profoundly changed in their social and cultural aspect, that we can speak of a new age of human history.[122] New ways are open, therefore, for the perfection and the further extension of culture. These ways have been prepared by the enormous growth of natural, human and social sciences, by technical progress, and advances in developing and organizing means whereby men can communicate with one another. Hence the culture of today possesses particular characteristics: sciences which are called exact greatly develop critical judgment; the more recent psychological studies more profoundly explain human activity; historical studies make it much easier to see things in their mutable and evolutionary aspects; customs and usages are becoming more and more uniform; industrialization, urbanization, and other causes which promote community living create a mass-culture from which are born new ways of thinking, acting and making use of leisure. The increase of commerce between the various nations and groups of men opens more widely to all the treasures of different civilizations and thus, little by little, there develops

a more universal form of human culture, which better promotes and expresses the unity of the human race to the degree that it preserves the particular aspects of the different civilizations.

55. From day to day, in every group or nation, there is an increase in the number of men and women who are conscious that they themselves are the authors and the artisans of the culture of their community. Throughout the whole world there is a mounting increase in the sense of autonomy as well as of responsibility. This is of paramount importance for the spiritual and moral maturity of the human race. This becomes more clear if we consider the unification of the world and the duty which is imposed upon us, that we build a better world based upon truth and justice. Thus we are witnesses of the birth of a new humanism, one in which man is defined first of all by this responsibility to his brothers and to history. 630

56. In these conditions, it is no cause of wonder that man, who senses his responsiblity for the progress of culture, nourishes a high hope but also looks with anxiety upon many contradictory things which he must resolve: 631

What is to be done to prevent the increased exchanges between cultures, which should lead to a true and fruitful dialogue between groups and nations, from disturbing the life of communities, from destroying the wisdom received from ancestors, or from placing in danger the character proper to each people? 632

How is the dynamism and expansion of a new culture to be fostered without losing a living fidelity to the heritage of tradition? This question is of particular urgency when a culture which arises from the enormous progress of science and technology must be harmonized with a culture nourished by classical studies according to various traditions. 633

How can we quickly and progressively harmonize the proliferation of particular branches of study with the necessity of forming a synthesis of them, and of preserving among men the faculties of contemplation and observation which lead to wisdom? 634

What can be done to make all men partakers of cultural values in the world, when the human culture of those who are 635 more competent is constantly becoming more refined and more complex?

636 Finally how is the autonomy which culture claims for itself to be recognized as legitimate without generating a notion of humanism which is merely terrestrial, and even contrary to religion itself?

637 In the midst of these conflicting requirements, human culture must evolve today in such a way that it can both develop the whole human person and aid man in those duties to whose fulfilment all are called, especially Christians fraternally united in one human family.

Section 2: Some Principles for the Proper Development of Culture

638 57. Christians, on pilgrimage toward the heavenly city, should seek and think of those things which are above.[123] This duty in no way decreases, rather it increases, the importance of their obligation to work with all men in the building of a more human world. Indeed, the mystery of the Christian faith furnishes them with an excellent stimulus and aid to fulfill this duty more courageously and especially to uncover the full meaning of this activity, one which gives to human culture its eminent place in the integral vocation of man.

639 When man develops the earth by the work of his hands or with the aid of technology, in order that it might bear fruit and become a dwelling worthy of the whole human family and when he consciously takes part in the life of social groups, he carries out the design of God manifested at the beginning of time, that he should subdue[124] the earth, perfect creation and develop himself. At the same time he obeys the commandment of Christ that he place himself at the service of his brethren.

640 Furthermore, when man gives himself to the various disciplines of philosophy, history and of mathematical and natural sciences, and when he cultivates the arts, he can do very much to elevate the human family to a more sublime understanding of truth, goodness, and beauty, and to the formation of considered opinions which have universal value. Thus mankind

may be more clearly enlightened by that marvelous Wisdom which was with God from all eternity, composing all things with Him, rejoicing in the earth, delighting in the sons of men.[125]

In this way, the human spirit, being less subjected to material things, can be more easily drawn to the worship and contemplation of the Creator. Moreoever, by the impluse of grace, he is disposed to acknowledge the Word of God, Who before He became flesh in order to save all and to sum up all in Himself was already "in the world" as "the true light which enlightens every man" (*John* 1:9-10).[126] 641

Indeed today's progress in science and technology can foster a certain exclusive emphasis on observable data, and an agnosticism about everything else. For the methods of investigation which these sciences use can be wrongly considered as the supreme rule of seeking the whole truth. By virtue of their methods these sciences cannot penetrate to the intimate notion of things. Indeed the danger is present that man, confiding too much in the discoveries of today, may think that he is sufficient unto himself and no longer seek the higher things. 642

These unfortunate results, however, do not necessarily follow from the culture of today, nor should they lead us into the temptation of not acknowledging its positive values. Among these values are included: scientific study and fidelity toward truth in scientific enquiries, the necessity of working together with others in technical groups, a sense of international solidarity, a clearer awareness of the responsibility of experts to aid and even to protect men, the desire to make the conditions of life more favorable for all, especially for those who are poor in culture or who are deprived of the opportunity to exercise responsibility. All of these provide some preparation for the acceptance of the message of the Gospel —a preparation which can be animated by divine charity through Him Who has come to save the world. 643

58. There are many ties between the message of salvation and human culture. For God, revealing Himself to His people to the extent of a full manifestation of Himself in His Incarnate Son, has spoken according to the culture proper to each epoch. 644

645 Likewise the Church, living in various circumstances in the course of time, has used the discoveries of different cultures so that in her preaching she might spread and explain the message of Christ to all nations, that she might examine it and more deeply understand it, that she might give it better expression in liturgical celebration and in the varied life of the community of the faithful.

646 But at the same time, the Church, sent to all peoples of every time and place, is not bound exclusively and indissolubly to any race or nation, any particular way of life or any customary pattern of life recent or ancient. Faithful to her own tradition and at the same time conscious of her universal mission, she can enter into communion with the various civilizations, to their enrichment and the enrichment of the Church herself.

647 The Gospel of Christ constantly renews the life and culture of fallen man; it combats and removes the errors and evils resulting from the permanent allurement of sin. It never ceases to purify and elevate the morality of peoples. By riches coming from above, it makes fruitful, as it were from within, the spiritual qualities and traditions of every people and of every age. It strengthens, perfects and restores[127] them in Christ. Thus the Church, in the very fulfillment of her own function[128] stimulates and advances human and civic culture; by her action, also by her liturgy, she leads men toward interior liberty.

648 59. For the above reasons, the Church recalls to the mind of all that culture is to be subordinated to the integral perfection of the human person, to the good of the community and of the whole society. Therefore it is necessary to develop the human faculties in such a way that there results a growth of the faculty of wonder, of intuition, of contemplation, of making personal judgment, of developing a religious, moral and social sense.

649 Culture, because it flows immediately from the spiritual and social character of man, has constant need of a just freedom in order to develop; it needs also the legitimate possiblity of exercising its autonomy according to its own principles. It therefore rightly demands respect and enjoys a certain in-

violability within the limits of the common good, as long, of course, as it preserves the rights of the individual and the community, whether particular or universal.

650 This Sacred Synod, therefore, recalling the teaching of the first Vatican Council, declares that there are "two orders of knowledge" which are distinct, namely faith and reason; and that the Church does not forbid that "the human arts and disciplines use their own principles and their proper method, each in its own domain"; therefore "acknowledging this just liberty," this Sacred Synod affirms the legitimate autonomy of human culture and especially of the sciences.[129]

651 All this supposes that, within the limits of morality and the common utility, man can freely search for the truth, express his opinion and publish it; that he can practice any art he chooses; that finally, he can avail himself of accurate information concerning events of a public nature.[130]

652 As for public authority, it is not its function to determine the character of the civilization, but rather to establish the conditions and to use the means which are capable of fostering the life of culture among all even within the minorities of a nation.[131] It is necessary to do everything possible to prevent culture from being turned away from its proper end and made to serve as an instrument of political or economic power.

Section 3: Some More Urgent Duties of Christians in Regard to Culture

653 60. It is now possible to free most of humanity from the misery of ignorance. Therefore the duty most consonant with our times, especially for Christians, is that of working diligently for fundamental decisions to be taken in economic and political affairs, both on the national and international level, which will everywhere recognize and satisfy the right of all to a human and social culture in conformity with the dignity of the human person without any discrimination based on race, sex, nation, religion or social condition. Therefore it is necessary to provide all with a sufficient quantity of cultural benefits, especially of those which constitute the so-called basic cul-

ture lest very many be prevented from cooperating in the promotion of the common good in a truly human manner because of illiteracy and a lack of responsible activity.

654 We must strive to provide for those men who are gifted the possiblity of pursuing higher studies; and in such a way that, as far as possible, they may occupy in society those duties, offices and services which are in harmony with their natural aptitude and the competence they have acquired.[132] Thus each man and the social groups of every people will be able to attain the full development of their culture in conformity with their qualities and traditions.

655 Everything must be done to make everyone conscious of the right to culture and the duty he has of developing himself culturally and of helping others. Sometimes there exist conditions of life and of work which impede the cultural striving of men and destroy in them the eagerness for culture. This is especially true of farmers and workers. It is necessary to provide for them those working conditions which will not impede their human culture but rather favor it. Women now engage in almost all spheres of activity. It is fitting that they are able to assume their proper role in accordance with their own nature. It is incumbent upon all to acknowledge and favor the proper and necessary participation of women in cultural life.

656 61. Today it is more difficult to form a synthesis of the various disciplines of knowledge and the arts than it was formerly. For while the mass and the diversity of cultural factors are increasing, there is a decrease in each man's faculty of perceiving and unifying these things, so that the image of "universal man" is being lost sight of more and more. Nevertheless it remains each man's duty to preserve an understanding of the whole human person in which the values of intellect, will, conscience and fraternity are pre-eminent. These values are all rooted in God the Creator and have been wonderfully restored and elevated in Christ.

657 The family is, as it were, the primary mother and nurse of this education. There, the children, in an atmosphere of love, more easily learn the correct order of things, while proper forms of human culture impress themselves in an almost un-

conscious manner upon the mind of the developing adolescent.

Opportunities for the same education are to be found also in the societies of today, due especially to the increased circulation of books and to the new means of cultural and social communication which can foster a universal culture. With the more or less universal reduction of working hours, the leisure time of most men has increased. May this leisure be used properly to relax, to fortify the health of soul and body through spontaneous study and activity, through tourism which refines man's character and enriches him with understanding of others, through sports activity which helps to preserve an equilibrium of spirit even in the community, and to establish fraternal relations among men of all conditions, nations and races. Let Christians cooperate so that the cultural manifestations and collective activity characteristic of our time may be imbued with a human and a Christian spirit. 658

All these leisure activities however cannot bring man to a full cultural development unless there is at the same time a profound inquiry into the meaning of culture and science for the human person. 659

62. Although the Church has contributed much to the development of culture, experience shows that, because of circumstances, it is sometimes difficult to harmonize culture with Christian teaching. These difficulties do not necessarily harm the life of faith, rather they can stimulate the mind to a deeper and more accurate understanding of the faith. The recent studies and findings of science, history and philosophy raise new questions which affect life and which demand new theological investigations. Furthermore, theologians, observing the requirements and methods proper to theology, are invited to seek continually for more suitable ways of communicating doctrine to the men of their times; for the deposit of Faith or the truths are one thing and the manner in which they are enunciated, in the same meaning and understanding, is another.[133] In pastoral care, sufficient use must be made not only of theological principles, but also of the findings of the secular sciences, especially of psychology and sociology, 660

so that the faithful may be brought to a more adequate and mature life of faith.

661 Literature and the arts are also, in their own way, of great importance to the life of the Church. They strive to make known the proper nature of man, his problems and his experiences in trying to know and perfect both himself and the world. They have much to do with revealing man's place in history and in the world; with illustrating the miseries and joys, the needs and strengths of man and with foreshadowing a better life for him. Thus they are able to elevate human life, expressed in manifold forms in various times and places.

662 Efforts must be made so that those who foster these arts feel that the Church recognizes their activity and so that, enjoying orderly freedom, they may initiate more friendly relations with the Christian community. The Church acknowledges also new forms of art which are adapted to our age and are in keeping with the characteristics of various nations and regions. They may be brought into the sanctuary since they raise the mind to God, once the manner of expression is adapted and they are conformed to liturgical requirements.[134]

663 Thus the knowledge of God is better manifested and the preaching of the Gospel becomes clearer to human intelligence and shows itself to be relevant to man's actual conditions of life.

664 May the faithful, therefore, live in very close union with the other men of their time and judging, as expressed in their culture. Let them blend new sciences and theories and the understanding of the most recent discoveries with Christian morality and the teaching of Christian doctrine, so that their religious culture and morality may keep pace with their scientific knowledge and with the constantly progressing technology. Thus they will be able to interpret and evaluate all things in a truly Christian spirit.

665 Let those who teach theology in seminaries and universities strive to collaborate with men versed in the other sciences through a sharing of their resources and points of view. Theological inquiry should pursue a profound understanding of revealed truth; at the same time it should not neglect close contact with its own time that it may be able to help those

men skilled in various disciplines to attain to a better understanding of the faith. This common effort will greatly aid the formation of priests, who will be able to present to our contemporaries the doctrine of the Church concerning God, man and the world, in a manner more adapted to them so that they may receive it more willingly.[135] Furthermore, it is to be hoped that many of the laity will receive a sufficient formation in the sacred sciences and that some will dedicate themselves professionally to these studies, developing and deepening them by their own labors. In order that they may fulfill their function, let it be recognized that all the faithful, whether clerics or laity, possess a lawful freedom of inquiry, freedom of thought and of expressing their mind with humility and fortitude in those matters on which they enjoy competence.[136]

CHAPTER III

Economic and Social Life

63. In the economic and social realms, too, the dignity and complete vocation of the human person and the welfare of society as a whole are to be respected and promoted. For man is the source, the center, and the purpose of all economic and social life. 666

Like other areas of social life, the economy of today is marked by man's increasing domination over nature, by closer and more intense relationships between citizens, groups, and countries and their mutual dependence, and by the increased intervention of the state. At the same time progress in the methods of production and in the exchange of goods and services has made the economy an instrument capable of better meeting the intensified needs of the human family. 667

Reasons for anxiety, however, are not lacking. Many people, especially in economically advanced areas, seem, as it were, to be ruled by economics, so that almost their entire personal and social life is permeated with a certain economic way of thinking. Such is true both of nations that favor a col- 668 lective economy and of others. At the very time when the development of economic life could mitigate social inequalities (provided that it be guided and coordinated in a reasonable and human way), it is often made to embitter them; or, in some places, it even results in a decline of the social status of the underprivileged and in contempt for the poor. While an immense number of people still lack the absolute necessities of life, some, even in less advanced areas, live in luxury or squander wealth. Extravagance and wretchedness exist side by side. While a few enjoy very great power of choice, the majority are deprived of almost all possibility of acting on their own initiative and responsibility, and often subsist in living and working conditions unworthy of the human person.

669 A similar lack of economic and social balance is to be noticed between agriculture, industry, and the services, and also between different parts of one and the same country. The contrast between the economically more advanced countries and other countries is becoming more serious day by day, and the very peace of the world can be jeopardized thereby.

670 Our contemporaries are coming to feel these inequalities with an ever sharper awareness, since they are thoroughly convinced that the ampler technical and economic possibilities which the world of today enjoys can and should correct this unhappy state of affairs. Hence, many reforms in the socio-economic realm and a change of mentality and attitude are required of all. For this reason the Church down through the centuries and in the light of the Gospel has worked out the principles of justice and equity demanded by right reason both for individual and social life and for international life, and she has proclaimed them especially in recent times. This Sacred Council intends to strengthen these principles according to the circumstances of this age and to set forth certain guidelines, especially with regard to the requirements of economic development.[137]

Section 1. Economic Development

64. Today more than ever before attention is rightly given to the increase of the production of agricultural and industrial goods and of the rendering of services, for the purpose of making provision for the growth of population and of satisfying the increasing desires of the human race. Therefore, technical progress, an inventive spirit, an eagerness to create and to expand enterprises, the application of methods of production, and the strenuous efforts of all who engage in production—in a word, all the elements making for such development—must be promoted. The fundamental purpose of this production is not the mere increase of products nor profit or control but rather the service of man, and indeed of the whole man with regard for the full range of his material needs and the demands of his intellectual, moral, spiritual, and religious life; this applies to every man whatsoever and to every group of men, of every race and of every part of the world. Consequently, economic activity is to be carried on according to its own methods and laws within the limits of the moral order,[138] so that God's plan for mankind may be realized.[139] 671

65. Economic development must remain under man's determination and must not be left to the judgment of a few men or groups possessing too much economic power or of the political community alone or of certain more powerful nations. It is necessary, on the contrary, that at every level the largest possible number of people and, when it is a question of international relations, all nations have an active share in directing that development. There is need as well of the coordination and fitting and harmonious combination of the spontaneous efforts of individuals and of free groups with the undertakings of public authorities. 672

Growth is not to be left solely to a kind of mechanical course of economic activity of individuals, nor to the authority of government. For this reason, doctrines which obstruct the necessary reforms under the guise of a false liberty, and those which subordinate the basic rights of individual persons 673 and groups to the collective organization of production must be shown to be erroneous.[140]

674 Citizens, on the other hand, should remember that it is their right and duty, which is also to be recognized by the civil authority, to contribute to the true progress of their own community according to their ability. Especially in underdeveloped areas, where all resources must urgently be employed, those who hold back their unproductive resources or who deprive their community of the material or spiritual aid that it needs—saving the personal right of migration—gravely endanger the common good.

675 66. To satisfy the demands of justice and equity, strenuous efforts must be made, without disregarding the rights of persons or the natural qualities of each country, to remove as quickly as possible the immense economic inequalities, which now exist and in many cases are growing and which are connected with individual and social discrimination. Likewise, in many areas, in view of the special difficulties of agriculture relative to the raising and selling of produce, country people must be helped both to increase and to market what they produce, and to introduce the necessary development and renewal and also obtain a fair income. Otherwise, as too often happens, they will remain in the condition of lower-class citizens. Let farmers themselves, especially young ones, apply themselves to perfecting their professional skill, for without it, there can be no agricultural advance.[141]

676 Justice and equity likewise require that the mobility, which is necessary in a developing economy, be regulated in such a way as to keep the life of individuals and their families from becoming insecure and precarious. When workers come from another country or district and contribute to the economic advancement of a nation or region by their labor, all discrimination as regards wages and working conditions must be carefully avoided. All the people, moreover, above all the public authorities, must treat them not as mere tools of production but as persons, and must help them to bring their families to live with them and to provide themselves with a decent dwelling; they must also see to it that these workers are incorporated into the social life of the country or region that receives

them. Employment opportunities, however, should be created in their own areas as far as possible.

In economic affairs which today are subject to change, as in the new forms of industrial society in which automation, for example, is advancing, care must be taken that sufficient and suitable work and the possibility of the appropriate technical and professional formation are furnished. The livelihood and the human dignity especially of those who are in very difficult conditions because of illness or old age must be guaranteed. 677

Section 2. Certain Principles Governing Socio-Economic Life as a Whole

67. Human labor which is expended in the production and exchange of goods or in the performance of economic services is superior to the other elements of economic life, for the latter have only the nature of tools. 678

This labor, whether it is engaged in independently or hired by someone else, comes immediately from the person, who as it were stamps the things of nature with his seal and subdues them to his will. By his labor a man ordinarily supports himself and his family, is joined to his fellow men and serves them, and can exercise genuine charity and be a partner in the work of bringing divine creation to perfection. Indeed, we hold that through labor offered to God man is associated with the redemptive work of Jesus Christ, Who conferred an eminent dignity on labor when at Nazareth He worked with His own hands. From this there follows for every man the duty of working faithfully and also the right to work. It is the duty of society, moreover, according to the circumstances prevailing in it, and in keeping with its role, to help the citizens to find sufficient employment. Finally, remuneration for labor is to be such that man may be furnished the means to cultivate worthily his own material, social, cultural, and spiritual life and that of his dependents, in view of the function and productiveness of each one, the conditions of the factory or workshop, and the common good.[142] 679

680 Since economic activity for the most part implies the associated work of human beings, any way of organizing and directing it which might be detrimental to any working men and women would be wrong and inhuman. It happens too often, however, even in our days, that workers are reduced to the level of being slaves to their own work. This is by no means justified by the so-called economic laws. The entire process of productive work, therefore, must be adapted to the needs of the person and to his way of life, above all to his domestic life, especially in respect to mothers of families, always with due regard for sex and age. The opportunity, moreover, should be granted to workers to unfold their own abilities and personality through the performance of their work. Applying their time and strength to their employment with a due sense of responsibility, they should also all enjoy sufficient rest and leisure to cultivate their familial, cultural, social and religious life. They should also have the opportunity freely to develop the energies and potentialities which perhaps they cannot bring to much fruition in their professional work.

681 68. In economic enterprises it is persons who are joined together, that is, free and independent human beings created to the image of God. Therefore, taking account of the prerogatives of each—owners or employers, management or labor—and without doing harm to the necessary unity of management, the active sharing of all in the administration and profits of these enterprises in ways to be properly determined should be promoted.[143] Since more often, however, decisions concerning economic and social conditions, on which the future lot of the workers and of their children depends, are made not within the business itself but by institutions on a higher level, the workers themselves should have a share also in determining these conditions—in person or through freely elected delegates.

682 Among the basic rights of the human person is to be numbered the right of freely founding unions for working people. These should be able truly to represent them and to contribute to the organizing of economic life in the right way. Included is the right of freely taking part in the activity of these

unions without risk of reprisal. Through this orderly participation joined to progressive economic and social formation, all will grow day by day in the awareness of their own function and responsibility, and thus they will be brought to feel that they are comrades in the whole task of economic development and in the attainment of the universal common good according to their capacities and aptitudes.

683 When, however, socio-economic disputes arise, efforts must be made to come to a peaceful settlement. Although recourse must always be had first to a sincere dialogue between the parties, the strike, nevertheless, can remain even in present-day circumstances a necessary, though ultimate, means for the defense of the workers' own rights and fulfillment of their just desires. As soon as possible, however, ways should be sought to resume negotations and discussions leading toward reconciliation.

684 69. God intended the earth with everything contained in it for the use of all human beings and peoples. Thus, under the guidance of justice together with charity, created goods should be in abundance for all in an equitable manner.[144] Whatever the forms of property may be, as adapted to the legitimate institutions of peoples, according to diverse and changeable circumstances, attention must always be paid to this universal goal of earthly goods. In using them, therefore, man should regard the external things that he legitimately possesses not only as his own but also as common in the sense that they should be able to benefit not only him but also others as well.[145] On the other hand, the right of having a share of earthly goods sufficient for oneself and one's family belongs to everyone. The Fathers and Doctors of the Church held this opinion, teaching that men are obliged to come to the relief of the poor and to do so not merely out of their superfluous goods.[146] If one is in extreme necessity, he has the right to procure for himself what he needs out of the riches of others.[147] Since there are so many people prostrate with hunger in the world, this Sacred Council urges all, both individuals and governments to remember the aphorism of the Fathers, "Feed the man dying of hunger, because if you have not fed him, you have killed him,"[148] and really to share

and use their earthly goods, according to the ability of each, especially by supporting individuals or peoples with the aid by which they may be able to help and develop themselves.

685 In economically less advanced societies the common destination of earthly goods is partly satisfied by means of the customs and traditions proper to the community, by which the absolute essentials are furnished to each member. An effort must be made, however, to avoid regarding certain customs as altogether unchangeable, if they no longer answer the new needs of this age. On the other hand, imprudent action should not be taken against respectable customs which, provided they are suitably adapted to present-day circumstances, do not cease to be very useful. Similarly in highly developed nations a body of social institutions dealing with protection and security can, for its own part, bring to reality the common destination of earthly goods. Family and social services, especially those that provide for culture and education, should be further promoted. When all these things are being organized, vigilance is necessary to prevent the citizens from being led into a certain inertia vis-a-vis society or from rejecting the burden of taking up office or from refusing to serve.

686 70. Investments, for their part, must be directed toward providing employment and sufficient income for the people both now and in the future. Whoever make decisions concerning these investments and the planning of the economy—whether they be individuals or groups or public authorities—are bound to keep these objectives in mind and to recognize their serious obligation of making sure, on the one hand, that provision be made for the necessities required for a decent life both of individuals and of the whole community and, on the other, of looking out for the future and of establishing a proper balance between the needs of present-day consumption, both individual and collective, and the demands of investing for the generation to come. They should also always bear in mind the urgent needs of underdeveloped countries or regions. In monetary matters they should beware of hurting the welfare of their own country or of other countries. Care should also be taken lest the economically weak countries unjustly suffer any loss from a change in the value of money.

71. Since property and other forms of private ownership of external goods contribute to the expression of the personality, and since, moreover, they furnish one an occasion to exercise his function in society and in the economy, it is very important that the access of both individuals and communities to some ownership of external goods be fostered. 687

Private property or some ownership of external goods confers on everyone a sphere wholly necessary for the autonomy of the person and the family, and it should be regarded as an extension of human freedom. Lastly, since it adds incentives for carrying on one's function and duty, it constitutes one of the conditions for civil liberties.[149] 688

The forms of such ownership of property are varied today and are becoming increasingly diversified. They all remain, however, a cause of security not to be underestimated, in spite of social funds, rights, and services provided by society. This is true not only of material goods but also of intangible goods such as professional skills. 689

The right of private ownership, however, is not opposed to the right inherent in various forms of public property. Goods can be transferred to the public domain only by the competent authority, according to the demands and within the limits of the common good, and with fair compensation. Furthermore, it is the right of public authority to prevent anyone from misusing his private property to the detriment of the common good.[150] 690

By its very nature private property has a social quality which is based on the law of the common destination of earthly goods.[151] If this social quality is overlooked, property often becomes an occasion of a passionate desire for wealth and serious disturbances, so that a pretext is given to those who attack private property for calling the right itself into question. 691

In many underdeveloped regions there are large or even extensive rural estates which are only slightly cultivated or lie completely idle for the sake of profit, while the majority of the people either are without land or have only very small fields, and, on the other hand, it is evidently urgent to increase the productivity of the fields. Not infrequently those 692 who are hired to work for the landowners or who till a portion of the land as tenants receive a wage or income unworthy of a human being, lack decent housing and are exploited by middlemen. Deprived of all security, they live under such personal servitude that almost every opportunity of acting on their own initiative and responsibility is denied to them and all advancement in human culture and all sharing in social and political life is forbidden to them. According to different circumstances, therefore, reforms are necessary: that income may grow, working conditions should be improved, security in employment increased, and an incentive to working on one's own initiative given. Indeed, insufficiently cultivated estates should be distributed to those who can make these lands fruitful; in this case, the necessary ways and means, especially educational aids and the right facilities for cooperative organization, must be supplied. Whenever, nevertheless, the common good requires expropriation, compensation must be reckoned in equity after all the circumstances have been weighed.

693 72. Christians who take an active part in present-day socio-economic development and fight for justice and charity should be convinced that they can make a great contribution to the prosperity of mankind and to the peace of the world. In these activities let them, either as individuals or as members of groups, give a shining example. Having acquired the skills and experience which are absolutely necessary, they should observe the right order in their earthly activities in faithfulness to Christ and His Gospel. Thus their whole life, both individual and social, will be permeated with the spirit of the beatitudes, notably with a spirit of poverty.

694 Whoever in obedience to Christ seeks first the Kingdom of God, takes therefrom a stronger and purer love for helping all his brethren and for perfecting the work of justice under the inspiration of charity.[152]

CHAPTER IV

The Life of the Political Community

73. In our day, profound changes are apparent also in the structure and institutions of peoples. These result from their cultural, economic and social evolution. Such changes have a great influence on the life of the political community, especially regarding the rights and duties of all in the exercise of civil freedom and in the attainment of the common good, and in organizing the relations of citizens among themselves and with respect to public authority. 695

The present keener sense of human dignity has given rise in many parts of the world to attempts to bring about a politico-juridical order which will give better protection to the rights of the person in public life. These include the right freely to meet and form associations, the right to express one's own opinion and to profess one's religion both publicly and privately. The protection of the rights of a person is indeed a necessary condition so that citizens, individually or collectively, can take an active part in the life and government of the state. 696

Along with cultural, economic and social development, there is a growing desire among many people to play a greater part in organizing the life of the political community. In the conscience of many there arises an increasing concern that the rights of minorities be recognized, without any neglect for their duties toward the political community. In addition, there is a steadily growing respect for men of other opinions or other religions. At the same time, there is wider cooperation to guarantee the actual exercise of personal rights to all citizens, and not only to a few privileged individuals. 697

However, those political systems, prevailing in some parts of the world are to be reproved which hamper civic or religious freedom, victimize large numbers through avarice and political crimes, and divert the exercise of authority from the 698 service of the common good to the interests of one or another faction or of the rulers themselves.

699 There is no better way to establish political life on a truly human basis than by fostering an inward sense of justice and kindliness, and of service to the common good, and by strengthening basic convictions as to the true nature of the political community and the purpose, right exercise, and sphere of action of public authority.

700 74. Men, families and the various groups which make up the civil community are aware that they cannot achieve a truly human life by their own unaided efforts. They see the need for a wider community, within which each one makes his specific contribution every day toward an ever broader realization of the common good.[153] For this purpose they set up a political community which takes various forms. The political community exists, consequently, for the sake of the common good, in which it finds its full justification and significance, and the source of its inherent legitmacy. Indeed, the common good embraces the sum of those conditions of the social life whereby men, families and associations more adequately and readily may attain their own perfection.[154]

701 Yet the people who come together in the political community are many and diverse, and they have every right to prefer divergent solutions. If the political community is not to be torn apart while everyone follows his own opinion, there must be an authority to direct the energies of all citizens toward the common good, not in a mechanical or despotic fashion, but by acting above all as a moral force which appeals to each one's freedom and sense of responsibility.

702 It is clear, therefore, that the political community and public authority are founded on human nature and hence belong to the order designed by God, even though the choice of a political regime and the appointment of rulers are left to the free will of citizens.[155]

703 It follows also that political authority, both in the community as such and in the representative bodies of the state, must always be exercised within the limits of the moral order and directed toward the common good—with a dynamic concept of that good—according to the juridical order legiti-

mately established or which should be established. When authority is so exercised, citizens are bound in conscience to obey.[156] Accordingly, the responsibility, dignity and importance of leaders are indeed clear.

But where citizens are oppressed by a public authority over-stepping its competence, they should not protest against those things which are objectively required for the common good; but it is legitimate for them to defend their own rights and the rights of their fellow citizens against the abuse of this authority, while keeping within those limits drawn by the natural law and the Gospels. 704

According to the character of different peoples and their historic development, the political community can, however, adopt a variety of concrete solutions in its structures and the organization of public authority. For the benefit of the whole human family, these solutions must always contribute to the formation of a type of man who will be cultivated, peace-loving and well-disposed towards all his fellow men. 705

75. It is in full conformity with human nature that there should be juridico-political structures providing all citizens in an ever better fashion and without any discrimination the practical possibility of freely and actively taking part in the establishment of the juridical foundations of the political community and in the direction of public affairs, in fixing the terms of reference of the various public bodies and in the election of political leaders.[157] All citizens, therefore, should be mindful of the right and also the duty to use their free vote to further the common good. The Church praises and esteems the work of those who for the good of men devote themselves to the service of the state and take on the burdens of this office. 706

If the citizens' responsible cooperation is to produce the good results which may be expected in the normal course of political life, there must be a statute of positive law providing for a suitable division of the functions and bodies of authority and an efficient and independent system for the protection of rights. The rights of all persons, families and groups, and their practical application, must be recognized, respected and furthered, together with the duties binding on all citizens.[158] 707

Among the latter, it will be well to recall the duty of rendering the political community such material and personal services as are required by the common good. Rulers must be careful not to hamper the development of family, social or cultural groups, nor that of intermediate bodies or organizations, and not to deprive them of opportunities for legitimate and constructive activity; they should willingly seek rather to promote the orderly pursuit of such activity. Citizens, for their part, either individually or collectively, must be careful not to attribute excessive power to public authority, not to make exaggerated and untimely demands upon it in their own interests, lessening in this way the responsible role of persons, families and social groups.

708 The complex circumstances of our day make it necessary for public authority to intervene more often in social, economic and cultural matters in order to bring about favorable conditions which will give more effective help to citizens and groups in their free pursuit of man's total well-being. The relations, however, between socialization[159] and the autonomy and development of the person can be understood in different ways according to various regions and the evolution of peoples. But when the exercise of rights is restricted temporarily for the common good, freedom should be restored immediately upon change of circumstances. Moreover, it is inhuman for public authority to fall back on dictatorial systems or totalitarian methods which violate the rights of the person or social groups.

709 Citizens must cultivate a generous and loyal spirit of patriotism, but without being narrow-minded. This means that they will always direct their attention to the good of the whole human family, united by the different ties which bind together races, people and nations.

710 All Christians must be aware of their own specific vocation within the political community. It is for them to give an example by their sense of responsibility and their service of the common good. In this way they are to demonstrate concretely how authority can be compatible with freedom, personal initiative with the solidarity of the whole social organism, and the advantages of unity with fruitful diversity. They must

recognize the legitimacy of different opinions with regard to temporal solutions, and respect citizens, who, even as a group, defend their points of view by honest methods. Political parties, for their part, must promote those things which in their judgment are required for the common good; it is never allowable to give their interests priority over the common good.

711 Great care must be taken with regard to civic and political formation, which is of the utmost necessity today for the population as a whole, and especially for youth, so that all citizens can play their part in the life of the political community. Those who are suited or can become suited should prepare themselves for the difficult, but at the same time, the very noble art of politics,[160] and should seek to practice this art without regard for their own interests or for material advantages. With integrity and wisdom, they must take action against any form of injustice and tyranny, against arbitrary domination by an individual or a political party, and any intolerance. They should dedicate themselves to the service of all with sincerity and fairness, indeed, with the charity and fortitude demanded by political life.

712 76. It is very important, especially where a pluralistic society prevails, that there by a correct notion of the relationship between the political community and the Church, and a clear distinction between the tasks which Christians undertake, individually or as a group, on their own responsibility as citizens guided by the dictates of a Christian conscience, and the activities which, in union with their pastors, they carry out in the name of the Church.

713 The Church, by reason of her role and competence, is not identified in any way with the political community nor bound to any political system. She is at once a sign and a safeguard of the transcendent character of the human person.

714 The Church and the political community in their own fields are autonomous and independent from each other. Yet both, under different titles, are devoted to the personal and social vocation of the same men. The more that both foster healthier cooperation between themselves with due consideration for the circumstances of time and place, the more effective will their service be exercised for the good of all. For man's hori-

zons are not limited only to the temporal order: while living in the context of human history, he preserves intact his eternal vocation. The Church, for her part, founded on the love of the Redeemer, contributes toward the reign of justice and charity within the borders of a nation and between nations. By preaching the truths of the Gospel, and bringing to bear on all fields of human endeavor the light of her doctrine and of a Christian witness, she respects and fosters the political freedom and responsibility of citizens.

715 The Apostles, their successors and those who cooperate with them, are sent to announce to mankind Christ, the Saviour. Their apostolate is based on the power of God, Who very often shows forth the strength of the Gospel in the weakness of its witnesses. All those dedicated to the ministry of God's Word must use the ways and means proper to the Gospel which in a great many respects differ from the means proper to the earthly city.

716 There are, indeed, close links betwen earthly things and those elements of man's condition which transcend the world. The Church herself makes use of temporal things insofar as her own mission requires it. She, for her part, does not place her trust in the privileges offered by civil authority. She will even give up the exercise of certain rights which have been legitimately acquired, if it becomes clear that their use will cast doubt on the sincerity of her witness or that new ways of life demand new methods. It is only right, however, that at all times and in all places, the Church should have true freedom to preach the faith, to teach her social doctrine, to exercise her role freely among men, and also to pass moral judgment in those matters which concern public order when the fundamental rights of a person or the salvation of souls require it. In this, she should make use of all the means—but only those—which accord with the Gospel and which correspond to the general good with due regard to the diverse circumstances of time and place.

717 While faithfully adhering to the Gospel and fulfilling her mission to the world, the Church, whose duty it is to foster and elevate[161] all that is found to be true, good and beauti-

ful in the human community, strengthens peace among men for the glory of God.[162]

CHAPTER V

The Fostering of Peace and the Promotion of a Community of Nations

77. In our generation when men continue to be afflicted by acute hardships and anxieties arising from the ravages of war or the threat of it, the whole human family faces an hour of supreme crisis in its advance toward maturity. Moving gradually together and everywhere more conscious already of its unity, this family cannot accomplish its task of constructing for all men everywhere a world more genuinely human unless each person devotes himself to the cause of peace with renewed vigor. Thus it happens that the Gospel message, which is in harmony with the loftier strivings and aspirations of the human race, takes on a new luster in our day as it declares that the artisans of peace are blessed "because they will be called the sons of God" (*Matt.* 5:9). 718

Consequently, as it points out the authentic and noble meaning of peace and condemns the frightfulness of war, the Council wishes passionately to summon Christians to cooperate, under the help of Christ, the author of peace, with all men in securing among themselves a peace based on justice and love and in setting up the instruments of peace. 719

78. Peace is not merely the absence of war; nor can it be reduced solely to the maintenance of a balance of power between enemies; nor is it brought about by dictatorship. Instead, it is rightly and appropriately called an enterprise of justice (*Is.* 32:7). Peace results from that order structured into human society by its divine Founder, and actualized by men as they thirst after ever greater justice. The common good of humanity finds its ultimate meaning in the eternal law. But since the concrete demands of this common good are constantly changing as time goes on, peace is never attained once and for all, but must be built up ceaselessly. Moreover, since the human will is unsteady and wounded by sin, the achieve- 720

ment of peace requires a constant mastering of passions and the vigilance of lawful authority.

721 But this is not enough. This peace on earth cannot be obtained unless personal well-being is safeguarded and men freely and trustingly share with one another the riches of their inner spirits and their talents. A firm determination to respect other men and peoples and their dignity, as well as the studied practice of brotherhood are absolutely necessary for the establishment of peace. Hence peace is likewise the fruit of love, which goes beyond what justice can provide.

722 That earthly peace which arises from love of neighbor symbolizes and results from the peace of Christ which radiates from God the Father. For by the Cross the Incarnate Son, the Prince of Peace reconciled all men with God. By thus restoring all men to the unity of one people and one body, He slew hatred in His own flesh;[163] and, after being lifted on high by His resurrection, He poured forth the spirit of love into the hearts of men.

723 For this reason, all Christians are urgently summoned to do in love what the truth requires (*Eph.* 4:15), and to join with all true peacemakers in pleading for peace and bringing it about.

724 Motivated by this same spirit, we cannot fail to praise those who renounce the use of violence in the vindication of their rights and who resort to methods of defense which are otherwise available to weaker parties too, provided this can be done without injury to the rights and duties of others or of the community itself.

725 Insofar as men are sinful, the threat of war hangs over them, and hang over them it will until the return of Christ. But insofar as men vanquish sin by a union of love, they will vanquish violence as well and make these words come true: "They shall turn their swords into plough-shares, and their spears into sickles. Nation shall not lift up sword against nation, neither shall they learn war any more" (*Isaias* 2:4).

Section I: The Avoidance of War

79. In spite of the fact that recent wars have wrought physical and moral havoc on our world, war produces its devastation day by day in some part of the world. Indeed, now that every kind of weapon produced by modern science is used in war, the fierce character of warfare threatens to lead the combatants to a savagery far surpassing that of the past. Furthermore, the complexity of the modern world and the intricacy of international relations allow guerrilla warfare to be carried on by new methods of deceit and subversion. In many cases the use of terrorism is regarded as a new way to wage war. 726

Contemplating this melancholy state of humanity, the Council wishes, above all things else, to recall the permanent binding force of universal natural law and its all-embracing principles. Man's conscience itself gives ever more emphatic voice to these principles. Therefore, actions which deliberately conflict with these same principles, as well as orders commanding such actions are criminal, and blind obedience cannot excuse those who yield to them. The most infamous among these are actions designed for the methodical extermination of an entire people, nation or ethnic minority. Such actions must be vehemently condemned as horrendous crimes. The courage of those who fearlessly and openly resist those who issue such commands merits the highest commendation. 727

On the subject of war, quite a large number of nations have subscribed to international agreements aimed at making military activity and its consequences less inhuman. Their stipulations deal with such matters as the treatment of wounded soldiers and prisoners. Agreements of this sort must be honored. Indeed they should be improved upon so that the frightfulness of war can be better and more workably held in check. All men, especially goverment officials and experts in these matters, are bound to do everything they can to effect these improvements. Moreover, it seems right that laws make humane provisions for the case of those who for reasons of 728 conscience refuse to bear arms, provided however, that they agree to serve the human community in some other way.

729 Certainly, war has not been rooted out of human affairs. As long as the danger of war remains and there is no competent and sufficiently powerful authority at the international level, governments cannot be denied the right to legitimate defense once every means of peaceful settlement has been exhausted. Government authorities and others who share public responsibility have the duty to conduct such grave matters soberly and to protect the welfare of the people entrusted to their care. But it is one thing to undertake military action for the just defense of the people, and something else again to seek the subjugation of other nations. Nor, by the same token, does the mere fact that war has unhappily begun mean that all is fair between the warring parties.

730 Those too who devote themselves to the military service of their country should regard themselves as the agents of security and freedom of peoples. As long as they fulfill this role properly, they are making a genuine contribution to the establishment of peace.

731 80. The horror and perversity of war is immensely magnified by the increase in the number of scientific weapons. For acts of war involving these weapons can inflict massive and indiscriminate destruction, thus going far beyond the bounds of legitimate defense. Indeed, if the kind of instruments which can now be found in the armories of the great nations were to be employed to their fullest, an almost total and altogether reciprocal slaughter of each side by the other would follow, not to mention the widespread devastation that would take place in the world and the deadly after effects that would be spawned by the use of weapons of this kind.

732 All these considerations compel us to undertake an evaluation of war with an entirely new attitude.[164] The men of our time must realize that they will have to give a somber reckoning of their deeds of war for the course of the future will depend greatly on the decisions they make today.

733 With these truths in mind, this most Holy Synod makes its own the condemnations of total war already pronounced by recent popes,[165] and issues the following declaration:

Any act of war aimed indiscriminately at the destruction of entire cities or extensive areas along with their population is a crime against God and man himself. It merits unequivocal and unhesitating condemnation. 734

The unique hazard of modern warfare consists in this: it provides those who possess modern scientific weapons with a kind of occasion for perpetrating just such abominations; moreover, through a certain inexorable chain of events, it can catapult men into the most atrocious decisions. That such may never happen in the future, the bishops of the whole world gathered together, beg all men, especially government officials and military leaders, to give unremitting thought to their tremendous responsibility before God and the entire human race. 735

81. Scientific weapons, to be sure, are not amassed solely for use in war. Since the defensive strength of any nation is considered to be dependent upon its capacity for immediate retaliation, this accumulation of arms, which increases each year, likewise serves, in a way heretofore unknown, as a deterrent to possible enemy attack. Many regard this as the most effective way by which peace of a sort can be maintained between nations at the present time. 736

Whatever be the facts about this method of deterrence, men should be convinced that the arms race in which an already considerable number of countries are engaged is not a safe way to preserve a steady peace, nor is the so-called balance resulting from this race a sure and authentic peace. Rather than being eliminated thereby, the causes of war are in danger of being gradually aggravated. While extravagant sums are being spent for the furnishing of ever new weapons, an adequate remedy cannot be provided for the multiple miseries afflicting the whole modern world. Disagreements between nations are not really and radically healed; on the contrary, they spread the infection to other parts of the earth. New approaches based on reformed attitudes must be taken to remove this trap and to emancipate the world from its crushing anxiety through the restoration of genuine peace. 737

Therefore, we say it again: the arms race is an utterly treacherous trap for humanity, and one which ensnares the 738 poor to an intolerable degree. It is much to be feared that if this race persists, it will eventually spawn all the lethal ruin whose path it is now making ready. Warned by the calamities which the human race has made possible, let us make use of the interlude granted us from above and for which we are thankful, to become more conscious of our own responsibility and to find means for resolving our disputes in a manner more worthy of man. Divine Providence urgently demands of us that we free ourselves from the age-old slavery of war. If we refuse to make this effort, we do not know where we will be led by the evil road we have set upon.

739 82. It is our clear duty, therefore, to strain every muscle in working for the time when all war can be completely outlawed by international consent. This goal undoubtedly requires the establishment of some universal public authority acknowledged as such by all and endowed with the power to safeguard on the behalf of all, security, regard for justice, and respect for rights. But before this hoped for authority can be set up, the highest existing international centers must devote themselves vigorously to the pursuit of better means for obtaining common security. Since peace must be born of mutual trust between nations and not be imposed on them through fear of the available weapons, everyone must labor to put an end at last to the arms race, and to make a true beginning of disarmament, not unilaterally indeed, but proceeding at an equal pace according to agreement, and backed up by adequate and workable safeguards.[166]

740 In the meantime, efforts which have already been made and are still under way to eliminate the danger of war are not to be underrated. On the contrary, support should be given to the good will of the very many leaders who work hard to do away with war, which they abominate. These men, although burdened by the extremely weighty preoccupations of their high office, are nonetheless moved by the very grave peacemaking task to which they are bound, even if they cannot ignore the complexity of matters as they stand. We should fervently ask God to give these men the strength to go forward perseveringly and to follow through courageously on this work of building peace with vigor. It is a work of supreme love for

mankind. Today it certainly demands that they extend their thoughts and their spirit beyond the confines of their own nation, that they put aside national selfishness and ambition to dominate other nations, and that they nourish a profound reverence for the whole of humanity, which is already making its way so laboriously toward greater unity.

741 The problems of peace and of disarmament have already been the subject of extensive, strenuous and constant examination. Together with international meetings dealing with these problems, such studies should be regarded as the first steps toward solving these serious questions, and should be promoted with even greater urgency by way of yielding concrete results in the future.

742 Nevertheless, men should take heed not to entrust themselves only to the efforts of others, while not caring about their own attitudes. For government officials who must at one and the same time guarantee the good of their own people and promote the universal good are very greatly dependent on public opinion and feeling. It does them no good to work for peace as long as feelings of hostility, contempt and distrust, as well as racial hatred and unbending ideologies, continue to divide men and place them in opposing camps. Consequently there is above all a pressing need for a renewed education of attitudes and for new inspiration in public opinion. Those who are dedicated to the work of education, particularly of the young, or who mold public opinion, should consider it their most weighty task to instruct all in fresh sentiments of peace. Indeed, we all need a change of heart as we regard the entire world and those tasks which we can perform in unison for the betterment of our race.

743 But we should not let false hope deceive us. For unless enmities and hatred are put away and firm, honest agreements concerning world peace are reached in the future, humanity, which already is in the middle of a grave crisis, even though it is endowed with remarkable knowledge, will perhaps be brought to that dismal hour in which it will experience no peace other than the dreadful peace of death. But, while we say this, the Church of Christ, present in the midst of the anxiety of this age, does not cease to hope most firmly. She

intends to propose to our age over and over again, in season and out of season, this apostolic message: "Behold, now is the acceptable time for a change of heart; behold! now is the day of salvation."[167]

Section II: Setting Up an International Community

744 83. In order to build up peace the causes of discord among men, especially injustice, which foment wars must above all be rooted out. Not a few of these causes come from excessive economic inequalities and from putting off the steps needed to remedy them. Other causes of discord, however, have their source in the desire to dominate and in a contempt for persons. And, if we look for deeper causes, we find them in human envy, distrust, pride, and other egotistical passions. Man cannot bear so many ruptures in the harmony of things. Consequently, the world is constantly beset by strife and violence between men, even when no war is being waged. Besides, since these same evils are present in the relations between various nations as well, in order to overcome or forestall them and to keep violence once unleashed within limits, it is absolutely necessary for countries to cooperate to better advantage, to work together more closely, and jointly to organize international bodies and to work tirelessly for the creation of organizations which will foster peace.

745 84. In view of the increasingly close ties of mutual dependence today between all the inhabitants and peoples of the earth, the fitting pursuit and effective realization of the universal common good now require of the community of nations that it organize itself in a manner suited to its present responsibilities, especially toward the many parts of the world which are still suffering from unbearable want.

746 To reach this goal, organizations of the international community, for their part, must make provision for men's different needs, both in the fields of social life—such as food supplies, health, education, labor and also in certain special circumstances which can crop up here and there, e.g., the need to promote the general improvement of developing countries,

or to alleviate the distressing conditions in which refugees dispersed throughout the world find themselves, or also to assist migrants and their families.

International and regional organizations which are already in existence are certainly well-deserving of the human race. These are the first efforts at laying the foundations on an international level for a community of all men to work for the solution to the serious problems of our times, to encourage progress everywhere, and to obviate wars of whatever kind. In all of these activities the Church rejoices in the spirit of true brotherhood flourishing between Christians and non-Christians as it strives to make ever more strenuous efforts to relieve widespread misery. 747

85. The present solidarity of mankind also calls for a revival of greater international cooperation in the economic field. Although nearly all peoples have become autonomous, they are far from being free of every form of undue dependence, and far from escaping all danger of serious internal difficulties. 748

The development of a nation depends on human and finanical aids. The citizens of each country must be prepared by education and professional training to discharge the various tasks of economic and social life. But this in turn requires the aid of foreign specialists who, when they give aid, will not act as overlords, but as helpers and fellow-workers. Developing nations will not be able to procure material assistance unless radical changes are made in the established procedures of modern world commerce. Other aid should be provided as well by advanced nations in the form of gifts, loans or financial investments. Such help should be accorded with generosity and without greed on the one side, and received with complete honesty on the other side. 749

If an authentic economic order is to be established on a world-wide basis, an end will have to be put to profiteering, to national ambition, to the appetite for political supremacy, to militaristic calculations, and to machinations for the purpose of spreading and imposing ideologies. 750

86. The following norms seem useful for such cooperation: 751

a) Developing nations should take great pains to seek as the object of progress to express and secure the total human fulfillment of their citizens. They should bear in mind that progress arises and grows above all out of the labor and genius of the nations themselves because it has to be based, not only on foreign aid, but especially on the full utilization of their own resources, and on the development of their own culture and traditions. Those who exert the greatest influence on others should be outstanding in this respect.

b) On the other hand, it is a very important duty of the advanced nations to help the developing nations in discharging their above-mentioned responsibilities. They should therefore gladly carry out on their own home front those spiritual and material readjustments that are required for the realization of this universal cooperation.

Consequently, in business dealings with weaker and proper nations, they should be careful to respect their welfare, for these countries need the income they receive on the sale of their homemade products to support themselves.

c) It is the role of the international community to coordinate and promote development, but in such a way that the resources earmarked for this purpose will be allocated as effectively as possible, and with complete equity. It is likewise this community's duty, with due regard for the principle of subsidiarity, so to regulate economic relations throughout the world that these will be carried out in accordance with the norms of justice.

Suitable organizations should be set up to foster and regulate international business affairs, particularly with the underdeveloped countries, and to compensate for losses resulting from an excessive inequality of power among the various nations. This type of organization, in unison with technical, cultural, and financial aid, should provide the help which developing nations need so that they can advantageously pursue their own economic advancement.

d) In many cases there is an urgent need to revamp economic and social structures. But one must guard against proposed technical solutions that are untimely. This is particularly true of those solutions providing man with material conveniences, which are nevertheless contrary to man's spiritual nature and advancement. For "not by bread alone does man live, but by every word which proceeds from the mouth of God" (*Matt.* 4:4). Every sector of the family of man carries within itself and in its best traditions some portion of the spiritual treasure entrusted by God to humanity, even though many may not be aware of the source from which it comes.

87. International cooperation is needed today especially for those peoples who, besides facing so many other difficulties, likewise undergo pressures due to a rapid increase in population. There is an urgent need to explore, with the full and intense cooperation of all, and especially of the wealthier nations, ways whereby the human necessities of food and a suitable education can be furnished and shared with the entire human community. But some peoples could greatly improve upon the conditions of their life if they would change over from antiquated methods of farming to the new technical methods, applying them with needed prudence according to their own circumstances. Their life would likewise be improved by the establishment of a better social order and by a fairer system for the distribution of land ownership. 752

Governments undoubtedly have rights and duties, within the limits of their proper competency, regarding the population problem in their respective countries, for instance, with regard to social and family life legislation, or with regard to information concerning the condition and needs of the country. Since men today are giving thought to this problem and are so greatly disturbed over it, it is desirable in addition that Catholic specialists, especially in the universities, skillfully pursue and develop studies and projects on all these matters. 753

But there are many today who maintain that the increase in world population, or at least the population increase in some countries, must be radically curbed by every means 754 possible and by any kind of intervention on the part of public authority. In view of this contention, the Council urges everyone to guard against solutions, whether publicly or privately supported, or at times even imposed, which are contrary to the moral law. For in keeping with man's inalienable right to marry and generate children, the decision concerning the number of children they will have depends on the correct judgment of the parents and it cannot in any way be left to the judgment of public authority. But since the judgment of the parents presupposes a rightly formed conscience, it is of the utmost importance that the way be open for everyone to develop a correct and genuinely human responsibility which respects the divine law and takes into consideration the circumstances of the place and the time. But sometimes this requires an improvement in educational and social conditions, and, above all, formation in religion or at least a complete moral training. Men should judiciously be informed, furthermore, of scientific advances in exploring methods whereby spouses can be helped in regulating the number of their children and whose safeness has been well proven and whose harmony with the moral order has been ascertained.

755 88. Christians should cooperate willingly and wholeheartedly in establishing an international order that includes a genuine respect for all freedoms and amicable brotherhoods between all. This is all the more pressing since the greater part of the world is still suffering from so much poverty that it is as if Christ Himself were crying out in these poor to beg the charity of the disciples. Do not let men, then be scandalized because some countries with a majority of citizens who are counted as Christians have an abundance of wealth, whereas others are deprived of the necessities of life and are tormented with hunger, disease, and every kind of misery. The spirit of poverty and charity are the glory and witness of the Church of Christ.

756 Those Christians are to be praised and supported, therefore, who volunteer their services to help other men and nations. Indeed, it is the duty of the whole People of God, following the word and example of the bishops, to alleviate as far as they are able the sufferings of the modern age. They should

do this too, as was the ancient custom in the Church, out of the substance of their goods, and not only out of what is superfluous.

757 The procedure of collecting and distributing aid, without being inflexible and completely uniform, should nevertheless be carried out in an orderly fashion in dioceses, nations, and throughout the entire world. Wherever it seems fitting, this activity of Catholics should be carried on in unison with other Christian brothers. For the spirit of charity does not forbid, but on the contrary commands that charitable activity be carried out in a careful and orderly manner. Therefore, it is essential for those who intend to dedicate themselves to the service of the developing nations to be properly trained in appropriate institutes.

758 89. Since, in virtue of her mission received from God, the Church preaches the Gospel to all men and dispenses the treasures of grace, she contributes to the ensuring of peace everywhere on earth and to the placing of the fraternal exchange between men on solid ground by imparting knowledge of the divine and natural law. Therefore, to encourage and stimulate cooperation among men, the Church must be clearly present in the midst of the community of nations, both through her official channels and through the full and sincere collaboration of all Christians—a collaboration motivated solely by the desire to be of service to all.

759 This will come about more effectively if the faithful themselves, conscious of their responsibility as men and as Christians, will exert their influence in their own milieu to arouse a ready willingness to cooperate with the international community. Special care must be given, in both religious and civic education, to the formation of youth in this regard.

760 90. An outstanding form of international activity on the part of Christians is found in the joint efforts which, both as individuals and in groups, they contribute to institutes already established or to be established for the encouragement of cooperation among nations. There are also various Catholic associations on the international level which can contribute in many ways to the building up of a peaceful and fraternal community of nations. These should be strengthened by

augmenting in them the number of well qualified collaborators, by increasing needed resources, and by a suitable coordination of their forces. For today both effective action and the need for dialogue demand joint projects. Moreover, such associations contribute much to the development of a universal outlook—something certainly appropriate for Catholics. They also help to form an awareness of genuine universal solidarity and responsibility.

761 Finally, it is very much to be desired that Catholics, in order to fulfill their role properly in the international community, should seek to cooperate actively and in a positive manner both with their separated brothers, who together with them profess the Gospel of charity, and with all men thirsting for true peace.

762 The Council, considering the immensity of the hardships which still afflict the greater part of mankind today, regards it as most opportune that an organism of the universal Church be set up in order that both the justice and love of Christ toward the poor might be developed everywhere. The role of such an organism would be to stimulate the Catholic community to promote progress in needy regions and international social justice.

CONCLUSION

763 91. Drawn from the treasures of Church teaching, the proposals of this Sacred Synod look to the assistance of every man of our time, whether he believes in God, or does not explicitly recognize Him. If adopted, they will promote among men a sharper insight into their full destiny, and thereby lead them to fashion the world more to man's surpassing dignity, to search for a brotherhood which is universal and more deeply rooted, and to meet the urgencies of our age with a gallant and unified effort born of love.

764 Undeniably this conciliar program is but a general one in several of its parts; and deliberately so, given the immense variety of situations and forms of human culture in the world. Indeed while it presents teaching already accepted in the

Church, the program will have to be followed up and amplified since it sometimes deals with matters in a constant state of development. Still, we have relied on the word of God and the spirit of the Gospel. Hence we entertain the hope that many of our proposals will prove to be of substantial benefit to everyone, especially after they have been adapted to individual nations and mentalities by the faithful, under the guidance of their pastors.

92. By virtue of her mission to shed on the whole world the radiance of the Gospel message, and to unify under one Spirit all men of whatever nation, race or culture, the Church stands forth as a sign of that brotherhood which facilitates and invigorates sincere dialogue. 765

Such a mission requires in the first place that we foster within the Church itself mutual esteem, reverence and harmony, through the full recognition of lawful diversity. Thus all those who compose the one People of God, both pastors and the general faithful, can engage in dialogue with ever increasing effectiveness. For the bonds which unite the faithful are mightier than anything dividing them. Hence, let there be unity in essentials; freedom in doubtful matters; and in all things charity. 766

Our hearts embrace also those brothers and communities not yet living with us in full communion; to them we are linked nonetheless by our profession of the Father and the Son and the Holy Spirit, and by the bond of charity. We are not unmindful of the fact that the unity of Christians is today awaited and desired by many, too, who do not believe in Christ; for the further it advances toward truth and love under the powerful impulse of the Holy Spirit, the more this unity will be a harbinger of unity and peace for the world at large. Therefore, by common effort and in ways which are today increasingly appropriate for seeking this splendid goal effectively, let us take pains to pattern ourselves after the Gospel more exactly every day, and thus work as brothers in rendering service to the human family. For, in Christ Jesus this family is constituted to the family of the sons of God. 767

We think cordially too of all who acknowledge God, and who preserve in their traditions precious elements of religion 768 and humanity. We want frank conversation to compel us all to receive the impulses of the Spirit faithfully and to act on them energetically.

769 For our part, the desire for such dialogue, which can lead to truth through love alone, excludes no one, though an appropriate measure of prudence must undoubtedly be exercised. We include those who cultivate outstanding qualities of the human spirit, but do not yet acknowledge the Source of these qualities. We include those who oppress the Church and harass her in manifold ways. Since God the Father is the origin and purpose of all men, we are all called to be brothers. Therefore, if we have been summoned to the same destiny, human and divine, we can and we should work together without violence and deceit in order to build up the world in genuine peace.

770 93. Mindful of the Lord's saying: "by this will all men know that you are my disciples, if you have love for one another" (*John* 13:35), Christians cannot yearn for anything more ardently than to serve the men of the modern world ever more generously and effectively. Therefore, by holding faithfully to the Gospel and benefiting from its resources, by joining with every man who loves and practices justice, Christians have shouldered a gigantic task to be carried out in this world, a task concerning which they must give a reckoning to Him who will judge every man on the last day.

771 Not everyone who cries, "Lord, Lord," will enter into the kingdom of heaven, but those who do the Father's will[168] by taking a strong grip on the work at hand. Now, the Father wills that in all men we recognize Christ our brother and love Him effectively, in word and in deed. By thus giving witness to the truth, we will share with others the mystery of the heavenly Father's love. As a consequence, men throughout the world will be aroused to a lively hope—the gift of the Holy Spirit—that finally they will be caught up in peace and utter happiness in that fatherland radiant with the glory of the Lord.

772 Now to Him who is able to accomplish all things in a measure far beyond what we ask or conceive, in keeping with the power that is at work in us—to Him be glory in the Church

and in Christ Jesus, down through all the ages of time without end. Amen (*Eph.* 3:20-21).

773 The entire text and all the individual elements which have been set forth in this Pastoral Constitution have pleased the Fathers. And by the Apostolic power conferred on us by Christ, we, together with the Venerable Fathers, in the Holy Spirit, approve, decree and enact them; and we order that what has been thus enacted in Council be promulgated, to the glory of God.

Rome, at St. Peter's 7 December, 1965.

Address of Pope Paul VI to the United Nations General Assembly October 4, 1965

As we begin our address to this unique world audience, we wish to thank your secretary general, U Thant, for the invitation which he extended to us to visit the United Nations on the occasion of the twentieth anniversary of the foundation of this world institution for peace and for collaboration between the peoples of the entire earth.

775 Our thanks also to the president of the General Assembly, Mr. Amintore Fanfani, who has used such kind language in our regard from the very day of his election.

776 We thank all of you here present for your kind welcome, and we present to each one of you our deferential and sincere salutation. In friendship you have invited us and admitted us to this meeting; and it is as a friend that we are here today.

777 We express to you our cordial personal homage, and we bring, you that of the entire Second Vatican Ecumenical Council now meeting in Rome, and represented here by the eminent cardinals who accompany us for this purpose.

778 In their name and in our own, to each and every one of you, honor and greeting!

779 This encounter, as you all understand, marks a simple and at the same time a great moment. It is simple because you have before you a man like you; your brother; and among you, all representatives of sovereign states, the

least-invested, if you wish to think of him thus, with a miniscule, as it were symbolic, temporal sovereignty, only as much as is necessary to be free to exercise his spiritual mission, and to assure all those who deal with him that he is independent of every other sovereignty of this world. But he, who now addresses you, has no temporal power, nor any ambition to compete with you. In fact, we have nothing to ask for, no question to raise; we have only a desire to express and a permission to request; namely, that of serving you insofar as we can, with disinterest, with humility and love.

This is our first declaration. As you can see, it is so simple as to seem insignificant to this Assembly which always treats of most important and most difficult matters. 780

We said also, however, and all here today feel it, that this moment is also a great one. Great for us, great for you. 781

For us: You know well who we are. Whatever may be the opinion you have of the Pontiff of Rome, you know our mission. We are the bearer of a message for all mankind. And this we are, not only in our own personal name and in the name of the great Catholic family; but also in that of those Christian brethren who share the same sentiments which we express here, particularly of those who so kindly charged us explicitly to be their spokesman here. Like a messenger who, after a long journey, finally succeeds in delivering the letter which has been entrusted to him, so we appreciate the good fortune of this moment, however brief, which fulfills a desire nourished in the heart for nearly twenty centuries. For, as you will remember, we are very ancient; we here represent a long history; we here celebrate the epilogue of a wearying pilgrimage in search of a conversation with the entire world, ever since the command was given to us: Go and bring the good news to all peoples. Now, you here represent all peoples. Allow us to tell you that we have a message, a happy message, to deliver to each one of you and to all. 782

1. We might call our message a ratification, a solemn moral ratification of this lofty institution. This message comes from our historical experience. As "an expert in humanity," 783

we bring to this organization the suffrage of our recent predecessors, that of the entire Catholic episcopate and our own, convinced as we are that this organization represents the obligatory path of modern civilization and of world peace. In saying this, we feel we are making our own the voice of the dead and of the living; of the dead, who fell in the terrible wars of the past; of the living who survived those wars, bearing in their hearts a condemnation of those who would try to renew wars; and also of those living who rise up fresh and confident, the youth of the present generation, who legitimately dream of a better human race. And we also make our own the voice of the poor, the disinherited, the suffering, of those who hunger and thirst for justice, for the dignity of life, for freedom, for well-being and progress. The peoples of the earth turn to the United Nations as the last hope of concord and peace; we presume to present here, with their tribute of honor and of hope, our own tribute also.

784 This is why this moment is great for you, also.

785 2. We feel that you are already aware of this. Hearken now to the continuation of our message. It becomes a message of good wishes for the future. The edifice which you have constructed must never fall; it must be perfected, and made equal to the needs which world history will present. You mark a stage in the development of mankind, from which retreat must never be admitted, but from which it is necessary that advance be made.

786 To the pluralism of states, which can no longer ignore one another, you offer an extremely simple and fruitful formula of coexistence. First of all, you recognize and distinguish the ones and the others. You do not confer existence upon states; but you qualify each single nation as fit to sit in the orderly congress of peoples. That is, you grant recognition, of the highest ethical and jurdical value, to each single sovereign national community guaranteeing it an honored international citizenship. This in itself is a great service to the cause of humanity, namely, to define clearly and to honor the national subjects of the world community, and to classify them in a juridical condition, worthy thereby of being recognized and respected by all, and from which there

may derive an orderly and stable system of international life. You give sanction to the great principle that the relations between peoples should be regulated by reason, by justice, by law, by negotiation; not by force, nor by violence, not by war, not by fear or by deceit. Thus it must be. Allow us to congratulate you for having had the wisdom to open this hall to the young peoples, to those states which have recently attained independence and national freedom. Their presence is the proof of the universality and magnanimity which inspire the principles of this institution.

787 Thus it must be. This is our praise and our good wish; and, as you can see, we do not attribute these as from outside; we derive them from inside, from the very genius of your institution.

788 3. Your charter goes further than this, and our message advances with it. You exist and operate to unite the nations, to bind states together. Let us use this second formula: to bring the ones together with the others. You are an association. You are a bridge between peoples. You are a network of relations between states. We would almost say that your chief characteristic is a reflection, as it were, in the temporal field, of what our Catholic Church aspires to be in the spiritual field: unique and universal. In the ideological construction of mankind, there is on the natural level nothing superior to this. Your vocation is to make brothers not only of some, but of all peoples. A difficult undertaking, indeed; but this it is, your most noble undertaking. Is there anyone who does not see the necessity of coming thus progressively to the establishment of a world authority, able to act efficaciously on the juridical and political levels?

789 Once more we reiterate our good wish: Advance always! We will go further, and say: Strive to bring back among you any who have separated themselves and study the right method of uniting to your pact of brotherhood, in honor and loyalty, those who do not yet share in it. Act so that those still outside will desire and merit the confidence of all; and then be generous in granting such confidence. You have the good fortune and honor of sitting in this assembly of peaceful community; hear us as we say: Ensure that the reciprocal

trust which here unites you, and enables you to do good and great things, may never be undermined or betrayed.

790 4. The inherent logic of this wish, which might be considered to pertain to the very structure of your organization, leads us to complete it with other formulas. Thus let no one, inasmuch as he is a member of your union, be superior to the others: never one above the other. This is the formula of equality. We are well aware that it must be completed by the evaluation of other factors besides simple membership in this institution; but equality, too, belongs to its constitution. You are not equal, but here you make yourselves equal. For several among you, this may be an act of high virtue; allow us to say this to you, as the representative of a religion which accomplishes salvation through the humility of its Divine Founder. Men cannot be brothers if they are not humble. It is pride, no matter how legitimate it may seem to be, which provokes tension and struggles for prestige, for predominance, colonialism, egoism; that is, pride disrupts brotherhood.

791 5. And now our message reaches its highest point, which is, at first, a negative point. You are expecting us to utter this sentence, and we are well aware of its gravity and solemnity: not the ones against the others, never again, never more! It was principally for this purpose that the organization of the United Nations arose: against war, in favor of peace! Listen to the lucid words of the great departed John Kennedy, who proclaimed four years ago, "Mankind must put an end to war or war will put an end to mankind." Many words are not needed to proclaim this loftiest aim of your institution. It suffices to remember that the blood of millions of men, that numberless and unheard-of sufferings, useless slaughter and frightful ruin are the sanction of the future history of the world: No more war, war never again! Peace, it is peace which must guide the destinies of people and of all mankind.

792 Gratitude to you, glory to you, who for twenty years have labored for peace. Gratitude and glory to you for the conflicts which you have prevented or have brought to an end. The results of your efforts in recent days in favor of peace,

even if not yet proved decisive, are such as to deserve that we, presuming to interpret the sentiments of the whole world, express to you both praise and thanks.

793 Gentlemen, you have performed and you continue to perform a great work: the education of mankind in the ways of peace. The U.N. is the great school where that education is imparted and we are today in the assembly hall of that school. Everyone taking his place here becomes a pupil and also a teacher in the art of building peace. When you leave this hall, the world looks upon you as the architects and constructors of peace.

794 Peace, as you know, is not built up only by means of politics, by the balance of forces and of interests. It is constructed with the mind, with ideas, with works of peace. You labor in this great construction. But you are still at the beginnings. Will the world ever succeed in changing that selfish and bellicose mentality which, up to now, has been interwoven in so much of its history? It is hard to foresee; but it is easy to affirm that it is toward that new history, a peaceful, truly human history, as promised by God to men of good will, that we must resolutely march. The roads thereto are already well marked out for you; and the first is that of disarmament.

795 If you wish to be brothers, let the arms fall from your hands. One cannot love while holding offensive arms. Those armaments, especially those terrible arms which modern science has given you, long before they produce victims and ruins, nourish bad feelings, create nightmares, distrust, and somber resolutions; they demand enormous expenditures; they obstruct projects of union and useful collaboration; they falsify the psychology of peoples. As long as man remains that weak, changeable and even wicked being that he often shows himself to be, defensive arms will, unfortunately, be necessary. You, however, in your courage and valiance, are studying the ways of guaranteeing the security of international life, without having recourse to arms. This is a most noble aim. This the peoples expect of you, this must be obtained! Let unanimous trust in this institution

grow, let its authority increase; and this aim, we believe, will be secured.

796 Gratitude will be expressed to you by all peoples, relieved as they will then be from the crushing expenses of armaments and freed from the nightmare of an ever imminent war.

797 We rejoice in the knowledge that many of you have considered favorably our invitation, addressed to all states in the cause of peace from Bombay last December, to divert to the benefit of the developing countries at least a part of the savings which could be realized by reducing armaments. We here renew that invitation, trusting in your sentiments of humanity and generosity.

798 6. In so doing, we become aware that we are echoing another principle which is structural to the United Nations, which is its positive and affirmative high point: namely, that you work here not only to avert conflicts beteen states, but also to make them capable of working the ones for the others. You are not satisfied with facilitating mere coexistence between nations: you take a much greater step forward, one deserving of our praise and our support—you organize the brotherly collaboration of peoples. In this way a system of solidarity is set up and its lofty civilized aims win the orderly and unanimous support of all the family of peoples for the common good and for the good of each individual. This aspect of the organization of the United Nations is the most beautiful; it is its most truly human visage; it is the ideal of which mankind dreams on its pilgrimage through time; it is the world's greatest hope; it is, we presume to say, the reflection of the loving and transcendent design of God for the progress of the human family on earth—a reflection in which we see the message of the Gospel, which is heavenly, become earthly. Indeed, it seems to us that here we hear the echo of the voice of our predecessors, and particularly of that of Pope John XXIII, whose message of *Pacem in Terris* was so honorably and significantly received among you.

799 You proclaim here the fundamental rights and duties of man, his dignity, his freedom—and above all his religious

freedom. We feel that you thus interpret the highest sphere of human wisdom and, we might add, its sacred character. For you deal here above all with human life; and the life of man is sacred; no one may dare offend it. Respect for life, even with regard to the great problem of birth, must find here in your assembly its highest affirmation and its most reasoned defense. You must strive to muliply bread so that it suffices for the tables of mankind, and not rather favor an artificial control of birth, which would be irrational, in order to diminish the number of guests at the banquet of life.

800 It does not suffice, however, to feed the hungry; it is necessary also to assure to each man a life conformed to his dignity. This too you strive to perform. We may consider this the fulfillment before our very eyes, and by your efforts, of that prophetical announcement so applicable to your institution: "They will melt down their swords into plowshares, their spears into pruningforks."[1] Are you not using the prodigious energies of the earth and the magnificent inventions of science, no longer as instruments of death but as tools of life for humanity's new era?

801 We know how intense and ever more efficacious are the efforts of the United Nations and its dependent world agencies to assist those government which need help to hasten their economic and social progress. We know how ardently you labor to overcome illiteracy and to spread culture throughout the world; to give man adequate modern medical assistance; to employ in man's service the marvelous resources of science, of technique and of organization—all of this is magnificent, and merits the praise and support of all, including our own.

802 We ourself wish to set a good example, even though our means may be inadequate to the practical and quantitative needs. We intend to intensify the development of our charitable institutions to combat world hunger and to meet world needs. It is thus, and in no other way, that peace can be built.

803 7. One more word, gentlemen, our final word: This edifice which you are constructing does not rest upon merely ma-

terial and earthly foundations, if so it would be a house built upon sand; above all, it is based on our own consciences. The hour has struck for our "conversion," for personal transformation, for interior renewal. We must get used to thinking of man in a new way; and in a new way also of men's life in common; in a new manner too conceiving the paths of history and the destiny of the world, according to the words of St. Paul: ". . .put on the new man, which has been created according to God in justice and holiness of truth."[2] The hour has struck for a halt, a moment of recollection, or reflection, almost of prayer, a moment to think anew of our common origin, our history, our common destiny. Today as never before, in our era so marked by human progress, there is need for an appeal to the moral conscience of man. For the danger comes, not from progress, nor from science–indeed, if properly utilized, these could rather resolve many of the grave problems which beset mankind. No, the real danger comes from man himself, wielding ever more powerful arms which can be employed equally as well for destruction as for the loftiest conquests.

804 In a word, the edifice of modern civilization must be built upon spiritual principles; the only principles capable not only of supporting it but also of enlightening and animating it. And these indispensable principles of higher wisdom can rest only–and you know that this is our conviction–upon faith in God; that unknown God, of whom St. Paul spoke to the Athenians in the Areopagus; unknown by them, although without realizing it they sought Him and He was close to them, as happens also to many men of our times. To us, in any case, and to all those who accept the ineffable revelation which Christ has given us of Him, He is the living God, the Father of all men.

POPULORUM PROGRESSIO

Encyclical Letter of
Pope Paul VI
On the Development of Peoples
March 26, 1967

The development of peoples has the Church's close attention, particularly the development of those peoples who are striving to escape from hunger, misery, endemic diseases and ignorance; of those who are looking for a wider share in the benefits of civilisation and a more active improvement of their human qualities; of those who are aiming purposefully at their complete fulfilment. Following on the Second Vatican Ecumenical Council a renewed consciousness of the demands of the Gospel makes it her duty to put herself at the service of all, to help them grasp their serious problem in all its dimensions, and to convince them that solidarity in action at this turning point in human history is a matter of urgency.

806

2. Our predecessors in their great encyclicals, Leo XIII in *Rerum Novarum,*[1] Pius XI in *Quadragesimo Anno*[2] and John XXIII in *Mater et Magistra*[3] and *Pacem in Terris*[4]—not to mention the messages of Pius XII[5] to the world—did not fail in the duty of their office of shedding the light of the Gospel on the social questions of their times.

807

3. Today the principal fact that we must all recognise is that the social question has become world-wide. John XXIII stated this in unambiguous terms[6] and the Council echoed him in its Pastoral Constitution on *The Church in the Modern World.*[7] This teaching is important and its application urgent. Today the peoples in hunger are making a dramatic appeal

to the peoples blessed with abundance. The Church shudders at this cry of anguish and calls each one to give a loving response of charity to this brother's cry for help.

808 4. Before We became Pope, two journeys, to Latin America in 1960 and to Africa in 1962, brought Us into direct contact with the acute problems pressing on continents full of life and hope. Then on becoming Father of all We made further journeys, to the Holy Land and India, and were able to see and virtually touch the very serious difficulties besetting peoples of long-standing civilisations who are at grips with the problem of development. While the Second Vatican Ecumenical Council was being held in Rome, providential circumstances permitted Us to address in person the General Assembly of the United Nations, and We pleaded the cause of poor peoples before this distinguished body.

809 5. Then quite recently, in Our desire to carry out the wishes of the Council and give specific expression to the Holy See's contribution to this great cause of peoples in development, We considered it Our duty to set up a Pontifical Commission in the Church's central administration, charged with "bringing to the whole of God's People the full knowledge of the part expected of them at the present time, so as to further the progress of poorer peoples, to encourage social justice among nations, to offer to less developed nations the means whereby they can further their own progress"[8]: its name, which is also its programme, is *Justice and Peace.* We think that this can and should bring together men of good will with our Catholic sons and our Christian brothers. So it is to all that We address this solemn appeal for concrete action towards man's complete development and the development of all mankind.

810 6. Freedom from misery, the greater assurance of finding subsistence, health and fixed employment; an increased share of responsibility without oppression of any kind and in security from situations that do violence to their dignity as men; better education—in brief, to seek to do more, know more and have more in order to be more: that is what men aspire to now when a greater number of them are condemned to live in conditions that make this lawful desire illusory. Be-

sides, peoples who have recently gained national independence experience the need to add to this political freedom a fitting autonomous growth, social as well as economic, in order to assure their citizens of a full human enchancement and to take their rightful place with other nations.

7. Though insufficient for the immensity and urgency of the task, the means inherited from the past are not lacking. It must certainly be recognised that colonising power have often furthered their own interests, power of glory, and that their departure has sometmes left a precarious economy, bound up for instance with the production of one kind of crop whose market prices are subject to sudden and considerable variation. Yet while recognising the damage done by a certain type of colonialism and its consequences, one must at the same time acknowledge the qualities and achievement of colonisers who brought their science and teachnical knowledge and left benefical results of their presence in so many underprivileged regions. The structures established by them persist, however incomplete they may be; they diminished ignorance and sickness, brought the benefits of communications and improved living conditions. 811

8. Yet once this is admitted, it remains only too true that the resultant situation is manifestly inadequate for facing the hard reality of modern economics. Left to itself it works rather to widen the differences in the world's levels of life, not to diminish them: rich peoples enjoy rapid growth whereas the poor develop slowly . The imbalance is on the increase: some produce a surplus of foodstuffs, others cruelly lack them and see their exports made uncertain. 812

9. At the same time social conflicts have taken on world dimensions. The acute disquiet which has taken hold of the poor classes in countries that are becoming industrialised, is not embracing those whose economy is almost exclusively agrarian: farming people, too, are becoming aware of their "undeserved hardship".[9] There is also the scandal of glaring inequalities not merely in the enjoyment of possessions but even more in the exercise of power. While a small restricted group enjoys a refined civilisation in certain 813

regions, the remainder of the population, poor and scattered, is "deprived of nearly all possibility of personal initiative and of responsibility, and oftentimes even its living and working conditions are unworthy of the human person".[10]

814 10. Furthermore, the conflict between traditional civilisation break down structures which do not adapt themselves to new conditions. Their framework, sometimes rigid, was the indispensable prop to personal and family life; older people remain attached to it, the young escape from it, as from a useless barrier, to turn eagerly to new forms of life in society. The conflict of the generations is made more serious by a tragic dilemma: whether to retain ancestral institutions and convictions and renounce progress, or to admit techniques and civilisations from outside and reject along with the traditions of the past all their human richness. In effect, the moral, spiritual and religious supports of the past too often give way without securing in return any guarantee of a place in the new world.

815 11. In this confusion the temptation becomes stronger to risk being swept away towards types of messianism which give promises but create illusions. The resulting dangers are patent: violent popular reactions, agitation towards insurrection, and a drifting towards totalitarian ideologies. Such are the data of the problem. Its seriousness is evident to all.

816 12. True to the teaching and example of her divine Founder, Who cited the preaching of the Gospel to the poor as a sign of His mission,[11] the Church has never failed to foster the human progress of the nations to which she brings faith in Christ. Her missionaries have built, not only churches, but also hostels and hospitals, schools and universities. Teaching the local populations the means of deriving the best advantages from their natural resources, missionaries have often protected them from the greed of foreigners. Without doubt their work, inasmuch as it was human, was not perfect, and sometimes the announcemnt of the authentic Gospel message was infiltrated by many ways of thinking and acting which were characteristic of their home country. But the missionaries were also able to develop and foster local

institutions. In many a region they were among the pioneers in material progress as well as in cultural advancement. Let it suffice to recall the example of Father Charles de Foucauld, whose charity earned him the title "Universal Brother", and who edited an invaluable dictionary of the Touareg language. We ought to pay tribute to these pioneers who have been too often forgotten, but who were urged on by the love of Christ, just as we honour their imitators and successors who today still continue to put themselves at the generous and unselfish service of those to whom they announce the Gospel.

13. However, local and individual undertakings are no longer enough. The present situation of the world demands concerted action based on a clear vision of all economic, social, cultural, and spiritual aspects. Experienced in human affairs, the Church, without attempting to interfere in any way in the politics of States, "seeks but a solitary goal: to carry forward the work of Christ Himself under the lead of the befriending Spirit. And Christ entered this world to give witness to the truth, to rescue and not to sit in judgment, to serve and not to be served".[12] Founded to establish on earth the Kingdom of Heaven and not to conquer any earthly power, the Church clearly states that the two realms are distinct, just as the two powers, ecclesiastical and civil, are supreme, each in its own domain.[13] But, since the Church lives in history, she ought to "scrutinize the signs of the times and interpret them in the light of the Gospel".[14] Sharing the noblest aspirations of men and suffering when she sees them not satisfied, she wishes to help them attain their full flowering, and that is why she offers men what she possesses as her characteristic attribute: a global vision of man and of the human race. 817

14. Development cannot be limited to mere economic growth. In order to be authentic, it must be complete: integral, that is, it has to promote the good of every man and of the whole man. As an eminent specialist has very rightly and emphatically declared: "We do not believe in separating the economic from the human, nor development from the civilisations in which it exists. What we hold important is man, 818

each man and each group of men, and we even include the whole of humanity".[15]

819 15. In the design of God, every man is called upon to develop and fulfill himself, for every life is a vocation. At birth, everyone is granted, in germ, a set of aptitudes and qualities for him to bring to fruition. Their coming to maturity, which will be the result of education received from the environment and personal efforts, will allow each man to direct himself toward the destiny intended for him by his Creator. Endowed with intelligence and freedom, he is responsible for his fulfilment as he is for his salvation. He is aided, or sometimes impeded, by those who educate him and those with whom he lives, but each one remains, whatever be these influences affecting him, the principal agent of his own success or failure. By the unaided effort of his own intelligence and his will, each man can grow in humanity, can enhance his personal worth, can become more a person.

820 16. However, this self-fulfilment is not something optional. Just as the whole of creation is ordained to its Creator, so spiritual beings should of their own accord orientate their lives to God, the first truth and the supreme good. Thus it is that human fulfilment constitutes, as it were, a summary of our duties. But there is much more: this harmonious enrichment of nature by personal and responsible effort is ordered to a further perfection. By reason of his union with Christ, the source of life, man attains to new fulfilment of himself, to a transcendent humanism which gives him his greatest possible perfection: this is the highest goal of personal development.

821 17. But each man is a member of society. He is part of the whole of mankind. It is not just certain individuals, but all men who are called to this fullness of development. Civilisations are born, develop and die. But humanity is advancing along the path of history like the waves of rising tide encroaching gradually on the shore. We have inherited from past generations, and we have benefitted from the work of our contemporaries: for this reason we have obligations towards all, and we cannot refuse to interest ourselves in those who will come after us to enlarge the human

family. The reality of human solidarity, which is a benefit for us, also imposes a duty.

18. This personal and communal development would be threatened if the true scale of values were underminded. The desire for necessities is legitimate, and work undertaken to obtain them is a duty: "If any man will not work, neither let him eat".[16] But the acquiring of temporal goods can lead to greed, to the insatiable desire for more, and can make increased power a tempting objective. Individuals, families and nations can be overcome by avarice, be they poor or rich, and all can fall victim to a stifling materialism. 822

19. Increased possession is not the ultimate goal of nations nor of individuals. All growth is ambivalent. It is essential if man is to develop as a man, but in a way it imprisons man if he considers it the supreme good, and it restricts his vision. Then we see hearts harden and minds close, and men no longer gather together in friendship but out of self-interest, which soon leads to oppositons and disunity. The exclusive pursuit of possessions thus becomes an obstacle to individual fulfilment and to man's true greatness. Both for nations and for individual men, avarice is the most evident form of moral underdevelopment. 823

20. If further development calls for the work of more and more technicians, even more necessary is the deep thought and reflection of wise men in search of a new humanism which will enable modern man to find himself anew by embracing the higher values of love and friendship, of prayer and contemplation.[17] This is what will permit the fullness of authentic development, a development which is for each and all the transition from less human conditions to those which are more human. 824

21. Less human conditions: the lack of material necessities for those who are without the minimum essential for life, the moral deficiencies of those who are mutilated by selfishness. Less human conditions: oppressive social structures, whether due to the abuses of ownership or to the abuses of power, to the exploitation of workers or to unjust transactions. Conditions that are more human: the passage from misery towards the possession of necessities, 825

victory over social scourges, the growth of knowledge, the acquisition of culture. Additional conditions that are more human: increased esteem for the dignity of others, the turning toward the spirit of poverty,[18] cooperation for the common good, the will and desire for peace. Conditions that are still more human: the acknowledgement by man of supreme values, and of God their source and their finality. Conditions that, finally and above all, are more human: faith, a gift of God accepted by the good will of man, and unity in the charity of Christ, Who calls us all to share as sons in the life of the living God, the Father of all men.

826 22. "Fill the earth and subdue it":[19] the Bible, from the first page on, teaches us that the whole of creation is for man, that it is his responsibility to develop it by intelligent effort and by means of his labour to perfect it, so to speak, for his use. If the world is made to furnish each individual with the means of livelihood and the instruments for his growth and progress, each man has therefore the right to find in the world what is necessary for himself. The recent Council reminded us of this "God intended the earth and all that it contains for the use of every human being and people. Thus, as all men follow justice and unite in charity, created goods should abound for them on a reasonable basis".[20] All other rights whatsoever, including those of property and of free commerce, are to be subordinated to this principle. They should not hinder but on the contrary favour its application. It is a grave and urgent social duty to redirect them to their primary finality.

827 23. "If someone who has the riches of this world sees his brother in need and closes his heart to him, how does the love of God abide in him?"[21] It is well known how strong were the words used by the Fathers of the Church to describe the proper attitude of persons who possess anything towards persons in need. To quote Saint Ambrose: "You are not making a gift of your possessions to the poor person. You are handing over to him what is his. For what has been given in common for the use of all, you have arrogated to yourself. The world is given to all, and not only to the rich".[22] That is, private property does not constitute for

anyone an absolute and unconditioned right. No one is justified in keeping for his exclusive use what he does not need, when others lack necessities. In a word, "according to the traditional doctrine as found in the Fathers of the Church and the great theologians, the right to property must never be exercised to the detriment of the common good". If there should arise a conflict "between acquired private rights and primary community exigencies", it is the responsibility of public authorities "to look for a solution, with the active participation of individuals and social groups".[23] 828

24. If certain landed estates impede the general prosperity because they are extensive, unused or poorly used, or because they bring hardship to peoples or are detrimental to the interests of the country, the common good sometimes demands their expropriation. While giving a clear statement on this,[24] the Council recalled no less clearly that the available revenue is not to be used in accordance with mere whim, and that no place must be given to selfish speculation. Consequently it is unacceptable that citizens with abundant incomes from the resources and activity of their country should transfer a considerable part of this income abroad purely for their own advantage, without care for the manifest wrong they inflict on their country by doing this.[25]

829 25. The introduction of industry is a necessity for economic growth and human progress; it is also a sign of development and contributes to it. By persistent work and use of his intelligence man gradually wrests nature's secrets from her and finds a better application for her riches. As his self-mastery increases, he develops a taste for research and discovery, an ability to take a calculated risk, boldness in enterprises, generosity in what he does and a sense of responsibility.

830 26. But it is unfortunate that on these new conditions of society a system has been constructed which considers profit as the key motive for economic progress, competition as the supreme law of economics, and private ownership of the means of production as an absolute right that has no limits and carries no corresponding social obligation. This unchecked liberalism leads to dictatorship right-

ly denounced by Pius XI as producing "the international imperialism of money".[26] One cannot condemn such abuses too strongly by solemnly recalling once again that the economy is at the service of man.[27] But if it is true that a type of capitalism has been the source of excessive suffering, injustices and fratricidal conflicts whose effects still persist, it would also be wrong to attribute to industrialisation itself evils that belong to the woeful system which accompanied it. On the contrary one must recognise in all justice the irreplaceable contribution made by the organisation of labour and of industry to what development has accomplished.

831 27. Similarly with work: while it can sometimes be given exaggerated significance, it is for all something willed and blessed by God. Man created to His image "must cooperate with his Creator in the perfecting of creation and communicate to the earth the spiritual imprint he himself has received".[28] God Who has endowed man with intelligence, imagination and sensitivity, has also given him the means of completing His work in a certain way: whether he be artist or craftsman, engaged in management, industry or agriculture, everyone who works is a creator. Bent over a material that resists his efforts, a man by his work gives his imprint for it, acquiring, as he does so, perseverance, skill and a spirit of invention. Further, when work is done in common, when hope, hardship, ambition and joy are shared, it brings together and firmly unites the wills, minds and hearts of men: in its accomplishment, men find themselves to be brothers.[29]

832 28. Work of course can have contrary effects, for it promises money, pleasure and power, invites some to selfishness, others to revolt; it also develops professional awareness, sense of duty and charity to one's neighbour. When it is more scientific and better organised, there is a risk of its dehumanising those who perform it, by making them its servants, for work is human only if it remains intelligent and free. John XXIII gave a reminder of the urgency of giving everyone who works his propter dignity by making him a true sharer in the work he does with others: "every

effort should be made that the enterprise become a community of persons in the dealings, activities and standing of all its members".[30] Man's labour means much more still for the Christian: the mission of sharing in the creation of the supernatural world[31] which remains incomplete until we all come to build up together that perfect Man of whom St. Paul speaks "who realises the fulness of Christ".[32]

29. We must make haste: too many are suffering, and the distance is growing that separates the progress of some and the stagnation, not to say the regression, of others. Yet the work required should advance smoothly if there is not to be the risk of losing indispensable equilibrium. A hasty agrarian reform can fail. Industrialisation if introduced suddenly can displace structures still necessary, and produce hardships in society which would be a setback in terms of human values. 833

30. There are certainly situations whose injustice cries to heaven. When whole populations destitute of necessities live in a state of dependence barring them from all initiative and responsibility, and all opportunity to advance culturally and share in social and political life, recourse to violence, as a means to right these wrongs to human dignity, is a grave temptation. 834

31. We know, however, that a revolutionary uprising—save where there is manifest, long-standing tyranny which would do great damage to fundamental personal rights and dangerous harm to the common good of the country—produces new injustices, throws more elements out of balance and brings on new disasters. A real evil should not be fought against at the cost of greater misery. 835

32. We want to be clearly understood: the present situation must be faced with courage and the injustices linked with it must be fought against and overcome. Development demands bold transformations, innovations that go deep. Urgent reforms should be undertaken without delay. It is for each one to take his share in them with generosity, particularly those whose education, position and opportunities afford them wide scope for action. May they show an ex- 836

ample, and give of their own possessions as several of Our brothers in the episcopacy have done.[33] In so doing they will live up to men's expectations and be faithful to the Spirit of God, since it is "the ferment of the Gospel which has aroused and continues to arouse in man's heart the irresistible requirements of his dignity".[34]

837 33. Individual initiative alone and the mere free play of competition could never assure successful development. One must avoid the risk of increasing still more the wealth of the rich and the dominion of the strong, whilst leaving the poor in their misery and adding to the servitude of the oppressed. Hence programmes are necessary in order "to encourage, stimulate, coordinate, supplement and integrate"[35] the activity of individuals and of intermediary bodies. It pertains to the public authorities to choose, even to lay down the objectives to be pursued, the ends to be achieved, and the means for attaining these, and it is for them to stimulate all the forces engaged in this common activity. But let them take care to associate private initiative and intermediary bodies with this work. They will thus avoid the danger of complete collectivisation or of arbitrary planning, which, by denying liberty, would prevent the exercise of the fundamental rights of the human person.

838 34. This is true since every programme, made to increase production, has, in the last analysis, no other *raison d'être* than the service of man. Such programmes should reduce inequalities, fight discriminations, free man from various types of servitude and enable him to be the instrument of his moral progress and of his spiritual growth. To speak of development, is in effect to show as much concern for social progress as for economic growth. It is not sufficient to increase overall wealth for it be distributed equitably. It is not sufficient to promote technology to render the world a more human place in which to live. The mistakes of their predecessors should warn those on the road to development of the dangers to be avoided in this field. Tomorrow's technocracy can beget evils no less redoubtable than those due to the liberalism of yesterday. Economics and technology have no meaning except from man whom they should

serve. And man is only truly man in as far as, master of his own acts and judge of their worth, he is author of his own advancement, in keeping with the nature which was given to him by his Creator and whose possibilities and exigencies he himself freely assumes.

35. It can even be affirmed that economic growth depends in the very first place upon social progress: thus basic education is the primary object of any plan of development. Indeed hunger for education is no less debasing than hunger for food: an illiterate is a person with an undernourished mind. To be able to read and write, to acquire a professional formation, means to recover confidence in oneself and to discover that one can progress along with the others. As We said in Our message to the UNESCO Congress held in 1965 at Teheran, for man literacy is "a fundamental factor of social integration, as well as of personal enrichment, and for society it is a privileged instrument of economic progress and of development".[36] We also rejoice at the good work accomplished in this field by private initiative, by the public authorities and by international organisations: these are the primary agents of development, because they render man capable of acting for himself. 839

36. But man finds his true identity only in his social milieu, where the family plays a fundamental role. The family's influence may have been excessive, at some periods of history and in some places, when it was exercised to the detriment of the fundamental rights of the individual. The long-standing social frameworks, often too rigid and badly organised, existing in developing countries, are, nevertheless, still necessary for a time, yet progressively relaxing their excessive hold on the population. But the natural family, monogamous and stable, such as the divine plan conceived it[37] and as Christianity sanctified it, must remain the place where "the various generations come together and help one another to grow wiser and to harmonise personal rights with the other requirements of social life".[38] 840

37. It is true that too frequently an accelerated demographic increase adds its own difficulties to the problems of development: the size of the population increases more 841

rapidly than available resources, and things are found to have reached apparently an impasse. From that moment the temptation is great to check the demographic increase by means of radical measures. It is certain that public authorities can intervene, within the limit of their competence, by favouring the availability of appropriate information and by adopting suitable measures, provided that these be in conformity with the moral law and that they respect the rightful freedom of married couples. Where the inalienable right to marriage and procreation is lacking, human dignity has ceased to exist. Finally, it is for the parents to decide, with full knowledge of the matter, on the number of their children, taking into account their responsibilities towards God, themselves, the children they have already brought into the world, and the community to which they belong. In all this they must follow the demands of their own conscience enlightened by God's law authentically interpreted, and sustained by confidence in Him.[39]

842 38. In the task of development, man, who finds his life's primary environment in the family, is often aided by professional organisations. If it is their objective to promote the interests of their members, their responsibility is also great with regard to the educative task which at the same time they can and ought to accomplish. By means of the information they provide and the formation they propose, they can do much to give to all a sense of the common good and of the consequent obligations that fall upon each person.

843 39. All social action involves a doctrine. The Christian cannot admit that which is based upon a materialistic and atheistic philosophy, which respects neither the religious orientation of life to its final end, nor human freedom and dignity. But, provided that these values are safeguarded, a pluralism of professional organisations and trade unions is admissible, and from certain points of view useful, if thereby liberty is protected and emulation stimulated. And We most willingly pay homage to all those who labour in them to give unselfish service to their brothers.

844 40. In addition to professional organisations, there are also institutions which are at work. Their role is no less

important for the success of development. "The future of the world stands in peril", the Council gravely affirms, "unless wiser men are forthcoming". And it adds: "many nations, poorer in economic goods, are quite rich in wisdom and able to offer noteworthy advantages to others".[40] Rich or poor, each country possesses a civilisation handed down by life in this world, and higher manifestations of the life of the spirit, manifestations of an artistic, intellectual and religious character. When the latter possess true human values, it would be grave error to sacrifice them to the former. A people that would act in this way would thereby lose the best of its patrimony; in order to live, it would be sacrificing its reasons for living. Christ's teaching also applied to people: "What does it profit a man to gain the whole world if he suffers the loss of his soul".[41]

41. Less well-off peoples can never be sufficiently on their guard against this temptation which comes to them from wealthy nations. For these nations all too often set an example of success in a highly technical and culturally developed civilization; they also provide the model for a way of acting that is principally aimed at the conquest of material prosperity. Not that material prosperity of itself precludes the activity of the human spirit. On the contrary, the human spirit, "increasingly free of its bondage to creatures, can be more easily drawn to the worship and contemplation of the Creator".[42] However, "modern civilization itself often complicates the approach to God, not for any essential reason, but because it is excessively engrossed in earthly affairs".[43] Developing nations must know how to discriminate among those things that are held out to them; they must be able to assess critically, and eliminate those deceptive goods which would only bring about a lowering of the human ideal, and to accept those values that are sound and beneficial, in order to develop them alongside their own, in accordance with their own genius. 845

42. What must be aimed at is complete humanism.[44] And what is that if not the fully-rounded development of the whole man and of all men? A humanism closed in on itself, and not open to the values of the spirit and to God 846

Who is their source, could achieve apparent success. True, man can organise the world apart from God, but "without God man can organise it in the end only to man's detriment. An isolated humanism is an inhuman humanism".[45] There is no true humanism but that which is open to the Absolute and is conscious of a vocation which gives human life its true meaning. Far from being the ultimate measure of all things, man can only realise himself by reaching beyond himself. As Pascal has said so well: "Man infinitely surpasses man".[46]

847 43. There can be no progress towards the complete development of man without the simultaneous development of all humanity in the spirit of solidarity. As We said at Bombay: "Man must meet man, nation meet nation, as brothers and sisters, as children of God. In this mutual understanding and friendship, in this sacred communion, we must also begin to work together to build the common future of the human race".[47] We also suggested a search for concrete and practical ways of organisation and cooperation, so that all available resources be pooled and thus a true communion among all nations be achieved.

848 44. This duty is the concern especially of better-off nations. Their obligations stem from a brotherhood that is at once human and supernatural, and take on a three-fold aspect: the duty of human solidarity—the aid that the rich nations must give to developing countries; the duty of social justice—the rectification of inequitable trade relations between powerful nations and weak nations; the duty of universal charity—the effort to bring about a world that is more human towards all men, where all will be able to give and receive, without one group making progress at the expense of the other. The question is urgent, for on it depends the future of the civilisation of the world.

849 45. "If a brother or a sister be naked", says Saint James; "if they lack their daily nourishment, and one of you says to them: 'Go in peace, be warmed and be filled', without giving them what is necessary for the body, what good does it do?".[48] Today no one can be ignorant any longer of the fact that in whole continents countless men and women are

ravished by hunger, countless numbers of children are undernourished, so that many of them die in infancy, while the physical growth and mental development of many others are retarded and as a result whole regions are condemned to the most depressing despondency.

46. Anguished appeals have already been sounded in the past: that of John XXIII was warmly received. We Ourselves repeated it in Our Christmas Message of 1963,[50] and again in 1966 on behalf of India.[51] The campaign against hunger being carried on by the Food and Agriculture Organisation (FAO) and encouraged by the Holy See, has been generously supported. Our *Caritas Internationalis* is at work everywhere, and many Catholics, at the urging of Our Brothers in the episcopacy, contribute generously of their means and spend themselves without counting the cost in assisting those who are in want, continually widening the circle of those they look upon as neighbours. 850

47. But neither all this nor the private and public funds that have been invested, nor the gifts and loans that have been made, can suffice. It is not just a matter of eliminating hunger, nor even of reducing poverty. The struggle against destitution, though urgent and necessary, is not enough. It is a question, rather, of building a world where every man, no matter what his race, religion or nationality, can live a fully human life, freed from servitude imposed on him by other men or by natural forces over which he has not sufficient control; a world where freedom is not an empty word and where the poor man Lazarus can sit down at the same table with the rich man.[52] This demands great generosity, much sacrifice and unceasing effort on the part of the rich man. Let each one examine his conscience, a conscience that conveys a new message for our times. Is he prepared to support out of his own pocket works and undertakings organised in favour of the most destitute? Is he ready to pay higher taxes so that the public authorities can intensify their efforts in favour of development? Is he ready to pay a higher price for imported goods so that the producer may be more justly rewarded? Or to leave his country, if necessary and if he 851

is young, in order to assist in this development of the young nations?

852 48. The same duty of solidarity that rests on individuals exists also for nations: "Advanced nations have a very heavy obligation to help the developing peoples".[53] It is necessary to put this teaching of the Council into effect. Although it is normal that a nation should be the first to benefit from the gifts that Providence has bestowed on it as the fruit of the labours of its people, still no country can claim on that account to keep its wealth for itself alone. Every nation must produce more and better quality goods to give to all its inhabitants a truly human standard of living, and also to contribute to the common development of the human race. Given the increasing needs of the under-developed countries, it should be considered quite normal for an advanced country to devote a part of its production to meet their needs, and to train teachers, engineers, technicians and scholars prepared to put their knowledge and their skill at the disposal of less fortunate peoples.

853 49. We must repeat once more that the superfluous wealth of rich countries should be placed at the service of poor nations. The rule which up to now held good for the benefit of those nearest to us, must today be applied to all the needy of this world. Besides, the rich will be the first to benefit as a result. Otherwise their continued greed will certainly call down upon them the judgement of God and the wrath of the poor, with consequences no one can foretell. If today's flourishing civilisations remain selfishly wrapped up in themselves, they could easily place their highest values in jeopardy, sacrificing their will to be great to the desire to possess more. To them, we could apply also the parable of the rich man whose fields yielded an abundant harvest and who did not know where to store his harvest: "God said to him: 'Fool, this night do they demand your soul of you' ".[54]

854 50. In order to be fully effective, these efforts ought not remain scattered or isolated, much less be in competition for reasons of power or prestige: the present situation calls for concerted planning. A planned programme is of course better and more effective than occasional aid left to individual

goodwill. It presupposes, as We said above, careful study, the selection of ends and the choice of means, as well as a re-organisation of efforts to meet the needs of the present and the demands of the foreseeable future. More important, a concerted plan has advantages that go beyond the field of economic growth and social progress; for in addition it gives significance and value to the work undertaken. While shaping the world it sets a higher value on man.

51. But it is necessary to go still further. At Bombay We called for the establishment of a great *World Fund,* to be made up of part of the money spent on arms, to relieve the most destitute of this world.[55] What is true of the immediate struggle against want, holds good also when there is a question of development. Only world-wide collaboration, of which a common fund would be both means and symbol, will succeed in overcoming vain rivalries and in establishing a fruitful and peaceful exchange between peoples. 855

52. There is certainly no need to do away with bilateral and multilateral agreements: they allow ties of dependence and feelings of bitterness, left over from the era of colonialism, to yield place to the happier relationship of friendship, based on a footing of constitutional and political equality. However, if they were to be fitted into the framework of world-wide collaboration, they would be beyond all suspicion, and as a result there would be less distrust on the part of the receiving nations. These would have less cause for fearing that, under the cloak of financial aid or technical assistance, there lurk certain manifestations of what has come to be called neo-colonialism, in the form of political pressures and economic suzerainty aimed at maintaining or acquiring complete dominance. 856

53. Besides, who does not see that such a fund would make it easier to take measures to prevent certain wasteful expenditures, the result of fear or pride? When so many people are hungry, when so many families suffer from destitution, when so many remain steeped in ignorance, when so many schools, hospitals and homes worthy of the name remain to be built, all public or private squandering of wealth, all expenditure prompted by motives of national or personal 857

ostentation, every exhausting armaments race, becomes an intolerable scandal. We are conscious of Our duty to denounce it. Would that those in authority listened to Our words before it is too late!

858 54. This means that it is absolutely necessary to create among all peoples that dialogue for whose establishment We expressed Our hope in Our first Encyclical *Ecclesiam Suam.*[56] This dialogue between those who contribute wealth and those who benefit from it, will provide the possibility of making an assessment of the contribution necessary, not only drawn up in terms of the generosity and the available wealth of the donor nation, but also conditioned by the real needs of the receiving countries and the use to which the financial assistance can be put. Developing countries will thus no longer risk being overwhelmed by debts whose repayment swallows up the greater part of their gains. Rates of interest and time for repayment of the loan could be so arranged as not to be too great a burden on either party, taking into account free gifts, interest-free or low-interest loans, and the time needed for liquidating the debts. Guarantees could be given to those who provide the capital that it will be put to use according to an agreed plan and with a reasonable measure of efficiency, since there is no question of encouraging parasites or the indolent. And the receiving countries could demand that there be no interference in their political life or subversion of their social structures. As sovereign states they have the right to conduct their own affairs, to decide on their policies and to move freely towards the kind of society they choose. What must be brought about, therefore, is a system of cooperation freely undertaken, an effective and mutual sharing, carried out with equal dignity on either side, for the construction of a more human world.

859 55. The task might seem impossible in those regions where the cares of day-to-day survival fill the entire existence of families incapable of planning the kind of work which would open the way to a future that is less desperate. These, however, are the men and women who must be helped, who must be persuaded to work for their own betterment and endeav-

our to acquire gradually the means to that end. This common task will not succeed without concerted, constant and courageous efforts. But let everyone be convinced of this: the very life of poor nations, civil peace in developing countries, and world peace itself are at stake.

56. The efforts which are being made to assist developing nations on a financial and technical basis, though considerable, would be illusory if their benefits were to be partially nullified as a consequence of the trade relations existing between rich and poor countries. The confidence of these latter would be severely shaken if they had the impression that what was being given them with one hand was being taken away with the other. 860

57. Of course, highly industrialised nations export for the most part manufactured goods, while countries with less developed economies have only food, fibres and other raw materials to sell. As a result of technical progress the value of manufactured goods is rapidly increasing and they can always find an adequate market. On the other hand, raw materials produced by under-developed countries are subject to wide and sudden fluctuations in price, a state of affairs far removed from the progressively increasing, value of industrial products. As a result, nations whose industrialisation is limited are faced with serious difficulties when they have to rely on their exports to balance their economy and to carry out their plans for development. The poor nations remain ever poor while the rich ones become still richer. 861

58. In other words, the rule of free trade, taken by itself, is no longer able to govern international relations. Its advantages are certainly evident when the parties involved are not affected by any excessive inequalities of economic power: it is an incentive to progress and a reward for effort. That is why industrially developed countries see in it a law of justice. But the situation is no longer the same when economic conditions differ too widely from country to county: prices which are "freely" set in the market can produce unfair results. One must recognise that it is the fundamental principle of liberalism, as the rule for commercial exchange, which is questioned here. 862

863 59. The teaching of Leo XIII in *Reum Novarum* is always valid: if the positions of the contracting parties are too unequal, the consent of the parties does not suffice to guarantee the justice of their contract, and the rule of free agreement remains subservient to the demands of the natural law.[57] What was true of the just wage for the individual is also true of international contracts: an economy of exchange can no longer be based solely on the law of free competition, a law which, in its turn, too often creates an economic dictatorship. Freedom of trade is fair only if it is subject to the demands of social justice.

864 60. Moreover, this has been understood by the developed nations themselves, which are striving, by means of appropriate measures, to re-establish within their own economies a balance, which competition, if left to itself, tends to compromise. Thus it happens that these nations often support their agriculture at the price of sacrifices imposed on economically more favoured sectors. Similarly, to maintain the commercial relations which are developing among themselves, especially within a common market, the financial, fiscal, and social policy of these nations tries to restore comparable opportunities to competing industries which are not equally prospering.

865 61. In this area one cannot employ two systems of weights and measures. What holds for a national economy or among developed countries is valid also in commercial relations between rich nations and poor nations. Without abolishing the competitive market, it should be kept within the limits which make it just and moral, and therefore human. In trade between developed and under-developed economies, conditions are too disparate and the degrees of genuine freedom available too unequal. In order that international trade be human and moral, social justice requires that it restore to the participants a certain equality of opportunity. This equality is a long-term objective, but to reach it, we must begin now to create true equality in discussions and negotiations. Here again international agreements on a rather wide scale would be helpful: they would establish general norms for regulating certain prices, for

guaranteeing certain types of production, for supporting certain new industries. Who is there who does not see that such a common effort aimed at increased justice in business relations between peoples would bestow on developing nations positive assistance, the effects of which would be not only immediate but lasting?

62. Among still other obstacles which are opposed to the formation of a world which is more just and which is better organised toward a universal solidarity, We wish to speak of nationalism and racism. It is only natural that communities which have recently reached their political independence should be jealous of a national unity which is still fragile, and that they should strive to protect it. Likewise, it is to be expected that nations endowed with an ancient culture should be proud of the patrimony which their history has bequeathed to them. But these legitimate feelings should be ennobled by that universal charity which embraces the entire human family. Nationalism isolates people from their true good. It would be especially harmful where the weakness of national economics demands rather the pooling of efforts, of knowledge and of funds, in order to implement programmes of development and to increase commercial and cultural exchange. 866

63. Racism is not the exclusive lot of young nations, where sometimes it hides beneath the rivalries of clans and political parties, with heavy losses for justice and at the risk of civil war. During the colonial period it often flared up between the colonists and the indigenous population, and stood in the wake of genuine injustices. It is still an obstacle to collaboration among disadvantaged nations and a cause of division and hatred within countries whenever individuals and families see the inviolable rights of the human person held in scorn, as they themselves are unjustly subjected to a regime of discrimination because of their race or their colour. 867

64. We are deeply distressed by such a situation which is laden with threats for the future. We are, nonetheless, hopeful: a more deeply felt need for collaboration, a heightened sense of unity will finally triumph over misunderstandings and selfishness. We hope that the countries whose develop- 868

ment is less advanced will be able to take advantage of their proximity in order to organise among themselves, on a broadened territorial basis, areas for concerted development: to draw up programmes in common, to coordinate investments, to distribute the means of production, and to organise trade. We hope also that multilateral and international bodies, by means of the reorganisation which seem to enclose them and to discover for themselves, in full fidelity to their own proper genius, the means for their social and human progress.

869 65. Such is the goal we must attain. World unity, ever more effective, should allow all peoples to become the artisans of their destiny. The past has too often been characterized by relationships of violence between nations; may the day dawn when international relations will be marked with the stamp of mutual respect and friendship, of interdependence in collaboration, the betterment of all seen as the responsibility of each individual. The younger or weaker nations ask to assume their active part in the construction of a better world, one which shows deeper respect for the rights and the vocation of the individual. This is a legitimate appeal; everyone should hear it and respond to it.

870 66. The world is sick. Its illness consists less in the unproductive monopolisation of resources by a small number of men than in the lack of brotherhood among individuals and peoples.

871 67. We cannot insist too much on the duty of welcoming others—a duty springing from human solidarity and Christian charity—which is incumbent both on the families and the cultural organisations of the host countries. Centres of welcome and hostels must be multiplied, especially for youth. This must be done first to protect them from loneliness, the feeling of abandonment and distress, which undermine all moral resistance. This is also necessary to protect them from the unhealthy situation in which they find themselves, forced as they are to compare the extreme poverty of their homeland with the luxury and waste which often surround them. It should be done also to protect them against the subversive teachings and temptations to aggression which assail them,

as they recall so much "unmerited misery".[58] Finally, and above all, this hospitality should aim to provide them, in the warm atmosphere of a brotherly welcome, with the example of wholesome living, an esteem for genuine and effective Christian charity, an esteem for spiritual values.

68. It is painful to think of the numerous young people who come to more advanced countries to receive the science, the competence, and the culture which will make them more qualified to serve their homeland, and who certainly acquire there a formation of high quality, but who too often lose the esteem for the spiritual values which often were to be found, as a precious patrimony, in the civilisations where they had grown up. 872

69. The same welcome is due to emigrant workers, who live in conditions which are often inhuman, and who economise on what they earn in order to send a little relief to their family living in misery in their native land. 873

70. Our second recommendation is for those whose business calls them to countries recently opened to industrialisation: industrialists, merchants, leaders or representatives of larger enterprises. It happens that they are not lacking in social sensitivity in their own country; why then do they return to the inhuman principles of individualism when they operate in less developed countries? Their advantaged situation should on the contrary move them to become the initiators of social progress and of human advancement in the area where their business calls them. Their very sense of organisation should suggest to them the means for making intelligent use of the labour of the indigenous population, of forming qualified workers, of training engineers and staffs, of giving scope to their initiative, of introducing them progressively into higher positions, thus preparing them to share, in the near future, in the responsibilities of management. At least let justice always rule the relations between superiors and their subordinates. Let standard contracts with reciprocal obligations govern these relationships. Finally, let no one, whatever his status, be subjected unjustly to the arbitrariness of others. 874

875 71. We are happy that experts are being sent in larger and larger numbers on development missions by institutions, whether international or bilateral, or by private organisations: "they ought not conduct themselves in a lordly fashion, but as helpers and co-workers".[59] A people quickly perceives whether those who come to help them do so with or without affection, whether they come merely to apply their techniques or to recognise in man his full value.

Their message is in danger of being rejected if it is not presented in the context of brotherly love.

876 72. Hence, necessary technical competence must be accompanied by authentic signs of disinterested love. Freed of all nationalistic pride and of every appearance of racism, experts should learn how to work in close collaboration with all. They realise that their competence does not confer on them a superiority in every field. The civilisation which formed them contains, without doubt, elements of universal humanism, but it is not the only civilisation nor does it enjoy a monopoly of valuable elements. Moreover it cannot be imported without undergoing adaptations. The men on these missions will be intent on discovering, along with its history, the component elements of the cultural riches of the country receiving them. Mutual understanding will be established which will enrich both cultures.

877 73. Between civilisations, as between persons, sincere dialogue indeed creates brotherhood. The work of development will draw nations together in the attainment of goals pursued with a common effort if all, from governments and their representatives to the last expert, are inspired by brotherly love and moved by the sincere desire to build a civilisation founded on world solidarity. A dialogue based on man, and not on commodities or technical skills, will then begin. It will be fruitful if it brings to the peoples who benefit from it the means of self-betterment an spiritual growth, if the technicians act as educators, and if the instruction imparted is characterised by so loftly a spiritual and moral tone that it guarantees not merely economic, but human development. When aid programmes have terminated, the relation-

ships thus established will endure. Who does not see of what importance they will be for the peace of the world?

74. Many young people have already responded with warmth and enthusiasm to the appeal of Pius XII for lay missionaries.[60] Many also are those who have spontaneously put themselves at the disposition of official or private organisations which are collaborating with developing nations. We are pleased to learn that in certain nations "military service" can be partially accomplished by doing "social service", a "service pure and simple". We bless these undertakings and the good will which inspires them. May all those who wish to belong to Christ hear His appeal: "I was hungry and you gave me to eat, thirsty and you gave me to drink, a stranger and you took me in, naked and you clothed me, sick and you visited me, a prisoner and you came to see me".[61] No one can remain indifferent to the lot of his brothers who are still buried in wretchedness, and victims of insecurity, slaves of ignorance. Like the heart of Christ, the heart of the Christian must sympathise with this misery: "I have pity on this multitude".[62] 878

75. The prayer of all ought to rise with fervour to the Almighty. Having become aware of such great misfortunes, the human race will apply itself with intelligence and steadfastness to abolish them. This prayer should be matched by the resolute commitment of each individual—according to the measure of his strength and possibilities—to the struggle against underdevelopment. May individuals, social groups, and nations join hands in brotherly fashion, the strong aiding the weak to grow, exerting all their competence, enthusiasm and disinterested love. More than any other, the individual who is animated by true charity labours skillfully to discover the causes of misery, to find the means to combat it, to overcome it resolutely. A creator of peace, he "will follow his path, lighting the lamps of joy and playing their brilliance and loveliness on the hearts of men across the surface of the globe, leading them to recognise, across all frontiers, the faces of their brothers, the faces of their friends".[63] 879

880 76. Excessive economic, social and cultural inequalities among peoples arouse tensions and conflicts, and are a danger to peace. As We said to the Fathers of the Council when We returned from Our journey of peace to the United Nations: "The condition of the peoples in process of development ought to be the object of our consideration; or better: our charity for the poor in the world—and there are multitudes of them—must become more considerate, more active, more generous".[64] To wage war on misery and to struggle against injustice is to promote, along with improved conditions, the human and spiritual progress of all men, and therefore the common good of humanity. Peace cannot be limited to a mere absence of war, the result of an ever precarious balance of forces. No, peace is something that is built up day after day, in the pursuit of an order intended by God, which implies a more perfect form of justice among men.[65]

881 77. The peoples themselves have the prime responsibility to work for their own development. But they will not bring this about in isolation. Regional agreements among weak nations for mutual support, understandings of wider scope entered into for their help, more far-reaching agreements to establish programmes for closer cooperation among groups of nations—these are the milestones on the road to development that leads to peace.

882 78. This international collaboration on a world-wide scale requires institutions that will prepare, coordinate and direct it, until finally there is established an order of justice which is universally recognised. With all Our heart, We encourage these organisations which have undertaken this collaboration for the development of the peoples of the world, and Our wish is that they grow in prestige and authority. "Your vocation", as We said to the representatives of the United Nations in New York, "is to bring not some people but all peoples to treat each other as brothers. . .Who does not see the necessity of thus establishing progressively a world authority, capable of acting effectively in the jurdical and political sectors?".[66]

883 79. Some would consider such hopes utopian. It may be that these persons are not realistic enough, and that they have not perceived the dynamism of a world which desires

to live more fraternally—a world which, in spite of its ignorance, its mistakes and even its sins, its relapses into barbarism and its wanderings far from the road of salvation, is, even unawares, taking slow but sure steps towards its Creator. This road towards a greater humanity requires effort and sacrifice; but suffering itself, accepted for the love of our brethren, favours the progress of the entire human family. Christians know that union with the sacrifice of our Saviour contributes to the building up of the Body of Christ in its plentitude: the assembled people of God.[67]

80. We are all united in this progress toward God. We have desired to remind all men how crucial is the present moment, how urgent the work to be done. The hour for action has now sounded. At stake are the survival of so many innoncent children and, for so many families overcome by misery, the access to conditions fit for human beings; at stake are the peace of the world and the future of civilisation. It is time for all men and all peoples so face up to their responsibilities. 884

81. First, We appeal to all Our sons. In countries undergoing development no less than in others, the laymen should take up as their own proper task the renewal of the temporal order. If the role of the Hierarchy is to teach and to interpret authentically the norms of morality to be followed in this matter, it belongs to the laymen, without waiting passively for orders and directives, to take the initiative freely and to infuse a Christian spirit into the mentality, customs, laws and structures of the community in which they live.[68] Changes are necessary, basic reforms are indispensable: the laymen should strive resolutely to permeate them with the spirit of the Gospel. We ask Our Catholic sons who belong to the more favoured nations, to bring their talents and give their active participation to organisations, be they of an official or private nature, civil or religious, which are working to overcome the difficulties of the developing nations. They will certainly desire to be in the first ranks of those who collaborate to establish as fact and reality an international morality based on justice and equity. 885

886 82. We are sure that all Christians, our brethren, will wish to expand their common cooperative effort in order to help mankind vanquish selfishness, pride and rivalries, to overcome ambitions and injustices, to open up to all the road to a more human life, where each man will be loved and helped as his brother, as his neighbour. And, still deeply impressed by the memory of Our unforgettable encounter in Bombay with our non-Christian brethren, We invite them anew to work with all their heart and their intelligence towards this goal, that all the children of men may lead a life worthy of the children of God.

887 83. Finally, We turn to all men of good will who believe that the way to peace lies in the area of development. Delegates to international organisations, government officials, gentlemen of the press, educators: all of you, each in your own way, are the builders of a new world. We entreat Almighty God to enlighten your minds and strengthen your determination to alert public opinion and to involve the peoples of the world. Educators, it is your task to awaken in persons, from their earliest years, a love for the peoples who live in misery. Gentlemen of the press, it is up to you to place before our eyes the story of the efforts exerted to promote mutual assistance among peoples, as well as the spectacle of the miseries which men tend to forget in order to quiet their consciences. Thus at least the wealthy will know that the poor stand outside their doors waiting to receive some left-overs from their banquets.

888 84. Government officials, it is your concern to mobilise your peoples to form a more effective world solidarity, and above all to make them accept the necessary taxes on their luxuries and their wasteful expenditures, in order to bring about development and to save the peace. Delegates to international organisations, it depends on you to see that the dangerous and futile rivalry of powers should give place to collaboration which is friendly, peaceful and free of vested interests, in order to achieve a responsible development of mankind, in which all men will have an opportunity to find their fulfilment.

85. If it is true that the world is in trouble because of the lack of thinking, then We call upon men of reflection and of learning, Catholics, Christians, those who hold God in honour, who thirst for an absolute, for justice and for truth: We call upon all men of good will. Following Christ, We make bold to ask you earnestly: "seek and you shall find",[69] open the paths which lead to mutual assistance among peoples, to a deepening of human knowledge, to an enlargement of heart, to a more brotherly way of living within a truly universal human society. 889

86. All of you who have heard the appeal of suffering peoples, all of you who are working to answer their cries, you are the apostles of a development which is good and genuine, which is not wealth that is self-centered and sought for its own sake, but rather an economy which is put at the service of man, the bread which is daily distributed to all, as a source of brotherhood and a sign of Providence. 890

87. With a full heart We bless you, and We appeal to all men of good will to join you in a spirit of brotherhood. For, if the new name for peace is development, who would not wish to labour for it with all his powers? Yes, We ask you, all of you, to heed Our cry of anguish, in the name of the Lord. 891

From the Vatican, on the Feast of Easter, the twenty-sixth day of March in the year one thousand nine hundred and sixty-seven.

HUMANAE VITAE
Encyclical Letter Of Pope Paul VI
On the Regulation of Birth
July 25, 1968

The most serious duty of transmitting human life, for which married persons are the free and responsible collaborators of God the Creator, has always been a source of great joys to them, even if sometimes accompanied by not a few difficulties and by distress.

893 At all times the fulfillment of this duty has posed grave problems to the conscience of married persons, but, with the recent evolution of society, changes have taken place that give rise to new questions which the Church could not ignore, having to do with a matter which so closely touches upon the life and happiness of men.

894 2. The changes which have taken place are in fact noteworthy and of varied kinds. In the first place, there is the rapid demographic development. Fear is shown by many that world population is growing more rapidly than the available resources, with growing distress to many families and developing countries, so that the temptation for authorities to counter this danger with radical measures is great. Moreover, working and lodging conditions, as well as increased exigencies both in the economic field and in that of education, often make the proper education of a larger number of children difficult today. A change is also seen both in the manner of considering the person of woman and her place in society, and in the value to be attributed to conjugal love in marriage, and also in the appreciation

to be made of the meaning of conjugal acts in relation to that love.

Finally and above all, man has made stupendous progress in the domination and rational organization of the forces of nature, such that he tends to extend this domination to his own total being: to the body, to psychical life, to social life and even to the laws which regulate the transmission of life. 895

3. This new state of things gives rise to new questions. Granted the conditions of life today, and granted the meaning which conjugal relations have with respect to the harmony between husband and wife and to their mutual fidelity, would not a revision of the ethical norms, in force up to now, seem to be advisable, especially when it is considered that they cannot be observed without sacrifices, sometimes heroic sacrifices? 896

And again: by extending to this field the application of the so-called "principle of totality," could it not be admitted that the intention of a less abundant but more rationalized fecundity might transform a materially sterilizing intervention into a licit and wise control of birth? Could it not be admitted, that is, that the finality of procreation pertains to the ensemble of conjugal life, rather than to its single acts? It is also asked whether, in view of the increased sense of responsibility of modern man, the moment has not come for him to entrust to his reason and his will, rather than to the biological rhythms of his organism, the task of regulating birth. 897

4. Such questions required from the teaching authority of the Church a new and deeper reflection upon the principles of the moral teaching on marriage: a teaching founded on the natural law, illuminated and enriched by divine revelation. 898

No believer will wish to deny that the teaching authority of the Church is competent to interpret even the natural moral law. It is, in fact, indisputable, as our predecessors have many times declared,[1] that Jesus Christ, when communicating to Peter and to the Apostles, His divine authority and sending them to teach all nations His command- 899 ments,[2] constituted them as guardians and authentic interpreters of all the moral law, not only, that is, of the law of the Gospel, but also of the natural law, which is also an expression of the will of God, the faithful fulfillment of which is equally necessary for salvation.[3]

900 Conformably to this mission of hers, the Church has always provided—and even more amply in recent times—a coherent teaching concerning both the nature of marriage and the correct use of conjugal rights and the duties of husband and wife.[4]

901 5. The consciousness of that same mission induced us to confirm and enlarge the study commission which our predecessor Pope John XXIII of happy memory had instituted in March, 1963. That commission which included, besides several experts in the various pertinent disciplines also married couples, had as its scope the gathering of opinions on the new questions regarding conjugal life, and in particular on the regulation of births, and of furnishing opportune elements of information so that the magisterium could give an adequate reply to the expectation not only of the faithful, but also of world opinion.[5]

902 The work of these experts, as well as the successive judgments and counsels spontaneously forwarded by or expressly requested from a good number of our brothers in the episcopate, have permitted us to measure more exactly all the aspects of this complex matter. Hence with all our heart we express to each of them our lively gratitude.

903 6. The conclusions at which the commission arrived could not, nevertheless, be considered by us as definitive, nor dispense us from a personal examination of this serious question; and this also because, within the commission itself, no full concordance of judgments concerning the moral norms to be proposed had been reached, and above all because certain criteria of solutions had emerged which departed from moral teaching on marriage proposed with constant firmness by the teaching authority of the Church.

904 Therefore, having attentively sifted the documentation laid before us, after mature reflection and assiduous prayers,

we now intend, by virture of the mandate entrusted to us by Christ, to give only reply to these grave questions.

7. The problem of birth, like every other problem regarding human life, is to be considered, beyond partial perspectives—whether of the biological or psychological, demographic or sociological orders—in the light of an integral vision of man and of his vocation, not only his natural and earthly, but also his supernatural and eternal vocation. And since, in the attempt to justify artificial methods of birth control, many have appealed to the demands both of conjugal love and of "responsible parenthood," it is good to state very precisely the true concept of these two great realities of married life, referring principally to what was recently set forth in this regard, and in a highly authoritative form, by the Second Vatican Council in its pastoral constitution *Gaudium et Spes.* 905

8. Conjugal love reveals its true nature and nobility when it is considered in its supreme origin, God, who is love,[6] "the Father, from whom every family in heaven and on earth is named."[7] 906

Marriage is not, then the effect of chance or the product of evolution of unconscious natural forces; it is the wise institution of the Creator to realize in mankind His design of love. By means of the reciprocal personal gift of self, proper and exclusive to them, husband and wife tend towards the communion of their beings in view of mutual personal perfection, to collaborate with God in the generation and education of new lives. 907

For baptized persons, moreover, marriage invests the dignity of a sacramental sign of grace, inasmuch as it represents the union of Christ and of the Church. 908

9. Under this light, there clearly appear the characteristic marks and demands of conjugal love, and it is of supreme importance to have an exact idea of these. 909

This love is first of all fully *human,* that is to say, of the senses and of the spirit at the same time. It is not, then, a simple transport of instinct and sentiment, but also, and principally, an act of the free will, intended to endure and 910 to grow by means of the joys and sorrows of daily life, in such a way that husband and wife become one only heart and one only soul, and together attain their human perfection.

911 Then, this love is *total,* that is to say, it is a very special form of personal friendship, in which husband and wife generously share everything, without undue reservations or selfish calculations. Whoever truly loves his marriage partner loves not only for what he receives, but for the partner's self, rejoicing that he can enrich his partner with the gift of himself.

912 Again, this love is *faithful* and *exclusive* until death. Thus in fact do bride and groom conceive it to be on the day when they freely and in full awareness assume the duty of the marriage bond. A fidelity, this, which can sometimes be difficult, but is always possible, always noble and meritorious, as no one can deny. The example of so many married persons down through the centuries shows, not only that fidelity is according to the nature of marriage, but also that it is a source of profound and lasting happiness.

913 And finally this love is *fecund* for it is not exhausted by the communion between husband and wife, but is destined to continue, raising up new lives. "Marriage and conjugal love are by their nature ordained toward the begetting and educating of children. Children are really the supreme gift of marriage and contribute very substantially to the welfare of their parents."[8]

914 10. Hence conjugal love requires in husband and wife an awareness of their mission of "responsible parenthood," which today is rightly much insisted upon, and which also must be exactly understood. Consequently it is to be considered under different aspects which are legitimate and connected with one another.

915 In relation to the biological processes, responsible parenthood means the knowledge and respect of their functions; human intellect discovers in the power of giving life biological laws which are part of the human person.[9]

916 In relation to the tendencies of instinct or passion, respon-

sible parenthood means that necessary dominion which reason and will must exercise over them.

In relation to physical, economic, psychological and social conditions, responsible parenthood is exercised, either by the deliberate and generous decision to raise a numerous family, or by the decision, made for grave motives and with due respect for the moral law, to avoid for the time being, or even for an indeterminate period, a new birth. 917

Responsible parenthood also and above all implies a more profound relationship to the objective moral order established by God, of which a right conscience is the faithful interpreter. The responsible exercise of parenthood implies, therefore, that husband and wife recognize fully their own duties towards God, towards themselves, towards the family and towards society, in a correct hierarchy of values. 918

In the task of transmitting life, therefore, they are not free to proceed completely at will, as if they could determine in a wholly autonomous way the honest path to follow; but they must conform their activity to the creative intention of God, expressed in the very nature of marriage and of its acts, and manifested by the constant teaching of the Church.[10] 919

11. These acts, by which husband and wife are united in chaste intimacy, and by means of which human life is transmitted, are, as the Council recalled, "noble and worthy,"[11] and they do not cease to be lawful if, for causes independent of the will of husband and wife, they are foreseen to be infecund, since they always remain ordained towards expressing and consolidating their union. In fact, as experience bears witness, not every conjugal act is followed by a new life. God has wisely disposed natural laws and rhythms of fecundity which, of themselves, cause a separation in the succession of births. Nonetheless the Church, calling men back to the observance of the norms of the natural law, as interpreted by their constant doctrine, teaches that each and every marriage act (*quilibet matrimonii usus*) must remain open to the transmission of life.[12] 920

12. That teaching, often set forth by the magisterium, is founded upon the inseparable connection, willed by God and 921

unable to be broken by man on his own initiative, between the two meanings of the conjugal act: the unitive meaning and the procreative meaning. Indeed, by its intimate structure, the conjugal act, while most closely uniting husband and wife, capacitates them for the generation of new lives, according to laws inscribed in the very being of man and of woman. By safeguarding both these essential aspects, the unitive and the procreative, the conjugal act preserves in its fullness the sense of true mutual love and its ordination towards man's most high calling to parenthood. We believe that the men of our day are particularly capable of seizing the deeply reasonable and human character of this fundamental principle.

922 13. It is in fact justly observed that a conjugal act imposed upon one's partner without regard for his or her condition and lawful desires is not a true act of love, and therefore denies an exigency of right moral order in the relationships between husband and wife. Likewise, if they consider the matter, they must admit that an act of mutual love, which is detrimental to the faculty of propagating life, which God the Creator of all, has implanted in it according to special laws, is in contradiction to both the divine plan, according to whose norm matrimony has been instituted, and the will of the Author of human life. To use this divine gift destroying, even if only partially, its meaning and its purpose is to contradict the nature both of man and of woman and of their most intimate relationship, and therefore it is to contradict also the plan of God and His will. On the other hand, to make use of the gift of conjugal love while respecting the laws of the generative process means to acknowledge oneself not to be the arbiter of the sources of human life, but rather the minister of the design established by the Creator. In fact, just as man does not have unlimited dominion over his body in general, so also, with particular reason, he has no such dominion over his generative faculties as such, because of their intrinsic ordination towards raising up life, of which God is the principle. "Human life is sacred," Pope John XXIII recalled; "from its very inception it reveals the creating hand of God."[13]

14. In conformity with these landmarks in the human and Christian vision of marriage, we must once again declare that the direct interruption of the generative process already begun, and, above all, directly willed and procured abortion, even if for therapeutic reasons, are to be absolutely excluded as licit means of regulating birth.[14] 923

Equally to be excluded, as the teaching authority of the Church has frequently declared, is direct sterilization, whether perpetual or temporary, whether of the man or of the woman.[15] Similarly excluded is every action which, either in anticipation of the conjugal act, or in its accomplishment, or in the development of its natural consequences, proposes, whether as an end or as a means, to render procreation impossible.[16] 924

To justify conjugal acts made intentionally infecund, one cannot invoke as valid reasons the lesser evil, or the fact that such acts would constitute a whole together with the fecund acts already performed or to follow later, and hence would share in one and the same moral goodness. In truth, if it is sometimes licit to tolerate a lesser evil in order to avoid a greater evil or to promote a greater good,[17] it is not licit, even for the gravest reasons, to do evil so that good may follow therefrom;[18] that is, to make into the object of a positive act of the will something which is intrinsically disorder, and hence unworthy of the human person, even when the intention is to safeguard or promote individual, family or social well-being. Consequently it is an error to think that a conjugal act which is deliberately made infecund and so is intrinsically dishonest could be made honest and right by the ensemble of a fecund conjugal life. 925

15. The Church, on the contrary, does not at all consider illicit the use of those therapeutic means truly necessary to cure diseases of the organism, even if an impediment to procreation, which may be foreseen, should result therefrom, provided such impediment is not, for whatever motive, directly willed.[19] 926

16. To this teaching of the Church on conjugal morals, the objection is made today, as we observed earlier (no. 3), 927

that it is the prerogative of the human intellect to dominate the energies offered by irrational nature and to orientate them towards an end comformable to the good of man. Now, some may ask: in the present case, is it not reasonable in many circumstances to have recourse to artifical birth control if, thereby, we secure the harmony and peace of the family, and better conditions for the education of the children already born? To this question it is necessary to reply with clarity: the Church is the first to praise and recommend the intervention of intelligence in a function which so closely associates the rational creature with his Creator; but she affirms that this must be done with respect for the order established by God.

928 If, then, there are serious motives to space out births, which derive from the physical or psychological conditions of husband and wife, or from external conditions, the Church teaches that it is then licit to take into account the natural rhythms immanent in the generative functions, for the use of marriage in the infecund periods only, and in this way to regulate birth without offending the moral principles which have been recalled earlier.[20]

929 The Church is coherent with herself when she considers recourse to the infecund periods to be licit, while at the same time condemning, as being always illicit, the use of means directly contrary to fecundation, even if such use is inspired by reasons which may appear honest and serious. In reality, there are essential differences between the two cases; in the former, the married couple make legitimate use of a natural disposition; in the latter, they impede the development of natural processes. It is true that, in the positive will of avoiding children for plausible reasons, seeking the certainty that offspring will not arrive; but it is also true that only in the former case are they able to renounce the use of marriage in the fecund periods when, for use of it during infecund periods to manifest their affection and to safeguard their mutual fidelity. By so doing, they give proof of a truly and integrally honest love.

930 17. Upright men can even better convince themselves of the solid grounds on which the teaching of the Church in

this field is based, if they care to reflect upon the consequences of methods of artificial birth control. Let them consider, first of all, how wide and easy a road would thus be opened up towards conjugal infidelity and the general lowering of morality. Not much experience is needed in order to know human weakness, and to understand that men—especially the young, who are so vulnerable on this point—have need of encouragement to be faithful to the moral law, so that they must not be offered some easy means of eluding its observance. It is also to be feared that the man, growing used to the employment of anti-conceptive practices, may finally lose respect for the woman and, no longer caring for her physical and psychological equilibrium, may come to the point of considering her as a mere instrument of selfish enjoyment, and no longer as his respected and beloved companion.

Let it be considered also that a dangerous weapon would thus be placed in the hands of those public authorities who take no heed of moral exigencies. Who could blame a government for applying to the solution of the problems of the community those means acknowledged to be licit for married couples in the solution of a family problem? Who will stop rulers from favoring, from even imposing upon their peoples, if they were to consider it necessary, the method of contraception which they judge to be more efficacious? In such a way men, wishing to avoid individual, family, or social difficulties encountered in the observance of the divine law, would reach the point of placing at the mercy of the intervention of public authorities the most personal and most reserved sector of conjugal intimacy. 931

Consequently, if the mission of generating life is not to be exposed to the arbitrary will of men, one must necessarily recognize insurmountable limits to the possibility of man's domination over his own body and its functions; limits which no man, whether a private individual or one invested with authority, may licitly surpass. And such limits cannot be determined otherwise than by the respect due to the integrity of the human organism and its functions, ac- 932 cording to the correct understanding of the "principle of totality" illustrated by our predecessor Pope Pius XII.[21]

933 18. It can be foreseen that this teaching will perhaps not be easily received by all: Too numerous are those voices—amplified by the modern means of propaganda—which are contrary to the voice of the Church. To tell the truth, the Church is not surprised to be made, like her divine Founder, a "sign of contradition,"[22] yet she does not because of this cease to proclaim with humble firmness the entire moral law, both natural and evangelical. Of such laws the Church was not the author, nor consequently can she be their arbiter; she is only their depositary and their interpreter, without ever being able to declare to be licit that which is not so by reason of its intimate and unchangeable opposition to the true good of man.

934 In defending conjugal morals in their integral wholeness, the Church knows that she contributes towards the establishment of a truly human civilization; she engages man not to abdicate from his own responsibility in order to rely on technical means; by that very fact she defends the dignity of man and wife. Faithful to both the teaching and the example of the Saviour, she shows herself to be the sincere and disinterested friend of men, whom she wishes to help, even during their earthly sojourn, "to share as sons in the life of the living God, the Father of all men."[23]

935 19. Our words would not be an adequate expression of the thought and solicitude of the Church, Mother and Teacher of all peoples, if, after having recalled men to the observance and respect of the divine law regarding matrimony, we did not strengthen them in the path of honest regulation of birth, even amid the difficult conditions which today afflict families and peoples. The Church, in fact, cannot have a different conduct towards men than that of the Redeemer: She knows their weaknesses, has compassion on the crowd, receives sinners; but she cannot renounce the teaching of the law which is, in reality, that law proper to a human life restored to its original truth and conducted by the spirit of God.[24]

936 20. The teaching of the Church on the regulation of birth, which promulgates the divine law, will easily appear to

many to be difficult or even impossible of actuation. And indeed, like all great beneficent realities, it demands serious engagement and much effort, individual, family and social effort. More than that, it would not be practicable without the help of God, who upholds and strengthens the good will of men. Yet, to anyone who reflects well, it cannot but be clear that such efforts ennoble man and are beneficial to the human community.

21. The honest practice of regulation of birth demands first of all that husband and wife acquire and possess solid convictions concerning the true values of life and of the family, and that they tend towards securing perfect self-mastery. To dominate instinct by means of one's reason and free will undoubtedly requires ascetical practices, so that the affective manifestations of conjugal life may observe the correct order, in particular with regard to the observance of periodic continence. Yet this discipline which is proper to the purity of married couples, far from harming conjugal love, rather confers on it a higher human value. It demands continual effort yet, thanks to its beneficent influence, husband and wife fully develop their personalities, being enriched with spiritual values. Such discipline bestows upon family life fruits of serenity and peace, and facilitates the solution of other problems; it favors attention for one's partner, helps both parties to drive out selfishness, the enemy of true love; and deepens their sense of responsibility. By its means, parents acquire the capacity of having a deeper and more efficacious influence in the education of their offspring; little children and youths grow up with a just appraisal of human values, and in the serene and harmonious development of their spiritual and sensitive faculties. 937

22. On this occasion, we wish to draw the attention of educators, and of all who perform duties of responsibility in regard to the common good of human society, to the need of creating an atmosphere favorable to education in chastity, that is, to the triumph of healthy liberty over license by means of respect for the moral order. 938

Everything in the modern media of social communications which leads to sense excitation and unbridled customs, as 939 well as every form of pornography and licentious performances, must arouse the frank and unanimous reaction of all those who are solicitous for the progress of civilization and the defense of the common good of the human spirit. Vainly would one seek to justify such depravation with the pretext of artistic or scientific exigencies,[25] or to deduce an argument from the freedom allowed in this sector by the public authorities.

940 23. To Rulers, who are those principally responsible for the common good, and who can do so much to safeguard moral customs, we say: Do not allow the morality of your peoples to be degraded; do not permit that by legal means practices contrary to the natural and divine law be introduced into that fundamental cell, the family. Quite other is the way in which public authorities can and must contribute to the solution of the demographic problem: namely, the way of a provident policy for the family, of a wise education of peoples in respect of moral law an the liberty of citizens.

941 We are well aware of the serious difficulties experienced by public authorities in this regard, especially in the developing countries. To their legitimate preoccupations we devoted our encyclical letter *Populorum Progressio*. But with our predecessor Pope John XXIII, we repeat: no solution to these difficulties is acceptable "which does violence to man's essential dignity" and is based only on an utterly materialistic conception of man himself and of his life. The only possible solution to this question is one which envisages the social and economic progress both of individuals and of the whole human society, and which respects and promotes true human values.[26] Neither can one, without grave injustice, consider divine providence to be responsible for what depends, instead, on a lack of wisdom in government, on an insufficient sense of social justice, on selfish monopolization, or again on blameworthy indolence in confronting the efforts and the sacrifices necessary to ensure the raising of living standards of a people and of all its sons.[27]

942 May all responsible public authorities—as some are already doing so laudably—generously revive their efforts. And may

mutual aid between all the members of the great human family never cease to grow: This is an almost limitless field which thus opens up to the activity of the great international organizations.

24. We wish now to express our encouragement to men of science, who "can considerably advance the welfare of marriage and the family, along with peace of conscience, if by pooling their efforts they labor to explain more thoroughly the various conditions favoring a proper regulation of births."[28] It is particularly desirable that, according to the wish already expressed by Pope Pius XII, medical science succeed in providing a sufficiently secure basis for a regulation of birth, founded on the observance of natural rhythms.[29] In this way, scientists and especially Catholic scientists will contribute to demonstrate in actual fact that, as the Church teaches, "a true contradiction cannot exist between the divine laws pertaining to the transmission of life and those pertaining to the fostering of authentic conjugal love."[30] 943

25. And now our words more directly address our own children, particularly those whom God calls to serve Him in marriage. The Church, while teaching imprescriptible demands of the divine law, announces the tidings of salvation, and by means of the sacraments opens up the paths of grace, which makes man a new creature, capable of corresponding with love and true freedom to the design of his Creator and Saviour, and of finding the yoke of Christ to be sweet.[31] 944

Christian married couples, then, docile to her voice, must remember that their Christian vocation, which began at baptism, is further specified and reinforced by the sacrament of matrimony. By it husband and wife are strengthened and as it were consecrated for the faithful accomplishment of their proper duties, for the carrying out of their proper vocation even to perfection, and the Christian witness which is proper to them before the whole world.[32] To them the Lord entrusts the task of making visible to men the holiness and sweetness of the law which unites the mutual love of husband and wife with their cooperation with the love of God the author of human life. 945

946 We do not at all intend to hide the sometimes serious difficulties inherent in the life of Christian married persons; for them as for everyone else, "the gate is narrow and the way is hard, that leads to life."[33] But the hope of that life must illuminate their way, as with courage they strive to live with wisdom, justice and piety in this present time,[34] knowing that the figure of this world passes away.[35]

947 Let married couples, then, face up to the efforts needed, supported by the faith and hope which "do not disappoint. . .because God's love has been poured into our hearts through the Holy Spirit, who has been given to us"[36]; let them implore divine assistance by persevering prayer; above all, let them draw from the source of grace and charity in the Eucharist. And if sin should still keep its hold over them, let them not be discouraged, but rather have recourse with humble perserverance to the mercy of God, which is poured forth in the sacrament of Penance. In this way they will be enabled to achieve the fullness of conjugal life described by the Apostle: "husbands, love your wives, as Christ loved the Church. . .husbands should love their wives as their own bodies. He who loves his wife loves himself. For no man ever hates his own flesh, but nourishes and cherishes it, as Christ does the Church. . .this is a great mystery, and I mean in referance to Christ and the Church. However, let each one of you love his wife as himself, and let the wife see that she respects her husband."[37]

948 26. Among the fruits which ripen forth from a generous effort of fidelity to the divine law, one of the most precious is that married couples themselves not infrequently feel the desire to communicate their experience to others. Thus there comes to be included in the vast pattern of the vocation of the laity a new and most noteworthy form of the apostolate of like to like; it is married couples themselves who become apostles and guides to other married couples. This is assuredly, among so many forms of apostolate, one of those which seem most opportune today.[38]

949 27. We hold those physicians and medical personnel in the highest esteem who, in the exercise of their profession, value above every human interest the superior demands of

their Christian vocation. Let them perservere, therefore, in promoting on every occasion the discovery of solutions inspired by faith and right reason, let them strive to arouse this conviction and this respect in their associates. Let them also consider as their proper professional duty the task of acquiring all the knowledge needed in this delicate sector, so as to be able to give to those married persons who consult them wise counsel and healthy direction, such as they have a right to expect.

28. Beloved priest sons, by vocation you are the counselors and spiritual guides of individual persons and of families. We now turn to you with confidence. Your first task—especially in the case of those who teach moral theology—is to expound the Church's teaching on marriage without ambiguity. Be the first to give, in the exercise of your ministry, the example of loyal internal and external obedience to the teaching authority of the Church. That obedience, as you know well, obliges not only because of the reasons adduced, but rather because of the light of the Holy Spirit, which is given in a particular way to the pastors of the Church in order that they may illustrate the truth.[39] You know, too, that it is of the utmost importance, for peace of consciences and for the unity of the Christian people, that in the field of morals as well as in that of dogma, all should attend to the magisterium of the Church, and all should speak the same language. Hence, with all our heart we renew to you the heartfelt plea of the great Apostle Paul: "I appeal to you, brethren, by the name of Our Lord Jesus Christ, that all of you agree and that there be no dissensions among you, but that you be united in the same mind and the same judgment."[40] 950

29. To diminish in no way the saving teaching of Christ constitutes an eminent form of charity for souls. But this must ever be accompanied by patience and goodness, such as the Lord himself gave example of in dealing with men. Having come not to condemn but to save,[41] he was indeed intransigent with evil, but merciful towards individuals. 951

In their difficulties, may married couples always find, in the words and in the heart of a priest, the echo of the voice and the love of the Redeemer. 952

953 And then speak with confidence, beloved sons, fully convinced that the spirit of God, while He assists the magisterium in proposing doctrine, illumines internally the hearts of the faithful inviting them to give their assent. Teach married couples the indispensable way of prayer; prepare them to have recourse often and with faith to the sacraments of the Eucharist and of Penance, without ever allowing themselves to be discouraged by their own weakness.

954 30. Beloved and venerable brothers in the episcopate, with whom we most intimately share the solicitude of the spiritual good of the People of God, at the conclusion of this encyclical our reverent and affectionate thoughts turn to you. To all of you we extend an urgent invitation. At the head of the priests, your collaborators, and of your faithful, work ardently and incessantly for the safeguarding and the holiness of marriage, so that it may always be lived in its entire human and Christian fullness. Consider this mission as one of your most urgent responsibilities at the present time. As you know, it implies concerted pastoral action in all the fields of human activity, economic, cultural and social; for, in fact, only a simultaneous improvement in these various sectors will make it possible to render the life of parents and of children within their families not only tolerable, but easier and more joyous, to render the living together in human society more fraternal and peaceful, in faithfulness to God's design for the world.

955 31. Venerable brothers, most beloved sons, and all men of good will, great indeed is the work of education, of progress and of love to which we call you, upon the foundation of the Church's teaching, of which the successor of Peter is, together with his brothers in the episcopate, the depositary and interpreter. Truly a great work, as we are deeply convinced, both for the world and for the Church, since man cannot find true happiness—towards which he aspires with all his being—other than in respect of the laws written by God in his very nature, laws which he must observe with intelligence and love. Upon this work, and upon all of you, and especially upon married couples, we invoke the abundant graces of the

God of holiness and mercy, and in pledge thereof we impart to you all our apostolic blessing.

Given at Rome, from St. Peter's, this 25th day of July, feast of St. James the Apostle, in the year 1968, the sixth of our pontificate. 956

A Call to Action
Apostolic Letter of Pope Paul VI to Cardinal Maurice Roy President of the Council of the Laity and of the Pontifical Commission Justice and Peace on the Occasion of the Eightieth Anniversary of the Encyclical Rerum Novarum
May 14, 1971

Venerable Brother,

The eightieth anniversary of the publication of the encyclical *Rerum Novarum,* the message of which continues to inspire action for social justice, prompts us to take up again and to extend the teaching of our predecessors, in response to the new needs of a changing world. The Church, in fact, travels forward with humanity and shares its lot in the setting of history. At the same time that she announces to men the Good News of God's love and of salvation in Christ, she clarifies their activity in the light of the Gospel and in this way helps them to correspond to God's plan of love and to realize the fullness of their aspirations.

958 2. It is with confidence that we see the Spirit of the Lord pursuing his work in the hearts of men and in every place gathering together Christian communities conscious of their responsibilities in society. On all the continents, among all races, nations and cultures, and under all conditions the Lord continues to raise up authentic apostles of the Gospel.

959 We have had the opportunity to meet these people, to admire them and to give them our encouragement in the course of our recent journeys. We have gone into the crowds and have heard their appeals, cries of distress and at the same time they are common to all mankind, which is questioning itself about its future and about the tendency and the mean-

ing of the changes taking place. Flagrant inequalities exist in the economic, cultural and political development of the nations: while some regions are heavily industrialized, others are still at the agricultural stage; while some countries enjoy prosperity, others are struggling against starvation; while some peoples have a high standard of culture, others are still engaged in eliminating illiteracy. From all sides there rises a yearning for more justice and a desire for a better guaranteed peace in mutual respect among individuals and peoples.

3. There is of course a wide diversity among the situations in which Christians—willingly or unwillingly—find themselves according to regions, socio-political systems and cultures. In some places they are reduced to silence, regarded with suspicion and as it were kept on the fringe of society, enclosed without freedom in a totalitarian system. In other places they are a weak minority whose voice makes itself heard with difficulty. In some other nations, where the Church sees her place recognized, sometimes officially so, she too finds herself subjected to the repercussions of the crisis which is unsettling society; some of her members are tempted by radical and violent solutions from which they believe that they can expect a happier outcome. While some people, unaware of present injustices, strive to prolong the existing situation, others allow themselves to be beguiled by revolutionary ideologies which promise them, not without delusion, a definitively better world. 960

4. In the face of such widely varying situations it is difficult for us to utter a unified message and to put forward a solution which has universal validity. Such is not our ambition, nor is it our mission. It is up to the Christian communities to analyze with objectivity the situation which is proper to their own country, to shed on it the light of the Gospel's unalterable words and to draw principles of reflection, norms of judgment and directives for action from the social teaching of the Church. This social teaching has been worked out in the course of history and notably, in this industrial era, since the historic date of the message of Pope Leo XIII on "the condition of the workers," and it is an honor and joy for us to cel- 961

ebrate today the anniversary of that message. It is up to these Christian communities, with the help of the Holy Spirit, in communion with the bishops who hold responsibility and in dialogue with other Christian brethren and all men of goodwill, to discern the options and commitments which are called for in order to bring about the social, political and economic changes seen in many cases to be urgently needed. In this search for the changes which should be promoted, Christians must first of all renew their confidence in the forcefulness and special character of the demands made by the Gospel. The Gospel is not out-of-date because it was proclaimed, written and lived in a different socio-cultural context. Its inspiration, enriched by the living experience of Christian tradition over the centuries, remains ever new for converting men and for advancing the life of society. It is not however to be utilized for the profit of particular temporal options, to the neglect of its universal and eternal message.[1]

962 5. Amid the disturbances and uncertainties of the present hour, the Church has a specific message to proclaim and a support to give to men in their efforts to take in hand and give direction to their future. Since the period in which the encyclical *Rerum Novarum* denounced in a forceful and imperative manner the scandle of the condition of the workers in the nascent industrial society, historical evolution has led to an awareness of other dimensions and other applications of social justice. The encyclicals *Quadragesimo Anno*[2] and *Mater et Magistra*[3] already noted this fact. The recent Council for its part took care to point them out, in particular in the Pastoral Constitution *Gaudium et Spes*. We ourself have already continued these lines of thought in our encyclical *Populorum Progressio*. "Today," we said, "the principal fact that we must all recognize is that the social question has become worldwide."[4] "A renewed consciousness of the demands of the Gospel makes it the Church's duty to put herself at the service of all, to help them grasp their serious problem in all its dimensions, and to convince them that solidarity in action at this turning point in human history is a matter of urgency."[5]

6. It will moreover be for the forthcoming Synod of Bishops itself to study more closely and to examine in greater detail the Church's mission in the face of grave issues raised today by the question of justice in the world. But the anniversary of *Rerum Novarum,* venerable brother, gives us the opportunity today to confide our preoccupations and thoughts in the face of this problem to you as President of the Pontifical Commission Justice and Peace and of the Council of Laity. In this way it is also our wish to offer these bodies of the Holy See our encouragement in their ecclesial activity in the service of men. 963

7. In so doing, our purpose—without however forgetting the permanent problems already dealt with by our predecessors—is to draw attention to a number of questions. These are questions which because of their urgency, extent and complexity must in the years to come take first place among the preoccupations of Christians, so that with other men the latter may dedicate themselves to solving the new difficulties which put the very future of man in jeopardy. It is necessary to situate the problems created by the modern economy in the wider context of a new civilization. These problems include human conditions of production, fairness in the exchange of goods and in the division of wealth, the significance of the increased needs of consumption and the sharing of responsibility. In the present changes, which are so profound and so rapid, each day man discovers himself anew, and he questions himself about the meaning of his own being and of his collective survival. Reluctant to gather the lessons of a past that he considers over and done with and too different from the present, man nevertheless needs to have light shed upon his future—a future which he perceives to be as uncertain as it is changing—by permanent eternal truths. These are truths which are certainly greater than man but, if he so wills, he can himself find their traces.[6] 964

8. A major phenomenon draws our attention, as much in the industrialized countries as in those which are developing: urbanization. 965

After long centuries, agrarian civilization is weakening. Is sufficient attention being devoted to the arrangement and im- 966 provement of the life of the country people, whose inferior and at all times miserable economic situation provokes the flight to the unhappy crowded conditions of the city outskirts, where neither employment nor housing awaits them?

967 This unceasing flight from the land, industrial growth, continual demographic expansion and the attraction of urban centers bring about concentrations of population, the extent of which is difficult to imagine, for people are already speaking in terms of a "megalopolis" grouping together tens of millions of persons. Of course there exist medium-sized towns, the dimension of which ensures a better balance in the population. While being able to offer employment to those that progress in agriculture makes available, they permit an adjustment of the human environment which better avoids the proletarianism and crowding of the great built-up areas.

968 9. The inordinate growth of these centers accompanies industrial expansion, without being identified with it. Based on technological research and the transformation of nature, industrialization constantly goes forward, giving proof of incessant creativity. While certain enterprises develop and are concentrated, others die or change their location. Thus new social problems are created: professional or regional unemployment, redeployment and mobility of persons, permanent adaptation of workers and disparity of conditions in the different branches of publicity incessantly launches new products and tries to attract the consumer, while earlier industrial installations which are still capable of functioning become useless. While very large areas of the population are unable to satisfy their primary needs, superfluous needs are ingeniously created. It can thus rightly be asked if, in spite of all his conquests, man is not turning back against himself the results of his activity. Having rationally endeavored to control nature,[7] is he not now becoming the slave of the objects which he makes?

969 10. Is not the rise of an urban civilization which accompanies the advance of industrial civilization a true challenge to the wisdom of man, to his capacity for organization and to his farseeing imagination? Within industrial society urbanization

upsets both the ways of life and the habitual structures of existence: the family, the neighborhood, and the very framework of the Christian community. Man is experiencing a new loneliness; it is not in the face of a hostile nature which it has taken him centuries to subdue, but in an anonymous crowd which surrounds him and in which he feels himself a stranger. Urbanization, undoubtedly an irreversible stage in the development of human societies, confronts man with difficult problems. How is he to master its growth, regulate its organization, and successfully accomplish its animation for the good of all?

970 In this disordered growth, new proletariats are born. They install themselves in the heart of the cities sometimes abandoned by the rich; they dwell on the outskirts—which become a belt of misery besieging in a still silent protest the luxury which blatantly cries out from centers of consumption and waste. Instead of favoring fraternal encounter and mutual aid, the city fosters discrimination and also indifference. It lends itself to new forms of exploitation and of domination whereby some people in speculating on the needs of others derive inadmissible profits. Behind the facades, much misery is hidden, unsuspected even by the closest neighbors; other forms of misery spread where human dignity founders: delinquency, criminality, abuse of drugs and eroticism.

971 11. It is in fact the weakest who are the victims of dehumanizing living conditions, degrading for conscience and harmful for the family institution. The promiscuity of working people's housing makes a minimum of intimacy impossible; young couples waiting in vain for a decent dwelling at a price they can afford are demoralized and their union can thereby even be endangered; youth escape from a home which is too confined and seek in the streets compensations and companionships which cannot be supervised. It is the grave duty of those responsible to strive to control this process and to give it direction.

972 There is an urgent need to remake at the level of the street, of the neighborhood or of the great agglomerative dwellings the social fabric whereby man may be able to develop the

needs of his personality. Centers of special interest and of culture must be created or developed at the community and parish levels with different forms of associations, recreational centers, and spiritual and community gatherings where the individual can escape from isolation and form anew fraternal relationships.

973 12. To build up the city, the place where men and their expanded communities exist, to create new modes of neighborliness and relationships, to perceive an original application of social justice and to undertake responsibility for this collective future, which is foreseen as difficult, is a task in which Christians must share. To those who are heaped up in an urban promiscuity which becomes intolerable it is necessary to bring a message of hope. This can be done by brotherhood which is lived and by concrete justice. Let Christians, conscious of this new responsibility, not lose heart in view of the vast and faceless society; let them recall Jonah who traversed Niniveh, the great city, to proclaim therein the good news of God's mercy and was upheld in his weakness by the sole strength of the word of Almighty God. In the Bible, the city is in fact often the place of sin and pride—the pride of man who feels secure enough to be able to build his life without God and even to affirm that he is powerful against God. But there is also the example of Jerusalem, the Holy City, the place where God is encountered, the promise of the city which comes from on high.[8]

974 13. Urban life and industrial change bring strongly to light questions which until now were poorly grasped. What place, for example, in this world being brought to birth, should be given to youth? Everywhere dialogue is proving to be difficult between youth, with its aspirations, renewal and also insecurity for the future, and the adult generations. It is obvious to all that here we have a source of serious conflicts, division and opting out, even within the family, and a questioning of modes of authority, education for freedom and the handing on of values and beliefs, which strikes at the deep roots of society.

975 Similarly, in many countries a charter for women which would put an end to an actual discrimination and would

establish relationships of equality in rights and of respect for their dignity is the object of study and at times of lively demands. We do not have in mind that false equality which would be in contradiction with woman's proper role, which is of such capital importance, at the heart of the family as well as within society. Developments in legislation should on the contrary be directed to protecting her proper vocation and at the same time recognizing her independence as a person, and her equal rights to participate in cultural, economic, social and political life.

976 14. As the Church solemnly reaffirmed in the recent Council, "the beginning, the subject and the goal of all social institutions is and must be the human person."[9] Every man has the right to work, to a chance to develop his qualities and his personality in the exercise of his profession, to equitable remuneration which will enable him and his family "to lead a worthy life on the material, social, cultural and spiritual level"[10] and to assistance in case of need arising from sickness or age.

977 Although for the defense of these rights democratic societies accept today the principle of labor union rights, they are not always open to their exercise. The important role of union organizations must be admitted: their object is the representation of the various categories of workers, their lawful collaboration in the economic advance of society, and the development of the sense of their responsibility for the realization of the common good. Their activity, however, is not without its difficulties. Here and there the temptation can arise of profiting from a position of force to impose, particularly by strikes—the right to which as a final means of defense remains certainly recognized—conditions which are too burdensome for the overall economy and for the social body, or to desire to obtain in this way demands of a directly political nature. When it is a question of public services, required for the life of an entire nation, it is necessary to be able to assess the limit beyond which the harm caused to society becomes inadmissible.

978 15. In short, progress has already been made in introducing, in the area of human relationships, greater justice and greater

sharing of responsibilities. But in this immense field much remains to be done. Further reflection, research and experimentation must be actively pursued, unless one is to be late in meeting the legitimate aspirations of the workers—aspirations which are being increasingly asserted according as their education, their consciousness of their dignity and the strength of their organizations increase.

979 Egoism and domination are permanent temptations for men. Likewise an ever finer discernment is needed, in order to strike at the roots of newly arising situations of injustice and to establish progressively a justice which will be less and less imperfect. In industrial change, which demands speedy and constant adaptation, those who will find themselves injured will be more numerous and at a greater disadvantage from the point of view of making their voices heard. The Church directs her attention to these new "poor"—the handicapped and the maladjusted, the old, different groups of those on the fringe of society, and so on—in order to recognize them, help them, defend their place and dignity in a society hardened by competition and the attraction of success.

980 16. Among the victims of situations of injustice—unfortunately no new phenomenon—must be placed those who are discriminated against, in law or in fact, on account of their race, origin, color, culture, sex or religion.

981 Racial discrimination possesses at the moment a character of very great relevance by reason of the tension which it stirs up both within certain countries and on the international level. Men rightly consider unjustifiable and reject as inadmissible the tendency to maintain or introduce legislation or behavior systematically inspired by racialist prejudice. The members of mankind share the same basic rights and duties, as well as the same supernatural destiny. Within a country which belongs to each one, all should be equal before the law, find equal admittance to economic, cultural, civic and social life and benefit from a fair sharing of the nation's riches.

982 17. We are thinking also of the precarious situation of a great number of emigrant workers whose condition as foreign-

ers makes it all the more difficult for them to make any sort of social vindication, in spite of their real participation in the economic effort of the country that receives them. It is urgently necessary for people to go beyond a narrowly nationalist attitude in their regard and to give them a charter which will assure them a right to emigrate, favor their integration, facilitate their professional advancement and give them access to decent housing where, if such is the case, their families can join them.[11]

983 Linked to this category are the people who, to find work, or to escape a disaster or a hostile climate, leave their regions and find themselves without roots among other people.

984 It is everyone's duty, but especially that of Christians,[12] to work with energy for the establishment of universal brotherhood, the indispensable basis for authentic justice and the condition for enduring peace: "We cannot in truthfulness call upon that God who is the Father of all if we refuse to act in a brotherly way toward certain men, created to God's image. A man's relationship with God the Father and his relationship with his brother men are so linked together that Scripture says: 'He who does not love does not know God' (1 *Jn* 4:8)."[13]

985 18. With demographic growth, which is particularly pronounced in the young nations, the number of those failing to find work and driven to misery or parasitism will grow in the coming years unless the conscience of man rouses itself and gives rise to a general movement of solidarity through an effective policy of investment and of organization of production and trade, as well as of education. We know the attention given to these problems within international organizations, and it is our lively wish that their members will not delay bringing their actions into line with their declarations.

986 It is disquieting in this regard to note a kind of fatalism which is gaining a hold even on people in positions of responsibility. This feeling sometimes leads to Malthusian solutions inculcated by active propaganda for contraception and abortion. In this critical situation, it must on the

contrary be affirmed that the family, without which no society can stand, has a right to the assistance which will assure it of the conditions for a healthy development. "It is certain," we said in our encyclical *Populorum Progressio,* "that public authorities can intervene, within the limit of their competence, by favoring the availability of appropriate information and by adopting suitable measures, provided that these be in conformity with the moral law and that they respect the rightful freedom of married couples. Where the inalienable right to marriage and procreation is lacking, human dignity has ceased to exist."[14]

987 19. In no other age has the appeal to the imagination of society been so explicit. To this should be devoted enterprises of invention and capital as important as those invested for armaments or technological achievements. If man lets himself rush ahead without foreseeing in good time the emergence of new social problems, they will become too grave for a peaceful solution to be hoped for.

988 20. Among the major changes of our times, we do not wish to forget to emphasize the growing role being assumed by the media of social communication and their influence on the transformation of mentalities, of knowledge, of organizations and of society itself. Certainly they have many positive aspects. Thanks to them news from the entire world reaches us practically in an instant, establishing contacts which supersede distances and creating elements of unity among all men. A greater spread of education and culture is becoming possible. Nevertheless, by their very action the media of social communication are reaching the point of representing as it were a new power. One cannot but ask about those who really hold this power, the aims that they pursue and the means they use, and finally, about the effect of their activity on the exercise of individual liberty, both in the political and ideological spheres and in social, economic and cultural life. The men who hold this power have a grave moral responsibility with respect to the truth of the information that they spread, the needs and the reactions that they generate and the values which they put forward. In the case of television, moreover, what is coming into being is an origi-

nal mode of knowledge and a new civilization: that of the image.

Naturally, the public authorities cannot ignore the growing power and influence of the media of social communication and the advantages and risks which their use involves for the civic community and for its development and real perfecting. 989

Consequently they are called upon to perform their own positive function for the common good by encouraging every constructive expression, by supporting individual citizens and groups in defending the fundamental values of the person and of human society, and also by taking suitable steps to prevent the spread of what would harm the common heritage of values on which orderly civil progress is based.[15] 990

21. While the horizon of man is thus modified being according to the images that are chosen for him, another transformation is making itself felt, one which is the dramatic and unexpected consequence of human activity. Man is suddenly becoming aware that by an ill-considered exploitation of nature he risks destroying it and becoming in his turn the victim of this degradation. Not only is the material environment becoming a permanent menace—pollution and refuse, new illnesses and absolute destructive capacity—but the human framework is no longer under man's control, thus creating an environment for tomorrow which may well be intolerable. This is a wide-ranging social problem which concerns the entire human family. 991

The Christian must turn to these new perceptions in order to take on responsibility, together with the rest of men, for a destiny which from now on is shared by all. 992

22. While scientific and technological progress continues to overturn man's surroundings, his patterns of knowledge, work, consumption and relationships, two aspirations persistently make themselves felt in these new contexts, and they grow stronger to the extent that he becomes better informed and better educated: the aspiration to equality and the aspiration to participation, two forms of man's dignity and freedom. 993

23. Through this statement of the rights of man and the seeking for international agreements for the application of 994

these rights, progress has been made towards inscribing these two aspirations in deeds and structures.[16] Nevertheless various forms of discrimination continually reappear—ethnic, cultural, religious, political and so on. In fact, human rights are still too often disregarded, if not scoffed at, or else they receive only formal recognition. In many cases legislation does not keep up with real situations. Legislation is necessary, but it is not sufficient for setting up true relationships of justice and equality. In teaching us charity, the Gospel instructs us in the preferential respect due to the poor and the special situation they have in society: the more fortunate should renounce some of their rights so as to place their goods more generously at the service of others. If, beyond legal rules, there is really no deeper feeling of respect for and service to others, then even equality before the law can serve as an alibi for flagrant discrimination, continued exploitation and actual contempt. Without a renewed education in solidarity, an overemphasis of equality can give rise to an individualism in which each one claims his own rights without wishing to be answerable for the common good.

995 In this field, everyone sees the highly important contribution of the Christian spirit, which moreover answers man's yearning to be loved. "Love for man, the prime value of the earthly order," ensures the conditions for peace, both social peace and international peace, by affirming our universal brotherhood.[17]

996 24. The two aspirations, to equality and to participation, seek to promote a democratic type of society. Various models are proposed, some are tried out, none of them gives complete satisfaction, and the search goes on between ideological and pragmatic tendencies. The Christian has the duty to take part in this search and in the organization and life of political society. As a social being, man builds his destiny within a series of particular groupings which demand, as their completion and as a necessary condition for their development, a vaster society, one of a universal character, the political society. All particular activity must be placed within that wider society, and thereby it takes on the dimension of the common good.[18]

This indicates the importance of education for life in society, in which there are called to mind, not only information on each one's rights, but also their necessary correlative: the recognition of the duties of each one in regard to others. The sense and practice of duty are themselves conditioned by self-mastery and by the acceptance of responsibility and of the limits placed upon the freedom of the individual or of the group. 997

25. Political activity—need one remark that we are dealing primarily with an activity, not an ideology?—should be the projection of a plan of society which is consistent in its concrete means and in its inspiration, and which springs from a complete conception of man's vocation and of its differing social expressions. It is not for the State or even for political parties, which would be closed unto themselves, to try to impose an ideology by means that would lead to a dictatorship over minds, the worst kind of all. It is for cultural and religious groupings, in the freedom of acceptance which they presume, to develop in the social body, disinterestedly and in their own ways, those ultimate convictions on the nature, origin and end of man and society. 998

In this field, it is well to keep in mind the principle proclaimed at the Second Vatican Council: "The truth cannot impose itself except by virtue of its own truth, and it makes its entrance into the mind at once quietly and with power."[19] 999

26. Therefore the Christian who wishes to live his faith in a political activity which he thinks of as service cannot without contradicting himself adhere to ideological systems which radically or substantially go against his faith and his concept of man. He cannot adhere to the Marxist ideology, to its atheistic materialism, to its dialectic of violence and to the way it absorbs individual freedom in the collectivity, at the same time denying all transcendence to man and his personal and collective history; nor can he adhere to the liberal ideology which believes it exalts individual freedom by withdrawing it from every limitation, by stimulating through exclusive seeking of interest and power, and by considering social solidarities as more or less automatic consequences of individual 1000

initiatives, not as an aim and a major criterion of the value of the social organization.

1001 27. Is there need to stress the possible ambiguity of every social ideology? Sometimes it leads political or social activity to be simply the application of an abstract, purely theoretical idea; at other times it is thought which becomes a mere instrument at the service of activity as a simple means of a strategy. In both cases is it not man that risks finding himself alienated? The Christian faith is above and is sometimes opposed to the ideologies, in that it recognizes God, who is transcendent and the Creator, and who, through all the levels of creation, calls on man as endowed with responsibility and freedom.

1002 28. There would also be the danger of giving adherence to an ideology which does not rest on a true and organic doctrine, to take refuge in it as a final and sufficient explanation of everything, and thus to build a new idol, accepting at times without being aware of doing so, its totalitarian and coercive character. And people imagine they find in it a justification for their activity, even violent activity, and an adequate response to a generous desire to serve. The desire remains but it allows itself to be consumed by an ideology which, even if it suggests certain paths to man's liberation, ends up by making him a slave.

1003 29. It has been possible today to speak of a retreat of ideologies. In this respect the present time may be favorable for an openness to the concrete transcendence of Christianity. It may also be a more accentuated sliding towards a new positivism: universalized technology as the dominant form of activity, as the overwhelming pattern of existence, even as a language, without the question of its meaning being really asked.

1004 30. But outside of this positivism which reduces man to a single dimension even if it be an important one today and by so doing mutilates him, the Christian encounters in his activity concrete historical movements sprung from ideologies and in part distinct from them. Our venerated predecessor Pope John XXIII in *Pacem in Terris* already showed that it is possible to make a distinction: "Neither can false philosophical teachings regarding the nature, origin and destiny of the universe and of man be identified with historical movements that have economic, social, cultural or political ends, not even when these movements have originated from those teachings and have drawn and still draw inspiration therefrom. Because the teachings, once they are drawn up and defined, remain always the same, while the movements, being concerned with hisorical situations in constant evolution, cannot but be influenced by these latter and cannot avoid, therefore, being subject to changes, even of a profound nature. Besides, who can deny that those movements, insofar as they conform to the dictates of right reason and are interpreters of the lawful aspirations of the human person, contain elements that are positive and deserving of approval?"[20]

1005

31. Some Christians are today attracted by socialist currents and their various developments. They try to recognize therein a certain number of aspirations which they carry within themselves in the name of their faith. They feel that they are part of that historical current and wish to play a part within it. Now this historical current takes on, under the same name, different forms according to different continents and cultures, even if it drew its inspiration, and still does in many cases, from ideologies incompatible with faith. Careful judgment is called for. Too often Christians attracted by socialism tend to idealize it in terms which, apart from anything else, are very general: a will for justice, solidarity and equality. They refuse to recognize the limitations of the historical socialist movements, which remain conditioned by the ideologies from which they originated. Distinctions must be made to guide concrete choices between the various levels of expression of socialism: a generous aspiration and a seeking for a more just society, historical movements with a political organization and aim, and an ideology which claims to give a complete and self-sufficient picture of man. Nevertheless, these distinctions must not lead one to consider such levels as completely separate and independent. The concrete link which, according to circumstances, exists between them must be clearly marked out. This insight will enable Christians to

see the degree of commitment possible along these lines, while safeguarding the values, especially those of liberty, responsibility and openness to the spiritual, which guarantee the integral development of man.

1006 32. Other Christians even ask whether an historical development of Marxism might not authorize certain concrete rapprochements. They note in fact that a certain splintering of Marxism, which until now showed itself to be a unitary ideology which explained in atheistic terms the whole of man and the world since it did not go outside their development process. Apart from the ideological confrontation officially separating the various champions of Marxism-Leninism in their individual interpretations of the thought of its founders, and apart from the open opposition between the political systems which make use of its name today, some people lay down distinctions between Marxism's various levels of expression.

1007 33. For some, Marxism remains essentially the active practice of class struggle. Experiencing the ever present and continually renewed force of the relationships of domination and exploitation among men, they reduce Marxism to no more than a struggle—at times with no other purpose—to be pursued and even stirred up in permanent fashion. For others, it is first and foremost the collective exercise of political and economic power under the direction of a single party, which would be the sole expression and guarantee of the welfare of all, and would deprive individuals and other groups of any possibility of initiative and choice. At a third level, Marxism, whether in power or not, is viewed as a socialist ideology based on historical materialism and the denial of everything transcendent. At other times, finally, it presents itself in a more attenuated form, one also more attractive to the modern mind: as a scientific activity, as a rigorous method of examining social and political reality, and as the rational link, tested by history, between theoretical knowledge and the practice of revolutionary transformation. Although this type of analysis gives a privileged position to certain aspects of reality to the detriment of the rest, and interprets them in the light of its ideology, it nevertheless furnishes some people not only with a working tool but also a certitude preliminary to action: the claim to decipher in a scientific manner the mainsprings of the evolution of society.

34. While, through the concrete existing form of Marxism, one can distinguish these various aspects and the questions they pose for the reflection and activity of Christians, it would be illusory and dangerous to reach a point of forgetting the intimate link which radically binds them together, to accept the elements of Marxist analysis without recognizing their relationships with ideology, and to enter into the practice of class struggle and its Marixist interpretations, while failing to note the kind of totalitartian and violent society to which this process leads. 1008

35. On another side, we are witnessing a renewal of the liberal ideology. This current asserts itself both in the name of economic efficiency, and for the defense of the individual against the increasingly overwhelming hold of organizations, and as a reaction against the totalitarian tendencies of political powers. Certainly, personal initiative must be maintained and developed. But do not Christians who take this path tend to idealize liberalism in their turn, making it a proclamation in favor of freedom? They would like a new model, more adapted to present-day conditions, while easily forgetting that at the very root of philosophical liberalism is an erroneous affirmation of the autonomy of the individual in his activity, his motivation and the exercise of his liberty. Hence, the liberal ideology likewise calls for careful discernment on their part. 1009

36. In this renewed encounter of the various ideologies, the Christian will draw from the sources of his faith and the Church's teaching the necessary principles and suitable criteria to avoid permitting himself to be first attracted by and then imprisoned within a system whose limitations and totalitarianism may well become evident to him too late, if he does not perceive them in their roots. Going beyond every system, without however failing to commit himself concretely to serving his brothers, he will assert, in the very 1010

midst of his options, the specific character of the Christian contribution for a positive transformation of society.[21]

1011 37. Today, moreover, the weaknesses of the ideologies are better perceived through the concrete systems in which they are trying to affirm themselves. Bureaucratic socialism, technocratic capitalism and authoritarian democracy are showing how difficult it is to solve the great human problem of living together in justice and equality. How in fact could they escape the materialism, egoism or constraint which inevitably go with them? This is the source of a protest which is springing up more or less everywhere, as a sign of a deep-seated sickness, while at the same time we are witnessing the rebirth of what it is agreed to call "utopias." These claim to resolve the political problem of modern societies better than the ideologies. It would be dangerous to disregard this. The appeal to a utopia is often a convenient excuse for those who wish to escape from concrete tasks in order to take refuge in an imaginary world. To live in a hypothetical future is a facile alibi for rejecting immediate responsibilities. But it must clearly be recognized that this kind of criticism of existing society often provokes the forward-looking imagination both to perceive in the present the disregarded possiblity hidden within it, and to direct itself towards a fresh future; it thus sustains social dynamism by the confidence that it gives to the inventive powers of the human mind and heart; and, if it refuses no overture, it can also meet the Christian appeal. The Spirit of the Lord, who animates man renewed in Christ, continually breaks down the horizons within which his understanding likes to find security and the limits to which his activity would willingly restrict itself; there dwells within him a power which urges him to go beyond every system and every ideology. At the heart of the world there dwells the mystery of man discovering himself to be God's son in the course of a historical and psychological process in which constraint and freedom as well as the weight of sin and the breath of the Spirit alternate and struggle for the upper hand.

The dynamism of Christian faith here triumphs over the narrow calculations of egoism. Animated by the power of the Spirit of Jesus Christ, the Saviour of mankind, and upheld by hope, the Christian involves himself in the building up of the human city, one that is to be peaceful, just and fraternal and acceptable as an offering to God.[22] In fact, "the expectation of a new earth must not weaken but rather stimulate our concern for cultivating this one. For here grows the body of a new human family, a body which even now is able to give some kind of foreshadowing of the new age."[23] 1012

38. In this world dominated by scientific and technological change, which threatens to drag it towards a new positivism, another more fundamental doubt is raised. Having subdued nature by using his reason, man now finds that he himself is as it were imprisoned within his own rationality; he in turn becomes the object of science. The "human sciences" are today enjoying a significant flowering. On the one hand they are subjecting to critical and radical examination the hitherto accepted knowledge about man, on the grounds that this knowledge seems either too empirical or too theoretical. On the other hand, methodological necessity and ideological presuppositions too often lead the human sciences to isolate, in the various situations, certain aspects of man, and yet to give these an explanation which claims to be complete or at least an interpretation which is meant to be all-embracing from a purely quantitative or phenomenological point of view. This scientific reduction betrays a dangerous presumption. To give a privileged position in this way to such an aspect of analysis is to mutilate man and, under the pretext of a scientific procedure, to make it impossible to understand man in his totality. 1013

39. One must be no less attentive to the action which the human sciences can instigate, giving rise to the elaboration of models of society to be subsequently imposed on men as scientifically tested types of behavior. Man can then become the object of manipulations directing his desires and needs and modifying his behavior and even his system of values. 1014

There is no doubt that there exists here a grave danger for the societies of tomorrow and for man himself. For even if all agree to build a new society at the service of men, it is still essential to know what sort of man is in question.

1015 40. Suspicion of the human sciences affects the Christian more than others, but it does not find him disarmed. For, as we ourself wrote in *Populorum Progressio*, it is here that there is found the specific contribution of the Church to civilizations: "Sharing the noblest aspirations of men and suffering when she sees them not satisfied, she wishes to help them attain their full flowering, and that is why she offers men what she possesses as her characteristic attribute: a global vision of man and of the human race."[24] Should the Church in its turn contest the proceedings of the human sciences, and condemn their pretentions? As in the case of the natural sciences, the Church has confidence in this research also and urges Christians to play an active part in it.[25] Prompted by the same scientific demands and the desire to know man better, but at the same time enlightened by their faith, Christians who devote themselves to the human sciences will begin a dialogue which promises to be fruitful. Of course, each individual scientific discipline will be able, in its own particular sphere, to grasp only a partial—yet true—aspect of man; the complete picture and the full meaning will escape it. But within these limits the human sciences give promise of a positive function that the Church willingly recognizes. They can even widen the horizons of human liberty to a greater extent than the conditioning circumstances perceived enable one to foresee. They could thus assist Christian social morality, which no doubt will see its field restricted when it comes to suggesting certain models of society, while its function of making a critical judgment and taking an overall view will be strengthened by its showing the relative character of the behavior and values presented by such and such a society as definitive and inherent in the very nature of man. These sciences are a condition at once indispensable and inadequate for a better discovery of what is human. They are a language which becomes more and more complex, yet one that deepens rather than solves the mystery of the heart of man; nor does it provide the complete and definitive answer to the desire which springs from his innermost being.

41. This better knowledge of man makes it possible to pass a better critical judgment upon and to elucidate a fundamental notion that remains at the basis of modern societies as their motive, their measure and their goal: namely, progress. Since the nineteenth century, western societies and, as a result, many others have put their hopes in ceaselessly renewed and indefinite progress. They saw this progress as man's effort to free himself in face of the demands of nature and of social constraints; progress was the condition for and the yardstick of human freedom. Progress, spread by the modern media of information and by the demand for wider knowledge and greater consumption, has become an omnipresent ideology. Yet a doubt arises today regarding both its value and its result. What is the meaning of this never-ending, breathless pursuit of a progress that always eludes one just when one believes one has conquered it sufficiently in order to enjoy it in peace? If it is not attained, it leaves one dissatisfied. Without doubt, there has been just condemnation of the limits and even the misdeeds of a merely quantitative economic growth; there is a desire to attain objectives of a qualitative order also. The quality and the truth of human relations, the degree of participation and of responsibility, are no less significant and important for the future of society than the quantity and variety of the goods produced and consumed. 1016

Overcoming the temptation to wish to measure everything in terms of efficiency and of trade, and in terms of the interplay of forces and interests, man today wishes to replace these quantitative criteria with the intensity of communication, the spread of knowledge and culture, mutual service and a combining of efforts for a common task. Is not genuine progress to be found in the development of moral consciousness, which will lead man to exercise a wider solidarity and to open himself freely to others and to God? For a Christian, progress necessarily comes up against the eschatological mystery of death. The death of Christ and his resurrection and the outpouring of the Spirit of the 1017

Lord help man to place his freedom, in creativity and gratitude, within the context of the truth of all progress and the only hope which does not deceive.[26]

1018 42. In the face of so many new questions the Church makes an effort to reflect in order to give an answer, in its own sphere, to men's expectations. If today the problems seem original in their breadth and their urgency, is man without the means of solving them? It is with all its dynamism that the social teaching of the Church accompanies men in their search. If it does not intervene to authenticate a given structure or to propose a ready-made model, it does not thereby limit itself to recalling general principles. It develops through reflection applied to the changing situations of this world, under the driving force of the Gospel as the source of renewal when its message is accepted in its totality and with all its demands. It also develops with the sensitivity proper to the Church which is characterized by a disinterested will to serve and by attention to the poorest.

1019 Finally, it draws upon its rich experience of many centuries which enables it, while continuing its permanent preoccupations, to undertake the daring and creative innovations which the present state of the world requires.

1020 43. There is need to establish a greater justice in the sharing of goods, both within national communities and on the international level. In international exhanges there is a need to go beyond relationships based on force, in order to arrive at agreements reached with the good of all in mind. Relationships based on force have never in fact established justice in a true and lasting manner, even if at certain times the alternation of positions can often make it possible to find easier conditions for dialogue. The use of force moreover leads to the setting in motion of opposing forces, and from this springs a climate of struggle which opens the way to situations of extreme violence and to abuses.[27]

1021 But, as we have often stated, the most important duty in the realm of justice is to allow each country to promote its own development, within the framework of a cooperation free from any spirit of domination, whether economic or political. The complexity of the problems raised is certainly great, in the present intertwining of mutual dependences. Thus it is necessary to have the courage to undertake a revision of the relationships between nations, whether it is a question of the international division of production, the structure of exchanges, the control of profits, the monetary system,—without forgetting the actions of human solidarity—to question the models of growth of the rich nations and change people's outlooks, so that they may realize the prior call of international duty, and to renew international organizations so that they may increase in effectiveness.

44. Under the driving force of new systems of production, national frontiers are breaking down, and we can see new economic powers emerging, the multinational enterprises, which by the concentration and flexibility of their means can conduct autonomous strategies which are largely independent of the national political powers and therefore not subject to control from the point of view of the common good. By extending their activities, these private organizations can lead to a new and abusive form of economic domination on the social, cultural and even political level. The excessive concentration of means and powers that Pope Pius XI already condemned on the fortieth anniversary of *Rerum Novarum* is taking on a new and very real image. 1022

45. Today men yearn to free themselves from need and dependence. But this liberation starts with the interior freedom that men must find again with regard to their goods and their powers; they will never reach it except through a transcendent love for man, and, in consequence, through a genuine readiness to serve. Otherwise, as one can see only too clearly, the most revolutionary ideologies lead only to a change of masters; once installed in power in their turn, these new masters surround themselves with privileges, limit freedoms and allow other forms of injustice to become established. 1023

Thus many people are reaching the point of questioning the very model of society. The ambition of many nations, in the competition that sets them in opposition and which carries them along, is to attain technological, economic and military power. This ambition then stands in the way of 1024 setting up structures in which the rhythm of progress would be regulated with a view to greater justice, instead of accentuating inequalities and living in a climate of distrust and struggle which would unceasingly compromise peace.

1025 46. Is it not here that there appears a radical limitation to economics? Economic activity is necessary and, if it is at the service of man, it can be "a source of brotherhood and a sign of Providence."[28] It is the occasion of concrete exchanges between man, of rights recognized, of services rendered and of dignity affirmed in work. Though it is often a field of confrontation and domination, it can give rise to dialogue and foster cooperation. Yet it runs the risk of taking up too much strength and freedom.[29] This is why the need is felt to pass from economics to politics. It is true that in the term "politics" many confusions are possible and must be clarified, but each man feels that in the social and economic field, both national and international, the ultimate decision rests with political power.

1026 Political power, which is the natural and necessary link for ensuring the cohesion of the social body, must have as its aim the achievement of the common good. While respecting the legitimate liberties of individuals, families and subsidiary groups, it acts in such a way as to create, effectively and for the well-being of all, the conditions required for attaining man's true and complete good, including his spiritual end. It acts within the limits of its competence, which can vary from people to people and from country to country. It always intervenes with care for justice and with devotion to the common good, for which it holds final responsibility. It does not, for all that, deprive individuals and intermediary bodies of the field of activity and responsibility which are proper to them and which lead them to collaborate in the attainment of this common good. In fact, "the true aim of all social activity should be to help individual members of the social body, but never to destroy or absorb them."[30] According to the vocation proper to it, the political power must know how to stand aside from particular interests in order to view its responsibility with regard to the good of all men, even going beyond national limits. To take politics seriously at its different levels—local, regional, national and worldwide—is to affirm the duty of man, of every man, to recognize the concrete reality and the value of the freedom of choice that is offered to him to seek to bring about both the good of the city and of the nation and of mankind. Politics are a demanding manner—but not the only one—of living the Christian commitment to the service of others. Without of course solving every problem, it endeavors to apply solutions to the relationships men have with one another. The domain of politics is wide and comprehensive, but it is not exclusive. An attitude of encroachment which would tend to set up politics as an absolute value would bring serious danger. While recognizing the autonomy of the reality of politics, Christians who are invited to take up political activity should try to make their choices consistent with the Gospel and, in the framework of a legitimate plurality, to give both personal and collective witness to the seriousness of their faith by effective and disinterested service of men.

1027

47. The passing to the political dimension also expresses a demand made by the man of today: a greater sharing in responsibility and in decision-making. This legitimate aspiration becomes more evident as the cultural level rises, as the sense of freedom develops and as man becomes more aware of how, in a world facing an uncertain future, the choices of today already condition the life of tomorrow. In *Mater et Magistra*[31] Pope John XXIII stressed how much the admittance to responsibility is a basic demand of man's nature, a concrete exercise of his freedom and a path to his development, and he showed how, in economic life and particularly in enterprise, this sharing in responsibilities should be ensured.[32] Today the field is wider, and extends to the social and political sphere in which a reasonable sharing in responsibility and in decisions must be established and strengthened. Admittedly, it is true that the choices proposed for a decision are more and more complex; the considerations that must be borne in mind are numerous and the foreseeing of the consequences involves risk, even if new sciences strive to enlighten freedom at these important moments.

However, although limits are sometimes called for, these obstacles must not slow down the giving of wider participation in working out decisions, making choices and putting them into practice. In order to counterbalance increasing technocracy, modern forms of democracy must be devised, not only making it possible for each man to become informed and to express himself, but also by involving him in a shared responsibility.

1028 Thus human groups will gradually begin to share and to live as communities. Thus freedom, which too often asserts itself as a claim for autonomy by opposing the freedom of others will develop in its deepest human reality: to involve itself and to spend itself in building up active and lived solidarity. But, for the Christian, it is by losing himself in God who sets him free that man finds true freedom, renewed in the death and resurrection of the Lord.

1029 48. In the social sphere, the Church has always wished to assume a double function: first to enlighten minds in order to assist them to discover the truth and to find the right path to follow amid the different teachings that call for their attention; and secondly to take part in action and to spread, with a real care for service and effectiveness, the energies of the Gospel. Is it not in order to be faithful to this desire that the Church has sent on an apostolic mission among the workers priests who, by sharing fully the condition of the worker, are at that level the witnesses to the Church's solicitude and seeking?

1030 It is to all Christians that we address a fresh and insistent call to action. In our encyclical on the Development of Peoples we urged that all should set themselves to the task: "Laymen should take up as their own proper task the renewal of the temporal order. If the role of the hierarchy is to teach and to interpret authentically the norms of morality to be followed in this matter, it belongs to the laity, without waiting passively for orders and directives, to take the initiative freely and to infuse a Christian spirit into the mentality, customs, laws and structures of the community in which they live."[33] Let each one examine himself, to see what he has done up to now, and what he ought to do. It is not enough to recall principles, state intentions, point to crying injustices and utter prophetic denunciations; these words, will lack real weight unless they are accompanied for each individual by a livelier awareness of personal responsibility and by effective action. It is too easy to throw back on others responsibility for injustices, if at the same time one does not realize how each one shares in it personally, and how personal conversion is needed first. This basic humility will rid action of all inflexibility and sectarianism; it will also avoid discouragement in the face of a task which seems limitless in size. The Christian's hope comes primarily from the fact that he knows that the Lord is working with us in the world, continuing in his Body which is the Church—and, through the Church, in the whole of mankind—the Redemption which was accomplished on the Cross and which burst forth in victory on the morning of the Resurrection.[34] This hope springs also from the fact that the Christian knows that other men are at work, to undertake actions of justice and peace working for the same ends. For beneath an outward appearance of indifference, in the heart of every man there is a will to live in brotherhood and a thirst for justice and peace, which is to be expanded.

1031

49. Thus, amid the diversity of situations, functions and organizations, each one must determine, in his conscience, the actions which he is called to share in. Surrounded by various currents into which, beside legitimate aspirations, there insinuate themselves more ambiguous tendencies, the Christian must make a wise and vigilant choice and avoid involving himself in collaboration without conditions and contrary to the principles of a true humanism, even in the name of a genuinely felt solidarity. If in fact he wishes to play a specific part as a Christian in accordance with his faith—a part that unbelievers themselves expect of him—he must take care in the midst of his active commitment to clarify his motives and to rise above the objectives aimed at, by taking a more all-embracing view which will avoid the danger of selfish particularism and oppressive totalitarianism.

1032

50. In concrete situations, and taking account of solidarity in each person's life, one must recognize a legitimate variety

of possible options. The same Christian faith can lead to different commitments.[35] The Church invites all Christians to take up a double task of inspiring and of innovating, in order to make structures evolve, so as to adapt them to the real needs of today. From Christians who at first sight seem to be in opposition, as a result of starting from differing options, she asks an effort at mutual understanding of the other's positions and motives; a loyal examination of one's behavior and its correctness will suggest to each one an attitude of more profound charity which, while recognizing the differences, believes nonetheless in the possibility of convergence and unity. "The bonds which unite the faithful are mightier than anything which divides them."[36]

1033 It is true that many people, in the midst of modern structures and conditioning circumstances, are determined by their habits of thought and their functions, even apart from the safeguarding of material interests. Others feel so deeply the solidarity of classes and cultures that they reach the point of sharing without reserve all the judgments and options of their surroundings.[37] Each one will take great care to examine himself and to bring about that true freedom according to Christ which makes one receptive to the universal in the very midst of the most particular conditions.

1034 51. It is in this regard too that Christian organizations, under their different forms, have a responsibility for collective action. Without putting themselves in the place of the institutions of civil society, they have to express, in their own way and rising above their particular nature, the concrete demands of the Christian faith for a just, and consequently necessary, transformation of society.[38]

1035 Today more than ever the Word of God will be unable to be proclaimed and heard unless it is accompanied by the witness of the power of the Holy Spirit, working within the action of Christians in the service of their brothers, at the points in which their existence and their future are at stake.

1036 52. In expressing these reflections to you, venerable brother, we are of course aware that we have not dealt with all the social problems that today face the man of faith and men of goodwill. Our recent declarations—to which has been added your message of a short time ago on the occasion of the launching of the Second Development Decade—particularly concerning the duties of the community of nations in the serious question of the integral and concerted development of man, are still fresh in people's minds. We address these present reflections to you with the aim of offering to the Council of the Laity and the Pontifical Commission Justice and Peace some fresh contributions, as well as an encouragement, for the pursuit of their task of "awakening the People of God to a full understanding of its role at the present time" and of "promoting the apostolate on the international level."[39]

1037 It is with these sentiments, venerable brother, that we impart to you our Apostolic Blessing.

From the Vatican, May 14, 1971.

Justice in the World
Synod of Bishops
November 30, 1971

Introduction

Gathered from the whole world, in communion with all who believe in Christ and with the entire human family, and opening our hearts to the Spirit who is making the whole of creation new, we have questioned ourselves about the mission of the People of God to further justice in the world.

1039 Scrutinizing the "signs of the times" and seeking to detect the meaning of emerging history, while at the same time sharing the aspirations and questionings of all those who want to build a more human world, we have listened to the Word of God that we might be converted to the fulfilling of the divine plan for the salvation of the world.

1040 Even though it is not for us to elaborate a very profound analysis of the situation of the world, we have nevertheless been able to perceive the serious injustices which are building around the world of men a network of domination, oppression and abuses which stifle freedom and which keep the greater part of humanity from sharing in the building up and enjoyment of a more just and more fraternal world.

1041 At the same time we have noted the inmost stirring moving the world in its depths. There are facts constituting a contribution to the furthering of justice. In associations of men and among peoples themselves there is arising a new awareness which shakes them out of any fatalistic resignation and which spurs them on to liberate themselves and to be responsible for their own destiny. Movements among men are seen which express hope in a better world and a will to change whatever has become intolerable.

Listening to the cry of those who suffer violence and are oppressed by unjust systems and structures, and hearing the appeal of a world that by its perversity contradicts the plan of its Creator, we have shared our awareness of the Church's vocation to be present in the heart of the world by proclaiming the Good News to the poor, freedom to the oppressed, and joy to the afflicted. The hopes and forces which are moving the world in its very foundations are not foreign to the dynamism of the Gospel, which through the power of the Holy Spirit frees men from personal sin and from its consequences in social life. 1042

The uncertainty of history and the painful convergences in the ascending path of the human community direct us to sacred history; there God has revealed himself to us, and make known to us, as it is brought progressively to realization, his plan of liberation and salvation which is once and for all fulfilled in the Paschal Mystery of Christ. Action on behalf of justice and participation in the transformation of the world fully appear to us as a constitutive dimension of the preaching of the Gospel, or, in other words, of the Church's mission for the redemption of the human race and its liberation from every oppressive situation. 1043

I

Justice and World Society

The world in which the Church lives and acts is held captive by a tremendous paradox. Never before have the forces working for bringing about a unified world society appeared so powerful and dynamic; they are rooted in the awareness of the full basic equality as well as of the human dignity of all. Since men are members of the same human family, they are indissolubly linked with one another in the one destiny of 1044 the whole world, in the responsibility for which they all share.

1045 The new technological possibilities are based upon the unity of science, on the global and simultaneous character of communications and on the birth of an absolutely interdependent economic world. Moreover, men are beginning to grasp a new and more radical dimension of unity; for they perceive that their resources, as well as the precious treasures of air and water—without which there cannot be life—and the small delicate biosphere of the whole complex of all life on earth, are not infinite, but on the contrary must be saved and preserved as a unique patrimony belonging to all mankind.

1046 The paradox lies in the fact that within this perspective of unity the forces of division and antagonism seem today to be increasing in strength. Ancient divisions between nations and empires, between races and classes, today possess new technological instruments of destruction. The arms race is a threat to man's highest good, which is life; it makes poor peoples and individuals yet more miserable, while making richer those already powerful; it creates a continuous danger of conflagration, and in the case of nuclear arms, it threatens to destroy all life from the face of the earth. At the same time new divisions are being born to separate man from his neighbour. Unless combatted and overcome by social and political action, the influence of the new industrial and technological order favours the concentration of wealth, power and decision-making in the hands of a small public or private controlling group. Economic injustice and lack of social participation keep a man from attaining his basic human and civil rights.

1047 In the last twenty-five years a hope has spread through the human race that economic growth would bring about such a quantity of goods that it would be possible to feed the hungry at least with the crumbs falling from the table, but this has proved a vain hope in underdeveloped areas and in pockets of poverty in wealthier areas, because of the rapid growth of population and of the labour force, because of rural stagnation and the lack of agrarian reform, and because of the massive migratory flow to the cities, where the industries, even though endowed with huge sums of money, nevertheless provide so few jobs that not infrequently one worker in four is left unemployed. These stifling oppressions constantly give rise to great numbers of "marginal" persons, ill-fed, inhumanly housed, illiterate and deprived of political power as well as of the suitable means of acquiring responsibility and moral dignity.

1048 Furthermore, such is the demand for resources and energy by the richer nations, whether capitalist or socialist, and such are the effects of dumping by them in the atmosphere and the sea that irreparable damage would be done to the essential elements of life on earth, such as air and water, if their high rates of consumption and pollution, which are constantly on the increase, were extended to the whole of mankind.

1049 The strong drive towards global unity, the unequal distribution which places decisions concerning three quarters of income, investment and trade in the hands of one third of the human race, namely the more highly developed part, the insufficiency of a merely economic progress, and the new recognition of the material limits of the biosphere—all this makes us aware of the fact that in today's world new modes of understanding human dignity are arising.

1050 In the face of international systems of domination, the bringing about of justice depends more and more on the determined will for development.

1051 In the developing nations and in the so-called socialist world, that determined will asserts itself especially in a struggle for forms of claiming one's rights and self-expression, a struggle caused by the evolution of the economic system itself.

1052 This aspiring to justice asserts itself in advancing beyond the threshold at which begins a consciousness of enchancement of personal worth (cf. *Populorum Progressio* 15; *A.A.S.* 59, 1967, p. 265) with regard both to the whole man and the whole of mankind. This is expressed in an awareness of the right to development. The right to development must be seen as a dynamic interpenetration of all those fundamental human rights upon which the aspiration of individuals and nations are based.

1053 This desire however will not satisfy the expectations of our time if it ignores the objective obstacles which social structures place in the way of conversion of hearts, or even of the realization of the ideal of charity. It demands on the contrary that the general condition of being marginal in society be overcome, so that an end will be put to the systematic barriers and vicious circles which oppose the collective advance towards enjoyment of adequate remuneration of the factors of production, and which strengthen the situation of discrimination with regard to access to opportunities and collective services from which a great part of the people are now excluded. If the developing nations and regions do not attain liberation through development, there is a real danger that the conditions of life created especially by colonial domination may evolve into a new form of colonialism in which the developing nations will be the victims of the interplay of international economic forces. That right to development is above all a right to hope according to the concrete measure of contemporary humanity. To respond to such a hope, the concept of evolution must be purified of those myths and false convictions which have up to now gone with a thought-pattern subject to a kind of deterministic and automatic notion of progress.

1054 By taking their future into their own hands through a determined will for progress, the developing peoples—even if they do not achieve the final goal—will authentically manifest their own personalization. And in order that they may cope with the unequal relationships within the present world complex, a certain responsible nationalism gives them the impetus needed to acquire an identity of their own. From this basic self-determination can come attempts at putting together new political groupings allowing full development to these peoples; there can also come measures necessary for overcoming the inertia which could render fruitless such an effort—as in some cases population pressure; there can also come new sacrifices which the growth of planning demands of a generation which wants to build its own future.

1055 On the other hand, it is impossible to conceive true progress without recognizing the necessity—within the political system chosen—of a development composed both of economic growth and participation; and the necessity too of an increase in wealth implying as well social progress by the entire community as it overcomes regional imbalance and islands of prosperity. Participation constitutes a right which is to be applied both in the economic and in the social and political field.

1056 While we again affirm the right of people to keep their own identity, we see ever more clearly that the fight against a modernization destructive of the proper characteristics of nations remains quite ineffective as long as it appeals only to sacred historical customs and venerable ways of life. If modernization is accepted with the intention that it serve the good of the nation, men will be able to create a culture which will constitute a true heritage of their own in the manner of a true social memory, one which is active and formative of authentic creative personality in the assembly of nations.

1057 We see in the world a set of injustices which constitute the nucleus of today's problems and whose solution requires the undertaking of tasks and functions in every sector of society, and even on the level of the global society towards which we are speeding in this last quarter of the twentieth centrury. Therefore we must be prepared to take on new functions and new duties in every sector of human activity and especially in the sector of world society, if justice is really to be put into practice. Our action is to be directed above all at those men and nations which because of various forms of oppression and because of the present character of our society are silent, indeed voiceless, victims of injustice.

1058 Take, for example, the case of migrants. They are often forced to leave their own country to find work, but frequently find the doors closed in their faces because of discriminatory attitudes, or, if they can enter, they are often obliged to lead an insecure life or are treated in an inhuman manner. The same is true of groups that are less well off on the social ladder such as workers and especially farm workers who play a very great part in the process of development.

1059 To be especially lamented is the condition of so many millions of refugees, and of every group or people suffering persecution—sometimes in institutionalized form—for racial or ethnic origin or on tribal grounds. This persecution on tribal grounds can at times take on the characteristics of genocide.

1060 In many areas justice is seriously injured with regard to people who are suffering persecution for their faith, or who are in many ways being ceaselessly subjected by political parties and public authorities to an action of oppressive atheization, or who are deprived of religious liberty either by being kept from honouring God in public worship, or by being prevented from publicly teaching and spreading their faith, or by being prohibited from conducting their temporal affairs according to the principles of their religion.

1061 Justice is also being violated by forms of oppression, both old and new, springing from restriction of the rights of individuals. This is occurring both in the form of repression by the political power and of violence on the part of private reaction, and can reach the extreme of affecting the basic conditions of personal integrity. There are well known cases of torture, especially of political prisoners, who besides are frequently denied due process or who are subjected to arbitrary procedures in their trial. Nor can we pass over the prisoners of war who even after the Geneva Convention are being treated in an inhuman manner.

1062 The fight against legalized aboriton and against the imposition of contraceptives and the pressures exerted against war are significant forms of defending the right to life.

1063 Furthermore, contemporary consciousness demands truth in the communications systems, including the right to the image offered by the media and the opportunity to correct its manipulation. It must be stressed that the right, especially that of children and the young, to education and to morally correct conditions of life and communications media is once again being threatened in our days. The activity of families in social life is rarely and insufficiently recognized by State institutions. Nor should we forget the growing number of persons who are often abandoned by their families and by the community: the old, orphans, the sick and all kinds of people who are rejected.

1064 To obtain true unity of purpose, as is demanded by the world society of men, a mediatory role is essential to overcome day by day the opposition, obstacles and ingrained privileges which are to be met with in the advance towards a more human society.

But effective mediation involves the creation of a lasting atmosphere of dialogue. A contribution to the progressive realization of this can be made by men unhampered by geopolitical, ideological or socioeconomic conditions or by the generation gap. To restore the meaning of life by adherence to authentic values, the participation and witness of the rising generation of youth is as necessary as communication among peoples. 1065

II

The Gospel Message and the Mission of the Church

In the face of the present-day situation of the world, marked as it is by the grave sin of injustice, we recognize both our responsibility and our inability to overcome it by our own strength. Such a situation urges us to listen with a humble and open heart to the word of God, as he shows us new paths towards action in the cause of justice in the world. 1066

In the Old Testament God reveals himself to us as the liberator of the oppressed and the defender of the poor, demanding from man faith in him and justice towards man's neighbour. It is only in the observance of the duties of justice that God is truly recognized as the liberator of the oppressed. 1067

By his action and teaching Christ united in an indivisible way the relationship of man to God and the relationship of man to other men. Christ lived his life in the world as a total giving of himself to God for the salvation and liberation of men. In his preaching he proclaimed the fatherhood of God towards all men and the intervention of God's justice on behalf of the needy and the oppressed (*Lk.* 6:21-23). In this way he identified himself with his "least brethren," as he stated: "As you did it to one of the least of these my brethren, you did it to me" (*Mt.* 25:40). 1068

1069 From the beginning the Church has lived and understood the Death and Resurrection of Christ as a call by God to conversion in the faith of Christ and in fraternal love, perfected in mutual help even to the point of a voluntary sharing of material goods.

1070 Faith in Christ, the Son of God and the Redeemer, and love of neighbour constitute a fundamental theme of the writers of the New Testament. According to St. Paul, the whole of the Christian life is summed up in faith effecting that love and service of neighbour which involve the fulfilment of the demands of justice. The Christian lives under the interior law of liberty, which is a permanent call to man to turn away from self-sufficiency to confidence in God and from concern for self to sincere love of neighbour. Thus takes place his genuine liberation and the gift of himself for the freedom of others.

1071 According to the Christian message, therefore, man's relationship to his neighbour is bound up with his relationship to God; his response to the love of God, saving us through Christ, is shown to be effective in his love and service of men. Christian love of neighbour and justice cannot be separated. For love implies an absolute demand for justice, namely a recognition of the dignity and rights of one's neighbour. Justice attains its inner fullness only in love. Because every man is truly a visible image of the invisible God and a brother of Christ, the Christian finds in every man God himself and God's absolute demand for justice and love.

1072 The present situation of the world, seen in the light of faith, calls us back to the very essence of the Christian message, creating in us a deep awareness of its true meaning and of its urgent demands. The mission of preaching the Gospel dictates at the present time that we should dedicate ourselves to the liberation of man even in his present existence in this world. For unless the Christian message of love and justice shows its effectiveness through action in the cause of justice in the world, it will only with difficulty gain credibility with the men of our times.

1073 The Church has received from Christ the mission of preaching the Gospel message, which contains a call to man to turn away from sin to the love of the Fathers, universal brotherhood and a consequent demand for justice in the world. This is the reason why the Church has the right, indeed the duty, to proclaim justice on the social, national and international level, and to denounce instances of injustice, when the fundamental rights of man and his very salvation demand it. The Church, indeed, is not alone responsible for justice in the world; however, she has a proper and specific responsibility which is identified with her mission of giving witness before the world of the need for love and justice contained in the Gospel message, a witness to be carried out in Church institutions themselves and in the lives of Christians.

1074 Of itself it does not belong to the Church, insofar as she is a religious and hierarchical community, to offer concrete solutions in the social, economic and political spheres for justice in the world. Her mission involves defending and promoting the dignity and fundamental rights of the human person.

1075 The members of the Church, as members of society, have the same right and duty to promote the common good as do other citizens. Christians ought to fulfill their temporal obligations with fidelity and competence. They should act as a leaven in the world, in their family, professional, social, cultural and political life. They must accept their responsibilities in this entire area under the influence of the Gospel and the teaching of the Church. In this way they testify to the power of the Holy Spirit through their action in the service of men in those things which are decisive for the existence and the future of humanity. While in such activities they generally act on their own initiative without involving the responsibility of the ecclesiastical hierarchy, in a sense they do involve the responsibility of the Church whose members they are.

III

The Practice of Justice

1076 Many Christians are drawn to give authentic witness on behalf of justice by various modes of action for justice, action inspired by love in accordance with the grace which they have received from God. For some of them, this action finds its place in the sphere of social and political conflicts in which Christians bear witness to the Gospel by pointing out that in history there are sources of progress other than conflict, namely love and right. This priority of love in history draws other Christians to prefer the way of non-violent action and work in the area of public opinion.

1077 While the Church is bound to give witness to justice, she recognizes that anyone who ventures to speak to people about justice must first be just in their eyes. Hence we must undertake an examination of the modes of acting and of the possessions and life style found within the Church herself.

1078 Within the Church rights must be preserved. No one should be deprived of his ordinary rights because he is associated with the Church in one way or another. Those who serve the Church by their labour, including priests and religious, should receive a sufficient livelihood and enjoy that social security which is customary in their region. Lay people should be given fair wages and a system for promotion. We reiterate the recommendations that lay people should exercise more important functions with regard to Church property and should share in its administration.

1079 We also urge that women should have their own share of responsibility and participation in the community life of soiety and likewise of the Church.

1080 We propose that this matter be subjected to a serious study employing adequate means: for instance, a mixed commission of men and women, religious and lay people, of differing situations and competence.

1081 The Church recognizes everyone's right to suitable freedom of expression and thought. This includes the right of everyone to be heard in a spirit of dialogue which preserves a legitimate diversity within the Church.

1082 The form of judicial procedure should give the accused the right to know his accusers and also the right to a proper defence. To be complete, justice should include speed in its procedure. This is especially necessary in marriage cases.

Finally, the members of the Church should have some share in the drawing up of decisions, in accordance with the rules given by the Second Vatican Ecumenical Council and the Holy See, for instance with regard to the setting up of councils at all levels. 1083

In regard to temporal possessions, whatever be their use, it must never happen that the evangelical witness which the Church is required to give becomes ambiguous. The preservation of certain positions of privilege must constantly be submitted to the test of this principle. Although in general it is difficult to draw a line between what is needed for right use and what is demanded by prophetic witness, we must certainly keep firmly to this principle: our faith demands of us a certain sparingness in use, and the Church is obliged to live and administers its own goods in such a way that the Gospel is proclaimed to the poor. If instead the Church appears to be among the rich and the powerful of this world its credibility is diminished. 1084

Our examination of conscience now comes to the life style of all: bishops, priests, religious and lay people. In the case of needy peoples it must abe asked whether belonging to the Church places people on a rich island within an ambient of poverty. In societies enjoying a higher level of consumer spending, it must be asked whether our life style exemplifies that sparingness with regard to consumption which we preach to others as necessary in order that so many millions of hungry people throughout the world may be fed. 1085

Christians' specific contribution to justice is the day-to-day life of the individual believer acting like the leaven of the Gospel in his family, his school, his work and his social and civic life. Included with this are the perspectives and meaning which the faithful can give to human effort. Accordingly, educational method must be such as to teach men to live their lives in its entire reality and in accord with the evangelical principles of personal and social morality which are expressed in the vital Christian witness of one's life. 1086

The obstacles to the progress which we wish for ourselves and for mankind are obvious. The method of education very 1087 frequently still in use today encourages narrow individualism. Part of the human family lives immersed in a mentality which exalts possessions. The school and the communications media, which are often obstructed by the established order, allow the formation only of the man desired by that order, that is to say, man in its image, not a new man but a copy of man as he is.

1088 But education demands a renewal of heart, a renewal based on the recognition of sin in its individual and social manifestations. It will also inculcate a truly and entirely human way of life in justice, love and simplicity. It will likewise awaken a critical sense, which will lead us to reflect on the society in which we live and on its values; it will make men ready to renounce these values when they cease to promote justice for all men. In the developing countries, the principal aim of this education for justice consists in an attempt to awaken consciences to a knowledge of the concrete situation and in a call to secure a total improvement; by these means the transformation of the world has already begun.

1089 Since this education makes men decidely more human, it will help them to be no longer the object of manipulation by communications media or political forces. It will instead enable them to take in hand their own destinies and bring about communities which are truly human.

1090 Accordingly, this education is deservedly called a continuing education, for it concerns every person and every age. It is also a practical education: it comes through action, participation and vital contact with the reality of injustice.

1091 Education for justice is imparted first in the family. We are well aware that not only Church institutions but also other schools, trade unions and political parties are collaborating in this.

1092 The content of this education necessarily involves respect for the person and for his dignity. Since it is world justice which is in question here, the unity of the human family within which, according to God's plan, a human being is born must first of all be seriously affirmed. Christians find a sign of this solidarity in the fact that all human beings are destined to become in Christ sharers in the divine nature.

The basic principles whereby the influence of the Gospel has made itself felt in contemporary social life are to be found in the body of teaching set out in a gradual and timely way from the encyclical *Rerum Novarum* to the letter *Octogesima Adveniens*. As never before, the Church has, through the Second Vatican Council's constitution *Gaudium et Spes*, better understood the situation in the modern world, in which the Christian works out his salvation by deeds of justice. *Pacem in Terris* gave us an authentic charter of human rights. In *Mater et Magistra* international justice begins to take first place; it finds more elaborate expression in *Populorum Progressio*, in the form of a true and suitable treatise on the right to development, and in *Octogesima Adveniens* is found a summary of guidelines for political action. 1093

Like the apostle Paul, we insist, welcome or unwelcome, that the Word of God should be present in the centre of human situations. Our interventions are intended to be an expression of that faith which is today binding on our lives and on the lives of the faithful. We all desire that these interventions should always be in conformity with circumstances of place and time. Our mission demands that we should courageously denounce injustice, with charity, prudence and firmness, in sincere dialogue with all parties concerned. We know that our denunciations can secure assent to the extent that they are an expression of our lives and are manifested in continuous action. 1094

The liturgy, which we preside over and which is the heart of the Church's life, can greatly serve education for justice. For it is a thanksgiving to the Father in Christ, which through its communitarian form places before our eyes the bonds of our brotherhood and again and again reminds us of the Church's mission. The liturgy of the world, catechesis and the celebration of the sacraments have the power to help us to discover the teaching of the prophets, the Lord and the Apostles on the subject of justice. The preparation for baptism is the beginning of the formation of the Christian conscience. The practice of penance should emphasize the social dimension of sin and of the sacrament. Finally, the Eucharist forms the community and places it at the service of men. 1095

1096 That the Church may really be the sign of that solidarity which the family of nations desires, it should show in its own life greater cooperation between the Churches of rich and poor regions through spiritual communion and division of human and material resources. The present generous arrangements for assistance between Churches could be made more effective by real coordination (Sacred Congregation for the Evangelization of Peoples and the Pontifical Council "*Cor Unum*"), through their overall view in regard to the common administration of the gifts of God, and through fraternal solidarity, which would always encourage autonomy and responsibility on the part of the beneficiaries in the determination of criteria and the choice of concrete programmes and their realization.

1097 This planning must in no way be restricted to economic programmes; it should instead stimulate activities capable of developing that human and spiritual formation which will serve as the leaven needed for the integral development of the human being.

1098 Well aware of what has already been done in this field, together with the Second Vatican Ecumenical Council we very highly commend cooperation with our separated Christian brethren for the promotion of justice in the world, for bringing about development of peoples and for establishing peace. This cooperation concerns first and foremost activities for securing human dignity and man's fundamental rights, especially the right to religious liberty. This is the source of our common efforts against discrimination on the grounds of differences of religion, race and colour, culture and the like. Collaboration extends also to the study of the teaching of the Gospel insofar as it is the source of inspiration for all Christian activity. Let the Secretariat for Promoting Christian Unity and the Pontifical Commission Justice and Peace devote themselves in common counsel to developing effectively this ecumenical collaboration.

1099 In the same spirit we likewise commend collaboration with all believers in God in the fostering of social justice, peace and freedom; indeed we commend collaboration also with those who, even though they do not recognize the Author of the world, nevertheless, in their esteem for human values, seek justice sincerely and by honourable means.

Since the Synod is of a universal character, it is dealing with those questions of justice which directly concern the entire human family. Hence, recognizing the importance of international cooperation for social and economic development, we praise above all else the inestimable work which has been done among the poorer peoples by the local Churches, the missionaries and the organizations supporting them; and we intend to foster those initiatives and institutions which are working for peace, international justice and the development of man. We therefore urge Catholics to consider well the following propositions: 1100

1. Let recognition be given to the fact that international order is rooted in the inalienable rights and dignity of the human being. Let the United Nations Declaration of Human Rights be ratified by all Governments who have not yet adhered to it, and let it be fully observed by all. 1101

2. Let the United Nations—which because of its unique purpose should promote participation by all nations—and international organizations be supported insofar as they are the beginning of a system capable of restraining the armaments race, discouraging trade in weapons, securing disarmament and settling conflicts by peaceful methods of legal action, arbitration and international police action. It is absolutely necessary that international conflicts should not be settled by war, but that other methods better befitting human nature should be found. Let a strategy of non-violence be fostered also, and let conscientious objection be recognized and regulated by law in each nation. 1102

3. Let the aims of the Second Development Decade be fostered. These include the transfer of a precise percentage of the annual income of the richer countries to the developing nations, fairer prices for raw materials, the opening of the markets of the richer nations and, in some fields, preferential treatment for exports of manufactured goods from the developing nations. These aims represent first guidelines for a graduated taxation of income as well as for an economic and social plan for the entire world. We grieve whenever richer na- 1103

tions turn their backs on this ideal goal of worldwide sharing and responsibility. We hope that no such weakening of international solidarity will take away their force from the trade discussions being prepared by the United Nations Conference on Trade and Development (UNCTAD).

1104 4. The concentration of power which consists in almost total domination of economics, research, investment, freight charges, sea transport and securities should be progressively balanced by institutional arrangements for strengthening power and opportunities with regard to responsible decision by the developing nations and by full and equal participation in international organizations concerned with development. Their recent *de facto* exclusion from discussions on world trade and also the monetary arrangments which vitally affect their destiny are an example of lack of power which is inadmissible in a just and responsible world order.

1105 5. Although we recognize that international agencies can be perfected and strengthened, as can any human instrument, we stress also the importance of the specialized agencies of the United Nations, in particular those directly concerned with the immediate and more acute questions of world poverty in the field of agrarian reform and agricultural development, health, education, employment, housing, and rapidly increasing urbanization. We feel we must point out in a special way the need for some fund to provide sufficient food and protein for the real mental and physical development of children. In the face of the population explosion we repeat the words by which Pope Paul VI defined the functions of public authority in his encyclical *Populorum Progressio*: "There is no doubt that public authorities can intervene, within the limit of their competence, by favouring the availability of appropriate information and by adopting suitable measures, provided that these can be in conformity with the moral law and that they absolutely respect the rightful freedom of married couples" (37; *A.A.S.* 59, 1967, p. 276).

1106 6. Let the governments continue with their individual contributions to a development fund, but let them also look for a way whereby most of their endeavours may follow multilateral channels, fully preserving the responsibility of the developing nations, which must be associated in decision-making concerning priorities and investments.

7. We consider that we must also stress the new worldwide preoccupation which will be dealt with for the first time in the conference on the human environment to be held in Stockholm in June 1972. It is impossible to see what right the richer nations have to keep up their claim to increase their own material demands, if the consequence is either that others remain in misery or that the danger of destroying the very physical foundations of life on earth is precipitated. Those who are already rich are bound to accept a less material way of life, with less waste, in order to avoid the destruction of the heritage which they are obliged by absolute justice to share with all other members of the human race. 1107

8. In order that the right to development may be fulfilled by action: 1108

a) people should not be hindered from attaining development in accordance with their own culture;

b) through mutual cooperation, all peoples should be able to become the principal architects of their own economic and social development;

c) every people, as active and responsible members of human society, should be able to cooperate for the attainment of the common good on an equal footing with other peoples.

The examination of conscience which we have made together, regarding the Church's involvement in action for justice, will remain ineffective if it is not given flesh in the life of our local Churches at all their levels. We also ask the episcopal conferences to continue to pursue the perspectives which we have had in view during the days of this meeting and to put our recommendations into practice, for instance by setting up centres of social and theological research. 1109

We also ask that there be recommended to the Pontifical Commission Justice and Peace, the Council of the Secretariat of the Synod and to competent authorities, the description, consideration and deeper study of the wishes and desires of our assembly, and that these bodies should bring to a successful conclusion what we have begun. 1110

IV

A Word of Hope

1111 The power of the Spirit, who raised Christ from the dead, is continuously at work in the world. Through the generous sons and daughters of the Church likewise, the People of God is present in the midst of the poor and of those who suffer oppression and persecution; it lives in its own flesh and its own heart the Passion of Christ and bears witness to his resurrection.

1112 The entire creation has been groaning till now in an act of giving birth, as it waits for the glory of the children of God to be revealed (cf. *Rom.* 8:22). Let Christians therefore be convinced that they will yet find the fruits of their own nature and effort cleansed of all impurities in the new earth which God is now preparing for them, and in which there will be the kingdom of justice and love, a kingdom which will be fully perfected when the Lord will come himself.

1113 Hope in the coming kingdom is already beginning to take root in the hearts of men. The radical transformation of the world in the Paschal Mystery of the Lord gives full meaning to the efforts of men, and in particular of the young, to lessen injustice, violence and hatred and to advance all together in justice, freedom, brotherhood and love.

1114 At the same time as it proclaims the Gospel of the Lord, its Redeemer and Saviour, the Church calls on all, especially the poor, the oppressed and the afflicted, to cooperate with God to bring about liberation from every sin and to build a world which will reach the fullness of creation only when it becomes the work of man for man.

Address of Pope Paul VI at Boy's Town in Rome January 1, 1972

On this the first day of the civil year, we are speaking of peace, celebrating peace, because peace is civilization's highest good, and because we must at the beginning of our work look to the goal, the final end that our work is intended to attain. Today is the day for plans, the day for resolutions. We want to be masters of time and spend it well. We want to give meaning to our lives. The value of our lives lies in the meaning we give them, the direction to which we stamp them, the goal, the aim at which we direct them. What is the goal? What is the aim? Peace.

1116

But what is peace? As we were saying, it is the good that, in this present temporal life, includes all the rest. It is order, true order, not just the order of external discipline, but the order that provides for the welfare of all men and the whole man. It is an order that presupposes that all have what is needed for life: food, clothing, housing, schooling, work, rest, respect, security, and so on. It is indeed a society that is free, harmonious, well-ordered, honoured all around, aware furthermore of life's destiny, and therefore cultured and above all else religious. For religion is the lamp of life: it, and it alone, if it is the true religion, the Christian religion, gives us light, reveals to us the meaning of our existence, and offers us the means to lead a good life and be saved, even beyond the end of the time granted us to live.

1117 We see at once that peace is something beautiful, but difficult. So difficult and complex is it that some think it a dream, a myth, a utopia. We, on the other hand, say that peace is something difficult; yes, yes indeed, very difficult; but it is possible, and it is a duty. That means that much work must be done in order to obtain peace. It does not come of itself. It does not stay of itself. It results from great efforts, from great plans. We must wish it; we must deserve it. We often think that his great plan of bringing order and peace to the world, of organizing society well, is a matter for those who govern the world and society. It is of course a matter for them, but not for them alone. Peace is everyone's good, and everyone must collaborate to keep it and make it advance. In some measure each and every one of us can and must collaborate. How is peace attained?

1118 But here another question comes up. Why is so lofty and difficult a talk being given here, to boys and young men like you, people already living in well-ordered, peaceful surroundings?

1119 We shall give you the answer. But the answer calls for another question: How is peace attained? Let us repeat that we are speaking of true peace, that resulting from true order. For there can be false order. Yes indeed! Order imposed by force, oppression, fear, threats, blackmail, abuse of other's weakness, a rooted habit of maintaining situations in which people suffer, unable even to raise themselves up and improve their own lives—is that true order? Is slavery true order? Is social misery true order? Is remediless, helpless poverty true order? Is domination and exploitation of the weak by the strong, or of the poor by the rich, true order? Is carelessness on the part of those who have responsibility with regard to neglect of others' rights or scandalous immorality, or tolerance of license damaging to the good of society true order? Where there is no reasonable effective law, or where it is not respected, is there true order? And so on! What we mean is, there are orders in appearance only, false orders, opposed to the common good, lawful freedom, the advance of the needy classes, and so forth; these do not deserve the beautiful authentic name of peace. They are tolerated or established disorders, rather than true balanced orders helpful for welfare and common progress. They are conditions capable of giving public life a certain fixity, and established custom, a resigned adaptation, but they cannot give rise to true peace.

1120 That much is clear. By now everyone has had some experience of it, and the conviction is spreading that there can be not true peace without—you say it—without justice.

1121 But another question comes up at this point, a hard one. However, it is a question that you boys, you young men especially, are able to answer; men especially, are able to answer immediately, as if by instinct, by intuition. What is justice?

1122 You have two answers in mind already. There is a justice of what is mine and yours, one defended by the famous commandment: You shall not steal. Nobody wants to be called a thief. And there is another justice, which concerns man's nature itself: the justice that wants every man to be treated as a man. You understand it immediately. Are all men equal? In substance, yes. Every man has his dignity, an inviolable dignity: woe betide anyone who touches it! It matters not whether he is little or great, poor or rich, white or black. Every man has his rights and duties, because of which he deserves to be treated as a person. Indeed, we Christians say that every man is our brother. He must be treated as a brother: that means he must be loved. (On the Day of Peace last year we meditated precisely on this reality: Every man is our brother). We can go further: the smaller, the poorer, the more suffering, the more defenceless, even the lower a man has fallen, the more he deserves to be assisted, raised up, cared for, and honoured. We learn this from the Gospel. But even one who does not believe in the authority of the Gospel feels this divine word to be right. This is justice! This is the way to order, that is to say, to man's rights and duties! This is where justice is, where peace is!

1123 So now we shall explain why we chose to come here, to be among you boys and young men for the celebration of the Day of Peace. It is because you, sooner and to a greater extent than others, have the sense of justice. Without much reasoning you understand that there is still need of justice in the world, even in our modern world. You understand it more than ever, precisely because you are people of the modern world. By that we mean that the social and cultural development that we have reached today has stirred up a human awareness that no longer remains insensitive to the disorders innate in our social arrangement. It cannot help noticing that progress itself produces maladies, which must be cured; it produces dangers of catastrophes, conflagrations, pollution, and the like, and action has to be taken against them. It is not just that you should be so! You understand that, and in your own way you are saying it; and you are saying it with a threat that can be fatal: there can be no peace without a new justice.

1124 As sons of the new generation, you immediately grasp the intrinsic necessity of this combination of two things: justice and peace. They go together. There can be no true peace without true justice. And just as justice must advance in keeping with the legitimate aspirations that have exploded in the evolved consciousness of modern man, so peace cannot be static. It cannot bolster up a state of affairs that takes no account of man's development and of his needs both old and new. It is a difficult equation, that between justice and peace. It will call for wisdom, prudence, patience, gradual advance, and not violence or revolution—these are other unjustices. It must instead be pursued with tenacity, self-sacrifice and deep sincere love for mankind.

1125 You young men, with your natural detachment from the past, with your easy critical genius, with your instinctive foresight, and with your ardour for human, noble and great enterprises, you can be in the prophetic vanguard of the joint cause of justice and peace.

1126 We tell you, too, these gentlemen who have wished to be present at the celebration, that we and you are carrying out of the Day of Peace, these illustrious qualified representatives of the world of those in responsibility—diplomats, political and municipal authorities (such as the Mayor of Rome), bishops and dignitaries of the Church, valiant lay people dedicated to the mission of good—these are with you.

1127 We thank you, boys and young men of this ideal town, for your welcome, and we thank all present for their significant support. With the wish of justice and peace, we bless you all from our heart.

Address of Pope Paul VI to the Diplomatic Corps January 10, 1972

We thank you, Mr. Ambassador, for the wise and kindly words that you, as Dean of the Diplomatic Corps accredited to the Holy See, have addressed to us, in your own name and in that of the other members of the Corps. You have synthesized the main lines of the document with which we commemorated the eightieth anniversary of the encyclical *Rerum Novarum* of our predecessor, Leo XIII, and you have well stressed what the Church is doing to make men more conscious of their responsibility, both on the individual and on the international level, to commit themselves to the task of uplifting society in a more just and true world, and to respect the freedom of others, by doing all they can "to build up active and lived solidarity" (*Octogesima Adveniens*, 47).

1129 For this we are grateful to you. We are likewise grateful to all of you, gentlemen, for this yearly encounter, which brings us special satisfaction.

1130 As you know, on the sixth of January is celebrated the solemnity of the Epiphany. This feast seems to us well suited for pointing out the value of your yearly visit to us, who feel ourselves so unequal to our task of representing Christ, God and Man, the Prince of Peace, the Author of Justice. The occasion enables us to speak to you, gentlemen, on a theme emerging from the reasons that underlie the presence of diplomats of the various States around the Vicar of Christ.

In other words, the occasion enables us to speak of the professional relationships between the Church and the civil world, or, to use openly a current phrase, on the so-called "policy of the Church." For this purpose we are immediately assisted by way the Council said on the matter. The Council spoke in affirmations so clear and luminous that from the very start they dispel any misunderstanding, let us say even any uneasiness, to which this phrase might give rise in the extremely sensitive minds of the men of today. 1131

The Church's policy? This is it, in the words of the Second Vatican Council: "The Church, founded on the Redeemer's love, contributes to the wider application of justice and charity within and between nations. By preaching the truth of the gospel and shedding light on all areas of human activity through her teaching and the example of the faithful, she shows respect for the political freedom and responsibility of citizens and fosters these values. . . It is always and everywhere legitimate for her to preach the faith with true freedom, to teach her social doctrine, and to discharge her duty among men without hindrance. She also has the right to pass moral judgments, even on matters touching the political order, whenever basic personal rights of the salvation of souls makes such judgments necessary" (*Gaudium et Spes*, 76). These words were echoed last autumn by the bishops gathered in the Synod. As you are well aware, the bishops chose, as one of the themes that were the object of the proposals recommended to us "Justice in the World" as a fruit of the Church's presence; and they expressed the hope that "every people, as active and responsible members of human society, should be able to cooperate for the attainment of the common good on an equal footing with other peoples" (III, *International Action*, 8c). 1132

Justice, gentlemen, is a value which resides in relationship in every field of living together: economic, social, political, cultural and religious. It is a value which involves all: individuals, families, social groups (whatever be the reason for their existence and operation), public powers and institutions working on a continental or world scale. All are therefore called to contribute to its realization, which is identical with 1133 the realization of genuine peace, each individual, however, making the contribution which corresponds to his nature and vocation. This is highly important and is also a demand of justice.

1134 Now we must ask ourselves these questions: what role does the Church have to play in this vast field, which involves all the political forces of the world? What is the task that she has the duty to carry out? What are the characteristics?

1135 We must first of all clearly affirm—though this may seem a paradox in view of the function that we have claimed for the Church in the international field—the Church's separateness from political activity as specifically understood. The Church's mission is different: it is essentially spiritual. In no way does she indulge in active political action, indeed she keeps herself distinct and aloof form it: "Render to Caesar the things that are Caesar's and to God the things that are God's" (*Mt.* 22:21). As was stressed by the Second Vatican Council, "the role and competence of the Church being what it is, she must in no way be confused with the political community, nor bound to any political system. For she is at once a sign and a safeguard of the transcendence of the human person. In their proper spheres, the political community and the Church are mutually independent and self-governing. Yet, by a different title, each serves the personal and social vocation of the same human beings" (*Gaudium et Spes*, 76). In like manner the Church shuns all violent action, for she takes as her sole model Christ, who was "gentle and humble in heart" (*Mt.* 11:29), she takes her inspiration from the Gospel law of love. She aims to persuade with her immeasurable store of hope, both present and eschatological, knowing that the law of true progress is not revolution but evolution and transformation. This presupposes a change from within, one whose fruits are lasting, for they spring from inner freedom, from the renewed vigour of resolutions that take their origin in "a love that transcends man" and therefore from " a genuine readiness to serve" (cf. *Octogesima Adveniens*, 45).

1136 Thus it is evident that this aloofness of the Church does not mean inaction and disengagement on the part of citizens, the laity, who are faithful to ecclesial life; in particular it does not mean absence from the life of the nation. Indeed they want to be the leaven in the flour (cf. *Mt.* 13:33). The Letter of Diognetus defines them, we may say, as the soul of the world: "Christians are to the world what the soul is to the body" (*Epistula ad Diognetum*, 6, 1:*PG* 2, 1173). As the Council stated, lay people, who draw their life from ecclesial communion, are called their "prophetic and royal" duty to being the forefront in collaborating "vigorously so that by human labour, technical skill, and civic culture created goods may be perfected for the benefit of every last man, according to the design of the Creator and the light of his Word. Let them work to see that created goods are more fittingly distributed among men, and that such goods in their own way lead to general progress in human and Christian liberty" (*Lumen Gentium*, 36).

1137 These therefore are the reason why the Church, though in herself and essentially aloof from political action, nevertheless claims a place in the civil world. In the first place, because she is made for men, and made up of men. By her profession of religious faith, and by her healing and sanctifying teaching, and by her upholding of the primacy of spiritual reality, she inculcates in them respect for the rights of each, and the fulfilment of the duties of each for the establishment of an organic and genuine brotherhood. The second and principle reason is that she is called to this mission by the mandate received from her Founder, that of saving man, communicating to him the Word that sets free and the Life that sanctifies, and thus of collaborating in the complete raising up of man.

1138 It is therefore obvious that the Church also cannot but feel herself obliged to make her own contribution to the realization in the world of peace in justice and justice in peace. And this contribution, as the constitution *Gaudium et Spes*, observes, she makes in particular by bringing "light kindled from the Gospel" and placing at mankind's" disposal those saving resources which the Church herself, under the guidance of the Holy Spirit, receives from her Founder" (*Gaudium et Spes*, 3).

1139 This is the reason for which we proposed in 1968 that in the whole world, and in particular within the Church, the

Day of Peace should be celebrated as a concrete testimony of that contribution to the building up of tranquillity of order to which the Church feels herself strictly obliged. We gladly take this occasion to express here also our heartfelt appreciation of the attention that individual Heads of State, the authorities and the peoples of their States, give each year to our initiative, and in particular, this year to our appeal, "If you want Peace, work for Justice," which, as you know, is the main theme of our message for the celebration of the fifth World Day of Peace.

1140 We must all work for this end, with complete sincerity, for the service of man. For the demands of justice, gentlemen, can only be gathered in the light of truth which is man—man, who is revealed in his essential components, in all his dimensions and in his lawful aspirations when he is seen in Christ, true God and true Man, in whom humanity finds it full expression and affirmation.

1141 The Church's contribution to the realization of justice takes concrete form firstly in an activity of educating its own members. This ceaseless and many-sided activity is aimed not solely at making men ever more conscious of the content of justice in its widening extent, but also at giving rise to, developing and strengthening the resolve to translate these demands into concrete terms of daily life. This will be done by conquering, through the power of love, the limitations of one's own selfishness and that of others, by influencing, in order also to humanize them, legal structures in cases in which these structures may have become an instrument of injustice.

1142 When necessary, therefore, the Church's presence—which finds its normal expression in positive forms, forms of advancement and exhortation—can sometimes become one of healthy criticism: it can be a touchstone encouraging a continuous testing as to whether the conditions reached really correspond to the ideal of justice and peace. The bishops meeting in the Synod noted this duty in their statment that educating to justice can "awaken a critical sense, which will lead us to reflect on the society in which we live and on its values," and in their recognition of the fact that in certain cases the mission of bishops "demands that we should courageously denounce injustice, with charity" (III, *Educating to Justice*).

In this regard, gentlemen, may we draw your attention for a few moments to what is perhaps the most disconcerting phenomenon of our time: the arms race. It is an epidemic phenomenon; no people now seems able to escape its contagion. 1143

The result is that world expenditure on armaments today already adds up to astronomical figures: every country shares in it; Great Powers and medium ones, even the weak nations or those of the so—called "Third World." 1144

What is most disconcerting is that this phenomenon is occurring at a time when men have become more aware of their own dignity and have a livelier sense of being members of the same human family; when individuals and peoples are more keenly aspiring to peace in justice, and when among the younger generation—for many of whom the human family is already a living unity—protests against the arms race are becoming ever more widespread. 1145

What is the explanation for so deep-rooted and distressing a contradiction within the human family, a contradiction between the growing sincere desire for peace on the one hand and the growing fearsome production of instruments of war on the other? 1146

There are some who see in armaments, at least for the great and medium Powers, as it were a necessity of their economic system, which is based on their production, if they are to avoid economic imbalance and mass unemployment. But such motivation is radically opposed to the spirit of civilization and still more to that of Christianity. How can it be admitted that there is no way of finding work for hundreds of thousands of workers other than setting them to making instruments of death? 1147

This is all the more true in that we are living in an era where there is an urgent need in many fields to undertake quite different constructive and beneficial works of vast proportions on a continental and world scale, in order to eliminate the scourges of hunger, ignorance and disease. For these unfortunately as yet, not all that the tragic human situation of so 1148 many of our brothers demands has been done, in spite of the generosity of so many people. There is likewise a need to safeguard goods that are indispensable for the lives of all, for example, the protection of the environment from the various polluting factor.

1149 It is further observed that there continues to be a widespread conviction that, while the policy of armaments cannot be justified in itself, it can however be explained by the fact that, if peace is possible today it can only be one based on a balance of armed forces.

1150 "Whatever is to be thought of this method of deterrence," declares the Constitution *Gaudium et Spes*, "men should be convinced that the arms race in which so many countries are engaged is not a safe way to preserve a ready peace. Nor is the so-called balance resulting from this race a sure and authentic peace" (*Gaudium et Spes*, 81).

1151 For this reason the realization of peace in justice demands—and attempts to attain this are already being carried out with courageous and wise initiatives—that the opposite road be followed: that of progressive disarmament. For its part, the Church, the People of God, cannot be enliven its commitment to educate man to have confidence in man; that is, to see others not as probable aggressors but as possible future collaborators, made capable of doing good for the building of a more human world.

1152 But ultimately this presence of the Church in civil society is not limited to being simply a presence. Where necessary, where possible, where required—always with respect for the exigencies of the Church's nature—this presence is also service: brotherly, humble and concerned service; for the Church, in carrying out her activity in the world, is not moved by ambition and earthly aims; she "seeks but a single goal: to carry forward the work of Christ himself under the lead of the befriending Spirit. Christ entered this world to give witness to the truth, to rescue and not to sit in judgment, to serve and not to be served," as was declared in that most widely quoted Constitution of the Council on the Church and the Modern World (*Gaudium et Spes*, 3). The image of herself that the Church presents today to the world is essentially that of being at the service of men, of being open to the world in order to serve it in its problems (cf. Y.M.–J. CONGAR, *Eglise et monde dans la perspective de Vatican II* in: *L'Eglise dans le monde de ce temps, T. III, Reflexions et perspectives*, Paris 1967, pp. 32 ff.).

1153 The Church wishes to serve the community of peoples by dedicating herself above all, as her essential and specific task, to educating consciences, to forming the hearts of men, who, when they accept the proclamation of salvation, know that they are loved by God, directed to him as the center of their lives, and united in him and for him in love for all their brethren, who are in his image and redeemed by his only begotten Son. It is an enterprise of universal and general scope, which by divine command knows no limit of people or time or space (cf. *Mt.* 28:18-20).

1154 In particular, furthermore, the Church offers her collaboration in serving mankind for the most urgent problems at given moments of history. Today she knows that this activity is especially to be directed on the level of culture and of social assistance, where the lamentable situations and tragic consequences of mankind's afflictions which we have already referred to are mainly to be seen. Thus the Church promotes the advance of culture also among the minority groups in individual nations (CONGAR, *op. cit.*, 59; vg. 53-62). This she does especially through fostering literacy, because "basic education is the first objective of a plan of development" (*Populorum Progressio*, 35). She strives that the most assiduous care be given to the field of education, so that schools may form the whole man for the professional, ethical and social responsibilities of life. This service, furthermore, is extended as far as possible to the various forms of assistance (the struggle against hunger, against unemployment, against disease and against social insecurity).

1155 Following the example of her founder, the Church cannot but be aware of the need to contribute to the realization of peace through these innumerable good initiatives. These initiatives of hers are undertaken in so many countries of the world, often in advance of, or in integration with, those fostered by civil society. They are aimed above all at relieving and raising up the poor, that is, those who are suffering or who are stricken with affliction or neglect or who are in a condition of weakness, of whatever nature this may be. Certainly, amid so much activity some defects or perhaps even some abuses and distortions may occur. But one cannot but feel amazed and saddened that such negative aspects, which are quite marginal, are taken as a pretext for discrediting the whole area of the initiatives that we have referred to. If they are evaluated with serene objectivity, these latter cannot but reveal themselves for what they really are: the testimony of an active love and the expression of an authentic human nobility, deserving rather of guidance and support than of indiscriminate aspersions.

1156 It is in this sense, gentlemen, that we speak of the "policy" of the Church: the Church's policy is nothing other than a keen readiness, a deeply felt demand to carryout her commitment, her mandate, and her vocation to announce the Gospel and to serve others. This was also the significance and the value of the recent Synod on the topic of justice; and, as we have said, the celebration of the Day of Peace has had, now has, and will have, no other purpose.

1157 The Church stands side by side with all nations that work sincerely for the raising up of their peoples; she does so at the cost of persevering service and even of sacrifice. She offers her collaboration to all, so that the strong desire, to be seen today at all levels, for greater respect for man may be no mere vague and empty Utopian aspiration, but may become a concrete reality. We invite everyone to work sincerely for this goal. We express the wish that the Church's offer may always receive a response in the good will and commitment of all States, while we pray the Lord to grant his aid where human strength fails.

1158 With these wishes we assure each of your nations of our great esteem and of our fatherly benevolvence. For each of them we desire the fulfilment of all the happiness they wish for, and we invoke upon all the blessing of God, without whom human fraility ultimately can do nothing. May he fulfil the aspirations we all share for the prosperity of the world, and may he grant to all your peoples to live in justice and in peace.

Message of Pope Paul VI
for the Celebration of the Day of Peace
January 1, 1973

You upon whose shoulders rests the responsibility for guiding the vital interests of mankind: statesmen, diplomats; and you, representatives of the nations of the world; men of philosophy, science and letters, industrialists, trade unionists, military men and artists, all you whose work influences the relations among peoples, states, tribes, classes and among the families of the human race; and you, citizens of the world; young people of this rising generation, students, teachers, workers, men and women; you who know what it means to search, to hope, to despair, to suffer; and you who are poor, who are orphans or victims of the hatred, selfishness and injustice that still exists in our world—do not be surprised if again you hear our voice. It is a voice that is weak but yet strong, like the voice of a prophet of the Word standing over us and filling us. We are your advocate who seeks not his own interests, for we are the brother of every man of good will, a Samaritan to whoever is weary and waits for help, a Servant—as we called ourself—of the servants of God, of truth, freedom, justice, development and hope. In the year 1973 we raise our voice to speak to you again of Peace. Yes, of Peace! Do not refuse to listen to us even though Peace is a theme about which you may be fully informed.

1160 Our message is as simple as an axiom: peace is possible! A chorus of voices assails us: we know it. Indeed it besets us and stifles us—peace is not just possible, it is real. Peace is already established, we are told. We still must grieve for the numberless victims of war whose blood has stained this century more than all centuries past, this century which is the highpoint of progress; the horrible scars of recent wars and civil strife still mark the faces of our adult generation; and even the still open wounds renew in the limbs of the new population a shudder of fear at the thought of the mere hypothesis of a new war.

1161 But wisdom has finally triumphed; weapons are still and are rusting in the armouries, useless instruments of a madness which has been overcome, worldwide and serious institutions guarantee safety and independence to all; international life is organized by now undisputed documents and instruments which immediately work to solve, through a listing of rights and justice, every possible controversy; dialogue between peoples is continuous and sincere; and in addition an immense intertwining of common interests brings about solidarity among peoples. Peace has now come to civilization. Do not disturb that peace, we are told, by calling it into question. We have other new and original questions which need to be treated: peace is a fact, peace is secure; it is no longer a matter for discussion!

1162 Really? Would that it were so!

1163 But then the voice of these spokesmen of peace, victorious over every contrary reality, becomes more timid and uncertain, and admits that there are truly unfortunate situations here and there, where war continues to rage fiercely even yet. Alas! It is not a question of wars buried in the sands of history; it is a question of wars here and now. Nor is it a question of passing episodes, but of wars which have been going on for years; nor is it a matter of superficial disturbances, because these wars weigh heavily upon the ranks of well-armed men and upon the unarmed masses of the civilian population. Nor are they easy to solve; they have exhausted and rendered impotent all the skills of negotiations and mediation. Nor is the general equilibrium of the world left undisturbed, since they breed an ever growing amount of injured prestige, of unrelenting desire for revenge and of endemic and organized disorder. They are not something that can be ignored, as though they will solve themselves with time, because their poison seeps into souls, corroding humanitarian ideologies, becoming contagious and transmitting itself to the youngest generation and carrying with it a fatal inherited commitment to revenge. Violence becomes fashionable again, and even clothes itself in the breastplate of justice. It becomes a way of life, abetted by all the ingredients of treacherous evildoing and by all the wiles of cowardice, of extortion and of complicity, and finally presents itself as an apocalyptic spectre armed with the unheard of instruments of murderous destruction. Collective selfishness comes to life again in the family, society, tribe, nation and race. Crime no longer horrifies. Cruelty becomes fatal, like the surgery of hate, declared legal. Genocide is seen as the possible monster of a radical solution. And behind all these horrible visions there grows through cold-blooded and unerring calculations the huge economy of arms, with its hunger-producing markets. And so politics resumes its unrenounceable programme of power.

1164 And peace?

1165 Yes, peace! Peace it is said, can survive equally in and to some extent exist side by side with the most unfavourable conditions of the world. Even in the frontline trenches, or in the lulls in warfare or amid the ruins of all normal order there are quiet corners, quiet moments. Peace immediately adapts itself to them and, in its own way, flourishes. But is this vestige of vitality, which we can speak of as true peace, mankind's ideal? Is it this modest and wonderful capacity for recovery and resistance, this desperate optimism that can slake man's supreme aspiration to order and the fullness of justice? Shall we give the name of peace to its counterfeits? *Ubi solitudinem faciunt pacem appellant* (TACITUS). Or shall we give the name of peace to a truce, to a mere laying down of arms, to an arrogant exercise of powers beyond revoke, to an external order based on violence and fear, or to a temporary balance of opposed forces, to a trial of strength consisting in the immobile tension of rival powers? This would be a necessary hypocrisy, with which history is filled. It is certainly true that many things can prosper peacefully even in precarious and unjust situations. We must be realistic, say the opportunists; the only possible kind of peace is this: a compromise, a fragile and partial settlement. Men, they say, are incapable of a better sort of peace.

1166 And so, at the end of the twentieth century, will mankind have to be content with a peace deriving from a diplomatic balance and from a certain regulation of rival interests, and nothing more?

1167 We admit that a perfect and stable *tranquillitas ordinis*, that is, an absolute and definitive peace among men—even if they have progressed to a universal high level of civilization—can only be a dream, not vain, but unfulfilled, an ideal, not unreal but still to be realized. This is so because everything in the course of history is subject to change, and because the perfection of man is neither univocal nor fixed. Human passions do not die. Selfishness is an evil root that can never be completely removed from man's psychology. In the psychology of whole peoples this evil commonly takes on the form and power of a *raison d'etre.* It acts as a philosophy of ideals. For this reason we are menaced by a doubt, a doubt that could be fatal: is peace ever possible? And in the minds of some this doubt very easily changes into a disastrous certainty: peace is impossible!

1168 A new, indeed an ancient anthropology arises: man is made to fight against man: *homo homini lupus*. War is inevitable. The arms race—how can it be avoided? It is a basic political necessity. And then it is a law of the international economy. It is a question of prestige. First the sword, then the plough. It seems as though this conviction prevails over every other, even for some developing peoples, which are struggling to enter into modern civilization, which are imposing upon themselves enormous sacrifices in the resources essential for life's basic needs, cutting down on food, medicine, education, road-building, housing and even sacrificing true economic and political independence, so that they can be armed and can inflict fear and slavery on their own neighbours, often with no more thought of offering friendship, cooperation, a common well-being, but showing a grim face of superiority in the art of offence and war. Peace, many people believe and say, is impossible, either as an ideal or a reality.

1169 Here on the contrary is our message, your message too, men of good will, the message of all mankind: peace is possible! It must be possible!

1170 Yes, because this is the message that arises from the battlefields of the two world wars and the other recent armed conflicts by which the earth has been stained with blood. It is the mysterious and frightening voice of the fallen and of the victims of past conflicts; it is the pitiable groan of the unnumbered graves in the military cemeteries and of the monuments dedicated to the Unknown Soldiers: peace, peace, not war. Peace is the necessary conditions and the summing up of human society.

1171 Yes, because peace has conquered the ideologies that oppose it. Peace is above all a state of mind. Peace has at last penetrated as a logical human need into the minds of many people, and especially of the young. It must be possible, they say, to live without hating and without killing. A new and universal pedagogy is gaining ascendancy—that of peace.

1172 Yes, because the maturity of civilized wisdom has expressed this obvious fact: instead of seeking the solution to human rivalries in the irrational and barbarous test of blind and murderous strength in arms, we shall build up new institutions, in which discussion, justice and right may be expressed and become a strict and peaceful law governing international relations. These institutions, and first among them the United Nations Organization, have been established. A new humanism supports them and holds them in honour. A solemn obligation unites their members. A positive and worldwide hope recognizes them as instruments of international order, of solidarity and of brotherhood among the peoples. In these institutions peace finds its own home and its own workshop.

1173 Yes, we repeat that peace is possible, since in these institutions it finds again its fundamental characteristic, which a wrong idea of peace easily makes one forget. Peace must be based on reason not inert and passive but dynamic, active and progressive according as the just demands of the declared and equitable rights of man require new and better expressions of peace. Peace must not be weak, inefficient and servile, but strong in the moral reasons that justify it and in the solid support of the nations which must uphold it. There follows an extremely important and delicate point: if these modern organizations which are to promote and protect peace were not fit for their specific function, what would be the fate of the world? If their inefficiency were to cause fatal disillusionment in the minds of men, peace would thereby be defeated, and with it the progress of civilization. Our hope and our conviction that peace is possible would be stifled, first by doubt, then by mockery and scepticism, and in the end by denial. And what an end this would be! One shrinks from thinking of such a downfall. It is necessary to repeat once more the basic statement that peace is possible, in these two complementary affirmations:

1174 Peace is possible, if it is truly willed; and

1175 If peace is possible, it is a duty.

1176 This involves discovering what moral forces are necessary for resolving positively the problem of peace. It is necessary to have—as we said on another occasion—the courage of peace. Courage of highest quality: not that of brute force, but that of love. We repeat: every man is my brother; there cannot be peace without a new justice.

1177 Men of strength and conscience, who through your collaboration have the power and duty to build and defend peace; you especially who are leaders and teachers of peoples: if ever the echo of this heartfelt message reaches your ears, may it enter also into your hearts and strengthen your consciences with the renewed certainty that peace is possible. Have the wisdom to fix your attention on this paradoxical certitude, devote your energy to it and, in spite of everything, give it your trust; with your powers of persuasion make it a theme for public opinion, not in order to weaken the spirits of the young but to strengthen them to more human and virile sentiments. Establish and build up in truth, in justice, in love and in freedom peace for the coming centuries; beginning with the year 1973, vindicate its possibility by accepting its reality. This was the programme which our predecessor John XXIII traced out in his Encyclical "Pacem in Terris," the tenth anniversary of which will fall in April 1973. And just as ten years ago you listened with respect and gratitude to his paternal voice, so we trust that the memory of that great flame which he kindled in the world will strengthen hearts to new and firmer resolutions for peace.

1178 We are with you.

1179 To you, brothers and sons and daughters in the Catholic communion, and to all united with us in the Christian faith, we extend once more the invitation to reflect upon the possibility of peace. We do this by indicating the way in which such reflection can be greatly deepened: through a realistic knowledge of anthropology, in which the mysterious causes of evil and good in history and in man's heart reveal to us why peace is always an open problem, always threatened by pessimistic solution and at the same time always encouraged not only by the obligation but also by the hope of happy solutions. We believe in the real, though often hidden sway of an infinite Goodness, which we call Providence and which rules over the destinies of humanity; we know the strange but tremendous reversibility of every human situation in a history of salvation (cf. *Rom.* 8:28); we bear engraved upon our memories the seventh beatitude of the Sermon of the Mount: "Happy the peacemakers: they shall be called sons of God" (*Mt.* 5:9); absorbed in a hope that does not deceive (cf. *Rom.* 5:5), we hear the Christmas proclamation of peace for men and good will (cf. *Lk.* 2:14); we have peace ever upon our lips and in our hearts as a gift and greeting and a biblical wish deriving from the Spirit, for we possess the secret and unfailing fount of peace, which is "Christ our peace" (*Eph.* 2:14). And if peace exists in Christ and through Christ, it is a possibility among men and for men.

1180 Let us not allow the idea of peace to perish, nor the hope of peace, nor the aspiration towards it, nor the experience of it; but let us renew the desire for peace in men's hearts, at all levels: in the inmost sanctuary of consciences, in family life, in the dialectic of social conflicts, in relations between classes and nations, in the support of initiatives and international institutions that have peace as their banner. Let us make peace possible by preaching friendship and practising love of neighbour, justice and Christian forgiveness; where peace has been cast out let us open the door to it through honest negotiations brought to a sincere and positive conclusion; let us not refuse any sacrifice which, without offending the dignity of any generous person, will make peace quicker, more heartfelt and more lasting.

1181 To the tragic and insuperable contradictions that seem to make up the grim reality of history in our day, to the attractions of aggressive force, to the blind violence that strikes the innocent, to the hidden snares that work to speculate on the big business of war and to oppress and enslave the weaker nations, to the anguished question, finally, that ever besets us; is peace ever possible among men? true peace?—to this question there springs from our heart, filled with faith and strong with love, the simple and victorious response: Yes! It is a response that impels us to be peacemakers, with sacrifice, with sincere and persevering love for mankind.

1182 Let this be an echo to our response, carrying with it blessing and good wishes in the name of Christ: Yes!

Letter of Pope Paul VI
to Leopoldo Benites
President of the XXVIII General Assembly
of the United Nations
December 10, 1973

Impelled by the consciousness of our mission to render immediate, living and actual to men the message of salvation which Christ proclaimed, we have not failed during our Pontificate repeatedly to offer our moral support to the United Nations' activities in favour of justice, peace and the progress of all the peoples of the world.

1184 As this eminent international assembly now prepares to commemorate the Twenty-fifth Anniversary of the Universal Declaration of Human Rights, we desire once more to express to you our great confidence and at the same time our firm approval of the continuing commitment of the United Nations Organization to promote, in an ever clearer, more authoritative and more effective manner, respect for the fundamental rights of man.

1185 As we stated on another occasion, the Declaration of Human Rights "in our view remains one of the finest titles to glory" (Message for the Twenty-fifth Anniversary of the United Nations Organization, *AAS* 62, 1970, p. 684) for your Organization, especially when one evaluates the importance which is attributed to it as a sure path to peace. In reality, peace and rights are two benefits directly related to each other as cause and effect. There can be no peace where there is no respect for, defence and promotion of human rights. While promotion of the rights of the human person leads to peace, at the same time peace contributes towards the realization of this aim.

1186 We cannot then remain indifferent in the face of the urgent need to construct a human coexistence which will everywhere guarantee to the individual, to communities, and particularly to minority groups, the right to live, to personal and social dignity, to development in a safe and improved environment, and to an equitable division of nature's resources and the fruits of civilization.

1187 "The Church, though concerned above all with the rights of God," as we said last year to the Secretary-General, Dr. Kurt Waldheim, "can never cease to be concerned with the rights to man, created in the image and likeness of his Creator.

1188 She feels herself to be wounded when the rights of one man are ignored and violated, whoever he may be and wherever this may occur" (Address to the new Secretary-General of the United Nations Organizations, *AAS* 64, 1972, p. 215).

1189 For this reason the Holy See gives its full moral support to the common ideal contained in the Universal Declaration, as also to the progressive affirmation of the human rights which are expressed in it.

1190 The rights of man are based upon the recognition of the dignity of all human beings and upon their equality and brotherhood. The duty of respecting these rights is a duty which is universal. The promotion of these rights is a factor for peace, and their violation is a cause of tensions and disturbances even in the international sphere.

1191 If it is in the interest of States to cooperate in scientific, economic, technological and ecological matters, it is even more in their interest to collaborate in the safeguarding and promotion of human rights. The United Nations Charter expressly obliges them to pursue this objective.

1192 The objection is sometimes raised that this collaboration of all States in promoting the rights of man constitutes interference in internal affairs. But surely it is true that the most certain means for a State to avoid external interference is precisely for it to recognize and ensure that in the territories under its jurisdiction fundamental rights and liberties are respected.

Without wishing to enter into the merits of the individual formulations, we consider that this outstanding document remains the question of the rights of the human person, and continues to represent the secure basis for the recognition of every man's title to worthy citizenship in the community of peoples. 1193

It would indeed be deplorable for mankind if this solemn pronouncement were to be reduced to an empty recognition of values or to an abstract doctrinal principle without a concrete and increasingly coherent application in the contemporary world, as you yourself rightly pointed out when you assumed the Presidency of this honourable Assembly. 1194

We are well aware that such application on the part of the public authorities is not without difficulties, but a concerted effort is required in order to ensure that these rights are respected and promoted by those with the power and the duty to do so, and that awareness of the fundamental rights and liberties of man is steadily developed among peoples. The cooperation of everyone must be sought to ensure that these principles are respected "by all, everywhere and for all" (Message to the Teheran Conference for the Twentieth Anniversary of the Declaration of Human Rights, *AAS* 60, 1968, p. 285). Is it really possible then without grave danger for the peaceful coexistence of peoples to remain indifferent in the face of the many grave and often systematic violations of those human rights clearly proclaimed in the Declaration as universal, inviolable and inalienable? 1195

We cannot conceal our serious anxiety at the persistence and aggravation of situations which we bitterly deplore—situations such as racial and ethnic discriminations; obstacles to the self-determination of peoples; the repeated violations of the sacred right to religious liberty in its various aspects and the absence of an international agreement supporting this right and specifying its consequences; the repression of the freedom to express wholesome opinions; the inhumane treatment of prisoners; the violent and systematic elimination of political opponents; other forms of violence, and attacks on human life, especially on life in the womb. To all the silent victims of injustice we lend our voice of protest and of en- 1196 treaty. But mere denunciation, often too late or ineffective, is not sufficient. There must be an analysis of the deep-rooted causes of such situations and a firm commitment to face up to them and resolve them correctly.

1197 It is encouraging, however, to note that the men of our time are showing that they are not insensible to the fundamental values contained in the Universal Declaration. Is not the ever increasing number of denunciations and of sensibility in the face of the multiplication of offences against the inalienable liberties of man both as an individual and in the community?

1198 We have learned with lively interest and deep satisfaction that this General Assembly, on the occasion of the Twenty-fifth Anniversary of the Universal Declaration, will hold a special session at which there will be proclaimed the Decade of Struggle against Racism and Racial Discrimination. This preeminently human undertaking will once again find the Holy See and the United Nations in close accord—albeit on different levels and with different means—in a common effort to defend and protect the freedom and dignity of every man and of every group, without distinction of race, colour, language, creed or any particular social condition.

1199 In this Message we also wish to underline the value and importance of the other documents on the rights of man previously approved by the United Nations. These documents, which came into being in accordance with the spirit and on the basis of the Universal Declaration of Human Rights, represent a sure step forward in the promotion and concrete safeguarding of certain of those rights, and seek to guarantee their careful and faithful application. Their ratification will ensure their effectiveness in both national and international circles. The Holy See gives its moral adherence and offers its support to the legitimate and praise worthy aspirations to which these documents are directed.

1200 While the fundamental rights of man represent a common good for the whole of mankind on its path towards the conquest of peace, it is necessary that all men, ever more conscious of this reality, should realize that in this sphere to speak of rights is the same as spelling out duties.

Thus we reiterate our good wishes to your noble and eminent Assembly, convinced as we are that it will continue tirelessly to promote among the Nations respect for and application of the principles solemnly enunicated in the Universal Declaration, with a sincere effort to transform the human family into a world community of brothers in which all the sons of men can lead a life worthy of the sons of God. **1201**

From the Vatican, 10 December 1973. **1202**

Message of Pope Paul VI
Issued in Union with the Synod of Bishops
October 23, 1974

Two anniversaries of special significance to the Church and the world have occurred since the synod of 1971: the 10th anniversary of Pope John's encyclical Pacem in Terris (1963) and the 25th anniversary of the United Nations Declaration of Human Rights (1948). Both documents remind us that human dignity requires the defense and promotion of human rights.

1204 We are gathered in a synod whose theme is evangelization, the proclamation of the good news of Jesus. While the truths about human dignity and rights are accessible to all, it is in the Gospel that we find their fullest expression and our strongest motive for commitment to their preservation and promotion. The relationship between this commitment and the ministry of the Church has been manifested in this synod in our sharing of pastoral experience, which reflect the transnational character of the Church, her entrance into the very consciences of people, and her participation in their suffering when rights are denied or violated.

1205 Reflecting on these experiences in light of the Gospel, we address this message on human rights and reconciliation to the Church and the entire world, especially to all in positions of responsibility. It is our desire to raise our voices on behalf of the voiceless victims of injustice.

1206 Human dignity is rooted in the image and reflection of God in each of us. It is this which makes all persons essentially equal. The integral development of persons makes more clear the divine image in them. In our time the Church has grown more deeply aware of this truth; hence she believes firmly that the promotion of human rights is required by the Gospel and is central to her ministry.

The Church desires to be more fully converted to the Lord and to perform her ministry by manifesting respect and regard for human rights in her own life. There is renewed consciousness in the Church of the role of justice in her ministry; Progress already made encourages us to continue efforts to conform ever more fully to the will of the Lord. 1207

From her own experience the Church knows that her ministry of fostering human rights in the world requires continued scrutiny and purification of her own life, her laws, institutions, and policies. The synod of 1971 declared that "anyone who ventures to speak to people about justice must first be just in their eyes," and failures in justice help us understand better the failings of other institutions and individuals. In the Church, as in other institutions and groups, purification is needed in internal practices and procedures, and in relationships with social structures and systems whose violations of human rights deserve censure. 1208

No nation today is faultless where human rights are concerned. It is not the role of the synod to identify specific violations; this can better be done at the local level. At the same time we desire by our words and actions to encourage those who work for human rights, to call upon those in authority to promote human rights and to give hope to those who suffer violations of their rights. We call attention here to certain rights most threatened today. 1209

The right to life: This right is basic and inalienable. It is grievously violated in our day by abortion and euthanasia, by widespread torture, by acts of violence against innocent parties, and by the scourge of war. The arms race is an insanity which burdens the world and creates the conditions for even more massive destruction of life. 1210

The right to eat: This right is directly linked to the right to life. Millions today face starvation. The nations and peoples of the world must make a concerted act of solidarity 1211 in the forthcoming United Nations Food Conference. We call upon the governments to undergo a conversion in their attitude toward the victims of hunger, to respond to the imperatives of justice and reconciliation, and speedily to find the means of feeding those who are without food.

1212 Socio-economic rights: Reconciliation is rooted in justice. Massive disparities of power and wealth in the world, and often within nations, are a grave obstacle to reconciliation. Concentration of economic power in the hands of a few nations and multinational groups, structural imbalances in trade relations and commodity prices, failure to balance economic growth with adequate distribution, both nationally and internationally, widespread unemployment and discriminatory employment practices, as well as patterns of global consumption of resources, all require reform if reconcilation is to be possible.

1213 Politico-cultural rights: Reconciliation in society and the rights of the person require that individuals have an effective role in shaping their own destinies. They have a right to participate in the political process freely and responsibly. They have a right to free access to information, freedom of speech and press, as well as freedom of dissent. They have a right to be educated and to determine the education of their children. Individuals and groups must be secure from arrest, torture and imprisonment for political or ideological reasons, and all in society, including migrant workers, must be guaranteed juridical protection of their personal, social, cultural and political rights. We condemn the denial or abridgement of rights because of race. We advocate that nations and contesting groups seek reconciliation by halting persecution of others and by granting amnesty, marked by mercy and equity, to political prisoners and exiles.

1214 The right of religious liberty: This right uniquely reflects the dignity of the person as this is known from the word of God and from reason itself. Today it is denied or restricted by diverse political systems in ways which impede worship, religious education and social ministry. We call upon all governments to acknowledge the right of religious liberty in words and foster it in deeds, to eliminate any type of discrimination, and to accord to all, regardless of their religious convictions, the full rights and opportunities of citizens.

1215

As we observe the Holy Year of renewal and reconciliation, recalling the great year of pardon (*Lv.* 25) and the gift of power of reconciliation offered us by Christ (*Lk.* 4:18-19; *Eph.* 2:13-17), we reassert that the Church must strive to be a sign and source of reconciliation among all peoples. People have a right to hope; the Church today should be a sign and source of hope. Hence the Church offers pardon to all who have persecuted or defamed her and pledges openness and sympathetic understanding to all who question, challenge and confront her. We call finally upon each person to recognize the responsibility which he or she has in conscience for the rights of others. Enlightened in our understanding of evangelization and strengthened in our commitment to proclaim the good news, we affirm our determination to foster human rights and reconciliation everywhere in the Church and the world today.

Address of Pope Paul VI
to the Participants of the World Food Conference
November 9, 1974

We are happy to greet you, the participants at the World Food Conference assembled in Rome under the auspices of the United Nations. There is no need to tell you that we share intensely in your preoccupations, for our mission is to carry on the teaching and activity of the Master from whom the sight of a hungry crowd prompted the moving exclamation: "I feel sorry for all these people; they. . .have nothing to eat. I do not want to send them off hungry, they might collapse on the way" (*Mt* 15:32).

1217 1. In the course of recent years, the situtation that we described in the Encyclical *Populorum Progressio* has reached still more alarming proportions, and what we said at that time has gained in relevance: "Today no one can be ignorant any longer of the fact that in whole continents countless men and women are ravished by hunger, countless numbers of children are undernourished, so that many of them die in infancy, while the physical growth and mental development of many others are retarded and as a result whole regions are condemned to the most depressing despondency" (45). The documentation prepared by your Conference describes the various aspects of hunger and of malnutrition, uncovers their causes and attempts to foresee their consequences, by recourse to statistics, market research and indices of production and consumption. In their accuracy, these indications take on a tragic eloquence: but what is it like then to come face to face, on the spot, with the realities that they represent? Recent disasters of every kind–drought, floods, wars–immediately give rise to pathetic cases of food scarcity. In a less spectacular but equally painful way, all are faced by the hardship created in the deprived classes by the rise in the cost of foodstuffs, which is a sign of their impending scarcity, and by the ever more marked lessening of international aid–given in the form of foodstuffs–which had powerfully contributed to the rehabilitation and progress of peoples after the last war.

1218

Lack of proper nourishment has long-term and sometimes unforeseeable effects. It has serious consequences on future generations and presents ecological and health hazards which cause damage to populations, more deep-seated than the maladies immediately apparent. It is truly painful to come to such a realization and to admit that, up to now, society seems incapable of tackling world hunger, although unprecedented technical progress has been achieved in all spheres of production. This is the case, for example, in regard to fertilizers and mechanization, and in regard to distribution and transport. A very few years ago, in fact, it was hoped that in one way or another the rapidity of the transmission of information and of goods, as well as the technological advances achieved, would be able speedily to eliminate the dangers of the ancient scourge of famine afflicting for a long period a nation or a whole region. That these hopes have not been realized explains the grave atmosphere surrounding your work. Hence also comes the hope mingled with anxiety with which the peoples of the world are watching your work. To use once again the words that we addressed in 1965 to the World Assembly of Youth gathered under the standard of the world campaign against hunger: "It is a drama of life or death for mankind, which must unite in order to survive and therefore must first learn to share the daily bread", which the Lord teaches us is ours, that is, for each and for all (allocution of 15 October 1965: *AAS* 57 (1965), p. 910).

1219

2. To you who are engaged in a task at once so difficult yet so rich in promise, we put forward two principles to guide your work: on the one hand, to face up to the data of

the problem without allowing yourselves to become bewildered in your evaluation of them through panic or through excessive timidity; and on the other hand to feel yourselves sufficiently stimulated by the absolute urgency and priority of the needs in question so that you will not be satisfied in any single case by delays or by half-measures. This Conference will not resolve everything on its own; it is not in its nature to do so. However, through the clarity and energy of its conclusions it will give the impetus to a series of effective and sincerely accepted commitments; or, contrary to the expectations placed in it and in spite of the good will of its members, it will have been held in vain. In order to beg you to avoid such a result, we do not hesitate to repeat, and adapt, the appeal that we made from the tribune of the United Nations: "No more war, war never again!" And we say to you: "No more hunger, hunger never again!"

1220 3. Ladies and gentlemen, this objective can be attained. The threat of hunger and the burden of malnutrition are not an inevitable destiny. In this crisis nature is not unfaithful to man. Its productive capcacity, on land and in the seas, remains immense and is still largely unexploited. While on the one hand fifty percent of arable land has, according to the generally accepted view, not yet been put to use, on the other hand we are faced by the scandal of enormous surpluses of foodstuffs that certain countries periodically destroy, because of the lack of a wise economy which would have guaranteed the useful employment of these surpluses. Here we have merely illustrations of a fact which no one challenges in its stark reality, even if some doubt whether it is possible to draw quickly enough from this potential what is needed to allay the hunger of expanding mankind. And when we speak of "allaying hunger" we are all in agreement that it is a question of more than just prolonging a minimal and subhuman biological existence. What is in question is "to provide each man with enough to live—to live a truly human life, to be capable by his own work of guaranteeing the upkeep of his family and to be able through the exercise of his intelligence to share in the common goods of society by a commitment freely agreed to and by an activity voluntarily assumed" (Speech to FAO, 16 November 1970: *AAS* 62 (1970), p. 831). It is of course with a view to this level of life that you have drawn up the calculations of your reports, according to which a campaign capable of feeding expanding mankind is possible on a technical level, but demands considerable effort.

1221

4. The present crisis appears in fact above all to be a crisis of civilization and of solidarity. A crisis of civilization and of method, which shows itself when the development of life in society that leads to an industrialized civilization is considered, that is to say, when too much confidence is placed in the automatic nature of purely technical solutions, while fundamental human values are forgotten. It is a crisis that shows itself when the accent is placed on the quest for mere economic success deriving from the large profits of industry, with a consequentail almost total abandonment of the agricultural sector, and the accompanying neglect of its highest human and spiritual values. It is also a crisis of solidarity, a crisis that sustains and sometimes accelerates the imbalances between individuals, groups and peoples, a crisis that is unfortunately the result—as is increasingly evident—of the insufficient willingness to contribute to a better distribution of available resources, especially to the countries that are lest well provided for and to the sections of mankind that live essentially on an agriculture which is still primitive.

1222

We thus touch upon the paradox of the present situation: mankind has at its disposal an unequalled mastery of the universe. It has means capable of making the resources of the universe yield their full potential. Will those who possess these means remain as though struck by paralysis when confronted with the absurdity of a situation in which the wealth of some can tolerate the enduring poverty of so many? Or a situation in which the highly enriched and diversified food consumption of some peoples can be satisfied at seeing the minimum necessary for existence doled out to all the others? Or a situation in which human intelligence could come to the aid of so many people afflicted by sickness, and yet evade the task of ensuring an adequate nourishment for the most defenceless sectors of mankind?

1223 5. One could not have arrived at that point without having committed serious errors of orientation, even if sometimes only through negligence or omission. It is indeed time to find out where the mechanisms have broken down, so that the situation can be corrected, or rather reordered from beginning to end. The right to satisfy one's hunger must finally be recognized for everyone, according to the specific requirements of his age and activity. This right is based on the fact that all the goods of the earth are destined primarily for universal use and for the subsistence of all men, before any individual appropriation. Christ based the judgment of each human being on respect for this right (cf. *Mt* 25:31 ff.). In examining the data of the problem, some facts are immediately evident. One of the most obvious causes of the present confusion is to be found in the increased prices of foodstuffs and of the materials needed for their production. An example is fertilizers. Their high price and scarcity are perhaps watering down the beneficial effects that were rightly hoped for from the "Green Revolution". Is not this a case intimately bound up with the fluctuations of a production based more on the calculations of profits to be gained than on satisfying the needs of mankind? The reduction of food supplies, which is also at the root of present worries, is at least partially due to certain commercial decisions which result in the lack of available reserves for victims of sudden and unforeseen shortages. A general food crisis is apparent and it is foreseen that it will worsen, while in some regions which are particularly well situated to ensure a surplus and emergency reserves the arable acreage has been reduced in an astonishing degree. Here we are face to face with the contradictions which characterize this acute crisis of civilization. At least when these phenomena are the result of ill-advised actions it must be possible to correct them and to put them right, provided that one employs the necessary wisdom and courage.

1224 We have spoken of the quantity of food necessary for the life of each and every man. But the problem of quality is equally important and also depends on an economic choice. In this matter the more industrialized nations are particularly concerned. In an atmosphere which is becoming polluted and in the face of the frenzied rush to create artificial substitutes, capable of quicker production, how shall we manage prudently to safeguard healthy nourishment with no serious risk for the health of the consumers, especially children and young people? And how, in these same nations, can we break with a consumption which is excessive because of the rich abundance of foodstuffs, which proves to be damaging to those concerned and which leaves others unprovided for? In this field too the situation calls for vigilance and courage.

1225

6. Other observations concern the flow of the resources which would allow the present situation to be remedied. All are agreed that multilateral and bilateral aid to the agricultural sector has been notoriously insufficient. In preparation for your Conference great care has been taken to list the requirements which would be entailed by the intensification of food production in the developing countries, by the drawing up of policies and programmes aimed at improving nutrition, and by measures for strengthening world food security. The sums arrived at by these calculations for the next ten years undoubtedly far surpass the effort so far made. But they are still quite modest in relation to the national budgets of the wealthy countries or those with international liquid assets. A recent crisis has modified the balance of these liquid assets but it has not reduced their volume. As far back as 1964, on the occasion of our journey to India, we launched an appeal to the nations, asking that, by a truly substantial commitment—the result mainly of a reduction in expenditure on arms—there be set up a Fund with the aim of giving a decisive impulse to the integral advancement of the less well-endowed sectors of mankind. Today the time has come for an energetic and binding decision along the same lines. Will such a decision—not yet obtained by a sense of solidarity or rather elementary social justice, which consists not only in not "stealing" but also in knowing how to share—finally be imposed by the perils of the present moment? Or will men obstinately close their eyes to their own fate and look for alibis, for instance an irrational and one-

sided campaign against demographic growth, rather than get down to the essential point?

1226 It is inadmissible that those who have control of the wealth and resources of mankind should try to resolve the problem of hunger by forbidding the poor to be born, or by leaving to die of hunger children whose parents do not fit into the framework of theoretical plans based on pure hypotheses about the future of mankind. In times gone by, in a past that we hope is now finished with, nations used to make war to seize their neighbours' riches. But is it not a new form of warfare to impose a restrictive demographic policy on nations, to ensure that they will not claim their just share of the earth's goods?

1227 We renew our full moral support for those who have repeatedly declared at international gatherings that they are not only ready to recognize the right of every man to enjoy the goods necessary for life but are equally ready, by agreeing voluntarily to a proportionate sacrifice of the resources and potential to place these goods effectively at the disposal of the individuals and peoples who need them, without any exclusion or discrimination. Thus we have the prospect of courageous reforms aimed at eliminating the obstacles and imbalances stemming also from out-of-date structures, which perpetuate inacceptable injustices or impede the dynamism of production and the impetus needed for an adequate circulation of the goods necessary for life.

1228 7. But the most widespread international aid, the increased tempo of research and of the application of agrarian technology and the most detailed planning of food production will have little effect unless one of the most serious gaps in technical civilization is filled as quickly as possible. The world food crises will not be solved without the participation of the agricultural workers, and this cannot be complete and fruitful without a radical revision of the underestimation by the modern world of the importance of agriculture. For agriculture is easily subordinated to the immediate interests of other sectors of the economy, even in countries which at present are trying to initiate the process of growth and economic autonomy.

Our predecessor John XXIII, who devoted a chapter of his Encyclical *Mater et Magistra* to agriculture, spoke of it in these terms: "The farming sector almost everywhere, is a depressed area, whether as regards the index of productivity or of the labour force, or as regards the standard of living of the agricultural rural populations" (*AAS* 53 [1961], p. 432). From this depression we shall only note two indices: first, the drop in the number of agricultural workers and sometimes also the reduction of cultivated land in the industrialized countries; secondly, the fact that in the developing nations of the world, although the great majority of the population work on the land, agriculture is the most underdeveloped of the sectors of underdevelopment. Whatever may be the value of the technical means employed, nothing will be achieved without the true reform represented by the rehabilitation of agriculture and the reversal of present attitudes towards it. 1229

It is the dignity of those who work on the land and of all those engaged in different levels of research and action in the field of agricultural development which must be unceasingly proclaimed and promoted. We said as much when we received, the FAO Conference in 1971: "It is no longer sufficient to stem the growing distortion of the situation of the members of the rural community in the modern world; it is necessary to make them an integral part of it in such a way that coming generations will no longer experience this debilitating feeling of being left aside, of being on the sidelines of modern progress where improvement is concerned." (*AAS* 63 [1971], p. 877). 1230

This will be achieved through a worldwide and balanced process of development supported by a political desire on the part of governments to give agriculture its rightful place. It is a question of putting an end to the pressure of the stronger economic sectors—a pressure which is stripping the countryside of those very energies which would be able to ensure high productivity agriculture. There must be established a policy which will guarantee to the young people of rural areas the fundamental personal right to a deliberate choice of a worthwhile profession, equal both in conditions and 1231 advantages to what only the exodus to the city and industry seems able to guarantee them today.

1232 8. Without any doubt, here again the reforms will have value only if individuals adapt themselves to them. That is why education and training have a fundamental role to play, by ensuring that proper preparation is not lacking. "The collaboration of the rural population is necessary; . . . agricultural workers must be faithful to the profession which they have chosen and which they value; . . . let them follow the programmes of cultural improvement which are essential if agriculture is to break out of its rooted and empirical immobility and adopt new forms of work, new machines, new methods." (Address to Italian Agricultural Workers, 13 November 1966: *L'Osservatore Romano,* 14-15 November 1966).

1233 What is especially important therefore to those afflicted with hunger is that governments should offer all agricultural workers the chance to learn how to cultivate the land, how to improve soils, how to avoid diseases in farm animals and how to increase yield. It is also important finally that, within the framework of an adequate preparation, agricultural workers should be granted the credit they need. In a word, it is necessary to give to the members of the farming community responsibility in their production and progress. Thus we find ourselves brought back to the notion of integral development embracing the whole man and all men. For our part we have never ceased to exhort humanity to work towards this goal.

1234 9. These are the thoughts which we offer you as our contribution to your work. They come from the awareness that we have of our pastoral duty and they are inspired by confidence in God who neglects none of his children, and by confidence in man, created in God's image and capable of accomplishing wonders of intelligence and of goodness. Faced with the hungry crowds, the Lord did not content himself with expressing his compassion. He gave his disciples a command: "Give them something to eat yourselves" (*Mt* 14:16), and his power came to the aid only of their helplessness, not of their selfishness. This episode of the multiplication of the loaves, then, contains many lessons that are applicable in view of the grave needs of the present moment. Today we wish primarily to re-echo this call to effective action. We must envisage the creation, on a long-term basis, of the possibility, for each people, of accurately ensuring its subsistence in the most suitable way. Nor must we forget in the immediate future to remedy, by sharing, the urgent needs that are experienced by a great part of mankind. Action must be united to charity.

1235

This progressive reorientation of production and distribution also involves an effort which must not be simply a constrant imposed by fear of want, but also a positive will not to waste thoughtlessly the goods which must be for everyone's benefit. After freely feeding the crowds, the Lord told his disciples–the Gospel relates–to gather up what was left over, lest anything should be lost (cf. *Jn* 6:12). What an excellent lesson in thrift–in the finest and fullest meaning of the term–for our age, given as it is to wastefulness! It carries with it the condemnation of a whole concept of society wherein consumption tends to become an end in itself, with contempt for the needy, and to the detriment, in the end, of those very people who believed themselves to be its beneficiaries, having become incapable of perceiving that man is called to a higher destiny. May our appeal then be clear and may it reach men's hearts. If the potential of nature is immense, if that of the mastery of the human genius over the universe seems almost unlimited what is it that is too often missing–in order that we should act with equity and with a desire for the well-being of all our brothers and sisters in the human race–except that generosity, that anxiety which is stimulated by the sight of the sufferings and the miseries of the poor, that deep conviction that the whole family suffers when one of its members is in distress? It is this solidarity which we hope to see inspiring your work, and, above all, your decisions. And we implore the Father of all light to grant you his grace.

The Church and Human Rights
Pontifical Commission "Justitia et Pax"
December 10, 1974

The twenty-fifth anniversary of the Universal Declaration of Human Rights (10 December 1948 - 10 December 1973) has afforded Christians another opportunity to reflect on their responsibilities in this area, both as Christians and as human beings.

1237 The Pontifical Commission Justice and Peace, in response to the Holy Father's mandate to promote justice and peace throughout the world, is especially committed to the struggle for the promotion and defence of human rights and to do all possible toward this end.

1238 2. This present document, which deals in a purposely limited way with the problem of human rights seen from a Christian perspective, is primarily intended to offer some reflections and practical criteria to the National Justice and Peace Commissions. It should be regarded as a "starting point" not as a finished product for its goal is simply to offer a few general considerations aimed at making the People of God more aware of their responsibilities and more ready to act in promotion and defence of human rights.

1239 3. First of all, the fundamental importance and the indivisible interrelationship between human rights and duties are emphasized. As the Holy Father affirmed in his Message to the United Nations on the occasion of the 25th anniversary of the Universal Declaration of Human Rights: "While the fundamental rights of man represent a common good for the whole of mankind on its path towards the conquest of peace, it is necessary that all men, ever more conscious of this reality, should realize that in this sphere to speak of rights is the same as spelling out duties."[1]

4. Modern man is so quick to defend his own right that he often seems to forget or at least underestimate the logical and real relationship which exists between the two aspects of the same right: *facultas* and *obligatio*, existence of right and its consequent responsibility. 1240

Man can demand complete respect for his fundamental rights only when he consciencіously respects the duties which such rights imply. 1241

5. The Encyclical *Pacem in Terris* demonstrates the psychological origin of the relation between rights and duties when it states that when man becomes conscious of his rights he must become equally aware of his duties. Thus he who possesses certain rights has likewise the duty to claim those rights as marks of his dignity, while all others have a similar obligation to acknowledge and respect those rights.[2] 1242

6. The fundamental correlation between rights and duties becomes manifest in two stages. The first stage occurs when the possessor of a right, aware of the right and the respect owed to it, also becomes aware of the duties which are inseparable from his right and of his obligation to discharge those duties. The same Encyclical states: "The natural rights with which we have been dealing [which refer to the fundamental rights of the human person set out in the Encyclical's preceding paragraphs] are, however, inseparably connected, in the very person who is their subject, with just as many respective duties; and rights as well as duties find their source, their sustenance and their inviolability in the Natural Law which grants or enjoins them. For example, the right of every man to life is correlative with the duty to preserve it; his right to a decent standard of living with the duty of living it becomingly; and his right to investigate the truth freely, with the duty of seeking it and of possessing it ever more completely and profoundly."[3] The second stage comes about in the relationship that exists between the right of one person and the obligation of others to recognize and respect it, since 1243

"in human society to one man's right there corresponds a duty in all other persons: the duty, namely, of acknowledging and respecting the right in question. For every fundamental human right draws its indestructible moral force from the Natural Law which in granting it imposes a corresponding obligation. Those, therefore, who claim their own rights, yet altogether forget or neglect to carry out their respective duties, are people who build with one hand and destroy with the other."[4]

1244 7. This reciprocity of rights and duties, besides being philosophically and juridically a unity of indivisible interrelationship, also provides men and women with a means of realizing integrally human, material and spiritual values. *Pacem in Terris* states: "When the relations of human society are expressed in terms of rights and duties, men become conscious of spiritual values, understand the meaning and significance of truth, justice, charity and freedom and become deeply aware that they belong to this world of values. Moreover, when moved by such concerns, they are brought to a better knowledge of the true God who is personal and transcendent, and thus they make the ties that bind them to God the solid foundations and supreme criterion of their lives."[5]

1245 8. Further, the present paper wants to call to mind that, in dealing with human rights, neither the defence of these rights nor the discharge of duties can be limited to the individual alone. It is necessary to open our minds and to widen the range of our actions beyond the sphere of the individual so as to include the rights and duties of whole societies with their groups and minorities.[6]

1246 To speak of human rights and responsibilities in fact means to speak not only of the rights and responsibilities of individuals but also those of the community.

1247 9. A study of the world today raises grave questions for serious consideration. A merely superficial glance is sufficient to recognize that the rights of the human person are systematically violated in an ever larger number of countries and communities. Racial and ethnic discrimination, the violent subjection of large majorities to the exercise of power by minorities, the persecution of dissident intellectuals, physical and mental torture, brutality and terrorism against defenceless peoples, deprivation of religious liberty even by force, widespread legalization of abortion, exploitation of migrant workers, extreme poverty, hunger and illiteracy, which are still the lot of large sections of mankind, are only some of the many examples of widespread offenses against human rights in various parts of the world, to the serious loss both of individuals and segments of society.

10. This state of affairs appears even more complex when one realizes that even people of good intent, who wish to exhort citizens to the defence of justice, in their exposition of injustices at times perhaps incomplete, often use the communications media in such a way that they frequently make the public less sensitive to injustice. 1248

Yet if we Christians wish to be peacemakers and to spread harmony among nations, we cannot "remain indifferent in the face of the many grave and often systematic violations of human rights."[7] "We cannot conceal our serious anxiety at the persistence and aggravation of situations we bitterly deplore."[8] 1249

11. This paper is not intended as an exhaustive handbook or guideline. Rather, as its prime goal, it seeks to encourage National Justice and Peace Commissions, and through them, to animate Christians, both individually and collectively, to engage in specific commitments and effective initiatives to redefine, defend and promote human rights on the national and international plane. 1250

12. Finally, this paper's aim, in the spirit of *Octogesima Adveniens* (no. 4), is not to assume the role of local churches but to stimulate them to act within the framework of their local and national situations, planning programmes that promote and defend the rights of the human person as an individual, a group or a society, according to the needs and circumstances of their countries. 1251

13. In 1963, Pope John XXIII in *Pacem in Terris* praised "an act of the highest importance"[9] performed by the United Nations, namely, the promulgation of the Universal Declaration of Human Rights. He traced the historic development which brought about this declaration on the dignity, liberty 1252

and equality of every human being, and, as the Church's Supreme Teacher, he took an unequivocal stand in respect to human rights. He was indeed restating the constant affirmation of liberty which Christianity from earliest times has ascribed to all men through the defence of religious liberty. This basically implied the gradual acquisition of complete liberty of thought, speech and assembly, now sanctioned by modern legislation. He was reaffirming the Church's adherence to all proclamations maintaining that everyone is a person endowed with rights and duties; and he was at the same time asserting that the effective realization of these convictions would depend on the emergence in history of an international community with fully developed and effective power to influence the behaviour of societies, if not of individuals.

1253 14. Human personality, through the emergence and exercise of conscience, is an ontological and psychological reality which is autonomous in the civil sphere. Within its own sphere its liberty and basic rights take precedence in certain cases over social and political structures. This insight is historically a typical affirmation of Christian social and political thought whose doctrinal formulation is intimately linked to the exegesis of the Biblical texts.

1254 15. Patristic and medieval Christian thought used various valid insights of ancient philosophy and jurisprudence, both Greek and Roman, and thus developed its social concept of man and of human personality. This led to the secure affirmation of the world as essentially personal, having as its centre the human person with all his rights, which thus provided the key to interpreting all of man's social and political life. Such thought reached its highest expression in the writings of Saint Augustine and Saint Thomas Aquinas.

1255 16. From the Renaissance onwards the numerous juridical, social and political problems which emerged, among other things, from the discovery of America and the first appearance of the modern State forced sixteenth century Christian thinkers to revise the doctrine of the human person and his basic rights. In this connection, it is enough to recall the works of Vittoria, Suarez, Las Casas and the whole Spanish school of law of that period.

17. However, there have been periods in the Church's history when in thought and action the rights of the human person have not been promoted or defended with sufficient clarity or energy. Today the Church, through her Magisterium and activity, represents an important factor in the field of human rights. Her contribution is keenly appreciated and her comment sought by civil society in the common effort to make the full affirmation of man's fundamental rights truly effective and operative. But we must recognize that this was not always so. 1256

There have been times when the historic evolution of the affirmation of human rights has been obscured both civilly and ecclesially by arguments and institutional structures which have impeded this process.[10] 1257

18. As we are well aware, the Church's attitude towards human rights during the last two centuries too frequently has been characterized by hesitations, objections, reservations and, on occasion, even vehement reaction on the Catholic side to any declaration of human rights made from the standpoint of liberalism and laicism. 1258

The profound changes kindled by the new ideals of liberty, progress and the defence of human or civic rights by the Illuminists and the French Revolution, the secularization of society in reaction to clericalism, the urgent need to resist indifferentism, naturalism and above all a totalitarian and anticlerical laicism (liberal in thought but hostile to any form of religion) were often factors in motivating Popes to adopt attitudes of caution, negation, and sometimes even of positive hostility and condemnation.[11] 1259

19. Then during the nineteenth century the Church's Magisterium gradually took up the theme of human rights, making needed interpretations of the "new freedoms"[12] proclaimed in the constitutions of modern States and inspired by the subjectivism and agnosticism of the French Revolution. These positions have often been viewed as a rejection of the modern world and its culture by the Church. 1260

20. A turning-point (albeit on a small scale) in the Church's attitude occurred during the pontificate of Leo XIII. In a series of encyclicals he examined the problems of the modern 1261

State and initiated a more open treatment of fundamental human rights and, more especially, the citizen's right to engage in political action.

1262 In the Thomist tradition, he recognized the State as existing in its own right and as enjoying a specific autonomy in its own order which implied a legitimate independence of ecclesiastical authority in its own field. While continuing to reaffirm the spiritual supremacy of the Church in tones which may seem to us over-insistent, Leo XIII undertook in his three great Encyclicals *Immortale Dei, Sapientiae Christianae* and *Libertas* a rehabilitation of the State and of the temporal order. Thus he incorporated whatever was true or healty in the liberal institutions, such as the juridical incarnation of "human rights" formulated in 1789, into a Catholic vision of the State and of society.

1263 21. Especially in his Encyclical *Libertas*, Leo XII began the intricate work of refurbishing those ideas of Christian origin which were included among the fundamental aspirations of modern lay democracies. By so doing he paved the way within the Church to the recent clear and decisive affirmations made by the Magisterium on the fundamental rights of the human person.

1264 22. In *Rerum Novarum*, Leo XIII placed particular emphasis on the social context of human rights, emphasizing the responsibility of public authority to insure that justice be observed in all labour relations.

1265 In this Encyclical, which is "rightly acknowledged as the *Magna Charta* of the economico-social reconstruction of the modern era,"[13] "whose message continues to inspire action for social justice,"[14] and which is an example of "the Church's prudent yet brave and generous concern for labour,"[15] Leo XIII first deplores the state of misery to which workers had been reduced and then makes their cause his own, pointing out very clearly the rights and duties both of employers and employees. He lays great emphasis on workers' rights and claims for workers the right to work, the right to a just wage, the right to a fair amount of rest, the safety of women and children in factories, and the right of association. Above all he affirms that workers are entitled to respect and dignity as human persons,[16] ennobled by Christian character.

23. Human rights receive forceful vindication in *Quadragesimo Anno*, where Pius XI sets out not merely a positive formulation of human rights but also the general requirements of the common good with the duty of public authority to ensure proper development of social and economic conditions as the pre-condition for the actual realization of the variety of human rights. Again in *Divini Redemptoris* he offers a synthesis of the Church teaching on the rights of the human person.[17] Nor should we overlook the same Pope's brave and vigorous defence of "freedom for conscience," of the natural rights of man and of the family against totalitarian Fascism (*Non abbiamo bisogno*), Nazism (*Mit brennender Sorge*), Soviet Communism (*Divini Redemptoris*), and of the Mexican regime of 1917-1937 (*Nos es muy conocida*). Thus it is useful to recall his fight against the State's monopoly of education (*Divini illius Magistri*); his condemnation of Nazi racism and of sterilization in itself or for political purposes; his statement on property having both an individual and a social character, on safeguarding the rights and dignity of labour, on the need for family allowances and on the advisability of effective trade or craft unions. 1266

24. With Pius XII the Church's Magisterium takes on an attitude and a positive defence even more sharply focussed on human rights. 1267

His messages in which he denounces violations of fundamental human rights, defends the cultural and political rights of the human person, and puts forward concrete proposals for the reconstruction of the human community after the havoc of the war greatly influenced world public opinion in that historical epoch. 1268

His Christmas Broadcasts of 1942 and 1944 are particularly concerned with basic human rights. 1269

In the first of these broadcasts Pius XII pleaded that the God-given dignity invested in man should be restored to the human person. Man should uphold respect for "the following fundamental rights: the right to maintain and develop one's corporal, intellectual and moral life and especially the right 1270 to religious formation and education; the right to worship God in private and public and to carry on religious works of charity; the right to marry and to achieve the aim of married life; the right to conjugal and domestic society; the right to work as the indispensable means toward the maintenance of family life; the right to free choice of a state of life, and hence, too, of the priesthood or religious life; the right to the use of material goods, in keeping with his duties and social limitations."[18]

1271 In his 1944 Christmas Broadcast Pius XII defends the right of all citizens to a share in public life and in the government of the State.[19]

1272 In other discourses he upholds such specific rights as the right of every family to adequate living space;[20] the elementary, primordial right of parents to choose which type of education to give their children; the right to life and to bodily and psychological health.

1273 Nor can it be forgotten that during the war years and in those immediately after, Pope Pius XII sought to create a peace which would be consonant with the dignity of the human person and with true equality among men and nations. He repeatedly called for the formation of a world-wide international agency to maintain the peace and to construct international institutions dedicated to safeguarding the vital fundamental rights of individuals and of whole peoples, and to prevent any possible usurpation of these rights.[21]

1274 In fact, in his speeches and writings Pius XII explored and expounded in detail a new analysis of the whole doctrine of human rights, especially in the social, political and cultural fields. He underlined the human person as subject, object and foundation for the reconstruction of the human community on the national and international plane.[22]

1275 25. During the pontificates of John XXIII and of Paul VI, especially in *Mater et Magistra, Pace in Terris,*[23] *Populorum Progressio*, and *Octogesima Adveniens*, there were further developed the central place and the dignity of the human person; the rights not only of individuals but also of peoples to the total progress of the civil community on the social, economic and human plane; the urgent need to make these human rights effective and the necessity for organic political action to defend and promote them both on the national and the international level.

26. At this historic moment, the fathers of the Second Vatical Council echoed the Supreme Pastor. 1276

The Pastoral Constitution *Gaudium et Spes* is clear proof that throughout the universal Church concern with the nature of man, his dignity and his role in the world and in contemporary history has reached a new depth, a new maturity. Greater stress is laid on the fact that human promotion cannot be realized through the affirmation of fundamental human rights, except in a civil community which is organized both juridically and politically. 1277

Man as a complete being is the key to the whole argument of the Pastoral Constitution. It proclaims the supreme grandeur of man's vocation, of his dignity, his fundamental rights, and affirms that there is a divine seed active within him. In this text the Council offers the whole of mankind the sincere cooperation of the Church in the attempt to establish the universal brotherhood which expresses his vocation.[24] 1278

27. Following the line and spirit of the Council, the Synod of Bishops in 1971 produced the document *Justice in the World* which states that only through service to the civil community can the People of God fulfil their duty and make a truly constructive and effective contribution to human liberation in the spirit of the Gospel. "Action on behalf of justice and participation in the transformation of the world fully appear to us as a constitutive dimension of the preaching of the Gospel, or, in other words, of the Church's mission for the redemption of the human race and its liberation from every oppressive situation."[25] 1279

In the latest Synod (27 September - 26 October 1974) on *Evangelization and the Contemporary World*, the Bishops, fully conscious of their pastoral duty to proclaim the Good News, issued a message in which they publicly affirmed "their determination to promote human rights and reconciliation everywhere, in the Church and in the contemporary world."[26] After stating that the Church "firmly . . . believes that the 1280 promotion of human rights is a requirement of the Gospel and as such must occupy a central position in its ministry,"[27] the declaration goes on to specify certain rights which are today more directly menaced, such as the right to live and to have enough to eat, the right to religious liberty, social and economic rights, and political and cultural rights. It encourages all those who work in defence of human rights; it invites public authorities to promote justice and to give hope to those who are the victims of violations, and insists that "reconciliation is impossible without justice."[28]

1281 28. This shows that the affirmation and defence of human rights is ever more closely linked with the need to transform social, political and economic structures. Thus the very terms in which the Magisterium defends the fundamental rights of the human person become more and more practical, explicit and incisive in relation to current social and political realities.

1282 29. No less important are the teachings in the human rights field undertaken by bishops and Episcopal Conferences throughout the world in conformity with the Church's Magisterium. National Commissions not only have a role of studying and reflecting upon their bishops' teaching but also of reciprocating and sharing their research, studies and experiences in order to promote practical action in defence of the dignity of the human person and of his fundamental rights.

1283 30. The Church then has flung open her windows. The Second Vatical Council formally approved this "opening" with the Constitutions *Dignitatis Humanae Personae* and *Gaudium et Spes*. This process shows the following stages: 1. radical changes in social structures enabling the Church to learn something of these changes in themselves; 2. the Industrial Revolution and the consequent advance of the common man calling out to the Church to defend workers' rights and the dignity of the human person (Leo XIII); 3. the rise of totalitarian States drawing the Church to a renewed consciousness of her duty to protect the natural and fundamental rights; 4. papal insistence that the old moral and paternalistic concept of the State be replaced by a juridical and constitutional one in which the true subject of politics is the human person, the citizen (Pius XII); 5. the demands and the prospects of the post World War II situation moving the Church yet further towards a recognition of the dignity of the human person and of his rights as the only sure foundation for justice (Pius XII, John XXIII, Paul VI).

31. Through all these tragedies the Church has come to realize not only the fact of human rights but also the fact that her own liberty is intimately bound up with respect for the inviolable rights of the human person. In *Gaudium et Spes* the Church, quite conscious of what she has given to the world, has recognized "how richly she has herself profited by the history and development of humanity";[29] she has further admitted that "in working out her relationship with the world she always has great need of the ripening which comes with the experience of the centuries."[30] 1284

32. In the last analysis the Church has widened the scope of her defensive action beyond the boundaries of Christendom—protecting her rights and her people—to the whole "society of man," safeguarding the rights of all on the basis of common human nature and natural law. 1285

33. Without exaggeration, one could say that the Church, especially in the second half of the twentieth century, has acquired an important position of responsibility towards human society and human rights, by way of spiritual leaven, claiming on behalf of all men, individually and collectively, an order of justice and love. Human rights, now sanctioned by the Universal Declaration, find in the Church's Magisterium not only a general consensus but a deeper understanding and a fuller expression that at times surpasses anything before it. 1286

34. Stimulated by the rapid advance of modern culture, the Church has enriched her own comprehensive notion of the rights of the human person, always fully human and open to his supernatural vocation, so that, without in any way weakening her condemnation of false rights, she has adopted an attitude which is positive and encouraging rather than negative and disapproving, and now supports and even reinforces the historical process, as it is. 1287

35. A function of the Church today is to guide and stimulate people concretely by means of the Magisterium to affirm the inalienable values of the person in social and political 1288

structures. This is the clear sign of the essential, and indeed irreplaceable, foundation of human rights.

1289 36. The teaching of the Magisterium on fundamental human rights is based in the first place or is suggested by the inherent requirements of human nature itself on the level of reason and within the sphere of Natural Law. Let us briefly recall some of the more important points.

1290 37. Recognizing that the social order is directed towards the good of the person,[31] that everyone is a person endowed with intelligence and free will[32] and that the human person is and must be the source, subject and goal of all social institutions,[33] the Magisterium affirms:

1) that any men are equal in nobility, dignity and nature,[34] without any distinction of race,[35] sex,[36] or religion;[37]

2) that everyone therefore has the same fundamental rights and duties;[38]

3) that the rights of the human person are inviolable, inalienable and universal;[39]

4) that everyone has a right to existence, to bodily integrity and well-being, to everything necessary to maintain a decent standard of living, such as food, clothing and shelter, means of subsistence and any other services indispensable to social security;[40]

5) that everyone has a right to a good reputation and respect,[41] to protection of privacy[42] and to an honest representation.[43]

6) that everyone has a right to act in accordance with the right norms of his own conscience[44] and to investigate the truth freely following the ways and means proper to man.[45] This may in certain circumstances involve the right of dissent for reasons of conscience from some rules of society;[46]

7) that everyone has the right to express his ideas and opinions freely[47] and to be correctly informed about public events;[48]

8) that everyone has the right to worship God according to the right norm of his own conscience, to practise his religion both in private and in public, and to enjoy religious liberty;[49]

9) that the person's fundamental right is to have all his rights safeguarded by law; namely, to a protection that is impartial, inspired by the true norm of justice, and at the same time effective.[50] This means that all are equal before the law[51] and any judicial procedure should give the accused the right to know his accusers and also the right to a proper defence;[52]

10) finally, the Magisterium asserts that fundamental human rights are inseparably interconnected in the very person who is their subject with just as many respective duties; and that rights as well as duties find their source, their sustenance and their inviolability in the Natural Law which grants or enjoins them.[53]

1291

38. In the context of civil, political, economic, social and cultural rights also, the Church's Magisterium throws light on some other fundamental liberties—rights of association, marriage and family, participation in public affairs, work, private property, education, and the development of peoples—which constitute the key sectors of all individual or collective action. According to this teaching:

1) all men have the right of free assembly and association,[54] as also the right to structure organizations according to the will of their members in order to achieve their desired objectives;[55]

2) every human being has the right to freedom of movement and of residence within the confines of his own country, and also the right to emigrate to other countries and to take up residence there;[56] special consideration and assistance should be extended to exiles and refugees,[57] in accordance with the humanitarian principle of the right to asylum;

3) every human being has the right to choose freely the state of life which he prefers, and to found a family with equal rights and duties for husband and wife or alternatively, the right to follow a vocation to the priesthood or the religious life;[58]

4) the family, grounded on marriage freely contracted, monogamous and indissoluble, is the primary and essential cell of human society, and must therefore be accorded every economic, social, cultural and moral consideration which will strengthen its stability, facilitate the fulfilment of its specific mission, and ensure an ambiance for its healthy development;[59]

5) parents have the right to beget children, and prior rights in their support and education within the family;[60]

6) children and young people have a special right to education and to morally correct conditions of life and communications media;[61]

7) women are entitled to the respect due to the dignity of the human person and must therefore be granted equality with men to participate in the educational, cultural, economic, social and political life of the state;[62]

8) old people, orphans, the sick, and those who are rejected have the right to such care and assistance as may be required;[63]

9) from the dignity of the human person derives everyone's right to take an active part in public affairs and to contribute personally to the common good,[64] as well as the right to vote and the right to have a voice in social decisions;[65]

10) everyone has the right to work, to develop his own personality and talents in the exercise of his profession[66] and also the right, exercised with due responsibility, to free initiative in the economic field.[67] These rights imply the right to working conditions in which physical health is not endangered, morals are safeguarded and young people's normal development is not impaired. Women have a special right to working conditions in accordance with their needs and their duties as wives and mothers;[68] everyone must be granted the right to a reasonable amount of free time and necessary recreation;[69]

11) everyone engaged in manual or intellectual work is entitled to a wage or salary determined according to justice and equity, and therefore sufficient to allow both the worker and his family to maintain a standard of living consonant with human dignity in due proportion to the resources available;[70]

12) workers have the right to strike as an ultimate means of defence of their other rights;[71]

13) everyone has the right to have a share of earthly goods sufficient for himself and his family. Private ownership, therefore, insofar as it provides everyone with a wholly necessary area of independence, both for himself and for his family, should be regarded as an extension of human freedom and as a right which is not absolute or unconditioned but limited. In fact, by its very nature private property has a social quality deriving from the law of the communal purpose of earthly goods as ordained by the Creator; earthly goods should in equity find their way into the hands of all men and all peoples, and should therefore never be used to the detriment of the common good;[72]

14) all men and nations enjoy the right to development, regarded as a dynamic interpretation of all those fundamental human rights on which the aspirations of individuals and nations are based;[73] this includes the right to equal opportunities in the cultural, civic, social and economic spheres and to an equitable distribution of national resources;[74]

15) everyone also has a natural right to share in the benefits of a culture, and therefore the right to basic education and to technical and professional training in keeping with the level of educational development of the country to which he belongs; every effort should be made to ensure that persons be enabled, on the basis of merit, to go on to higher studies so that they may occupy posts and take on responsibilities in accordance with their natural gifts and acquired skills;[75]

16) not only individuals but also communities and particularly minority groups enjoy the right to life, to personal and social dignity, to free association, to development within a safe and improved environment, and to an equitable distribution of natural resources and of the fruits of civilization;[76] the Magisterium makes a special plea on behalf of minorities, claiming the need for public authorities to promote their betterment with effective measures, to conserve their language, their culture, their ancestral customs and their accomplishments and endeavours in the economic order;[77]

17) the right of every people to keep its own identity is affirmed.[78]

1292 39. The value which the Church ascribes to man, then, is one of incomparable greatness. In this connection, Pope Paul VI said a few years ago: "No anthropology equals that of the Church in its evaluation of the human person. This is true as regards man's individuality, his originality, his dignity; as regards the intangible richness arising from his fundamental rights; as regards his sacredness, his capacity for education, his aspiration to complete development, his immortality, etc. A code could be composed out of the rights which the Church recognizes in man, and it will always be difficult to limit the fulness of the rights which derive from man's elevation to the supernatural by reason of his insertion in Christ."[79]

1293 40. The mystery of the Incarnation—the Son of God assuming human nature—threw a new light on the concept of man and of his dignity suggested by natural reason. "The truth is that only in the mystery of the Incarnate Word does the mystery of man take on light . . .. Christ, by the revelation of the mystery of the Father and His love, fully reveals man to man himself."[80]

1294 The ordinary Magisterium of the Church has provided teaching on fundamental human rights in the light of faith and of Christian perspectives which enrich the meaning of the rights by explaining them in depth and in the context of contemporary facts.

1295 *Pacem in Terris* emphasizes the principle that every human being is a person and adds: "If we look upon the dignity of the human person in the light of divinely revealed truth, we cannot help but esteem it far more highly; for men are redeemed by the blood of Jesus Christ, they are by grace the children and friends of God and heirs of eternal glory."[81]

1296 "The dignity of man is the dignity of the image of God," said Pius XII in his famous Christmas Broadcast of 1944.[82]

1297 This Christian view of man is the basis of the Church's pastoral motivation for defending human rights, whether of individuals or of groups.

41. "By virtue of the Gospel committed to her, the Church proclaims the rights of man. She acknowledges and greatly esteems the dynamic movements of today by which these rights are everywhere fostered. Yet these movements must be penetrated by the spirit of the Gospel and protected against any kind of false autonomy. For we are tempted to think that our personal rights are fully ensured only when we are exempt from every requirement of divine law. But this way lies not the maintainance of the dignity of the human person, but its annihilation."[83] 1298

Pope Paul VI, in a communication to the United Nations' Secretary-General, Dr. Kurt Waldheim, reaffirmed this view of faith in the defence of the rights of the human person. "The Church, concerned above all with the rights of God, can never dissociate herself from the rights of man, created in the image and likeness of his Creator. She feels injured when the rights of a man, whoever he may be, and wherever he may be, are ignored and violated."[84] 1299

The Holy Father spoke out ever more clearly, however, in the opening passages of his recent Message to the United Nations on the occasion of the 25th anniversary of the Universal Declaration of Human Rights. He reaffirmed his endorsement of the United Nations' initiatives for justice and peace and therefore of the general ideal contained in the Universal Declaration, "impelled by the consciousness of Our mission which is to render immediate, living and actual to men the message of salvation which Christ proclaimed."[85] 1300

This faith vision in the defence and the promotion of human rights, both of individuals and of groups, is based upon and explicated by Christian Revelation which paves the way to a simpler, surer and more comprehensive knowledge of human rights and of the laws which are inscribed by the Creator in man's moral and spiritual nature and which govern his social activities. 1301

42. No one can doubt that there is a continuously growing awareness of the exalted dignity of the human person not only among Christians but also throughout the human family. It is the ferment of the Gospel which "has aroused and contin- 1302

ues to arouse in man's heart the irresistible requirements of his dignity," proclaims the Second Vatican Council. "God's Spirit, with a marvelous providence . . . is not absent from this development."[86] Indeed Christ is still at work in the hearts of men through the power of his Spirit. Not only does he arouse a desire for the age to come, but also "animates, purifies and strengthens those noble longings too by which the human family strives to make its life more human."[87]

1303 Coming down to practical consequences, the Council condemns whatever is opposed to life itself, both individuals and of groups, such as any type of murder, willful self-destruction, genocide, euthanasia, abortion, contraception and sterilization. It condemns whatever violates the integrity of the human person such as mutilation, corporal or mental torture, attempts to coerce the will itself. It condemns whatever offends human dignity such as subhuman living conditions, arbitrary imprisonment, deportation, slavery, prostitution, the selling of women and children, disgraceful working conditions. "All these . . . poison human society . . .. Moreover they are a supreme dishonour to the Creator."[88]

1304 43. The Second Vatican Council further acknowledges that all men share a basic equality since they all have the same nature and origin, are all created in God's likeness, and, in fact, "have all been redeemed by Christ and enjoy the same divine calling and destiny."[89] For this reason, "with respect to the fundamental rights of the person, every type of discrimination, whether social or cultural, whether based on sex, race, colour, social status, language or religion, is to be overcome and eradicated as contrary to God's intent."[90]

1305 This equal dignity of persons and groups demands that a more humane and just condition of life be realized, eliminating "excessive economic and social differences between the members of the one human family or population groups"[91] as contrary to the Christian law of brotherhood and love.

1306 This is the reason why Pope Paul VI, speaking of the right of peoples to development and self-fulfilment, considers it an obligation of his apostolic mission to endorse "the legitimate aspirations of men today, not hesitating, to see there the action of 'evangelical ferment in the human heart,' calling with deep concern and hope on all men to live as brothers, since they are all sons of the living God."[92]

44. In short, the Church's defence of human rights is an inescapable requirement of her mission of justice and love in the spirit of the Gospel message. 1307

Indeed the 1971 Synod of Bishops clearly states: "Of itself it does not belong to the Church, insofar as she is a religious and hierarchical community, to offer concrete solutions in the social, economic and political spheres for justice in the world. Her mission involves defending and promoting the dignity and fundamental rights of the human person."[93] 1308

To accomplish her evangelical mission for the salvation of mankind, the Church has the right, as the Second Vatican Council teachers, "to pass moral judgment, even on matters touching the political order, whenever basic personal rights or the salvation of souls make such judgments necessary."[94] 1309

45. On the basis of the statements formulated by the Church's Magisterium regarding the dignity and fundamental rights of the human person, both individually and in groups, modern theologians have intensified their study of these problems, developing ideas and drawing practical conclusions notably from the theologies of the *imago Dei,* of the Incarnation, of the Church and of liberation. 1310

The chief elements of this study on the nature of man may be briefly summarized as follows. 1311

46. According to the teaching of the Book of Genesis, man is made in the image of God (Cf. *Gn* 1:26-27). This signifies that every human being is endowed with intelligence, will and power which exist in this full perfection, free of contingency, only in God. These gifts of God constitute the essential basis of the rights and dignity enjoyed by man as such, independent of his particular personal talents, background, education or social status. Everyone, therefore, has imprinted on his conscience the moral sense which moves him to act according to the laws laid down by the Creator (Cf. *Rm* 2:15). Man's freedom to behave according to the dictates of conscience constitutes the most forceful expression of his inalienable nobility. As he preached the message of the Kingdom of God 1312

to the crowds in Palestine, Christ, himself, fully respected man's genuine freedom, not in any way forcing man but inviting him to respond freely to the Gospel message (Cf. *Mk* 8:34). As he died upon the cross for all mankind and became through his resurrection the second Adam and the universal source of salvation, Jesus won for all men the power to become sons of God (Cf. *Jn* 1:12) and to be changed by the Holy Spirit into a new creature.[95] All those who are in fact incorporated in Christ by faith and baptism from the People of God, in which "there are henceforth no more distinctions between Jew and Greek, slave and free, male and female, but all of you are one in Christ Jesus" (Cf. *Ga* 3:28). All men of all times and places are destined to share in this sublime equality and supernatural brotherhood.

1313 These truths, as set out in Holy Scripture, form the biblical foundation and theological basis of man's dignity and fundamental rights. Insofar as man was created by God and for God, by the power of the Word of the Almighty, which called him into existence, he is destined and orientated towards God as his ultimate goal and perfection.[96]

1314 47. Being an image of God, man possesses and truly enjoys a spiritual nature, subsisting itself and constituting an ontological whole, open to truth, goodness and beauty–qualities which man is constantly seeking in order to achieve his own perfection until he finds absolute truth, goodness and beauty in God himself.[97] But man is not merely a natural being; he is also an historical one, and as one century succeeds another, by discerning the signs of the times, he continually finds the divine likeness shining through his being with brighter and brighter light.

1315 The consequence of this fundamental ontological datum at the level of consciousness is the fact that man is by his very nature open to the Absolute and can indeed find his perfection and final satisfaction only in God[98] who has made man for himself and to whom man has to give himself unreservedly. "Thou hast made us, O Lord, for thyself, and our hearts are restless until they rest in thee."[99]

1316 It is God, therefore, who created human life and who has loving dominion over it. Every man has a right to life insofar as this is given him by God himself; and together with the right to life he has also been given by the Creator the right to his own full self-development.[100]

48. For us Christians, the human person is the apex of everything created. His great dignity is like a reflection of the divine image, an indelible imprint on his very being, and as such ranks above all other things,[101] "so that man can never be considered a mere instrument to be used for the benefit of others. Unfortunately, modern technological and political mentality sometimes seems to ignore this, forgetting the values and the rights of the human spirit."[102] 1317

Since man is a person and the subject of any action, there is no human reason or pretext in the scientific or in the social, political and economic order which could ever justify a change in his function or status from subject to object. 1318

49. Furthermore, every person has a special relation with God, grounded in the mystery of the Incarnate Word. When the Son of God became man, he entered into the world's history as Perfect Man.[103] He lived in a particular nation, a particular culture, even in a particular minority group, and thus raised the whole human family and its members, which is to say human nature with all its prerogatives, to the dignity of Sons of God. Thus in a definite way he sanctified all humanity. 1319

It is precisely this choice by our Saviour of a particular nation or people, heirs of blessings destined for all nations, which gives value and dignity to every particular people, culture or nation. 1320

By his death on the cross Christ has redeemed through his blood every man, every race, every group, every culture. 1321

His life on earth was one total gift of himself to the Father for the salvation and liberation of men. He proclaimed the universal fatherhood of God to all mankind, the law of love for one's neighbour, and the intervention of divine justice in favour of the needy and the oppressed.[104] His supreme revelation was that "god is love" (1 *Jn* 4:8); he therefore taught that the fundamental law of human perfection, and of the transformation of the world, is "the new commandment": "A new commandment I give unto you, that you love one 1322 another; even as I have loved you, that you also love one another" (*Jn* 13:34).

1323 50. Christ made this law of love for one's neighbour his own personal commandment and enriched it with a new meaning. For he wanted to identify himself with his brethren as the object of love. Indeed, by "taking on human nature he bound the whole human race to himself as a family through a certain supernatural solidarity and established charity as the mark of his disciples, saying, 'By this will all men know that you are my disciples, if you have love for one another' " (*Jn* 13:35).[105] "To those therefore who believe in divine charity he gives assurance that the way of love lies open to all men and that the effort to establish a universal brotherhood is not a hopeless one."[106]

1324 51. At that point Christ carried his solidarity with even "the least" of his brethren to the point of affirming: "Whatever you have done for any one of these brothers of mine, even the least, you have done it to me" (*Mt* 25:40). He furthermore commanded the Apostles to go out and proclaim the Good News to all men, because it was in brotherhood and solidarity that the human race would become God's family, in which love would be the fulfilment of the law. In this way man's commitment to his neighbour becomes merged with his commitment to God, and his response to God's love is expressed in love and service to men.

1325 52. But Christian love "implies an absolute demand for justice, namely a recognition of the dignity and rights of one's neighbour. Justice attains its inner fulness only in love. Because every man is truly a visible image of the invisible God and a brother of Christ, the Christian finds in every man God himself and God's absolute demand for justice and love."[107] The practice of brotherly love and human and Christian solidarity to promote and defend human rights must therefore conform to the true sense of that central message of the Gospel and to the needs of men to whom it is addressed.

1326 53. Through the Paschal Mystery Christ has restored the unity of all men in one people and one body. He has spread the Spirit of love abroad in the hearts of men. That is why all Christians are called upon everywhere "to live the truth in love" (*Ep* 4:15).

54. These truths, revealed by God to man through Christ, are not only the basis and foundation of the Church's teaching on human nature and human rights, both individually and collectively. They also establish the Church's responsibility in her mission of actively advancing persons and nations together with their fundamental rights. 1327

55. The problems of human rights are manifest and operative, not only for the individual, but also to a higher degree in society and public affairs; for this reason they have both a private and public aspect. 1328

Although the Church with her religious role has no proper mission in the political, social or economic order, she is far from looking on religion as purely private and has always firmly stated that "out of this religious mission itself comes a function, a light and an energy which can serve to structure and consolidate the human community according to the divine law."[108] 1329

That is why the Catholic Church has never confined her moral teaching to private or individual ethics; but on the contrary, and with ever greater insistence in modern times, she has spoken out to the world on questions of public morality such as social justice, the development of peoples, human rights, war and peace, and racism. This is part of her pastoral mission. 1330

56. The Church is the continuation and the presence of Christ in the world and in history. She continues the prophetic mission of Jesus, whose words and actions are all for the good of men to save, heal, liberate and assist them all. 1331

The Bible, and in particular the New Testament, presents Christ's work as one of liberation. God himself in the fulness of time sent his Incarnate Son into the world to free men from every form of slavery to which they were subject by reason of sin and of human egoism,—from ignorance, destitution, hunger, oppression, hatred or injustice (Cf. *Ga* 4:4-5). 1332

Jesus' first preaching was to proclaim the liberation of the oppressed. By his death on Calvary Christ freed us from sin that we may enjoy the fulness of true freedom (Cf. *Ga* 5:13). Sin, the root of all injustice and oppression, is in fact an egoistic turning-back upon ourselves, a refusal to love others 1333 and therefore to love God himself. The fulness of liberation consists in communion with God and with all our fellowmen.

1334 57. In continuing the prophetic mission of her founder the Church must also preach more forcefully and realize more effectively this liberation of the poor, the oppressed and the outcast, working with others "building a world where every man, no matter what his race, religion or nationality, can live a fully human life, freed from servitude imposed on him by other men or by natural forces over which he has not sufficient control."[109]

1335 Today there are structural impediments which deny access of large sections of society to the spiritual and material goods which belong to the community in which they live. These obstacles foment alienation. They offend the dignity of the human person, and in effect estrange large masses of people who have no normal outlets or means of expression to claim and establish their fundamental rights.

1336 The irresponsible behaviour of those who allow such a state of affairs to continue is incompatible with the demands of the Gospel and must be boldly condemned. "This is the reason why the Church has the right, indeed the duty, to proclaim justice on the social, national and international level, and to denounce instances of injustice, when the fundamental rights of man and his very salvation demand it."[110]

1337 The proof that such prophetic denunciation is authentic and sincere can be seen in readiness to accept suffering, persecution, even death as Christ himself did.

1338 58. To imitate Christ and to be his true continuation in the world, the Church as a whole, like every Christian community, is called to work for the dignity and rights of man, both individually and collectively; to protect and promote the dignity of the human person; and to denounce and oppose every sort of human oppression. It is the risen Christ who inspires the Church in the campaign for human rights; and she knows that the prayers and sufferings of the People of God, particularly those who are victims of injustice in the field of human rights, are the noblest and most effective contribution to this activity.

59. Finally, theological reflection urgently reminds us of one final aspect which is of supreme importance for the Christian–namely, the eschatological view of man and of his fundamental rights. 1339

We know by Revelation that the Kingdom of God is already mysteriously present here on this earth, and that when the Lord returns on the Day of Judgment this Kingdom will reach its perfection: a new heaven and a new earth (*Rv* 21:1), the place where righteousness,[111] perfect felicity and lasting peace await us at the end of time. 1340

Only then, "after we have obeyed the Lord and in his Spirit nurtured on earth the values of human dignity, brotherhood and freedom, and indeed all the good fruits of our nature and enterprise," will we find them again, "but freed of stain, burnished and transfigured."[112] Then will Christ deliver up to the Father his everlasting and universal kingdom. But even if these good fruits, which constitute human values, liberties and rights, will not be completely and perfectly realized except in our future homeland, this should not be an excuse for slackening our speed or effort in the struggle for justice. Rather it should impel us to even greater commitment in order to offer people a definite approximation or anticipation of the new world. 1341

60. The mission of the Church, in obedience to God's command and in response to the grace and love of the Holy Spirit, is to be fully present to all men and nations, to lead them by the example of her life, her preaching, the Sacraments and other means of grace to live the faith, in the freedom and the grace of Christ, strengthening them so that they can participate fully in the Christian mystery.[113] 1342

61. The way in which the Church carries out this mission, through the collaboration and prayers of every member of the People of God, is commonly called "pastoral." 1343

Guided by the bishops and promoted by appropriate institutes and other organizations, pastoral activity has developed methods and techniques which naturally need constant review to keep them up to date but which are nonetheless certainly tried and proved instruments of the apostolate among men today. Pastoral activity to protect and promote human 1344 rights among the People of God can be developed in many ways. It is helpful to be aware of them; some constitute a positive mission to affirm and promote human rights, together with others which are negative, prophetically denouncing violations of such rights when they occur.

1345 Both functions of affirmation and of denunciation must not be regarded as two separate or self-sufficient enterprises but rather as complementary and interdependent. These two aspects of pastoral activity may well develop along different lines within the context of a local church, but they will always be of an apostolic and missionary character.

1346 62. It is the mission of the hierarchy to be a source of inspiration, support and guidance in the struggle for human rights. If her evangelical mission is to be effective, the Church must first and foremost stimulate in the world the recognition, observance, protection and promotion of the rights of the human person, beginning with an act of self-examination, a hard look at the manner and degree in which fundamental rights are observed and applied within her own organization.

1347 In this connection the Synod of Bishops in 1971 frankly and logically observed: "While the Church is bound to give witness to justice, she recognizes that anyone who ventures to speak to people about justice must first be just in their eyes."[114]

1348 With equal clarity, the 1974 Synod has recently declared: "From her own experience the Church knows that her ministry of fostering human rights in the world requires continued scrutiny and purification of her own life, her laws, institutions and policies . . . In the Church, as in other institutions and groups, purification is needed in internal practices and procedures, and in relationships with social structures and systems whose violations of human rights deserve censure."[115]

1349 63. The pastoral function of the Church in defending and promoting human rights inevitably leads us to consider the relations between pastoral activity and politics. Local churches and many other Christian groups have recently become concerned with this theme. We should like to emphasize the importance of their concern and of their contributions to better understanding. Indeed, from *Pacem in Terris* until today the Papal Magisterium has repeatedly intervened to explore the basic principles of this problem in depth with the hope of developing such spiritual conditions as may enable both Christians and Christian communities, even with the wide variety of conditions in which they find themselves, to make specific choices and to determine political decision and action.[116] In the face of such widely varying situations it is more and more difficult for the Magisterium in a single statement to put forward a solution which has universal validity.[117]

64. There can be no doubt, however, that the Catholic Church, as indeed the other Christian Churches, has a collective responsibility where politics are concerned. 1350

There is a tendency in some quarters to discredit any social or corporate witness by Christians as "triumphalist" and to reserve approval solely to individual, anonymous intervention. But this would seem to forget that the Church is herself a social body. "She would fail in her mission if she omitted to bear a common witness on the great questions where the spiritual and temporal good of man is at stake."[118] 1351

65. Therefore, Christian communities and the Church's numerous organizations, both local and regional, must take up responsibly and realistically the specific problems of society today. These must include certain aspects of politics in order to treat them with due discernment in the light of the Gospel.[119] Christians, especially those who professionally engage in politics, must have the courage "to define the evangelical significance of their action and to start discussions on precise points of interest today,"[120] such as war, violence, international injustice and, what primarily concerns us here, the promotion of human rights, knowing that politics "are a demanding manner—but not the only one—of living the Christian commitment to the service of others."[121] 1352

66. Contact with real life will sharpen their consciences so that they may see in the often confused succession of political events the eager aspirations which the Spirit of God has planted in men's hearts. In this way Christians may quickly uncover "the injustices and sufferings that the present evolution secretes, in order to convert the minds of men and 1353

guide towards the structural changes likely to remedy them."[122] In this sense faith appeals to politics.

1354 67. It is furthermore imperative to find common guidelines for concrete political action by Christians, in order to unite their energies for more effective combined effort without artifically diminishing the legitimate variety of possible options.[123]

1355 In this regard, the Apostolic Letter *Octogesima Adveniens* observes that "Christian organizations, under their different forms, have a responsibility for collective action. Without putting themselves in the place of the institutions of civil society, they have to express, in their own way and rising above their particular nature, the concrete demands of the Christian faith for a just, and consequently necessary, transformation of society."[124]

1356 This collective action, however, presupposes a greater sharing of responsibility and of decision-making among citizens. This admission to responsibility is in turn a basic demand of man's nature, a concrete exercise of his freedom and an indispensable path to his development.[125]

1357 68. The whole Church, then, is called to be an active leaven in political society. In return for this collaboration she will receive from political society "precious stimuli to adapt her own internal life to the exigencies thus perceived. In this sense there is a certain appeal to the Church by politics."[126]

1358 69. Conscious both of her prophetic mission in the political sphere and of her own specific nature and identity, the Church by casting a new light on man in every sector of his existence is active in the political world, intervening daily in its operations and giving it practical assistance without becoming identified or confused with it. As the Second Vatican Council teaches, the Church's role is to be "a sign and a safeguard of the transcendence of the human person."[127] Indeed, by teaching that man will exhaust his human aspirations and potentialities only if he fails to transcend temporal values, even those of greatest importance, the Church at the same time makes clear to the civil community the existence of values, goods and ends of a higher order—moral, spiritual and religious values which determine the destiny of the human person and which necessarily are projected on society. Since the Church's mission is to promote and defend these values in every man's conscience and life, and since every man is a member of the political community, the Church is also in this way able to influence the life of the community, affirming and promoting principles of the highest consequence in political and social life such as the principles of human dignity, universal brotherhood, freedom and responsibility, justice and love, and solidarity among citizens and peoples.

1359 The Church's prophetic mission is not, however, exhausted by simple acts of assent or dissent, but must in virtue of her eschatological hopes and promises throw into sharp relief the fulfilment of all things in the world to come, and the contingent character of the present. It is through her pastoral activity that the Church discharges this prophetic mission in the political field. Now, when one considers that politics play a large part in fundamental human rights, all that we have said above is easily applied without argument. Common testimony, doctrinal reflection, sensitization of consciences to uncover injustcies, collective or individual action by Christians must constitute the obligatory stages of a true pastoral policy to promote the fundamental rights of the human person.

1360 70. The Church's first duty in this field is to proclaim by word and by example the Gospel message of peace and justice in regard to human rights. The words of their pastors should always encourage Christians to devote themselves, singly or in groups, to promoting these rights, and thus join in support of both those who are engaged in this hard battle and those who are victims of oppression.

1361 Pastoral proclamation will find its chief force in demonstrating how the Christian basis of any theory of human rights is respect for the human person as an end in himself, not as a social instrument, and how the content of human rights is at the very heart of the Gospel itself. More particularly, the Church will always present the defence of the rights of the human person, singly or collectively, in the light of the

Gospel of love for one's neighbour: "Thou shalt love thy neighbour as thyself" (*Mt* 22:39).

1362 71. This faith in love which inspires the Church to undertake the promotion of man's inalienable rights is the faith which obliges each of us to take on the responsibility for helping our brethren, all our brethren, both near and far, to mature as men and women, children of God.

1363 72. Testimony in word and deed by local churches and by individual Christians will make a particularly strong and lasting contribution if it is properly planned and organized.

1364 This is why *Octogesima Adveniens* in discussing the choices and commitments which the Christian community has to make in order to bring about the social, political and economic changes urgently needed in their nations points out that it is up to these Christian communities to act "with the help of the Holy Spirit, in communion with the bishops who hold responsibility and in dialogue with other Christian brethren and all men of good will."[128] A valid pastoral activity of approbation and reprobation in favour of human rights will thus bear the marks of charismatic inspiration, hierarchical and ecclesial order, joint action with other Christian churches and with non-Christian religions, openness to the world of today and collaboration with it. In its search for adequate means and forms of promoting the human person and his rights, the People of God will find its inspiration, strength and creativity in the Gospel which "has truly been a leaven of liberty and progress in human history . . . and always proves itself a leaven of brotherhood, of unity, and of peace."[129]

1365 Impelled by this faith, the Pontifical Commission Justice and Peace and the World Council of Churches, on the occasion of the 25th anniversary of the Universal Declaration of Human Rights, issued a joint appeal "to local churches, and particularly to Christian leaders and educators, to initiate or intensify programmes of instruction and sensitization on human rights, and corresponding duties so that every person . . . may be aware of the quality of human life to which he is entitled."[130]

73. Every dynamic movement in human history for making the world a better, more just and brotherly place, for overcoming social inequalities, and for freeing man from whatever dehumanizes him while making him more aware of his dignity, has its source, its motive power, and its final perfection in Christ's works of salvation. Freedom is a gift from Christ, and every promotion of human rights is a thrust to liberation, to repulse egoism which is the negation of love. 1366

74. Therefore, to take part in the process of liberating the whole man, as seen in the light of the Gospel, is an indispensable element in any genuine pastoral mission of effective and authentic proclamation. 1367

75. It is an accepted fact that renewal in the temporal order is the specific province of the laity. The Second Vatican Council teaches that the laity must take on the renewal of the temporal order as their own special obligation. "Led by the light of the Gospel and the mind of the Church, and motivated by Christian love, let them act directly and definitely in the temporal sphere. As citizens they must co-operate with other citizens, using their own particular skills and acting on their own responsibility. Everywhere and in all things they must seek the justice characteristic of God's Kingdom."[131] 1368

Human rights, deriving from man's human and intrinsically social nature, are not merely natural humanitarian rights or, as some people believe, non-political rights, but rather have a content and political implications. 1369

There can be no question but that their observance and application belong to the social sphere and are in a special sense the work of the laity, men and women. 1370

76. Nonetheless, priests and men and women religious, in their capacity as citizens of the earthly community and in fulfilment of their pastoral mission, are called upon to defend and promote human rights. For this reason the Synod of Bishops in 1971 affirmed in *The Ministerial Priesthood:* "Together with the entire Church, priests are obliged, to the utmost of their ability, to select a definite pattern of action, when it is a question of the defence of fundamental human 1371

rights, the promotion of the full development of persons and the pursuit of the cause of peace and justice; the means must indeed always be consonant with the Gospel. These principles are all valid not only in the individual sphere, but also in the social field; in this regard priests should help the laity to devote themselves to forming their consciences rightly."[132]

1372 77. As in the past, so today in many local churches there has been no dearth of devoted Christians, priests and laymen, missionaries and natives, men and women, who have fought for the rights of the poor and of minority groups. Today in many countries the Church is involved in the fight against every type of discrimination or oppression, claiming for all men fair and equal access to economic, cultural, social and spiritual benefits.

1373 Unfortunately, this is too often left to isolated efforts. Often there is lacking the planning and coordination which are indispensable to the exertion of effective influence on public opinion, government policy, and economic, social and political structures.

1374 78. Today more than ever the Church appears to be committed to the service of mankind, "open to the world in order to help it solve its problems."[133] Her own credibility requires her to make specific acts or statements in condemnation of aggression and aggressors.

1375 The defence of human rights to which the Church is committed implies protest against any violation of these rights, past or present, temporary or permanent.[134] This is all the more necessary when the victims of such injustice cannot defend themselves.

1376 79. In 1972 Pope Paul VI, addressing the Diplomatic Corps, repeated the words of the 1971 Synod of Bishops and emphasized that "the mission of bishops demands that we should denounce injustice courageously, with charity."[135] In his message to the United Nations, 10 December 1973, the Pope referred to the persistent and steadily increasing violations of human rights and forcefully asserted: "To all the silent victims of injustice, We lend Our voice of protest and of entreaty."[136] Certain categories of these victims had already been singled out by His Holiness for special attention–victims of racial or ethnic discrimination, victims of colonial oppression, those who suffer from the suppresssion of religious liberty, those who are denied freedom of expression, prisoners who are ill-treated or tortured, political opponents who are eliminated by violence, and finally, those human beings who are weak and defenceless such as babies not yet weaned.

1377 80. In certain periods or circumstances of real difficulty in the history of nations, only the voice of the Church, stern and decisive, can make herself heard, to protest and to condemn. Any such protest demands courage, charity, prudence and firmness. Above all it must be a truly human and Christian testimony, in sincere dialogue with all parties concerned, and based on justice and objectivity.[137] The Church cannot remain neutral when human rights are truly violated. But the charity which she has for all men will lead her, on the one side, to reprove tyranny and injustice according to circumstances, place and time and, on the other, to relieve distress according to the words of the *Didaché*: "Thou shalt not hate any man, but shalt reprove some and show mercy to others" (*Didaché*, Chap. II).

1378 81. The hierarchical Church is able to set a truly evangelical example when in such situations she makes every effort to bring the guilty to understand the process which led to the violation of human rights, to convince them of their responsibility and to lead them to conversion. In this way the Church clearly demonstrates that her mission is not only one of defending truth and denouncing error but also of affirming and protecting genuine human values, both temporal and eternal, in the best and fullest way.

1379 82. We all know how current human situations become daily more complex, more unstable and more ambiguous. Before making any formal judgment or taking action against apparent violations, it is imperative to obtain a reliable and objective knowledge of all the facts and then to act only after deep and serious reflection.

1380 83. Not only the denunciation itself but its form and content should be decided in agreement with other members of the Church's family. It is most desirable that any such decisions will be taken in cooperation with our separated Christian brethren and indeed with all men of good will."[138]

1381 84. It would be a very grave error to regard prophetic protest as the exclusive testimony of bishops, priests or religious. Within the Church, denunciation of any violation of human rights is the duty of the laity no less than of the hierarchy if and when circumstances demand it.

1382 Everyone who has been baptized has his own particular and indisputable responsibility within the Church. Where human rights are violated the laity have a special duty to denounce such violations and at the same time ensure that whatever action they take is coherent and well coordinated. In this way, their words will not be empty and they will be an effective witness in the name of the Church for the whole community. This support for human rights opens up a vast field of possibilities for the faithful, especially for National Justice and Peace Commissions.

1383 85. However, denunciation is not the only method of putting things right; there are other ways of acting which may be better in certain circumstances, such as "symbolic acts" or "acts of solidarity" with the poor and the oppressed when their human rights are injured.

1384 86. In any case, where local political conditions are unfavourable and where open protest would expose individuals to further repression by governments, some way must be found of expressing the universal Church's concern for intolerable conditions of this sort.

1385 87. At the same time, as the Holy Father Observed: "Mere denunciation, often too late or ineffective, is not sufficient. There must be an analysis of the deep-rooted causes of such situations and a firm commitment to face up to them and resolve them correctly."[139]

1386 It is not enough, therefore, simply to utter prophetic denunciations if we are really to fulfil our obligations to renew the temporal order on sound principles. "These words will lack real weight unless they are accompanied for each individual by a livelier awareness of personal responsibility and by effective action. It is too easy to throw back on to others responsibility for injustices."[140] In every nation it is important to make a close detailed examination of the relations between theory and practice, between protection of fundamental human rights and liberties as expressed by signed or ratified international treaties and declarations, on the one hand, and, on the other, the day-to-day struggle within each nation for social and economic justice, for real equality without any discrimination, and for a higher standard of living. It is a sad fact that numerous principles sanctioned by the United Nations which bear directly on the urgent needs of people in the developing countries are often openly flouted or ignored with impunity.

88. There is a serious discrepancy between official declarations on human rights and their observance in practice. It may be that this glaring contrast between theory and practice is due to the fact that very often human rights are wrongly considered as a political weapon, not as an effective and well-tried means of securing justice and peace. Often violations of human rights can be traced to specific economic or political situations which at least indirectly encourage such violations. 1387

This factor needs to be studied in depth, because this very day the principal violations of human rights stem from the type of regime whose very structure, even if more or less disguised, is conducive to violence. This violence inevitably leads to failure to respect human rights. It is a mistake to suppose that these violations occur only at the individual level. Violations of individual rights are often easiest to denounce because they are the most conspicuous. But they are certainly not the only ones. 1388

89. Looking at the current situation today, no form of government seems to take sufficient account of all human rights. Yet it is certain that one of the gravest forms of oppression with major consequences for social and individual rights is found in governments which consider man nothing more than an instrument of production or a necessary item in a consumer economy or in one which makes economic gain its ultimate goal. Freedom and the dignity of the human person suffer equal harm from governments which consider man as purely material and so reduce him to a mere "cog in the wheel" of the social system. This whole philosophy makes 1389

man an instrument to the supposed good of society ignoring individual rights and liberties.[141]

1390 90. Local churches, and above all National Commissions, should therefore investigate and study the causes which underlie particular violations of human rights in their own country. If they are to make an effective contribution to a pastoral activity of protest in order to effect change they must try thoroughly to understand the mechanisms which sustain and govern the social and economic structures in which human rights are not and cannot be respected.

1391 91. The Church's mission of peace covers the whole human race. "Peace and rights," says Pope Paul VI, "are two benefits directly related to each other as cause and effect. There can be no peace where there is no respect for, defence and promotion of human rights."[142] From this it follows that the Church is obliged to work for both peace and human rights at the same time because both are the fruit of the love and liberation which Our Saviour came to bring to men.

1392 The Church's main contribution to the realization of human rights consists in a continuous and eminently practical process of education, first of all among her own members. The purpose of this education is to make Christians ever more conscious of the dignity of the human person, the brotherhood of man, the liberty and equality which all men share. Above all the Church endeavours to implant, foster and bring to flower the will to respect these fundamental rights in every moment of daily life.

1393 92. What matters in education in respect for human rights is much the same thing as education for justice: "to teach men to live their lives in its entire reality and in accord with the evangelical principles of personal and social morality which are expressed in the vital Christian witness of one's life."[143]

1394 All this implies a continuously growing awareness of the Christian's special vocation in the social and political community and a profound sense of responsibility and dedication for the achievement of the common good.

1395 Education for life in society involves "not only information on each one's rights, but also their necessary correlative: the recognition of the duties of each one in regard to others,"[144] since the performance of duties depends upon self-discipline as well as acceptance of responsibilities and limitations on the exercise of personal and social freedom.[145]

Experience shows, however, that many Christians today are still a long way from bearing witness to respect for and observance of their duties in regard to the inviolable rights of man, particularly in the sphere of work, society, politics and economics, and even in education. It may be that the form of education which many members of the Church have received has given rise to a narrow individualism which is slow to recognize the rights of others, whereas they should have been made more open and ready to live together in brotherly fellowship guaranteeing true peace and unity upon earth. 1396

93. According to the Second Vatican Council, "a true education aims at the formation of the human person with respect to his ultimate goal, and simultaneously with respect to the good of those societies of which, as a man, he is a member, and in whose responsibilities, as an adult, he will share."[146] 1397

It cannot be denied that in this matter, too, the family, the school, the parish and many ecclesiastical and civil organizations such as political parties, trade unions and the communications media play an important role.[147] 1398

But, as the Pastoral Constitution *Gaudium et Spes* admonishes us, educators particularly of the young "should regard as their most weighty task the effort to instruct all in fresh sentiments of peace"[148] and to cooperate readily with the rest of the community both at national and at international levels.[149] 1399

A continuing education in understanding other people, which individuals will be able to receive from the social agencies mentioned above and more particularly from their educators, is the surest way to inculate genuine respect for fundamental human rights.[150] 1400

94. Indeed, education in human rights means in effect education in awareness of the existence of other people, of one's neighbours; to be aware that they have as much right to live as we have, to recognize the relations which bind us to them 1401

and for that very reason make us social. Education in human rights means education in respect for other people, in respect for differences of opinion, of activity and even of singular traits of individuals or of groups. All too often we judge others too harshly and unjustly because of our own prejudice or preconceived ideas, though their intrinsic validity and historic background is easily explained by the fact of cultural pluralism. This means finding a place in our own cultural pattern or setting for other people's equally legitimate cultural traditions and expressions. In short, education to human rights means learning to respect the legitimate differences which distinguish every human being or cultural group and at the same time learning to perceive the identity of nature, the basic resemblance between human beings as between brothers and sisters.

1402 95. Man is a social, indeed a communal being. The human person as such has a profound value of its own, but needs to be developed and can reach its fulfilment only through interaction with other people. "In the design of God every man is called to develop and fulfil himself, for every life is a vocation."[151] In this way education in human rights must call on a man's creative talents, his responsibility and his capacity for full growth. Before birth every man has in germ a set of aptitudes and qualities for him to bring to fruition. The development of these will be the result of the education he receives together with his own personal efforts.

1403 But it is obvious that education in human rights cannot be given piecemeal. Wherever men live and have to meet the demands of living with others, questions of justice and of fundamental human rights are closely interwoven. Man is a single whole, a comprehensive entity, and all authentic education must be equally comprehensive in its outlook and approach.[152]

1404 96. Educators for peace and human respect will run counter to their responsibility if they confine these profound truths to mere precept and do not go on to bear living witness to them by their example. They ought not put their faith in a socialization based only on moral and disciplinary constrictions.

97. For every man the first fundamental right without which the others make no sense is the right to be really and truly a person. It is therefore necessary for education in human rights to help every person to become truly what he is; to jettison certain ideas and attitudes based on power and possession, to establish norms of conduct which may safeguard those rights and duties by virtue of which, on the basis of equality, liberty, fraternity and love, "each man can grow in humanity, can enhance his personal worth, can become more a person"[153] without any increase in possessions. 1405

98. It is not difficult then to comprehend that every educator who tries to promote human rights must have a keen critical sense, tact and discretion if he is going to call in question certain individual or collective customs or attitudes based on defending one's self against others and to replace such attitudes with new ones of responsibility, respect and cooperation. For this reason it will be necessary to pay great attention to preparing every person practically to cope with social and cultural pluralism and to realize brotherhood and equality not merely in theory but in practice. This implies, at the same time, the recognition of other peoples' rights to legitimate freedom. 1406

Human rights cannot be just an object of purely theoretical teaching without any relation to the conditions in which they may be realized. They must be put squarely in the actual context and dynamics of the society in which the person lives. Hence the importance of studying a right balance between the rights of the human person and the functions of groups or of whole societies. 1407

99. The natural and human content of this educational process will be raised to a higher plane by theological reflection on the main points already expounded in the Church's teaching on the dignity of the human person. All persons are made in the image of God, the Father of all. They thus feel themselves, and indeed truly are, brothers and sisters, equal in dignity and freedom. "By reason of his union with Christ, the source of life, man attains to new fulfilment of himself, to a transcendant humansim which gives him his 1408

greatest possible perfection. This is the highest goal of personal development."[154]

1409 100. If the defence and promotion of human rights are to be an effective, credible and truly evangelical witness, there must be a joint effort especially on the part of all those who, as followers of Christ, are called to put into practice Christian charity, mutual understanding, respect for others, justice, solidarity, and collaboration for the common good.

1410 101. The 1971 Synod of Bishops in the document *Justice in the World* repeated the teaching of the Second Vatican Council and emphasized the importance of cooperation with separated brethren to promote peace in the world and to establish this on a firm basis by encouraging the development of peoples. To this end it urged the Pontifical Commission Justice and Peace in conjunction with the Secretariat for Christian Unity to devote itself to developing this effective ecumenical collaboration. "This cooperation concerns first and foremost," the Synod stressed, "activities for securing human dignity and man's fundamental rights, especially the right to religious liberty. This is the source of our common efforts against discrimination on the grounds of differences of religion, race and colour, culture and the like."[155]

1411 102. From the dignity of the human person who has been created in the image and likeness of God, the Father of all men, and who has further been redeemed by the blood of Christ, must arise the spontaneous witness of all Christians to their faith. They should, as followers of Christ, demonstrate their awareness of their responsibility to defend the rights of their neighbours, male and female, individuals and groups, regardless of race, sex, class, religion, or political opinion.

1412 103. The Joint Declaration of the Pontifical Commission Justice and Peace and of the World Council of Churches on the occasion of the 25th Anniversary of the Universal Declaration of Human Rights is intended to be at once an appeal and a spur to action in this matter for every Christian community.

1413 There have been other similar initiatives in ecumenical collaboration organized by SODEPAX; such as the Beirut

Conference (21-28 April 1968), the World Conference at Montreal (9-12 May 1969) and, above all, the Consultation at Baden in Austria (3-9 April 1970), where human rights and their promotion as a contribution to peace were fully discussed.

The Baden Consultation affirmed: "In order to ensure the more effective protection of human rights it is urged that the Churches should promote an active educational campaign to ensure a fuller knowledge of the provisions of the Universal Declaration of Human Rights and subsequent instruments for the protection of human rights and their wider public diffusion; such an educational programme should be undertaken at pastoral level and through all the educational institutions under the control of the Churches. In school programmes the scope and importance of human rights should be highlighted by concrete practical examples by way of illustration."[156] 1414

This statement was repeated and reaffirmed by the World Conference on Religion and Peace held at Kyoto (16-21 October 1970), where representatives of the world's major religions, Christian and non-Christian, discussed problems of disarmament, development and human rights.[157] 1415

104. The possibilities of ecumenical action are countless, ranging from meetings for prayer together to prophetic denounciation, from initiatives to educate people on human rights, *en masse* or through small groups, to active intervention with the relevant authorities to defend a claim to some particular right or to safeguard some other right which has been violated. Every National Commission can and should encourage this sort of ecumenical collaboration between Churches or local Christian institutions, according to the needs and present circumstances of each country, in whatever ways seem best for the times. 1416

105. It is by inspiring Christians to take specific, practical initiatives in the field of human rights that local churches and, more particularly, National Justice and Peace Commissions find effective outlets for their pastoral activity. 1417

One indispensable premise is careful research and study on the problems of human rights through an objective analysis 1418 of the causes of violations with a view to finding appropriate solutions and proposing practical remedies.

1419 The Second Vatican Council teaches that when man consciously takes part in the various forms of social life, he carries out God's design that he should develop himself, exercise Christian charity and spend himself in the service of his fellows.[158] Would it not then be desirable for every local church to encourage the faithful to form study circles, forums, seminars and lecture courses on human rights to highlight by free and frank discussion the most urgent problems and their fundamental causes?

1420 In these matters National Commissions can act in a variety of ways and in a wide range of sectors, both at national and at international planes. There have already been several experiments in meetings on various topics both at regional and at continental levels, chiefly through the National Commissions in Europe and Latin America. On these occasions it has been possible to single out points of considerable importance for joint action by all Christians.

1421 106. It is well known that human rights are a world-wide concern, transcending all national frontiers or regional cultures. But this "universality" does not mean that human rights are something abstract or static. Rather they are a matter of hard fact in constant evolution which everyone should observe and comprehend, especially in the context of the social conditions in his own country.

1422 107. Collaboration with governmental and non-governmental organizations which help to defend and promote human rights within the community is an absolute necessity and a duty incumbent on every citizen and every Christian.

1423 The choice of such collaboration may take one of many forms according to need or the exigencies of the moment. There is an almost infinite variety of choice. We here suggest a few, as simple examples, though we call attention of the National Commissions to the fact that some of the international instruments listed below should be treated with some reserve on certain points, despite their genuine desire to defend human rights.

Here then are a few points on which collaboration is possible: 1424

108. To press for the application of international legal instruments, which provide concrete protection for human rights. 1425

Special attention should be paid to: 1426

1) The two International Covenants already quoted on "Economic, Social, and Cultural Rights" and on "Civil and Political Rights" with its relevant Optional Protocol (1966). It is urgent that these be ratified everywhere.[159]

2) The International Convention on the "Elimination of All Forms of Racial Discrimination," and appropriate measures to apply the norms set out therein (21 December 1965).

3) The UNESCO Convention on "Discrimination in Education," (14 December 1960).

4) The procedure laid down in Resolution 1503 (48th Session), approved in 1970 by the United Nations Economic and Social Council, which authorized the Sub-Committee for the campaign against acts of discrimination and for protecting minorities to set up a work group to study reports of any violations of human rights according to certain criteria of admissibility.

109. To follow with interest the progress of certain important draft conventions, some of which are still under review by the competent UN Commission. 1427

1) The draft of the "International Convention on the Elimination of All Forms of Religious Intolerance." If there are serious disagreements on the text of this Convention, it might be advisable to insist at least on a declaration on this matter.

2) The draft "Convention on the Right of Asylum."

3) The draft "Convention on Freedom of Information."

4) Measures to reinforce the protection of freedom of association and of peaceful assembly.

5) Due protection of the freedom and welfare of the family (*Statut de la famille*).

6) More effective legislation at the national and international level to protect children in society, especially in the labour field.

1428 110. To demand more effective protection against racial discrimination, especially during the "Decade against Racial Discrimination" launched by the United Nations on 10 December 1973.

1) To determine what can be done about Apartheid and every socio-economic system which is based on racial, cultural, religious, ethnic or political discrimination.
2) To stimulate specialized studies of these problems.
3) To examine new forms of action and intervention for eradicating racism.

1429 111. To protect the rights of women.

1) To press for the ratification by all nations of the "Convention on Political Rights of Women."
2) To support and publicize the existing "Declaration on the Elimination of Discrimination against Women."
3) To protect woman's role as mother, responsible for the home and the fonts of life, and the first teacher of the next generation.
4) To encourage a better social status for married and working women and a fairer recognition of their rights, especially those of protecting their children in case of legal separation or of widowhood.
5) To determine a plan of action with specific practical initiatives within the context of each national society for defending women's rights, especially on the occasion of "International Woman's Year (1975)."

1430 112. To demand greater protection for ethnic, linguistic or religious minorities.

1) Minority groups who play their part in a nation's life need adequate protection for their traditional customs and

values, both religious and cultural. As social life becomes more and more pluralistic, the need for appropriate legislation increases.

113. To promote legislation on the social and economic rights of developing nations and peoples. 1431

1) The rights of all peoples to political autonomy, which were so strongly affirmed in the post-colonial period, need to be complemented by the recognition of those social and economic rights urgently needed for the proper development of many peoples in the Third World, at the same time avoiding the dangers of neo-colonialism.

2) In the light of *Populorum Progressio* and of *Octogesima Adveniens* attempts must be made to form a body of international law on this subject, taking full account of the experiences of the three UNCTAD Conferences.

114. To favour a fuller personalization of human rights to a greater extent by examining ways of extending and applying them to cover the needs of particular categories of people in special circumstances, for example, the elderly, the sick, the disabled. 1432

115. To take steps to provide more effective social and legal safeguards for certain rights, notably those which bear most directly on the dignity of the human person, such as: 1433

1) The right to religious liberty

2) The right to be born, to live and to be adequately fed

3) The right to be educated and to enjoy the benefit of culture

4) The rights of foreign workers

5) The right to decent working conditions, whether through workers' participation in management or through a wage sufficient to support the development of the worker's own person and that of his family.

1434 116. National Commissions must pay particular attention to the defence of religious liberty, which is the basis of all other liberties and inseparably bound up with them. As the Holy Father states, "Alas, this most sacred of all rights is for millions of men, innocent victims of intolerant religious discrimination, ridiculed with impunity. And so We turn with confidence toward your distinguished assembly, in the hope that it will be able to promote, in such a basic area of man's life, an attitude in conformity with the unsuppressable voice of conscience and to banish conduct incompatible with the dignity of mankind."[160]

1435 117. To provide new legal measures at regional and international levels to strengthen the executive power protecting human rights.

1) To support the plan to create a World Court or Tribunal for Human Rights as a final court of appeal in this matter.[161]

2) To support the plan to create a High Commission for Human Rights within the structure of the United Nations, which would be supernational making full allowance both for the independence of each State in respect of its internal affairs and, at the same time, for the necessary observance of certain principles of international law which are already recognized and in process of being codified by the United Nations—an observance which national governments should not be free to disregard at whim.

3) To support the proposal to create Regional Courts or Tribunals and Regional Commissions for human rights since agencies of this sort would be better able to hear local or regional cases of infringement of human rights which might arise, following the example of the Council of Europe or of the Inter-American Commission.

1436 118. To support the general recognition of every man's right of appeal to International Tribunals on rights of the human person.

1) It is imperative that associations, groups and individuals be granted the right of individual recourse in international assemblies. If human rights are to be protected effectively, every man must be able to have such recourse as a guarantee against governmental and ideological pressures on the human person.

2) Furthermore, to ensure this observance and the due application of human rights, might it perhaps be useful to suggest that the UN lay upon Members States the obligation to reply to enquiries into any violations of human rights, adopting judicial machinery like that of the European Commission for Human Rights? In the same way might it be a good thing to encourage the formation of a system of periodic inspection on the observance of human rights within the jurisdiction of individual States, similar to the permanent inspectorate of the International Labour Organization (ILO)?

3) It would seem advisable, in any case, whenever circumstances permit or demand, to back up the UN in its protests against violations of human rights by offering whatever moral support may be needed.

119. This is where National Commissions are most especially called on to make an objective diagnosis of certain local conditions which infringe human rights in some particular sector and at the same time offer a choice of remedies. But it will not be possible for human rights to be studied and understood in the home, the school, the parish, the diocese, indeed throughout the nation, without using all the media of social communication, such as: 1437

4) The press, preparing, for example, popular editions of the Universal Declaration of Human Rights with quotations of passages from the social doctrine of the Church; the text and a short commentary of *Pacem in Terris* with it *Magna Charta* on human rights; pamphlets on racism, on people's rights to self-determination, on the right to development, on the right to be born; brief, succinct articles explaining the problems of human rights to appear in daily or weekly newspapers or periodicals, both Catholic and non-Catholic;

5) Radio and television, with talks or group discussions on any rights which have been particularly violated in their own society.

1438 At parochial or diocesan levels it should be possible to organize Human Rights Campaigns at particular periods of the liturgical year, incorporating appropriate means of publicity, such as speaches, leaflets, posters, handbills and streamers, lecture courses, films, sermons and religious services. It is important, indeed imperative, that such campaigns should be planned by both clergy and laity together.

1439 120. National Commissions also contribute by making Christians better informed and more sensitive about these matters by reminding them of:

1) their duty to watch out for any action or behaviour, in any quarter whatsoever, which is an affront to human rights;[162]

2) the need to bring pressure to bear on public authorities to ensure that those human rights which have already been affirmed by the United Nations in numerous Declarations and Conventions are incorporated into legal systems and given effect in administrative regulations of their own state;

3) the usefulness and need of making public those rights which have suffered most violation in their own country, and to correct these abuses by informing the competent authorities both in the Church and the State and by alerting public opinion and keeping it regularly informed;

4) the need and opportunity to make the public aware of the attitude of the national government towards ratifying the UN Convention for safeguarding fundamental human rights, especially the two Covenants with the additional Protocol of 1966;

5) the need to welcome and encourage young people to play their part in defending and promoting human rights and to make their distinctive contribution towards social development in this field.[163]

121. In conclusion, whatever action we take whether at national or international levels must always bear the stamp of healthy realism and Christian optimism. 1440

While fundamental human rights are in incalculable social benefit for every culture, we must not forget their historic background or their dynamic dimension. In every age rights emerge in new dimensions, and old problems are seen in a new light. "On a permanent basis, therefore, law in continually developing. It is thus necessary to be involved in the search for new aspects of human rights at the same time as one works on the institution of those already acquired. This is one of the tasks of the Christian's prophetic role."[164] 1441

122. At times the grave problems of human rights may make it seem as if their full realization is, humanly speaking, a Utopia; but then the eschatological dimension will inspire us to continue working with undiminished fidelity and zeal towards the coming of a new heaven and a new earth (*Rv* 21:1). 1442

We know that legal means are not enough by themselves to ensure the protection of human rights. The lack of success of international agencies in this respect makes us daily more conscious of their limitations. For this reason it is necessary to endeavour to create, both at national and international levels, a new social and political order, which will have structures capable of satisfying the demand for justice among peoples, societies and individuals. 1443

The very concept of human rights may perhaps reflect too closely the Western humanist tradition; but in fact its worldwide range and universal character should make it possible, with a reasonable degree of flexibility and a pluralist outlook, to embrace the widely differing thinking and circumstances of all the nations in the world. Here again the cooperation of National Commissions should prove invaluable. 1444

Finally, the dynamism of our faith always accompanies us as we defend and promote human rights, carefully scrutinizing the signs of the times in all circumstances in order to build up for all men "a human city, one that is to be peaceful, just and fraternal and acceptable as an offering to God."[165] 1445

EVANGELII NUNTIANDI

Apostolic Exhortation of Pope Paul VI
on Evangelization in the Modern World
December 8, 1975

There is no doubt that the effort to proclaim the Gospel to the people of today, who are buoyed up by hope but at the same time often oppressed by fear and distress, is a service rendered to the Christian community and also to the whole of humanity.

1447 For this reason the duty of confirming the brethren—a duty which with the office of being the Successor of Peter[1] we have received from the Lord, and which is for us a "daily preoccupation,"[2] a program of life and action, and a fundamental commitment of our Pontificate—seems to us all the more noble and necessary when it is a matter of encouraging our brethren in their mission as evangelizers, in order that, in this time of uncertainty and confusion, they may accomplish this task with ever increasing love, zeal and joy.

1448 2. This is precisely what we wish to do here, at the end of this Holy Year during which the Church, "striving to proclaim the Gospel to all people,"[3] has had the single aim of fulfilling her duty of being the messenger of the Good News of Jesus Christ—the Good News proclaimed through two fundamental commands: "Put on the new self"[4] and "Be reconciled to God."[5]

1449 We wish to do so on this tenth anniversary of the closing of the Second Vatican Council, the objectives of which are definitively summed up in this single one: to make the Church of the twentieth century ever better fitted for proclaiming the Gospel to the people of the twentieth century.

We wish to do so one year after the Third General Assembly of the Synod of Bishops, which, as is well known, was devoted to evangelization; and we do so all the more willingly because it has been asked of us by the Synod Fathers themselves. In fact, at the end of that memorable Assembly, the Fathers decided to remit to the Pastor of the universal Church, with great trust and simplicity, the fruits of all their labors, stating that they awaited from him a fresh forward impulse, capable of creating within a Church still more firmly rooted in the undying power and strength of Pentecost a new period of evangelization.[6] 1450

3. We have stressed the importance of this theme of evangelization on many occasions, well before the Synod took place. On 22 June 1973 we said to the Sacred College of Cardinals: "The conditions of the society in which we live oblige all of us therefore to revise methods, to seek by every means to study how we can bring the Christian message that modern man can find the answer to his questions and the energy for his commitment of human solidarity."[7] And we added that in order to give a valid answer to the demands of the Council which call for our attention, it is absolutely necessary for us to take into account a heritage of faith that the Church has the duty of preserving in its untouchable purity, and of presenting it to the people of our time, in a way that is as understandable and persuasive as possible. 1451

4. This fidelity both to a message whose servants we are and to the people to whom we must transmit it living and intact is the central axis of evangelization. It poses three burning questions, which the 1974 Synod kept constantly in mind: 1452

— In our day, what has happened to that hidden energy of the Good News, which is able to have a powerful effect on man's conscience?

— To what extent and in what way is that evangelical force capable of really transforming the people of this century?

– What methods should be followed in order that the power of the Gospel may have its effect?

1453 Basically, these inquiries make explicit the fundamental question that the Church is asking herself today and which may be expressed in the following terms: after the Council and thanks to the Council, which was a time given her by God, at this turning-point of history, does the Church or does she not find herself better equipped to proclaim the Gospel and to put it into people's hearts with conviction, freedom of spirit and effectiveness?

1454 5. We can all see the urgency of giving a loyal, humble and courageous answer to this question, and of acting accordingly.

1455 In our "anxiety for all the Churches,"[8] we would like to help our Brethren and sons and daughters to reply to these inquiries. Our words come from the wealth of the Synod and are meant to be a meditation on evangelization. May they succeed in inviting the whole People of God assembled in the Church to make the same meditation; and may they give a fresh impulse to everyone, especially those "who are assiduous in preaching and teaching,"[9] so that each one of them may follow "a straight course in the message of the truth,"[10] and may work as a preacher of the Gospel and acquit himself perfectly of his ministry.

1456 Such an exhortation seems to us to be of capital importance, for the presentation of the Gospel message is not an optional contribution for the Church. It is the duty incumbent on her by the command of the Lord Jesus, so that people can believe and be saved. This message is indeed necessary. It is unique. It cannot be replaced. It does not permit either difference, syncretism or accommodation. It is a question of people's salvation. It is the beauty of the Revelation that it represents. It brings with it a wisdom that is not of this world. It is able to stir up by itself faith—faith that rests on the power of God.[11] It is truth. It merits having the apostle consecrate to it all his time and all his energies, and to sacrifice for it, if necessary, his own life.

6. The witness that the Lord gives of himself and that Saint Luke gathered together in his Gospel—"I must proclaim the Good News of the kingdom of God"[12]—without doubt has enormous consequences, for it sums up the whole mission of Jesus: "That is what I was sent to do."[13] These words take on their full significance if one links them with the previous verses, in which Christ has just applied to himself the words of the Prophet Isaiah: "The Spirit of the Lord has been given to me, for he has anointed me. He has sent me to bring the good news to the poor."[14] 1457

Going from town to town, preaching to the poorest—and frequently the most receptive—the joyful news of the fulfillment of the promises and of the Covenant offered by God is the mission for which Jesus declares that he is sent by the Father. And all the aspects of his mystery—the incarnation itself, his miracles, his teaching, the gathering together of the disciples, the sending out of the Twelve, the Cross and the Resurrection, the permanence of his presence in the midst of his own—were components of his evangelizing activity. 1458

7. During the Synod, the Bishops very frequently referred to this truth: Jesus himself, the Good News of God,[15] was the very first and the greatest evangelizer; he was so through and through: to perfection and to the point of the sacrifice of his earthly life. 1459

To evangelize: what meaning did this imperative have for Christ? It is certainly not easy to express in a complete synthesis the meaning, the content and the modes of evangelization as Jesus conceived it and put it into practice. In any case the attempt to make such a synthesis will never end. Let it suffice for us to recall a few essential aspects. 1460

8. As an evangelizer, Christ first of all proclaims a kingdom, the Kingdom of God; and this is so important that, by comparison, everything else becomes "the rest," which is "given in addition."[16] Only the Kingdom therefore is absolute, and it makes everything else relative. The Lord will delight in describing in many ways the happiness of belonging to this Kingdom (a paradoxical happiness which is made up of things that the world rejects),[17] the demands of the King- 1461

dom and its Magna Charta,[18] the heralds of the Kingdom,[19] its mysteries,[20] its children,[21] the vigilance and fidelity demanded of whoever awaits its definitive coming.[22]

1462 9. As the kernel and center of his Good News, Christ proclaims salvation, this great gift of God which is liberation from sin and the Evil One, in the joy of knowing God and being known by him, of seeing him, and of being given over to him. All of this is begun during the life of Christ and definitely accomplished by his death and Resurrection. But it must be patiently carried on during the course of history, in order to be realized fully on the day of the final coming of Christ, whose date is known to no one except the Father.[23]

1463 10. This Kingdom and this salvation, which are the key words of Jesus Christ's evangelization, are available to every human being as grace and mercy, and yet at the same time each individual must gain them by force—they belong to the violent, says the Lord,[24] through toil and suffering, through a life lived according to the Gospel, through abnegation and the Cross, through the spirit of the beatitudes. But above all each individual gains them through a total interior renewal which the Gospel calls metanoia; it is a radical conversion, a profound change of mind and heart.[25]

1464 11. Christ accomplished this proclamation of the Kingdom of God through the untiring preaching of a word which, it will be said, has no equal elsewhere: "Here is a teaching that is new, and with authority behind it."[26] "And he won the approval of all, and they were astonished by the gracious words that came from his lips."[27] "There has never been anybody who has spoken like him."[28] His words reveal the secret of God, his plan and his promise, and thereby change the heart of man and his destiny.

1465 12. But Christ also carries out this proclamation by innumerable signs, which amaze the crowds and at the same time draw them to him in order to see him, listen to him and allow themselves to be transformed by him: the sick are cured, water is changed into wine, bread is multiplied, the dead come back to life. And among all these signs there is the one to which he attaches great importance: the humble and the poor are evangelized, become his disciples and gather together "in his name" in the great community of those who believe in him. For this Jesus who declared, "I must preach the Good News of the Kingdom of God,"[29] is the same Jesus of whom John the Evangelist said that he had come and was to die "to gather together in unity the scattered children of God."[30] Thus he accomplishes his revelation, completing it and confirming it by the entire revelation that he makes of himself, by words and deeds, by signs and miracles, and more especially by his death, by his Resurrection and by the sending of the Spirit of Truth.[31]

13. Those who sincerely accept the Good News, through the power of this acceptance and of shared faith, therefore gather together in Jesus' name in order to seek together the Kingdom, build it up and live it. They make up a community which is in its turn evangelizing. The command to the Twelve to go out and proclaim the Good News is also valid for all Christians, though in a different way. It is precisely for this reason that Peter calls Christians "a people set apart to sing the praises of God,"[32] those marvellous things that each one was able to hear in his own language.[33] Moreover, the Good News of the Kingdom which is coming and which has begun is meant for all people of all times. Those who have received the Good News and who have been gathered by it into the community of salvation can and must communicate and spread it. 1466

14. The Church knows this. She has a vivid awareness of the fact that the Saviour's words, "I must proclaim the Good News of the kingdom of God,"[34] apply in all truth to herself. She willingly adds with Saint Paul: "Not that I boast of preaching the gospel, since it is a duty that has been laid on me; I should be punished if I did not preach it!"[35] It is with joy and colsolation that at the end of the great Assembly of 1974 we heard these illuminating words: "We wish to confirm once more that the task of evangelizing all people constitutes the essential mission of the Church."[36] It is a task and mission which the vast and profound changes of present-day society make all the more urgent. Evangelizing is in fact the grace and vocation proper to the Church, her deepest 1467

identity. She exists in order to evangelize, that is to say in order to preach and teach, to be the channel of the gift of grace, to reconcile sinners with God, and to perpetuate Christ's sacrifice in the Mass, which is the memorial of his death and glorious Resurrection.

1468 15. Anyone who re-reads in the New Testament the origins of the Church, follows her history step by step and watches her live and act, sees that she is linked to evangelization in her most intimate being:

– The Church is born of the evangelizing activity of Jesus and the Twelve. She is the normal, desired, most immediate and most visible fruit of this activity: "Go, therefore, make disciples of all the nations."[37] Now, "they accepted what he said and were baptized. That very day about three thousand were added to their number. . . . Day by day the Lord added to their community those destined to be saved."[38]

– Having been born consequently out of being sent, the Church in her turn is sent by Jesus. The Church remains in the world when the Lord of glory returns to the Father. She remains as a sign–simultaneously obscure and luminous–of a new presence of Jesus, of his departure and of his permanent presence. She prolongs and continues him. And it is above all his mission and his condition of being an evangelizer that she is called upon to continue.[39] For the Christian community is never closed in upon itself. The intimate life of this community–the life of listening to the Word and the Apostles' teaching, charity lived in a fraternal way, the sharing of bread[40]–this intimate life only acquires its full meaning when it becomes a witness, when it evokes admiration and conversion, and when it becomes the preaching and proclamation of the Good News. Thus it is the whole Church that receives the mission to evangelize, and the work of each individual member is important for the whole.

– The Church is an evangelizer, but she begins by being evangelized herself. She is the community of believers, the community of hope lived and communicated, the community of brotherly love; and she needs to listen unceasingly to what she must believe, to her reasons for hoping, to the new commandment of love. She is the People of God immersed in the world, and often tempted by idols, and she always needs to hear the proclamation of the "mighty works of God"[41] which converted her to the Lord; she always needs to be called together afresh by him and reunited. In brief, this means that she has a constant need of being evangelized, if she wishes to retain freshness, vigor and strength in order to proclaim the Gospel. The Second Vatican Council recalled[42] and the 1974 Synod vigorously took up again this theme of the Church which is evangelized by constant conversion and renewal in order to evangelize the world with credibility.

– The Church is the depositary of the Good News to be proclaimed. The promises of the New Alliance in Jesus Christ, the teaching of the Lord and the Apostles, the Word of life, the sources of grace and of God's loving kindness, the path of salvation–all these things have been entrusted to her. It is the content of the Gospel, and therefore of evangelization, that she preserves as a precious living heritage, not in order to keep it hidden but to communicate it.

– Having been sent and evangelized, the Church herself sends out evangelizers. She puts on their lips the saving Word, she explains to them the message of which she herself is the depositary, she gives them the mandate which she herself has received and she sends them out to preach. To preach not their own selves or their personal ideas,[43] but a Gospel of which neither she nor they are the absolute masters and owners, to dispose of it as they wish, but a Gospel of which they are the ministers, in order to pass it on with complete fidelity.

16. There is thus a profound link between Christ, the Church and evangelization. During the period of the Church that we are living in, it is she who has the task of evangelizing. This mandate is not accomplished without her, and still less against her. 1469

1470 It is certainly fitting to recall this fact at a moment like the present one when it happens that not without sorrow we can hear people—whom we wish to believe are well-intentioned but who are certainly misguided in their attitude—continually claiming to love Christ but without the Church, to listen to Christ but not the Church, to belong to Christ but outside the Church. The absurdity of this dichotomy is clearly evident in this phrase of the Gospel: "Anyone who rejects you rejects me."[44] And how can one wish to love Christ without loving the Church, if the finest witness to Christ is that of Saint Paul: "Christ loved the Church and sacrificed himself for her?"[45]

1471 17. In the Church's evangelizing activity there are of course certain elements and aspects to be specially insisted on. Some of them are so important that there will be a tendency simply to identify them with evangelization. Thus it has been possible to define evangelization in terms of proclaiming Christ to those who do not know him, of preaching, of catechesis, of conferring Baptism and the other Sacrements.

1472 Any partial and fragmentary definition which attempts to render the reality of evangelization in all its richness, complexity and dynamism does so only at the risk of impoverishing it and even of distorting it. It is impossible to grasp the concept of evangelization unless one tries to keep in view all its essential elements.

1473 These elements were strongly emphasized at the last Synod and are still the subject of frequent study, as a result of the Synod's work. We rejoice in the fact that these elements basically follow the lines of those transmitted to us by the Second Vatican Council, especially in *Lumen Gentium, Gaudium et Spes* and *Ad Gentes.*

1474 18. For the Church, evangelizing means bringing the Good News into all the strata of humanity, and through its influence transforming humanity from within and making it new: "Now I am making the whole of creation new."[46] But there is no new humanity if there are not first of all new persons renewed by Baptism[47] and by lives lived according to the Gospel.[48] The purpose of evangelization is therefore precisely this interior change, and if it has to be expressed in one sentence the best way of stating it would be to say that the Church evangelizes when she seeks to convert,[49] solely through the divine power of the Message she proclaims, both the personal and collective consciences of people, the activities in which they engage, and the lives and concrete milieux which are theirs.

19. Strata of humanity which are transformed: for the Church it is a question not only of preaching the Gospel in ever wider geographic areas or to ever greater numbers of people, but also of affecting and as it were upsetting, through the power of the Gospel, mankind's criteria of judgment, determining values, points of interest, lines of thought, sources of inspiration and models of life, which are in contrast with the Word of God and the plan of salvation. 1475

20. All this could be expressed in the following words: what matters is to evangelize man's culture and cultures (not in a purely decorative way as it were by applying a thin veneer, but in a vital way, in depth and right to their very roots), in the wide and rich sense which these terms have in *Gaudium et Spes,*[50] always taking the person as one's starting point and always coming back to the relationships of people among themselves and with God. 1476

The Gospel, and therefore evangelization, are certainly not identical with culture, and they are independent in regard to all cultures. Nevertheless, the Kingdom which the Gospel proclaims is lived by men who are profoundly linked to a culture, and the building up of the Kingdom cannot avoid borrowing the elements of human culture or cultures. Though independent of cultures, the Gospel and evangelization are not necessarily incompatible with them; rather they are capable of permeating them all without becoming subject to any one of them. 1477

The split between the Gospel and culture is without a doubt the drama of our time, just as it was of other times. Therefore every effort must be made to ensure a full evangelization of culture, or more correctly of cultures. They have to be regenerated by an encounter with the Gospel. But 1478 this encounter will not take place if the Gospel is not proclaimed.

1479 21. Above all the Gospel must be proclaimed by witness. Take a Christian or a handful of Christians who, in the midst of their own community, show their capacity for understanding and acceptance, their sharing of life and destiny with other people, their solidarity with the efforts of all for whatever is noble and good. Let us suppose that, in addition, they radiate in an altogether simple and unaffected way their faith in values that go beyond current values, and their hope in something that is not seen and that one would not dare to imagine. Through this wordless witness these Christians stir up irresistible questions in the hearts of those who see how they live: Why are they like this? Why do they live in this way? What or who is it that inspires them? Why are they in our midst? Such a witness is already a silent proclamation of the Good News and a very powerful and effective one. Here we have an initial act of evangelization. The above questions will perhaps be the first that many non-Christians will ask, whether they are people to whom Christ has never been proclaimed, or baptized people who do not practice, or people who live as nominal Christians but according to principles that are in no way Christian, or people who are seeking, and not without suffering, something or someone whom they sense but cannot name. Other questions will arise, deeper and more demanding ones, questions evoked by this witness which involves presence, sharing, solidarity, and which is an essential element, and generally the first one, in evangelization.[51]

1480 All Christians are called to this witness, and in this way they can be real evangelizers. We are thinking especially of the responsibility incumbent on immigrants in the country that receives them.

1481 22. Nevertheless this always remains insufficient, because even the finest witness will prove ineffective in the long run if it is not explained, justified—what Peter called always having "your answer ready for people who ask you the reason for the hope that you all have"[52]—and made explicit by a clear and unequivocal proclamation of the Lord Jesus. The Good

News proclaimed by the witness of life sooner or later has to be proclaimed by the word of life. There is no true evangelization if the name, the teaching, the life, the promises, the Kingdom and the mystery of Jesus of Nazareth, the Son of God are not proclaimed. The history of the Church, from the discourse of Peter on the morning of Pentecost onwards, has been intermingled and identified with the history of this proclamation. At every new phase of human history, the Church, constantly gripped by the desire to evangelize, has but one preoccupation: whom to send to proclaim the mystery of Jesus? In what way is this mystery to be proclaimed? How can one ensure that it will resound and reach all those who should hear it? This proclamation—*kerygma,* preaching or catechesis—occupies such an important place in evangelization that it has often become synonymous with it; and yet it is only one aspect of evangelization.

23. In fact the proclamation only reaches full development when it is listened to, accepted and assimilated, and when it arouses a genuine adherence in the one who has thus received it. An adherence to the truths which the Lord in his mercy has revealed; still more, an adherence to a program of life—a life henceforth transformed—which he proposes. In a word, adherence to the Kingdom, that is to say the "new world" to the new state of things, to the new manner of being, of living, of living in community, which the Gospel inaugurates. Such an adherence, which cannot remain abstract and unincarnated, reveals itself concretely by a visible entry into a community of believers. Thus those whose life has been transformed enter a community which is itself a sign of transformation, a sign of newness of life: it is the Church, the visible sacrament of salvation.[53] But entry into the ecclesial community will in its turn be expressed through many other signs which prolong and unfold the sign of the Church. In the dynamism of evangelization, a person who accepts the Church as the Word which saves[54] normally translates it into the following sacramental acts: adherence to the Church, and acceptance of the Sacraments, which manifest 1482

and support this adherence through the grace which they confer.

1483 24. Finally: the person who has been evangelized goes on to evangelize others. Here lies the test of truth, the touchstone of evangelization: it is unthinkable that a person should accept the Word and give himself to the Kingdom without becoming a person who bears witness to it and proclaims it in his turn.

1484 To complete these considerations on the meaning of evangelization, a final observation must be made, one which we consider will help to clarify the reflections that follow.

1485 Evangelization, as we have said, is a complex process made up of varied elements: the renewal of humanity, witness, explicit proclamation, inner adherence, entry into the community, acceptance of signs, apostolic initiative. These elements may appear to be contradictory, indeed mutually exclusive. In fact they are complementary and mutually enriching. Each one must always be seen in relationship with the others. The value of the last Synod was to have constantly invited us to relate these elements rather than to place them in opposition one to the other, in order to reach a full understanding of the Church's evangelizing activity.

1486 It is this global vision which we now wish to outline, by examining the content of evangelization and the methods of evangelizing and by clarifying to whom the Gospel message is addressed and who today is responsible for it.

1487 25. In the message which the Church proclaims there are certainly many secondary elements. Their presentation depends greatly on changing circumstances. They themselves also change. But there is the essential content, the living substance, which cannot be modified or ignored without seriously diluting the nature of evangelization itself.

1488 26. It is not superfluous to recall the following points: to evangelize is first of all to bear witness, in a simple and direct way, to God revealed by Jesus Christ, in the Holy Spirit; to bear witness that in his Son God has loved the world—that in his Incarnate Word he has given being to all things and has called men to eternal life. Perhaps this attestation of God will be for many people the unknown God[55] whom they adore without giving him a name, or whom they seek by a secret call of the heart when they experience the emptiness of all idols. But it is fully evangelizing in manifesting the fact that for man the Creator is not an anonymous and remote power; he is the Father: " . . . that we should be called children of God; and so we are."[56] And thus we are one another's brothers and sisters in God.

27. Evangelization will also always contain—as the foundation, center and at the same time summit of its dynamism—a clear proclamation that, in Jesus Christ, the Son of God made man, who died and rose from the dead, salvation is offered to all men, as a gift of God's grace and mercy.[57] And not an immanent salvation, meeting material or even spiritual needs, restricted to the framework of temporal existence and completely identified with temporal desires, hopes, affairs and struggles, but a salvation which exceeds all these limits in order to reach fulfillment in a communion with the one and only divine Absolute: a transcendent and eschatological salvation, which indeed has its beginning in this life but which is fulfilled in eternity. 1489

28. Consequently evangelization cannot but include the prophetic proclamation of a hereafter, man's profound and definitive calling, in both continuity and discontinuity with the present situation: beyond time and history, beyond the transient reality of this world, and beyond the things of this world, of which a hidden dimension will one day be revealed—beyond man himself, whose true destiny is not restricted to his temporal aspect but will be revealed in the future life.[58] Evangelization therefore also includes the preaching of hope in the promises made by God in the new Covenant in Jesus Christ, the preaching of God's love for all men—the capacity of giving and forgiving, of self-denial, of helping one's brother and sister—which, springing from the love of God, is the kernel of the Gospel; the preaching of the mystery of evil and of the active search for good. The preaching likewise—and this is always urgent—of the search for God himself through prayer which is principally that of adoration and thanksgiving, but also through communion with the visible sign of the encounter with God which is the Church of Jesus 1490

Christ; and this communion in its turn is expressed by the application of those other signs of Christ living and acting in the Church which are the Sacraments. To live the Sacraments in this way, bringing their celebration to a true fullness, is not, as some would claim, to impede or to accept a distortion of evangelization: it is rather to complete it. For in its totality, evangelization—over and above the preaching of a message—consists in the implantation of the Church, which does not exist without the driving force which is the sacramental life culminating in the Eucharist.[59]

1491 29. But evangelization would not be complete if it did not take account of the unceasing interplay of the Gospel and of man's concrete life, both personal and social. This is why evangelization involves an explicit message, adapted to the different situations constantly being realized, about the rights and duties of every human being, about family life without which personal growth and development is hardly possible,[60] about life in society, about international life, peace, justice and development—a message especially energetic today about liberation.

1492 30. It is well known in what terms numerous Bishops from all the continents spoke of this at the last Synod, especially the Bishops from the Third World, with a pastoral accent resonant with the voice of the millions of sons and daughters of the Church who make up those peoples. Peoples, as we know, engaged with all their energy in the effort and struggle to overcome everything which condemns them to remain on the margin of life: famine, chronic disease, illiteracy, poverty, injustices in international relations and especially in commercial exchanges, situations of economic and cultural neo-colonialism sometimes as cruel as the old political colonialism. The Church, as the Bishops repeated, has the duty to proclaim the liberation of millions of human beings, many of whom are her own children—the duty of assisting the birth of this liberation, of giving witness to it, of ensuring that it is complete. This is not foreign to evangelization.

1493 31. Between evangelization and human advancement—development and liberation—there are in fact profound links. These include links of an anthropological order, because the man who is to be evangelized is not an abstract being but is subject to social and economic questions. They also include links in the theological order, since one cannot dissociate the plan of creation from the plan of Redemption. The latter plan touches the very concrete situations of injustice to be combatted and of justice to be restored. They include links of the eminently evangelical order, which is that of charity: how in fact can one proclaim the new commandment without promoting in justice and in peace the true, authentic advancement of man? We ourself have taken care to point this out, by recalling that it is impossible to accept "that in evangelization one could or should ignore the importance of the problems so much discussed today, concerning justice, liberation, development and peace in the world. This would be to forget the lesson which comes to us from the Gospel concerning love of our neighbor who is suffering and in need."[61]

1494

The same voices which during the Synod touched on this burning theme with zeal, intelligence and courage have, to our great joy, furnished the enlightening principles for a proper understanding of the importance and profound meaning of liberation, such as it was proclaimed and achieved by Jesus of Nazareth and such as it is preached by the Church.

1495

32. We must not ignore the fact that many, even generous Christians who are sensitive to the dramatic questions involved in the problem of liberation, in their wish to commit the Church to the liberation effort are frequently tempted to reduce her mission to the dimensions of a simply temporal project. They would reduce her aims to a man-centered goal; the salvation of which she is the messenger would be reduced to material well-being. Her activity, forgetful of all spiritual and religious preoccupation, would become initiatives of the political or social order. But if this were so, the Church would lose her fundamental meaning. Her message of liberation would no longer have any originality and would easily be open to monopolization and manipulation by ideological systems and political parties. She would have no more authority to proclaim freedom as in the name of God. This is why we have wished to emphasize, in the same address at the opening of the Synod, "the need to restate clearly the specifically reli-

gious finality of evangelization. This latter would lose its reason for existence if it were to diverge from the religious axis that guides it: the Kingdom of God, before anything else, in its fully theological meaning. . . ."[62]

1496 33. With regard to the liberation which evangelization proclaims and strives to put into practice one should rather say this:

— it cannot be contained in the simple and restricted dimension of economics, politics, social or cultural life; it must envisage the whole man, in all his aspects, right up to and including his openness to the absolute, even the divine Absolute;

— it is therefore attached to a certain concept of man, to a view of man which it can never sacrifice to the needs of any strategy, practice or short-term efficiency.

1497 34. Hence, when preaching liberation and associating herself with those who are working and suffering for it, the Church is certainly not willing to restrict her mission only to the religious field and dissociate herself from man's temporal problems. Nevertheless she reaffirms the primacy of her spiritual vocation and refuses to replace the proclamation of the Kingdom by the proclamation of forms of human liberation; she even states that her contribution to liberation is incomplete if she neglects to proclaim salvation in Jesus Christ.

1498 35. The Church links human liberation and salvation in Jesus Christ, but she never identifies them, because she knows through revelation, historical experience and the reflection of faith that not every notion of liberation is necessarily consistent and compatible with an evangelical vision of man, of things and of events; she knows too that in order that God's Kingdom should come it is not enough to establish liberation and to create well-being and development.

1499 And what is more, the Church has the firm conviction that all temporal liberation, all political liberation—even if it endeavors to find its justification in such a page of the Old or New Testament, even if it claims for its ideological postulates and its norms of action theological data and conclusions, even if it pretends to be today's theology—carries within itself the germ of its own negation and fails to reach the ideal that it proposes for itself, whenever its profound motives are not those of justice in charity, whenever its zeal lacks a truly spiritual dimension and whenever its final goal is not salvation and happiness in God.

36. The Church considers it to be undoubtedly important to build up structures which are more human, more just, more respectful of the rights of the person and less oppressive and less enslaving, but she is conscious that the best structures and the most idealized systems soon become inhuman if the inhuman inclinations of the human heart are not made wholesome, if those who live in these structures or who rule them do not undergo a conversion of heart and of outlook. 1500

37. The Church cannot accept violence, especially the force of arms—which is uncontrollable once it is let loose—and indiscriminate death as the path to liberation, because she knows that violence always provokes violence and irresistibly engenders new forms of oppression and enslavement which are often harder to bear than those from which they claimed to bring freedom. We said this clearly during our journey in Colombia: "We exhort you not to place your trust in violence and revolution: that is contrary to the Christian spirit, and it can also delay instead of advancing that social uplifting to which you lawfully aspire."[63] "We must say and reaffirm that violence is not in accord with the Gospel, that it is not Christian; and that sudden or violent changes of structures would be deceitful, ineffective of themselves, and certainly not in conformity with the dignity of the people."[64] 1501

38. Having said this, we rejoice that the Church is becoming ever more conscious of the proper manner and strictly evangelical means that she possesses in order to collaborate in the liberation of many. And what is she doing? She is trying more and more to encourage large numbers of Christians to devote themselves to the liberation of men. She is providing these Christian "liberators" with the inspiration of faith, the motivation of fraternal love, a social teaching which the true Christian cannot ignore and which he must make the foundation of his wisdom and of his experience in order to translate it 1502

concretely into forms of action, participation and commitment. All this must characterize the spirit of a committed Christian, without confusion with tactical attitudes or with the service of a political system. The Church strives always to insert the Christian struggle for liberation into the universal plan of salvation which she herself proclaims.

1503 What we have just recalled comes out more than once in the Synod debates. In fact we devoted to this theme a few clarifying words in our address to the Fathers at the end of the Assembly.[65]

1504 It is to be hoped that all these considerations will help to remove the ambiguity which the word "liberation" very often takes on in ideologies, political systems or groups. The liberation which evangelization proclaims and prepares is the one which Christ himself announced and gave to man by his sacrifice.

1505 39. The necessity of ensuring fundamental human rights cannot be separated from this just liberation which is bound up with evangelization and which endeavors to secure structures safeguarding human freedoms. Among these fundamental human rights, religious liberty occupies a place of primary importance. We recently spoke of the relevance of this matter, emphasizing "how many Christians still today, because they are Christians, because they are Catholics, live oppressed by systematic persecution! The drama of fidelity to Christ and of the freedom of religion continues, even if it is disguised by categorical declarations in favor of the rights of the person and of life in society!"[66]

1506 40. The obvious importance of the content of evangelization must not overshadow the importance of the ways and means.

1507 This question of "how to evangelize" is permanently relevant, because the methods of evangelizing vary according to the different circumstances of time, place and culture, and because they thereby present a certain challenge to our capacity for discovery and adaptation.

1508 On us particularly, the pastors of the Church, rests the responsibility for reshaping with boldness and wisdom, but in complete fidelity to the content of evangelization, the means that are most suitable and effective for communication the Gospel message to the men and women of our times.

Let it suffice, in this meditation, to mention a number of methods which, for one reason or another, have a fundamental importance. 1509

41. Without repeating everything that we have already mentioned, it is appropriate first of all to emphasize the following point: for the Church, the first means of evangelization is the witness of an authentically Christian life, given over to God in a communion that nothing should destroy and at the same time given to one's neighbor with limitless zeal. As we said recently to a group of law people, "Modern man listens more willingly to witnesses than to teachers, and if he does listen to teachers, it is because they are witnesses."[67] Saint Peter expressed this well when he held up the example of a reverent and chaste life that wins over even without a word those who refuse to obey the word.[68] It is therefore primarily by her conduct and by her life that the Church will evangelize the world, in other words, by her living witness of fidelity to the Lord Jesus—the witness of poverty and detachment, of freedom in the face of the powers of this world, in short, the witness of sanctity. 1510

42. Secondly, it is not superfluous to emphasize the importance and necessity of preaching. "And how are they to believe in him of whom they have never heard? And how are they to hear without a preacher? . . . So faith comes from what is heard and what is heard comes by the preaching of Christ."[69] This law once laid down by the Apostle Paul maintains its full force today. 1511

Preaching, the verbal proclamation of a message, is indeed always indispensable. We are well aware that modern man is sated by talk;he is obviously often tired of listening and, what is worse, impervious to words. We are also aware that many psychologists and sociologists express the view that modern man has passed beyond the civilization of the word, which is now ineffective and useless, and that today he lives in the civilization of the image. These facts should certainly impel us to employ, for the purpose of transmitting the Gospel message, the modern means which this civilization has produced. 1512

Very positive efforts have in fact already been made in this sphere. We cannot but praise them and encourage their further development. The fatigue produced these days by so much empty talk and the relevance of many other forms of communication must not however diminish the permanent power of the word, or cause a loss of confidence in it. The word remains ever relevant, especially when it is the bearer of the power of God.[70] This is why Saint Paul's axiom, "Faith comes from what is heard,"[71] also retains its relevance: it is the Word that is heard which leads to belief.

1513 43. This evangelizing preaching takes on many forms, and zeal will inspire the reshaping of them almost indefinitely. In fact there are innumerable events in life and human situations which offer the opportunity for a discreet but incisive statement of what the Lord has to say in this or that particular circumstance. It suffices to have true spiritual sensitivity for reading God's message in events. But at a time when the liturgy renewed by the Council has given greatly increased value to the Liturgy of the Word, it would be a mistake not to see in the homily an important and very adaptable instrument of evangelization. Of course it is necessary to know and put to good use the exigencies and the possibilities of the homily, so that it can acquire all its pastoral effectiveness. But above all it is necessary to be convinced of this and to devote oneself to it with love. This preaching, inserted in a unique way into the Eucharistic celebration, from which it receives special force and vigor, certainly has a particular role in evangelization, to the extent that it expresses the profound faith of the sacred minister and is impregnated with love. The faithful assembled as a Paschal Church, celebrating the feast of the Lord present in their midst, expect much from this preaching, and will greatly benefit from it provided that it is simple, clear, direct, well-adapted, profoundly dependent on Gospel teaching and faithful to the Magisterium, animated by a balanced apostolic ardor coming from its own characteristic nature, full of hope, fostering belief, and productive of peace and unity. Many parochial or other communities live and are held together thanks to the Sunday homily, when it possesses these qualities.

Let us add that, thanks to the same liturgical renewal, the Eucharistic celebration is not the only appropriate moment for the homily. The homily has a place and must not be neglected in the celebration of all the Sacraments, at paraliturgies, and in assemblies of the faithful. It will always be a privileged occasion for communicating the Word of the Lord. 1514

44. A means of evangelization that must not be neglected is that of catechetical instruction. The intelligence, especially that of children and young people, needs to learn through systematic religious instruction the fundamental teachings, the living content of the truth which God has wished to convey to us and which the Church has sought to express in an ever richer fashion during the course of her long history. No one will deny that this instruction must be given to form patterns of Christian living and not to remain only notional. Truly the effort for evangelization will profit greatly—at the level of catechetical instruction given at church, in the schools, where this is possible, and in every case in Christian homes—if those giving catechetical instruction have suitable texts, updated with wisdom and competence, under the authority of the Bishops. The methods must be adapted to the age, culture and aptitude of the persons concerned; they must seek always to fix in the memory, intelligence and heart the essential truths that must impregnate all of life. It is necessary above all to prepare good instructors—parochial catechists, teachers, parents—who are desirous of perfecting themselves in this superior art, which is indispensable and requires religious instruction. Moreover, without neglecting in any way the training of children, one sees that present conditions render ever more urgent catechetical instruction, under the form of the catechumenate, for innumerable young people and adults who, touched by grace, discover little by little the face of Christ and feel the need of giving themselves to him. 1515

45. Our century is characterized by the mass media or means of social communication, and the first proclamation, catechesis or the further deepening of faith cannot do without these means, as we have already emphasized. 1516

When they are put at the service of the Gospel, they are capable of increasing almost indefinitely the area in which 1517 the Word of God is heard; they enable the Good News to reach millions of people. The Church would feel guilty before the Lord if she did not utilize these powerful means that human skill is daily rendering more perfect. It is through them that she proclaims "from the housetops"[72] the message of which she is the depositary. In them she finds a modern and effective version of the pulpit. Thanks to them she succeeds in speaking to the multitudes.

1518 Nevertheless the use of the means of social communication for evangelization presents a challenge: through them the evangelical message should reach vast numbers of people, but with the capacity of piercing the conscience of each individual, of implanting itself in his heart as though he were the only person being addressed, with all his most individual and personal qualities, and evoke an entirely personal adherence and commitment.

1519 46. For this reason, side-by-side with the collective proclamation of the Gospel, the other form of transmission, the person-to-person one, remains valid and important. The Lord often used it (for example with Nicodemus, Zacchaeus, the Samaritan woman, Simon the Pharisee), and so did the Apostles. In the long run, is there any other way of handing on the Gospel than by transmitting to another person one's personal experience of faith? It must not happen that the pressing need to proclaim the Good News to the multitudes should cause us to forget this form of proclamation whereby an individual's personal conscience is reached and touched by an entirely unique word that he receives from someone else. We can never sufficiently praise those priests who through the Sacrament of Penance or through pastoral dialogue show their readiness to guide people in the ways of the Gospel, to support them in their efforts, to raise them up if they have fallen, and always to assist them with discernment and availability.

1520 47. Yet, one can never sufficiently stress the fact that evangelization does not consist only of the preaching and teaching of a doctrine. For evangelization must touch life: the natural life to which it gives a new meaning, thanks to the evangelical perspectives that it reveals; and the supernatural life, which is not the negation but the purification and elevation of the natural life.

This supernatural life finds its living expression in the seven Sacraments and in the admirable radiation of grace and holiness which they possess. 1521

Evangelization thus exercises its full capacity when it achieves the most intimate relationship, or better still a permanent and unbroken intercommunication, between the Word and the Sacraments. In a certain sense it is a mistake to make a contrast between evangelization and sacramentalization, as is sometimes done. It is indeed true that a certain way of administering the Sacraments, without the solid support of catechesis regarding these same Sacraments and a global catechesis, could end up by depriving them of their effectiveness to a great extent. The role of evangelization is precisely to educate people in the faith in such a way as to lead each individual Christian to live the Sacraments as true Sacraments of faith—and not to receive them passively or to undergo them. 1522

48. Here we touch upon an aspect of evangelization which cannot leave us insensitive. We wish to speak about what today is often called popular religiosity. 1523

One finds among the people particular expressions of the search for God and for faith, both in the regions where the Church has been established for centuries and where she is in the course of becoming established. These expressions were for a long time regarded as less pure and were sometimes despised, but today they are almost everywhere being rediscovered. During the last Synod the Bishops studied their significance with remarkable pastoral realism and zeal. 1524

Popular religiosity of course certainly has its limits. It is often subject to penetration by many distortions of religion and even superstitions. It frequently remains at the level of forms of worship not involving a true acceptance by faith. It can even lead to the creation of sects and endanger the true ecclesial community. 1525

But if it is well oriented, above all by a pedagogy of evangelization, it is rich in values. It manifests a thirst for God 1526 which only the simple and poor can know. It makes people capable of generosity and sacrifice even to the point of heroism, when it is a question of manifesting belief. It involves an acute awareness of profound attributes of God: fatherhood, providence, loving and constant presence. It engenders interior attitudes rarely observed to the same degree elsewhere: patience, the sense of the Cross in daily life, detachment, openness to others, devotion. By reason of these aspects, we readily call it "popular piety," that is, religion of the people, rather than religiosity.

1527 Pastoral charity must dictate to all those whom the Lord has placed as leaders of the ecclesial communities the proper attitude in regard to this reality, which is at the same time so rich and so vulnerable. Above all one must be sensitive to it, know how to perceive its interior dimensions and undeniable values, be ready to help it to overcome its risks of deviation. When it is well oriented, this popular religiosity can be more and more for multitudes of our people a true encounter with God in Jesus Christ.

1528 49. Jesus' last words in Saint Mark's Gospel confer on the evangelization which the Lord entrusts to his Apostles a limitless universality: "Go out to the whole world; proclaim the Good News to all creation."[73]

1529 The Twelve and the first generation of Christians understood well the lesson of this text and other similar ones; they made them into a program of action. Even persecution, by scattering the Apostles, helped to spread the Word and to establish the Church in ever more distant regions. The admissions of Paul to the rank of the Apostles and his charism as the preacher to the pagans (the non-Jews) of Jesus' Coming underlined this universality still more.

1530 50. In the course of twenty centuries of history, the generations of Christians have periodically faced various obstacles to this universal mission. On the one hand, on the part of the evangelizers themselves, there has been the temptation for various reasons to narrow down the field of their missionary activity. On the other hand, there has been the often humanly insurmoutable resistance of the people being addressed by the evangelizer. Furthermore, we must note with sadness that the evangelizing work of the Church is strongly opposed, if not prevented, by certain public powers. Even in our own day it happens that preachers of God's Word are deprived of their rights, persecuted, threatened or eliminated solely for preaching Jesus Christ and his Gospel. But we are confident that despite these painful trials the activity of these apostles will never meet final failure in any part of the world.

Despite such adversities the Church constantly renews her deepest inspiration, that which comes to her directly from the Lord: To the whole world! To all creation! Right to the ends of the earth! She did this once more at the last Synod, as an appeal not to imprison the proclamation of the Gospel by limiting it to one sector of mankind or to one class of people or to a single type of civilization. Some examples are revealing. 1531

51. To reveal Jesus Christ and his Gospel to those who do not know them has been, ever since the morning of Pentecost, the fundamental program which the Church has taken on as received from her Founder. The whole of the New Testament, and in a special way the Acts of the Apostles, bears witness to a privleged and in a sense exemplary moment of this missionary effort which will subsequently leave its mark on the whole history of the Church. 1532

She carries out this first proclamation of Jesus Christ by a complex and diversified activity which is sometimes termed "preevangelization" but which is already evangelization in a true sense, although at its initial and still incomplete stage. An almost indefinite range of means can be used for this purpose: explicit preaching, of course, but also art, the scientific approach, philosophical research and legitimate recourse to the sentiments of the human heart. 1533

52. This first proclamation is addressed especially to those who have never heard the Good News of Jesus, or to children. But, as a result of the frequent situations of dechristianization in our day, it also proves equally necessary for innumerable people who have been baptized but who live quite outside Christian life, for simple people who have a certain faith but an imperfect knowledge of the foundations of that faith, for intellectuals who feel the need to know Jesus Christ in a light 1534

different from the instruction they received as children, and for many others.

1535 53. This first proclamation is also addressed to the immense sections of mankind who practice non-Christian religions. The Church respects and esteems these non-Christian religions because they are the living expression of the soul of vast groups of people. They carry within them the echo of thousands of years of searching for God, a quest which is incomplete but often made with great sincerity and righteousness of heart. They possess an impressive patrimony of deeply religious texts. They have taught generations of people how to pray. They are all impregnated with innumerable "seeds of the Word"[74] and can constitute a true "preparation for the Gospel,"[75] to quote a felicitous term used by the Second Vatican Council and borrowed from Eusebius of Caesarea.

1536 Such a situation certainly raises complex and delicate questions that must be studied in the light of Christian Tradition and the Church's Magisterium, in order to offer to the missionaries of today and of tomorrow new horizons in their contacts with non-Christian religions. We wish to point out, above all today, that neither respect and esteem for these religions nor the complexity of the questions raised is an invitation to the Church to withhold from these non-Christians the proclamation of Jesus Christ. On the contrary the Church holds that these multitudes have the right to know the riches of the mystery of Christ[76]—riches in which we believe that the whole of humanity can find, in unsuspected fullness, everything that it is gropingly searching for concerning God, man and his destiny, life and death, and truth. Even in the face of natural religious expressions most worthy of esteem, the Church finds support in the fact that the religion of Jesus, which she proclaims through evangelization, objectively places man in relation with the plan of God, with his living presence and with his action; she thus causes an encounter with the mystery of divine paternity that bends over towards humanity. In other words, our religion effectively establishes with God an authentic and living relationship which the other religions do not succeed in doing, even though they have, as it were, their arms stretched out towards heaven.

This is why the Church keeps her missionary spirit alive, and even wishes to intensify it in the moment of history in which we are living. She feels responsible before entire peoples. She has no rest so long as she has not done her best to proclaim the Good News of Jesus the Saviour. She is always preparing new generations of apostles. Let us state this fact with joy at a time when there are not lacking those who think and even say that ardor and the apostolic spirit are exhausted, and that the time of the missions is now past. The Synod has replied that the missionary proclamation never ceases and that the Church will always be striving for the fulfillment of this proclamation. 1537

54. Nevertheless the Church does not feel dispensed from paying unflagging attention also to those who have received the faith and who have been in contact with the Gospel often for generations. Thus she seeks to deepen, consolidate, nourish and make ever more mature the faith of those who are already called the faithful or believers, in order that they may be so still more. 1538

This faith is nearly always today exposed to secularism, even to militant atheism. It is a faith exposed to trials and threats, and even more, a faith besieged and actively opposed. It runs the risk of perishing from suffocation or starvation if it is not fed and sustained each day. To evangelize must therefore very often be to give this necessary food and sustenance to the faith of believers, especially through a catechesis full of Gospel vitality and in a language suited to people and circumstances. 1539

The Church also has a lively solicitude for the Christians who are not in full communion with her. While preparing with them the unity willed by Christ, and precisely in order to realize unity in truth, she has the consciousness that she would be gravely lacking in her duty if she did not give witness before them of the fullness of the revelation whose deposit she guards. 1540

55. Also significant is the preoccupation of the last Synod in regard to two spheres which are very different from one another but which at the same time are very close by reason 1541

of the challenge which they make to evangelization, each in its own way.

1542 The first sphere is the one which can be called the increase of unbelief in the modern world. The Synod endeavored to describe this modern world: how many currents of thought, values and countervalues, latent aspirations or seeds of destruction, old convictions which disappear and new convictions which arise are covered by this generic name!

1543 From the spiritual point of view, the modern world seems to be for ever immersed in what a modern author has termed "the drama of atheistic humanism."[77]

1544 On the one hand one is forced to note in the very heart of this contemporary world the phenomenon which is becoming almost its most striking characteristic: secularism. We are not speaking of secularization, which is the effort, in itself just and legitimate and in no way incompatible with faith or religion, to discover in creation, in each thing or each happening in the universe, the laws which regulate them with a certain autonomy, but with the inner conviction that the Creator has placed these laws there. The last Council has in this sense affirmed the legitimate autonomy of culture and particularly of the sciences.[78] Here we are thinking of a true secularism: a concept of the world according to which the latter is self-explanatory, without any need for recourse to God, who thus becomes superfluous and an encumbrance. This sort of secularism, in order to recognize the power of man, therefore ends up by doing without God and even by denying him.

1545 New forms of atheism seem to flow from it: a man-centered atheism, no longer abstract and petaphysical but pragmatic, systematic and militant. Hand in hand with this atheistic secularism, we are daily faced, under the most diverse forms, with a consumer society, the pursuit of pleasure set up as the supreme value, a desire for power and domination, and discrimination of every kind: the inhuman tendencies of this "humanism."

1546 In this same modern world, on the other hand, and this is a paradox, one cannot deny the existence of real stepping-stones to Christianity, and of evangelical values at least in the form of a sense of emptiness or nostalgia. It would not be an exaggeration to say that there exists a powerful and tragic appeal to be evangelized.

56. The second sphere is that of those who do not practice. Today there is a very large number of baptized people who for the most part have not formally renounced their Baptism but who are entirely indifferent to it and not living in accordance with it. The phenomenon of the non-practicing is a very ancient one in the history of Christianity; it is the result of a natural weakness, a profound inconsistency which we unfortunately bear deep within us. Today however it shows certain new characteristics. It is often the result of the uprooting typical of our time. It also springs from the fact that Christians live in close proximity with nonbelievers and constantly experience the effects of unbelief. Furthermore, the non-practicing Christians of today, more so than those of previous periods, seek to explain and justify their position in the name of an interior religion, of personal independence or authenticity. 1547

Thus we have atheists and unbelievers on the one side and those who do not practice on the other, and both groups put up a considerable resistance to evangelization. The resistance of the former takes the form of a certain refusal and an inability to grasp the new order of things, the new meaning of the world, of life and of history; such is not possible if one does not start from a divine absolute. The resistance of the second group takes the form of inertia and the slightly hostile attitude of the person who feels that he is one of the family, who claims to know it all and to have tried it all and who no longer believes it. 1548

Atheistic secularism and the absence of religious practice are found among adults and among the young, among the leaders of society and among the ordinary people, at all levels of education, and in both the old Churches and the young ones. The Church's evangelizing action cannot ignore these two worlds, nor must it come to a standstill when faced with them; it must constantly seek the proper means and language for presenting, or re-presenting, to them God's revelation and faith in Jesus Christ. 1549

1550 57. Like Christ during the time of his preaching, like the Twelve on the morning of Pentecost, the Church too sees before her an immense multitude of people who need the Gospel and have a right to it, for God "wants everyone to be saved and reach full knowledge of the truth."[79]

1551 The Church is deeply aware of her duty to preach salvation to all. Knowing that the Gospel message is not reserved to a small group of the initiated, the privileged or the elect but is destined for everyone, she shares Christ's anguish at the sight of the wandering and exhausted crowds "like sheep without a shepherd" and she often repeats his words: "I feel sorry for all these people."[80] But the Church is also conscious of the fact that, if the preaching of the Gospel is to be effective, she must address her message to the heart of the multitudes, to communities of the faithful whose action can and must reach others.

1552 58. The last Synod devoted considerable attention to these "small communities," or *communautés de base,* because they are often talked about in the Church today. What are they, and why should they be the special beneficiaries of evangelization and at the same time evangelizers themselves?

1553 According to the various statements heard in the Synod, such communities flourish more or less throughout the Church. They differ greatly among themselves, both within the same region and even more so from one region to another.

1554 In some regions they appear and develop, almost without exception, within the Church, having solidarity with her life, being nourished by her teaching and united with her pastors. In these cases, they spring from the need to live the Church's life more intensely, or from the desire and quest for a more human dimension such as larger ecclesial communities can only offer with difficulty, especially in the big modern cities which lend themselves both to life in the mass and to anonymity. Such communities can quite simply be in their own way an extension on the spiritual and religious level—worship, deepening of faith, fraternal charity, prayer, contact with pastors—of the small sociological community such as the village, etc. Or again their aim may be to bring together, for the purpose of listening to and meditating on the Word, for the

Sacraments and the bond of the agape, groups of people who are linked by age, culture, civil state or social situation: married couples, young people, professional people, etc., people who already happen to be united in the struggle for justice, brotherly aid to the poor, human advancement. In still other cases they bring Christians together in places where the shortage of priests does not favor the normal life of a parish community. This is all presupposed within communities constituted by the Church, especially individual Churches and parishes.

In other regions, on the other hand, *communautés de base* come together in a spirit of bitter criticism of the Church, which they are quick to stigmatize as "institutional" and to which they set themselves up in opposition as charismatic communities, free from structures and inspired only by the Gospel. Thus their obvious characteristic is an attitude of fault-finding and of rejection with regard to the Church's outward manifestations: her hierarchy, her signs. They are radically opposed to the Church. By following these lines their main inspiration very quickly becomes ideological, and it rarely happens that they do not quickly fall victim to some political option or current of thought, and then to a system, even a party, with all the attendant risks of becoming its instrument. 1555

The difference is already notable: the communities which by their spirit of opposition cut themselves off from the Church, and whose unity they wound, can well be called *communautés de base,* but in this case it is a strictly sociological name. They could not, without a misuse of terms, be called ecclesial *communautés de base,* even if, while being hostile to the hierarchy, they claim to remain within the unity of the Church. This name belongs to the other groups, those which come together within the Church in order to unite themselves to the Church and to cause the Church to grow. 1556

These latter communities will be a place of evangelization, for the benefit of the bigger communities, especially the individual Churches. And, as we said at the end of the last Synod, they will be a hope for the universal Church to the extent: 1557

— that they seek their nourishment in the Word of God and do not allow themselves to be ensnared by political polarization or fashionable ideologies, which are already to exploit their immense human potential;

— that they avoid the ever present temptation of systematic protest and a hypercritical attitude, under the pretext of authenticity and a spirit of collaboration;

— that they remain firmly attached to the local Church in which they are inserted, and to the universal Church, thus avoiding the very real danger of becoming isolated within themselves, then of believing themselves to be the only authentic Church of Christ, and hence of condemning the other ecclesial communities;

— that they maintain a sincere communion with the pastors whom the Lord gives to his Church, and with the Magisterium which the Spirit of Christ has entrusted to these pastors;

— that they never look on themselves as the sole beneficiaries or sole agents of evangelization—or even the only depositaries of the Gospel—but, being aware that the Church is much more vast and diversified, accept the fact that this Church becomes incarnate in other ways than through themselves;

— that they constantly grow in missionary consciousness, fervor, commitment and zeal;

— that they show themselves to be universal in all things and never sectarian.

1558 On these conditions, which are certainly demanding but also uplifting, the ecclesial *communautés de base* will correspond to their most fundamental vocation: as hearers of the Gospel which is proclaimed to them and privileged beneficiaries of evangelization, they will soon become proclaimers of the Gospel themselves.

1559 59. If people proclaim in the world the Gospel of salvation, they do so by the command of, in the name of and with the grace of Christ the Saviour. "They will never have a preacher unless one is sent,"[81] wrote he who was without doubt one of the greatest evangelizers. No one can do it without having been sent.

1560 But who then has the mission of evangelizing?

The Second Vatican Council gave a clear reply to this question: it is upon the Church that "there rests, by divine mandate, the duty of going out into the whole world and preaching the gospel to every creature."[82] And in another text: ". . . the whole Church is missionary, and the work of evangelization is a basic duty of the People of God."[83] 1561

We have already mentioned this intimate connection between the Church and evangelization. While the Church is proclaiming the Kingdom of God and building it up, she is establishing herself in the midst of the world as the sign and instrument of this Kingdom which is and which is to come. The Council repeats the following expression of Saint Augustine on the missionary activity of the Twelve: "They preached the word of truth and brought forth Church."[84] 1562

60. The observation that the Church has been sent out and given a mandate to evangelize the world should awaken in us two convictions. 1563

The first is this: evangelization is for no one an individual and isolated act; it is one that is deeply ecclesial. When the most obscure preacher, catechist or pastor in the most distant land preaches the Gospel, gathers his little community together or administers a Sacrament, even alone, he is carrying out an ecclesial act, and his action is certainly attached to the evangelizing activity of the whole Church by institutional relationships, but also by profound invisible links in the order of grace. This presupposes that he acts not in virtue of a mission which he attributes to himself or by a personal inspiration, but in union with the mission of the Church and in her name. 1564

From this flows the second conviction: if each individual evangelizes in the name of the Church, who herself does so by virtue of a mandate from the Lord, no evangelizer is the absolute master of his evangelizing action, with a discretionary power to carry it out in accordance with individualistic criteria and perspectives; he acts in communion with the Church and her pastors. 1565

We have remarked that the Church is entirely and completely evangelizing. This means that, in the whole world and 1566 in each part of the world where she is present, the Church feels responsible for the task of spreading the Gospel.

1567 61. Brothers and sons and daughters, at this stage of our reflection, we wish to pause with you at a question which is particularly important at the present time. In the celebration of the liturgy, in their witness before judges and executioners and in their apologetical texts, the first Christians readily expressed their deep faith in the Church by describing her as being spread throughout the universe. They were fully conscious of belonging to a large community which neither space nor time can limit: "From the just Abel right to the last of the elect,"[86] "indeed to the ends of the earth,"[86] "to the end of time."[87]

1568 This is how the Lord wanted his Church to be: universal, a great tree whose branches shelter the birds of the air,[88] a net which catches fish of every kind[89] or which Peter drew in filled with one hundred and fifty-three big fish,[90] a flock which a single shepherd pastures.[91] A universal Church without boundaries or frontiers except, alas, those of the heart and mind of sinful man.

1569 62. Nevertheless this universal Church is in practice incarnate in the individual Churches made up of such or such an actual part of mankind, speaking such and such a language, heirs of a cultural patrimony, of a vision of the world, of an historical past, of a particular human substratum. Receptivity to the wealth of the individual Church corresponds to a special sensitivity of modern man.

1570 Let us be very careful not to conceive of the universal Church as the sum, or, if one can say so, the more or less anomalous federation of essentially different individual Churches. In the mind of the Lord the Church is universal by vocation and mission, but when she puts down her roots in a variety of cultural, social and human terrains, she takes on different external expressions and appearances in each part of the world.

1571 Thus each individual Church that would voluntarily cut itself off from the universal Church would lose its relationship to God's plan and would be impoverished in its ecclesial dimension. But, at the same time, a Church *toto orbe diffusa* would become an abstraction if she did not take body and life precisely through the individual Churches. Only continual attention to these two poles of the Church will enable us to perceive the richness of this relationship between the universal Church and the individual Churches.

63. The individual Churches, intimately built up not only of people but also of aspirations, of riches and limitations, of ways of praying, of loving, of looking at life and the world which distinguish this or that human gathering, have the task of assimilating the essence of the Gospel message and of transposing it, without the slightest betrayal of its essential truth, into the language that these particular people understand, then of proclaiming it in this language. 1572

The transposition has to be done with the discernment, seriousness, respect and competence which the matter calls for in the field of liturgical expression,[92] and in the areas of catechesis, theological formulation, secondary ecclesial structures, and ministries. And the word "language" should be understood here less in the semantic or literary sense than in the sense which one may call anthropological and cultural. 1573

The question is undoubtedly a delicate one. Evangelization loses much of its force and effectiveness if it does not take into consideration the actual people to whom it is addressed, if it does not use their language, their signs and symbols, if it does not answer the questions they ask, and if it does not have an impact on their concrete life. But on the other hand evangelization risks losing its power and disappearing altogether if one empties or adulterates its content under the pretext of translating it; if, in other words, one sacrifices this reality and destroys the unity without which there is no universality, out of a wish to adapt a universal reality to a local situation. Now, only a Church which preserves the awareness of her universality and shows that she is in fact universal is capable of having a message which can be heard by all, regardless of regional frontiers. 1574

Legitimate attention to individual Churches cannot fail to enrich the Church. Such attention is indispensable and urgent. It responds to the very deep aspirations of peoples and human communities to find their own identity ever more clearly. 1575

1576 64. But this enrichment requires that the individual Churches should keep their profound openness towards the universal Church. It is quite remarkable, moreover, that the most simple Christians, the ones who are most faithful to the Gospel and most open to the true meaning of the Church, have a completely spontaneous sensitivity to this universal dimension. They instictively and very strongly feel the need for it, they easily recognize themselves in such a dimension. They feel with it and suffer very deeply within themselves when, in the name of theories which they do not understand, they are forced to accept a Church deprived of this universality, a regionalist Church, with no horizon.

1577 As history in fact shows, whenever an individual Church has cut itself off from the universal Church and from its living and visible center—sometimes with the best of intentions, with theological, sociological, political or pastoral arguments, or even in the desire for a certain freedom of movement or action—it has escaped only with great difficulty (if indeed it has escaped) from two equally serious dangers. The first danger is that of a withering isolationism, and then, before long, of a crumbling away, with each of its cells breaking away from it just as it itself has broken away from the central nucleus. The second danger is that of losing its freedom when, being cut off from the center and from the other Churches which gave it strength and energy, it finds itself all alone and a prey to the most varied forces of enslavery and exploitation.

1578 The more an individual Church is attached to the universal Church by solid bonds of communion, in charity and loyalty, in receptiveness to the Magisterium of Peter, in the unity of the *lex orandi* which is also the *lex credendi,* in the desire for unity with all the other Churches which make up the whole—the more such a Church will be capable of translating the treasure of faith into the legitimate variety of expressions of the profession of faith, of prayer and worship, of Christian life and conduct and of the spiritual influence on the people among which it dwells. The more will it also be truly evangelizing, that is to say capable of drawing upon the universal patrimony in order to enable its own people to profit from it, and capable too of communicating to the universal Church the experience and the life of this people, for the benefit of all.

65. It was precisely in this sense that at the end of the last Synod we spoke clear words full of paternal affection, insisting on the role of Peter's Successor as a visible, living and dynamic principle of the unity between the Churches and thus of the universality of the one Church.[93] We also insisted on the grave responsibility incumbent upon us, but which we share with our Brothers in the Episcopate, of preserving unaltered the content of the Catholic faith which the Lord entrusted to the Apostles. While being translated into all expressions, this content must be neither impaired nor mutilated. While being clothed with the outward forms proper to each people, and made explicit by theological expression which takes account of differing cultural, social and even racial milieux, it must remain the content of the Catholic faith just exactly as the ecclesial Magisterium has received it and transmits it. 1579

66. The whole Church therefore is called upon to evangelize, and yet within her we have different evangelizing tasks to accomplish. This diversity of services in the unity of the same mission makes up the richness and beauty of evangelization. We shall briefly recall these tasks. 1580

First, we would point out in the pages of the Gospel the insistence with which the Lord entrusts to the Apostles the task of proclaiming the Word. He chose them,[94] trained them during several years of intimate company,[95] constituted[96] and sent them out[97] as authorized witnesses and teachers of the message of salvation. And the Twelve in their turn sent out their successors who, in the apostolic line, continue to preach the Good News. 1581

67. The Successor of Peter is thus, by the will of Christ, entrusted with the pre-eminent ministry of teaching the revealed truth. The New Testament often shows Peter "filled with the Holy Spirit" speaking in the name of all.[98] It is precisely for this reason that Saint Leo the Great describes him as he who has merited the primacy of the apostolate.[99] This is also why the voice of the Church shows the Pope "at the 1582

highest point—in apice, in specula—of the apostolate."[100] The Second Vatican Council wished to reaffirm this when it declared that "Christ's mandate to preach the Gospel to every creature (cf. *Mk* 16:15) primarily and immediately concerns the Bishops with Peter and under Peter."[101]

1583 The full, supreme and universal power[102] which Christ gives to his Vicar for the pastoral government of his Church is thus specially exercised by the Pope in the activity of preaching and causing to be preached the Good News of salvation.

1584 68. In union with the Successor of Peter, the Bishops, who are successors of the Apostles, receive through the power of their episcopal ordination the authority to teach the revealed truth in the Church. They are teachers of the faith.

1585 Associated with the Bishops in the ministry of evangelization and responsible by a special title are those who through priestly ordination "act in the person of Christ."[103] They are educators of the People of God in the faith and preachers, while at the same time being ministers of the Eucharist and of the other Sacraments.

1586 We pastors are therefore invited to take note of this duty, more than any other members of the Church. What identifies our priestly service, gives a profound unity to the thousand and one tasks which claim our attention day by day and throughout our lives, and confers a distinct character on our activities, is this aim, ever present in all our action: to proclaim the Gospel of God.[104]

1587 A mark of our identity which no doubts ought to encroach upon and no objection eclipse is this: as pastors, we have been chosen by the mercy of the Supreme Pastor,[105] in spite of our inadequacy, to proclaim with authority the Word of God, to assemble the scattered People of God, to feed this People with the signs of the action of Christ which are the Sacraments, to set this People on the road to salvation, to maintain it in that unity of which we are, at different levels, active and living instruments, and unceasingly to keep this community gathered around Christ faithful to its deepest vocation. And when we do all these things, within our human limits and by the grace of God, it is a work of evangelization that we are carrying out. This includes ourself as Pastor of the universal Church, our Brother Bishops at the head of the individual Churches, priests and deacons united with their Bishops and whose assistants they are, by a communion which has its source in the Sacrament of Orders and in the charity of the Church.

69. Religious, for their part, find in their consecrated life a privileged means of effective evangelization. At the deepest level of their being they are caught up in the dynamism of the Church's life, which is thirsty for the divine Absolute and called to holiness. It is to this holiness that they bear witness. They embody the Church in her desire to give herself completely to the radical demands of the beatitudes. By their lives they are a sign of total availability to God, the Church and the brethren. 1588

As such they have a special importance in the context of the witness which, as we have said, is of prime importance in evangelization. At the same time as being a challenge to the world and to the Church herself, this silent witness of poverty and abnegation, of purity and sincerity, of self-sacrifice in obedience, can become an eloquent witness capable of touching also non-Christians who have good will and are sensitive to certain values. 1589

In this perspective one perceives the role played in evangelization by religious men and women consecrated to prayer, silence, penance and sacrifice. Other religious, in great numbers, give themselves directly to the proclamation of Christ. Their missionary activity depends clearly on the hierarchy and must be coordinated with the pastoral plan which the latter adopts. But who does not see the immense contribution that these religious have brought and continue to bring to evangelization? Thanks to their consecration they are eminently willing and free to leave everything and to go and proclaim the Gospel even to the ends of the earth. They are enterprising and their apostolate is often marked by an originality, by a genius that demands admiration. They are generous: often they are found at the outposts of the mission, and they take the greatest of risks for their health and their very lives. Truly the Church owes them much. 1590

1591 70. Lay people, whose particular vocation places them in the midst of the world and in charge of the most varied temporal tasks, must for this very reason exercise a very special form of evangelization.

1592 Their primary and immediate task is not to establish and develop the ecclesial community—this is the specific role of the pastors—but to put to use every Christian and evangelical possibility latent but already present and active in the affairs of the world. Their own field of evangelizing activity is the vast and complicated world of politics, society and economics, but also the world of culture, of the sciences and the arts, of international life, of the mass media. It also includes other realities which are open to evangelization, such as human love, the family, the education of children and adolescents, professional work, suffering. The more Gospel-inspired lay people there are engaged in these realities, clearly involved in them, competent to promote them and conscious that they must exercise to the full their Christian powers which are often buried and suffocated, the more these realities will be at the service of the Kingdom of God and therefore of salvation in Jesus Christ, without in any way losing or sacrificing their human content but rather pointing to a transcendent dimension which is often disregarded.

1593 71. One cannot fail to stress the evangelizing action of the family in the evangelizing apostolate of the laity.

1594 At different moments in the Church's history and also in the Second Vatican Council, the family has well deserved the beautiful name of "domestic Church."[106] This means that there should be found in every Christian family the various aspects of the entire Church. Furthermore, the family, like the Church, ought to be a place where the Gospel is transmitted and from which the Gospel radiates.

1595 In a family which is conscious of this mission, all the members evangelize and are evangelized. The parents not only communicate the Gospel to their children, but from their children they can themselves receive the same Gospel as deeply lived by them.

1596 And such a family becomes the evangelizer of many other families, and of the neighborhood of which it forms part.

Families resulting from a mixed marriage also have the duty of proclaiming Christ to the children in the fullness of the consequences of a common Baptism; they have moreover the difficult task of becoming builders of unity.

72. Circumstances invite us to make special mention of the young. Their increasing number and growing presence in society and likewise the problems assailing them should awaken in everyone the desire to offer them with zeal and intelligence the Gospel ideal as something to be known and lived. And on the other hand, young people who are well trained in faith and prayer must become more and more the apostles of youth. The Church counts greatly on their contribution, and we ourself have often manifested our full confidence in them. 1597

73. Hence the active presence of the laity in the temporal realities takes on all its importance. One cannot, however, neglect or forget the other dimension: the laity can also feel themselves called, or be called, to work with their pastors in the service of the ecclesial community, for its growth and life, by exercising a great variety of ministries according to the grace and charisms which the Lord is pleased to give them. 1598

We cannot but experience a great inner joy when we see so many pastors, religious and lay people, fired with their mission to evangelize, seeking ever more suitable ways of proclaiming the Gospel effectively. We encourage the openness which the Church is showing today in this direction and with this solicitude. It is an openness to meditation first of all, and then to ecclesial ministries capable of renewing and strengthening the evangelizing vigor of the Church. 1599

It is certain that, side-by-side with the ordained ministries, whereby certain people are appointed pastors and consecrate themselves in a special way to the service of the community, the Church recognizes the place of non-ordained ministries which are able to offer a particular service to the Church. 1600

A glance at the origins of the Church is very illuminating, and gives the benefit of an early experience in the matter of ministries. It was an an experience which was all the more valuable in that it enabled the Church to consolidate herself and to grow and spread. Attention to the sources however has to be complemented by attention to the present needs 1601 of mankind and of the Church. To drink at these ever inspiring sources without sacrificing anything of their values, and at the same time to know how to adapt oneself to the demands and needs of today—these are the criteria which will make it possible to seek wisely and to discover the ministries which the Church needs and which many of her members will gladly embrace for the sake of ensuring greater vitality in the ecclesial commmunity. These ministries will have a real pastoral value to the extent that they are established with absolute respect for unity and adhering to the directives of the pastors, who are the ones who are responsible for the Church's unity and the builders thereof.

1602 These ministires, apparently new but closely tied up with the Church's living experience down the centuries—such as catechists, directors of prayer and chant, Christians devoted to the service of God's Word or to assisting their brethren in need, the heads of small communities, or other persons charged with the responsibility of apostolic movements—these ministries are valuable for the establishment, life, and growth of the Church, and for her capacity to influence her surroundings and to reach those who are remote from her. We owe also our special esteem to all the laypeople who accept to consecrate a part of their time, their energies, and sometimes their entire lives, to the service of the missions.

1603 A serious preparation is needed for all workers for evangelization. Such preparation is all the more necessary for those who devote themselves to the ministry of the Word. Being animated by the conviction, ceaselessly deepened, of the greatness and riches of the Word of God, those who have the mission of transmitting it must give the maximum attention to the dignity, precision and adaptation of their language. Everyone knows that the art of speaking takes on today a very great importance. How would preachers and catechists be able to neglect this?

1604 We earnestly desire that in each individual Church the Bishops should be vigilant concerning the adequate formation of all the ministers of the Word. This serious preparation will increase in them the indispensable assurance and also the enthusiasm to proclaim today Jesus Christ.

74. We would not wish to end this encounter with our beloved Brethren and sons and daughters without a pressing appeal concerning the interior attitudes which must animate those who work for evangleization. 1605

In the name of the Lord Jesus Christ, and in the name of the Apostles Peter and Paul, we wish to exhort all those who, thanks to the charisms of the Holy Spirit and to the mandate of the Church, are true evangelizers, to be worthy of this vocation, to exercise it without the reticence of doubt or fear, and not to neglect the conditions that will make this evangelization not only possible but also active and fruitful. These, among many others, are the fundamental conditions which we consider it important to emphasize. 1606

75. Evangelization will never be possible without the action of the Holy Spirit. The Spirit descends on Jesus of Nazareth at the moment of his baptism when the voice of the Father—"This is my beloved Son with whom I am well pleased"[107]—manifests in an external way the election of Jesus and his mission. Jesus is "led by the Spirit" to experience in the desert the decisive combat and the supreme test before beginning this mission.[108] It is "in the power of the Spirit"[109] that he returns to Galilee and begins his preaching at Nazareth, applying to himself the passage of Isaiah: "The Spirit of the Lord is upon me." And he proclaims: "Today this Scripture has been fulfilled."[110] To the disciples whom he was about to send forth he says, breathing on them: "Receive the Holy Spirit."[111] 1607

In fact, it is only after the coming of the Holy Spirit on the day of Pentecost that the Apostles depart to all the ends of the earth in order to begin the great work of the Church's evangelization. Peter explains this event as the fulfillment of the prophecy of Joel: "I will pour out my Spirit."[112] Peter is filled with the Holy Spirit so that he can speak to the people about Jesus, the Son of God.[113] Paul too is filled with the Holy Spirit[114] before dedicating himself to his apostolic ministry, as is Stephen when he is chosen for the ministry of service and later on for the witness of blood.[115] The Spirit, who causes Peter, Paul and the Twelve to speak, and who in- 1608 spires the words that they are to utter, also comes down "on those who heard the word."[116]

1609 It is in the "consolation of the Holy Spirit" that the Church increases.[117] The Holy Spirit is the soul of the Church. It is he who explains to the faithful the deep meaning of the teaching of Jesus and of his mystery. It is the Holy Spirit who, today just as at the beginning of the Church, acts in every evangelizer who allows himself to be possessed and led by him. The Holy Spirit places on his lips the words which he could not find by himself, and at the same time the Holy Spirit predisposes the soul of the hearer to be open and receptive to the Good News and to the Kingdom being proclaimed.

1610 Techniques of evangelization are good, but even the most advanced ones could not replace the gentle action of the Spirit. The most perfect preparation of the evangelizer has no effect without the Holy Spirit. Without the Holy Spirit the most convincing dialectic has no power over the heart of man. Without him the most highly developed schemas resting on a sociological or psychological basis are quickly seen to be quite valueless.

1611 We live in the Church at a privileged moment of the Spirit. Everywhere people are trying to know him better, as the Scripture reveals him. They are happy to place themselves under his inspiration. They are gathering about him; they want to let themselves be led by him. Now if the Spirit of God has a pre-eminent place in the whole life of the Church, it is in her evangelizing mission that he is most active. It is not by chance that the great inauguration of evangelization took place on the morning of Pentecost, under the inspiration of the Spirit.

1612 It must be said that the Holy Spirit is the principal agent of evangelization: it is he who impels each individual to proclaim the Gospel, and it is he who in the depths of consciences causes the word of salvation to be accepted and understood.[118] But it can equally be said that he is the goal of evangelization: he alone stirs up the new creation, the new humanity of which evangelization is to be the result, with that unity in variety which evangelization wishes to achieve within the Christian community. Through the Holy Spirit the

Gospel penetrates to the heart of the world, for it is he who causes people to discern the signs of the times—signs willed by God—which evangelization reveals and puts to use within history.

The Bishops' Synod of 1974, which insisted strongly on the place of the Holy Spirit in evangelization, also expressed the desire that pastors and theologians—and we would also say the faithful marked by the seal of the Spirit by Baptism—should study more thoroughly the nature and manner of the Holy Spirit's action in evangelization today. This is our desire too, and we exhort all evangelizers, whoever they may be, to pray without ceasing to the Holy Spirit with faith and fervor and to let themselves prudently be guided by him as the decisive inspirer of their plans, their initiatives and their evangelizing activity. 1613

76. Let us now consider the very persons of the evangelizers. 1614

It is often said nowadays that the present century thirsts for authenticity. Especially in regard to young people it is said that they have a horror of the artificial or false and that they are searching above all for truth and honesty. 1615

These "signs of the times" should find us vigilant. Either tacitly or aloud—but always forcefull—we are being asked: Do you really believe what you are proclaiming? Do you live what you believe? Do you really preach what you live? The witness of life has become more than ever an essential condition for real effectiveness in preaching. Precisely because of this we are, to a certain extent, responsible for the progress of the Gospel that we proclaim. 1616

"What is the state of the Church ten years after the Council?" we asked at the beginning of this meditation. Is she firmly established in the midst of the world and yet free and independent enough to call for the world's attention? Does she testify to solidarity with people and at the same time to the divine Absolute? Is she more ardent in contemplation and adoration and more zealous in missionary, charitable and liberating action? Is she ever more committed to the effort to search for the restoration of the complete unity of Christians, a unity that makes more effective the common witness, "so 1617 that the world may believe"?[119] We are all responsible for the answers that could be given to these questions.

1618 We therefore address our exhortation to our brethren in the Episcopate, placed by the Holy Spirit to govern the Church.[120] We exhort the priests and deacons, the Bishops' collaborators in assembling the People of God and in animating spiritually the local communities. We exhort the religious, witnesses of a Church called to holiness and hence themselves invited to a life that bears testimony to the beatitudes of the Gospel. We exhort the laity: Christian families, youth, adults, all those who exercise a trade or profession, leaders, without forgetting the poor who are often rich in faith and hope—all lay people who are conscious of their evangelizing role in the service of their Church or in the midst of society and the world. We say to all of them: our evangelizing zeal must spring from true holiness of life, and, as the Second Vatican Council suggests, preaching must in its turn make the preacher grow in holiness, which is nourished by prayer and above all by love for the Eucharist.[121]

1619 The world which, paradoxically, despite innumerable signs of the denial of God, is nevertheless searching for him in unexpected ways and painfully experiencing the need of him—the world is calling for evangelizers to speak to it of a God whom the evangelists themselves should know and be familiar with as if they could see the invisible.[122] The world calls for and expects from us simplicity of life, the spirit of prayer, charity towards all, especially towards the lowly and the poor, obedience and humility, detachment and self-sacrifice. Without this mark of holiness, our word will have difficulty in touching the heart of modern man. It risks being vain and sterile.

1620 77. The power of evangelization will find itself considerably diminished if those who proclaim the Gospel are divided among themselves in all sorts of ways. Is this not perhaps one of the great sicknesses of evangelization today? Indeed, if the Gospel that we proclaim is seen to be rent by doctrinal disputes, ideological polarizations or mutual condemnations among Christians, at the mercy of the latters' differing views on Christ and the Church and even because of their different concepts of society and human institutions, how can those to whom we address our preaching fail to be disturbed, disoriented, even scandalized?

The Lord's spiritual testament tells us that unity among his followers is not only the proof that we are his but also the proof that he is sent by the Father. It is the test of the credibility of Christians and of Christ himself. As evangelizers, we must offer Christ's faithful not the image of people divided and separated by unedifying quarrels, but the image of people who are mature in faith and capable of finding a meeting-point beyond the real tensions, thanks to a shared, sincere and disinterested search for truth. Yes, the destiny of evangelization is certainly bound up with the witness of unity given by the Church. This is a source of responsibility and also of comfort. 1621

At this point we wish to emphasize the sign of unity among all Christians as the way and instrument of evangelization. The division among Christians is a serious reality which impedes the very work of Christ. The Second Vatican Council states clearly and emphatically that this division "damages the most holy cause of preaching the Gospel to all men, and it impedes many from embracing the faith."[123] For this reason, in proclaiming the Holy Year we considered it necessary to recall to all the faithful of the Catholic world that "before all men can be brought together and restored to the grace of God our Father, communion must be re-established between those who by faith have acknowledged and accepted Jesus Christ as the Lord of mercy who sets men free and unites them in the Spirit of love and truth."[124] 1622

And it is with a strong feeling of Christian hope that we look to the efforts being made in the Christian world for this restoration of the full unity willed by Christ. Saint Paul assures us that "hope does not disappoint us."[125] While we still work to obtain full unity from the Lord, we wish to see prayer intensified. Moreover we make our own the desire of the Fathers of the Third General Assembly of the Synod of Bishops, for a collaboration marked by greater commitment with the Christian brethren with whom we are not yet united in perfect unity, taking as a basis the foundation of Baptism 1623 and the patrimony of faith which is common to us. By doing this we can already give a greater common witness to Christ before the world in the very work of evangelization. Christ's command urges us to do this; the duty of preaching and of giving witness to the Gospel requires this.

1624 78. The Gospel entrusted to us is also the word of truth. A truth which liberates[126] and which alone gives peace of heart is what people are looking for when we proclaim the Good News to them. The truth about God, about man and his mysterious destiny, about the world; the difficult truth that we seek in the Word of God and of which, we repeat, we are neither the masters nor the owners, but the depositaries, the heralds and the servants.

1625 Every evangelizer is expected to have a reverence for truth, especially since the truth that he studies and communicates is none other than revealed truth and hence, more than any other, a sharing in the first truth which is God himself. The preacher of the Gospel will therefore be a person who even at the price of personal renunciation and suffering always seeks the truth that he must transmit to others. He never betrays or hides truth out of a desire to please men, in order to astonish or to shock, nor for the sake of originality or a desire to make an impression. He does not refuse truth. He does not obscure revealed truth by being too idle to search for it, or for the sake of his own comfort, or out of fear. He does not neglect to study it. He serves it generously, without making it serve him.

1626 We are the pastors of the faithful people, and our pastoral service impels us to preserve, defend, and to communicate the truth regardless of the sacrifices that this involves. So many eminent and holy pastors have left us the example of this love of truth. In many cases it was an heroic love. The God of truth expects us to be the vigilant defenders and devoted preachers of truth.

1627 Men of learning—whether you be theologians, exegetes or historians—the work of evangelization needs your tireless work of research, and also care and tact in transmitting the truth to which your studies lead you but which is always greater than the heart of men, being the very truth of God.

Parents and teachers, your task—and the many conflicts of the present day do not make it an easy one—is to help our children and your students to discover truth, including religious and spiritual truth. 1628

79. The work of evangelization presupposes in the evangelizer an ever increasing love for those whom he is evangelizing. That model evangelizer, the Apostle Paul, wrote these words to the Thessalonians, and they are a program for us all: "With such yearning love we chose to impart to you not only the gospel of God but our very selves, so dear had you become to us."[127] What is this love? It is much more than that of a teacher; it is the love of a father; and again, it is the love of a mother.[128] It is this love that the Lord expects from every preacher of the Gospel, from every builder of the Church. A sign of love will be the concern to give the truth and to bring people into unity. Another sign of love will be a devotion to the proclamation of Jesus Christ, without reservation or turning back. Let us add some other signs of this love. 1629

The first is respect for the religious and spiritual situation of those being evangelized. Respect for their tempo and pace; no one has the right to force them excessively. Respect for their conscience and convictions, which are not to be treated in a harsh manner. 1630

Another sign of this love is concern not to wound the other person, especially if he or she is weak in faith,[129] with statements that may be clear for those who are already initiated but which for the faithful can be a source of bewilderment and scandal, like a wound in the soul. 1631

Yet another sign of love will be the effort to transmit to Christians, not doubts and uncertainties born of an erudition poorly assimilated but certainties that are solid because they are anchored in the Word of God. The faithful need these certainties for their Christian life; they have a right to them, as children of God who abandon themselves entirely into his arms and to the exigencies of love. 1632

80. Our appeal here is inspired by the fervor of the greatest preachers and evangelizers, whose lives were devoted to the apostolate. Among these we are glad to point out those whom we have proposed to the veneration of the faithful during 1633

the course of the Holy Year. They have known how to overcome many obstacles to evangelization.

1634 Such obstacles are also present today, and we shall limit ourself to mentioning the lack of fervor. It is all the more serious because it comes from within. It is manifested in fatigue, disenchantment, compromise, lack of interest and above all lack of joy and hope. We exhort all those who have the task of evangelizing, by whatever title and at whatever level, always to nourish spiritual fervor.[130]

1635 This fervor demands first of all that we should know how to put aside the excuses which would impede evangelization. The most insidious of these excuses are certainly the ones which people claim to find support for in such and such a teaching of the Council.

1636 Thus one too frequently hears it said, in various terms, that to impose a truth, be it that of the Gospel, or to impose a way, be it that of salvation, cannot but be a violation of religious liberty. Besides, it is added, why proclaim the Gospel when the whole world is saved by uprightness of heart? We know likewise that the world and history are filled with "seeds of the Word"; is it not therefore an illusion to claim to bring the Gospel where it already exists in the seeds that the Lord himself has sown?

1637 Anyone who takes the trouble to study in the Council's documents the questions upon which these excuses draw too superficially will find quite a different view.

1638 It would certainly be an error to impose something on the consciences of our brethren. But to propose to their consciences the truth of the Gospel and salvation in Jesus Christ, with complete clarity and with a total respect for the free options which it presents—"without coercion, or dishonorable or unworthy presure"[131]—far from being an attack on religious liberty is fully to respect that liberty, which is offered the choice of a way that even nonbelievers consider noble and uplifting. Is it then a crime against others' freedom to proclaim with joy a Good News which one has come to know through the Lord's mercy?[132] And why should only falsehood and error, debasement and pornography have the right to be put before people and often unfortunately imposed on them by the destructive propaganda of the mass media, by the tolerance of legislation, the timidity of the good and the impudence of the wicked? The respectful presentation of Christ and his Kingdom is more than the evangelizer's right; it is his duty. It is likewise the right of his fellowmen to receive from him the proclamation of the Good News of salvation. God can accomplish this salvation in whomsoever he wishes by ways which he alone knows.[133] And yet, if his Son came, it was precisely in order to reveal to us, by his word and by his life, the ordinary paths of salvation. And he has commanded us to transmit this revelation to others with his own authority. It would be useful if every Christian and every evangelizer were to pray about the following thought: men can gain salvation also in other ways, by God's mercy, even though we do not preach the Gospel to them; but as for us, can we gain salvation if through negligence or fear or shame—what Saint Paul called "blushing for the Gospel"[134]—or as a result of false ideas we fail to preach it? For that would be to betray the call of God, who wishes the seed to bear fruit through the voice of the ministers of the Gospel; and it will depend on us whether this grows into trees and produces its full fruit.

Let us therefore preserve our fervor of spirit. Let us preserve the delightful and comforting joy of evangelizing, even when it is in tears that we must sow. May it mean for us—as it did for John the Baptist, for Peter and Paul, for the other Apostles and for a multitude of splendid evangelizers all through the Church's history—an interior enthusiasm that nobody and nothing can quench. May it be the great joy of our consecrated lives. And may the world of our time, which is searching, sometimes with anguish, sometimes with hope, be enabled to receive the Good News not from evangelizers who are dejected, discouraged, impatient or anxious, but from ministers of the Gospel whose lives glow with fervor, who have first received the joy of Christ, and who are willing to risk their lives so that the Kingdom may be proclaimed and the Church established in the midst of the world. 1639

81. This then, Brothers and sons and daughters, is our heartfelt plea. It echoes the voice of our Brethren assembled for the 1640

Third General Assembly of the Synod of Bishops. This is the task we have wished to give you at the close of a Holy Year which has enabled us to see better than ever the needs and the appeals of a multitude of brethren, both Christians and non-Christians, who await from the Church the Word of salvation.

1641 May the light of the Holy Year, which has shone in the local Churches and in Rome for millions of consciences reconciles with God, continue to shine in the same way after the Jubilee through a program of pastoral action with evangelization as its basic feature, for these years which mark the eve of a new century, the eve also of the third millennium of Christianity.

1642 82. This is the desire that we rejoice to entrust to the hands and the heart of the Immaculate Blessed Virgin Mary, on this day which is especially consecrated to her and which is also the tenth anniversary of the close of the Second Vatican Council. On the morning of Pentecost she watched over with her prayer the beginning of evangelization prompted by the Holy Spirit: may she be the Star of the evangelization ever renewed which the Church, docile to her Lord's command, must promote and accomplish, especially in these times which are difficult but full of hope!

1643 In the name of Christ we bless you, your communities, your families, all those who are dear to you, in the words which Paul addressed to the Philippians: "I give thanks to my God every time I think of you—which is constantly, in every prayer I utter—rejoicing, as I plead on your behalf, at the way you have all continually helped to promote the gospel . . . I hold all of you dear—you who . . . are sharers of my gracious lot . . . to defend the solid grounds on which the gospel rests. God himself can testify how much I long for each of you with the affection of Christ Jesus!"[135]

1644 Given in Rome, at Saint Peter's, on the Solemnity of the Immaculate Conception of the Blessed Virgin Mary, December 8, 1975, the thirteenth year of our Pontificate.

Address of Pope Paul VI to the Congregation of the Italian Women's Center December 6, 1976

Dear Daughters in Christ, You have come in great numbers to Rome as delegates of your various regions and provinces to the National Congress of the Italian Women's Center and in order to elect National Council which will hold office for the next three years.

1646 The theme of your discussion is "The Condition of Women." A vast and many faceted theme, indeed, but surely a highly topical and compelling one as well. With it you enter in an authoritative way—into the worldwide debate on the status and advancement of women. It is a debate which, in various and often quite lively forms, is a characteristic of contemporary society.

1647 The entire Church is following with great interest and concern the various movements in behalf of women's rights, the aim of which is to win "legal and practical equality with men."[1] For, in Christianity more than in any other religion, women have from the very beginning been accorded an especially high dignity. The New Testament bears witness to various important aspects of this dignity.

1648 The New Testament tells us of "Mary the mother of Jesus,"[2] whose extraordinary and holy role makes her the most revered of women. It tells us of the women who followed and assisted the Lord during the time of his public ministry[3] and who later were graced by the early appearances of the risen Christ.[4] It tells us of the women who were with the 12 in the upper room on Pentecost[5] and of the many women whom Paul mentions by name in his letters because of the numerous roles they had in the first churches.[6] From all this it is clear that women have an important place in the living, dynamic structure of Christianity—so much so that all the implications and possibilities of their role have perhaps not yet come to light. If to the valuable information provided by the New Testament we add all the texts which urge respect for every woman and a special love of husband for wife,[7] we have further confirmation that in this area the Church has shown a creative originality ever since her first appearance in the world.

1649 Like the Church of the first age, the Church of today cannot but be on the side of women, especially where, instead of being treated as active, responsible subjects, they are reduced to the status of passive, insignificant objects, as happens in some work situations, in degenerate exploitation of the mass media, in social relations and in the family. It might be said that for some men women are the easiest tool to use in expressing their impulses to outrageous violence. This explains and to some extent makes intelligible the bitterness and vehemence with which various feminist movements seek to retaliate.

1650 We are entirely convinced that the participation of women at the various levels of social life must not only be recognized but promoted and, above all, sincerely valued. In this respect, much progress undoubtedly has yet to be made.

1651 At the same time, let us remember that, according to the statement of the Second Vatican Council, "women . . . should assume their proper role in accordance with their own nature."[8] This special nature, women must not surrender. In fact, the very "image and likeness" of God[9] that makes her fully like and equal to man is realized in her in a special way which distinguishes her from man, just as man is distinct from woman. The difference is not in dignity of nature but in diversity of function. Woman must be on guard against an insidious kind of depreciation of the womanly state, which she can fall into today where there is an attempt being made to misconceive the differentiating characteristics which are determined by nature itself in the two sexes.

It is in keeping with the very order of creation, then, that woman should seek it, that is, not be an effort to win the upper hand in a confrontation with man but by a harmonious, fruitful integration with man, based on a respectful recognition of the roles proper to each. For that reason it is most desirable that to the various spheres of life in society in which she works woman should bring that unmistakably human quality of sensitivity and concern which is uniquely hers. 1652

In particular, We very much encourage you, the women of the Italian Women's Center, to pursue with enthusiasm, fidelity and joy your commitment to giving witness as citizens and Christians in contemporary Italian life. We also take the liberty of inviting you to extend the activity of your organization, and to make it ever more responsive to the changing needs of the times by not only directing it to specific social services which promote the good of mankind generally but also applying yourselves with unwearying concern to the specific problems of the world of women. The task of promoting a feminist movement on a mass scale could stimulate and concentrate your powers of generous understanding in a very profitable manner. You would, thus, achieve a greater presence and influence both in the world of women in particular and in society at large, so as to make the latter more sensitive to the problems of women and to a more satisfactory and honorable way of facing these problems and solving them. 1653

What is being asked of you, then, is to evolve a prudent overall strategy and opportune ways of implementing it, not in a partisan and polemical spirit but with serene, unyeilding dedication to an ideal which, being based on faith, is destined to make its way by reason of its radiant beauty and beneficient value. 1654

Because of the special charism you possess as individuals and as a group, the entire community expects of you a selfless energetic witness to the Christian presence of wom- 1655 an in the world, a witness of which you alone are capable and which you certainly know how to give. To you, then, members of the Italian Women's Center. We entrust this mission, in the name of the Lord. You represent in Italy a well-organized and experienced Catholic feminist movement and you are called on to accept this responsibility which is surely worthy of your best efforts, to dedicate yourselves, that is, to a task for which you are uniquely fitted and in which your best selves can shine forth resplendent.

1656 As a pledge of future success We bestow on you Our fatherly Apostolic Blessing, in order that the Lord may be always with you, sustaining you and strengthening you with his energizing inspiration.

Message of Pope Paul VI
for the World Day of Environment
June 5, 1977

"And God saw everything he had made and behold it was very good" (*Genesis* 1:31).

This ancient text, so simple and yet so profound, is a reminder to all of us today that the world we live in, this creation, is to be seen and embraced by all people in its totality as good: good because it is a gift from God; good because it is the environment in which all of us have been placed and in which we are called to live out our vocations in solidarity with one another. 1658

In recent years there has arisen around the world an increasing awareness that "the environment conditions in an essential way the life and development of man and that man, in turn, perfects and ennobles his milieu by his presence, his work and his contemplation." (Message to the Conference on the Environment, Stockholm, 1972 in *Insegnamenti di Paolo VI*, 1972, 606). 1659

Because of this, it is very heartening to see the members of the United Nations setting aside a world-wide Day of the Environment so that people everywhere can take this opportunity to celebrate the good things of this earth and to share them more consciously and more equitably with all their brothers and sisters. 1660

This consciousness of the environment around us is more pressing today than ever. For men who have the means and the ability to construct and ennoble the world about them 1661 can also destroy it and squander its goods. Human science and technology have made marvelous gains. But care must be taken that they are used to enhance human life and not to diminish it. Human effort has brought forth much wealth from the earth. But this wealth should not be squandered superfluously by a small minority nor selfishly hoarded for a few at the expense of the rest of mankind in need.

1662 For these reasons, this Day of celebration of the environment we live in should also be a day of appeal to all of us to be united as custodians of God's creation. It should be a day of re-dedication to the enterprise of preserving, improving and handing over to future generations a healthy environment in which every person is truly at home. (cf. Message . . . *Ibid.*, p. 607).

1663 The intent of such an appeal demands more than just a renewal of effort. It calls for a change of mentality, for a conversion of attitude and of practice so that the rich willingly use less and share the earth's goods more widely and more wisely. It calls for a simplicity of life style and a society that intelligently conserves rather than needlessly consumes. It calls finally for a universal sense of solidarity in which each person and every nation plays its proper and interdependent role to ensure an ecologically sound environment for people today as well as for future generations.

1664 "Everything created by God is good," wrote the apostle Paul. It is our earnest prayer that this Day of the Environment might be a time in which all people everywhere rejoice in the wisdom of that cry and commit themselves to a fraternal sharing and protection of a good environment, the common patrimony of mankind.

Message of Pope Paul VI
for World Peace Day, 1977
December 8, 1976

Men and women in high and responsible places! Men and women unknown to Us—and you are countless! Men and women—friends!

Once again, for the 10th time, We address you and enter into dialogue with you. As the new year, 1977, dawns, We stand at your door and knock.[1] Open to Us, We beg you! We are, as always, a pilgrim walking the world's roads, never wearying, never losing Our way. We have been sent to bring you the same message, to be the prophet of peace. Yes, We go Our way crying "Peace! Peace!" We are messengers with a single thought. It is an old idea but it is also ever new because new situations call it forth, as though it were newly discovered, as though it were a duty newly revealed and carring a hitherto unknown promise of happiness. 1666

I. PEACE IS POSSIBLE AND NECESSARY

The idea of peace seems well established today, being almost a synonym for the perfect civilization. Civilization is impossible apart from peace and, yet, peace is never entire, never assured! You have surely observed that the very progress men make can be a source of conflicts—and what staggering conflicts they are! Therefore, do not think of Our annual peace message as unnecessary and wearisome. 1667

1668 In terms of the psychology of mankind, peace entered upon a favorable period after the last World War. Over the vast ruins—different in different countries but everywhere to be seen—peace at last rose up, the sole victor, to dominate the scene. Suddenly the works and institutions proper to peace flowered like the greenery of spring. Many of these works and institutions have lasted and are still vigorous. They are the conquests a new world has made and the world does well to be proud of them and to see to it that they remain effective and grow. They are works and institutions that mark a step forward and upward in the advancement of mankind.

1669 Let us listen here for a moment to an authoritative voice which was both fatherly and prophetic, the voice of Our esteemed predecessor, Pope John XXIII: "And so, dearest sons and daughters, we must think of human society as being primarily a spiritual reality. By its means enlightened men can share their knowledge of the truth, can claim their rights and fulfill their duties, receive encouragement in their aspirations for the goods of the spirit, share their enjoyment of all the wholesome pleasures of the world and strive continually to pass on to others all that is best in themselves and to make their own the spiritual riches of others. It is these spiritual values which exercise a guiding influence on culture, economics, social institutions, political movements and forms, laws and all the other components which go to make up the external community of men and its continual development."[2]

1670 The period when peace thus exercised its healing ministry has been terminated by new disputes. At times these are revivals of conflicts only temporarily resolved. At times they are new historical phenomena attributable to social structures which are continually evolving. Peace is once again suffering as a result. It suffers in the hearts of men; it suffers from limited local conflicts; it suffers from dreadful armament programs which coldly calculate their terrifying potential for destruction, a potential so great that we cannot measure it in concrete terms. Praiseworthy efforts are being made here and there to avert such a catastrophe; We hope that they will prevail over the unthinkable dangers they seek to prevent.

1671 Men and women! Brothers and sisters! That kind of effort is not enough. The idea of peace as an ideal which effectively directs the activity of the human community seems to be succumbing and yielding a deadly upper hand to the world's inability to govern itself in and with peace. Peace will not come about of itself, even though the deepest impulses of human nature are directed toward it. Peace is order and every being and action aspires to order as to its preordained destiny and the preestablished reason for its existence. Yet, peace comes to pass only through a cooperation which involves many factors. That is why peace is a high point and must have beneath it an internally complex system of support. It is like boneless flesh that needs to be stiffened by a strong skeletal structure. It is a building that owes it solidity and completeness to the foundational strength of causes and conditions which are in fact frequently lacking to it. Even when they are operative, they do not always perform their assigned function which would make the pyramid of peace strong both at the base and at the summit.

1672 Given this analysis of peace, an analysis which indicates its excellence and necessity but also its instability and fragility, We state once more Our conviction that peace is a duty and that peace is possible. That has been Our constant message: one that embraces the ideal to which civilization tends, one that echoes the longing of the peoples, one that strengthens the hope of weak men in lowly places and adorns the security of the strong with the nobility accruing from justice. It is an optimistic message and a prophecy of the future. Peace is not a dream, it is not a utopian illusion nor is its achievement a Sisyphean labor. No, peace can be prolonged and strengthened. It can lead to the finest pages of man's history and adorn them not only with the pomp of power and glory but even more with those greater glories of human virtue, widespread goodness and the collective prosperity which marks a true civilization: the civilization based on love.

1673 Is all that really possible? Yes, it is! It must be! We speak from the heart: peace is a duty and a possibility but it will not come to pass without the concurrence of many conditions which are not easily assured. It is a difficult and lengthy task to discourse on the conditions of peace; of this We are well aware, and We shall not undertake that task here. We leave it to the experts. One aspect of the task, however, We are unwilling to pass over in silence; the aspect is of primordial importance, and it will be enough to mention it and commend it to the thoughtful consideration of intelligent men of good will. We are referring to the connection between peace and the conception the world has of life.

1674 Peace and life are the supreme goods of the civic order and they are interdependent. Do we want peace? Then let us defend life!

II. THE INTERDEPENDENCE OF PEACE AND LIFE

1675 "Peace and Life" may seem a tautology or a rhetorical slogan. It is neither. It represents an insight achieved only slowly in the course of man's development, a development we cannot regard as yet complete. How often in the dramatic history of mankind peace and life have failed to embrace as brothers but instead have fought each other bitterly! Peace is so often sought and won through death, not through life. Life so often asserts itself not throught peace but through conflict which is regarded as a sad necessity of self-defense.

1676 The connection between peace and life seems to spring from the very nature of things, yet, the connection is not always reflected in the logic of men's thinking and acting. That is the paradox, the new insight, which we must assert in this year of grace, 1977, and henceforth, if we want to grasp the dynamics of human progress. It is not an easy or simple matter to make men see the paradox. Too many formidable objections in the immense arsenal of false convictions, concrete utilitarian prejudices, "reasons of state" and traditional customs inherited from the past create obstacles, even in our day, which seem insuperable.

1677 The tragic conclusion we must draw is that if peace and life can be thus illogically dissociated in practice, then on the horizon of the future of a catastrophe awaits us which in our time can be so extreme as to be irremediable in terms either of peace or of life. Hiroshima stands as a terribly eloquent proof of this possibility and as a frighteningly prophetic example. If peace is thought of (as it need not be!) without relation to man's connatural respect for life, then death will certainly keep its sad court. The words of Tacitus come to mind: "They make a wilderness and call it peace."[3] Conversely: if the life of a privileged few is given selfish and almost idolatrous priority at the cost of the oppression or elimination of others, is that to be called peace?

1678 In order to find the true answer to this opposition between peace and life which passes from the level of moral theory to become tragically real and which so often profanes society and leaves it blood-covered, even in our day, we must acknowledge the importance of life as a value and as a condition for peace. Whence the formula: "If you want peace, defend life!" Life is the crown of peace. If the logic of our actions is based on the sacredness of life, war will be virtually outlawed as a normal and habitual means of asserting rights and achieving peace. Peace will simply be a consequence of giving law and right an unchallengeable place. In the last analysis, peace will be the joyous celebration of life.

1679 There is no end to the examples which might be given here, just as there is no end to the list of the adventures or, more accurately, misadventures which befall life when it is regarded as opposed to peace. We shall adopt here the classification according to the "three essential imperatives." These imperatives would have it that, in order to obtain authentic and truly blessed peace, we must *defend life, heal life and promote life.*

1680 These imperatives are a direct challenge to the politics which relies on extensive armaments. The ancient saying which has been and still is accepted in politics: "If you want peace, prepare for war," is not admissible without reservations which cut to the very heart of it.[4] Openly, and with a boldness that matches Our principles, We denounce the false and dangerous policy of "recourse to armaments" and to an unadmitted competition between nations for military superiority. Even if, because of a luckily surviving measure of prudence or because of an unasserted but fearful "iron arm," the balance of opposing forces is maintained and war (what a war it would be!) does not break out, how can we not bemoan the incalculable expenditure of economic and human energies which is required for each state to maintain its carapace of weapons which are ever more costly and ever more effective. What a loss in terms of education, culture, agriculture, health and civic life! True peace and life struggle on under an enormous, incalculable burden so that a peace based on the perpetual threat to life may be maintained and life may be defended by a constant threat to peace!

1681 "It is inevitable," you say? Perhaps, it is indeed inevitable when men still have so imperfect a concept of civilization. But let us, at least, recognize that the ingrained distrust which the competition in armaments fosters between peace and life is based on falsehood and must be overcome and eliminated. All praise, then, for the efforts already being made to reduce and finally put an end to the absurd cold war which results from the progressive development of each nation's military potential, as though nations must inevitably be hostile to each other and as though they could not see that such a conception of international relations must inevitably lead some day to the end both of peace and of countless human lives.

1682 But is it not only war which kills peace. Every crime against life is an attack on peace, especially if such crime infects a people's way of life, as it frequently does today, now that it is so terribly easy, and sometimes legal, to suppress new life through abortion. Reasons such as the following are usually given for abortion: abortion slows down population growth with its problems; it does away with human beings who are condemned to be deformed or social outcasts or part of a wretched proletariat, and so forth. All in all, it is said, abortion seems helpful rather than harmful to peace.

1683 Not so! The suppression of a living human being, whether still in the womb or already born, violates, above all, the sacred moral principle which must always be the starting point for a philosophy of human life: the principle that human life is sacred from the first moment of conception to the last moment of natural survival in time. What does it mean to say that human life is "sacred"? It means that it is not subject to any arbitrary power which wishes to suppress it; it is inviolable; it deserves all respect, every care, every rightful sacrifice.

1684 For anyone who believes in God, such respect is spontaneous and instinctive; transcendent religious law makes it a duty. Even for someone who does not have the good fortune of believing that God protects the rights of every human being. This same sense of the sacred, that is, inviolable character of the living human being is and should be intuitively present simply because the thinker is himself a human being. They know this truth, they are well aware of it indeed, who have had the misfortune, the inexorable sense of guilt, the ever-living remorse, of having deliberately ended a life. The voice of innocent blood cries out in the heart of the killer with torturing insistence and tells the person that sophistries in the service of self-satisfaction cannot bring interior peace.

1685 If life is indeed sacred, then an attack on peace, that is, on the general framework which protects order and a humane, safe coexistence, has been committed; the individual life and the general peace are always inseparably bound up together. If we want to build a progressive social order on inviolable principles, we must not attack the very heart of such an order namely, the respect for human life. From this point of view, too, peace and life together form the basis of order and civilization.

1686 We might continue by reviewing the countless ways in which the attack on life seems to be becoming habitual today, wherever individual criminality gets organized and becomes a collective affair, winning the connivance and complicity of whole classes of the citizenry and turning the private vendetta into a vile collective duty, terrorism into a supposedly legitimate means of political or social self-assertion and torture by the police into an effective weapon of the public authorities, not for establishing order but for imposing a base form of repression. How can peace flourish where the preservation of life is so compromised? Where violence rages, true peace is no more but where the rights of men are sincerely professed and publicly acknowledged and defended, peace becomes the joyous atmosphere in which social coexistence flourishes.

1687 The progress society has made is proved by the texts of international commitments to the defense of human rights, the protection of children and the safeguarding of man's basic freedoms. Such commitments are the epic poetry of peace because they are a shield protecting life. But are they perfect? Are they observed? We all know that civilized man expresses himself in such declarations and finds in them the guarantee of his own reality—a reality which is full and glorious if the declarations permeate the minds and hearts of men but violated and treated with contempt if they remain a dead letter.

III: CLOSING EXHORTATION

1688 Men and women of the late 20th century, you have signed the charters which, if sincerely meant, are the glorious proof that you have recovered your full humanity. But you have written your own moral condemnation into the book of history if they are but pages full of rhetorical velleities or juridical hypocrises. How measure which they are? The measure is the extent to which you link true peace with the dignity accorded human life.

1689 Hear Our suppliant prayer that the link may become a reality and mark a new summit of achievement in a civilization built of life and peace, a civilization (let Us repeat) built on love.

1690 Has everything now been said? No. There remains an unanswered question: How is such a program for a civilization to be carried out? How are life and peace to be linked as they should?

1691 We shall answer in terms that may be unintelligible to those who have limited the horizons of reality to what the natural eye can see for we must have recourse to that religious world we call the "supernatural." That is, we need faith to discover the system which effectively operates amid the complexity of human circumstance when the transcendent God takes a hand and makes possible the attainment of results which, humanly speaking, are impossible. We need a religion which is true and vital, if these goals are to be possible. We need the help of "the God of peace."[5]

Happy are we if we understand and believe all this and if in the light of faith we know how to uncover and actuate the relation between life and peace! 1692

We make this last statement because there is an important exception to the reasoning proposed above which gives priority to life over peace and makes peace depend on life's being held inviolable. It is the exception which occurs when a good higher than life itself comes upon the scene. For there are values which surpass even life: for example, truth, justice, civil liberty, love of neighbor and faith. Then the words of Christ reveal their meaning: "The man who loves his life [more than these higher values] loses it."[6] These words tell us that just as peace is to be conceived of in relation to life and just as from life, when its ordered well-being is assured, peace should result as the harmony which renders human existence both interiorly and socially well-ordered and happy, so in turn human existence or life cannot and may not reject those higher goals which give it its true meaning. 1693

Why, after all, do we live? What is it which gives life not only the ordered tranquility of peace but also its dignity, its spiritual fulfillment, its moral grandeur and its religious finality? Will peace—authentic peace—perhaps be lost if love in its highest expression, sacrifice, is allowed to become part of our life? By no means! And if sacrifice is part of a redemptive plan and a source of merit in relation to an existence which transcends temporal form and measure, will not human existence find at a higher, everlasting level the true hundredfold peace of eternal life?[7] Any student in the school of Christ can understand this language of transcendence.[8] Is there any reason why we cannot be such students? After all, he, Christ, "is our peace"![9] 1694

We hope that all who hear this blessed message of peace and life will indeed become disciples of Christ. 1695

The Vatican, December 8, 1976. 1696

References

MATER ET MAGISTRA, Encyclical Letter of Pope John XXIII on Christianity and Social Progress, May 15, 1961.

1 Cf. 1 *Tim.* 3, 15.

2 *John* 14, 6.

3 *John* 8, 12.

4 *Mark* 8, 2.

5 *Acta Leonis* XIII, XI (1891), p. 97-144.

6 *Ibid.*, p. 107.

7 St. Thomas, *De regimine principum,* I, 15,

8 Cf. *Acta Apostolicae Sedis*, XXIII (1931), p. 185.

9 Cf. *Ibid.*, p. 189.

10 *Ibid.*, p. 177-228.

11 Cf. *Ibid.*, p. 199.

12 Cr. *Ibid.*, p. 200.

13 Cf. *Ibid.*, p. 201.

14 Cf. *Ibid.*, p. 210f.

15 Cf. *Ibid.*, p. 211.

16 Cf. *Acta Apostolicae Sedis*, XXXIII (1941), p. 196.

17 Cf. *Ibid.*, p. 197.

18 Cf. *Ibid.*, p. 196.

19 Cf. *Ibid.*, p. 198f.

20 Cf.*Ibid.*, p. 199.

21 Cf. *Ibid.*, p. 201.

22 Cf. *Ibid.*, p. 202.

23 Cf. *Ibid.*, p. 203.

24 *Acta Apostolicae Sedis*, XXIII (1931), p. 203.

25 *Ibid.*, p. 203.

26 Cf. *Ibid.*, p. 222f.

27 Cf. *Acta Apostolicae Sedis,* XXXIII (1941), p. 200.

28 *Acta Apostolicae Sedis*, XXIII (1931), p. 195.

29 *Ibid.*, p. 198.

30 Radio Broadcast, September 1, 1944; cf. *A.A.S.*, XXXVI (1944), p. 254.

31 Allocution, October 8, 1956; cf. *A.A.S.*, XLVIII (1956), p. 799-800.

32 Radio Broadcast, September 1, 1944; cf. *A.A.S.*, XXXVI (1944), p. 253.

33 Radio Broadcast, December 24, 1942; cf. *A.A.S.*, XXXV (1943), p. 17.

34 Cf. *Ibid.*, p. 20.

35 Encyclical Letter *Quadragesimo Anno:A.A.S.*, XXIII (1943), p. 17.

36 *Acta Leonis* XIII, XI (1891), p. 114.

37 *Matt.* 6, 19-20.

38 *Matt.* 25, 40.

39 Ct. *Acta Apostolicae Sedis,* XXIII (1931), p. 202.

40 *Allocution,* May 3, 1960; cf. *A.A.S.*, LII (1960), p. 465.

41 Cf. *Ibid.*

42 1 *John* 3, 16-17.

43 Encyclical Letter *Summi Pontificatus; A.A.S.*, XXXI (1939), p. 428-29.

44 *Gen.*, 1, 28.

45 *Ibid.*

46 *Confessions,* 1, 1.

47 *Ps.* 126, 1.

48 *Acta Apostolicae Sedis,* XXIII (1931), p. 221f.

49 Radio Broadcast, Christmas Eve., 1953; cf. *A.A.S.,* XLVI (1954), p. 10.

50 *Ps.* 113, 4.

51 *Matt.* 16, 26.

52 *Exod.* 20, 8.

53 *John* 17, 15.

54 1 *Cor.* 10, 31.

55 *Col.* 3, 17.

56 *Matt.* 6, 33.

57 *Eph.* 5, 8.

58 Cf. *Ibid.*

59 1 *Cor.* 13, 4-7.

60 1 *Cor.,* 12, 12.

61 *John* 15, 5.

62 *Ibid.*

63 *Preface of Jesus Christ the King.*

64 *Ps.* 84, 9ff.

65 1 *Cor.* 1, 30.

PACEM IN TERRIS, Encyclical Letter of Pope John XXIII on Establishing Universal Peace in Truth, Justice, Charity and Liberty, April 11, 1963.

1 *Ps.* 8, 1.

2 *Ps.* 103, 24.

3 Ct. *Gen.* 1, 26.

4 *Ps.* 8, 6-8.

5 *Rom.* 2, 15.

6 Cf. *Ps.* 18, 8-11.

7 Cf. Radio Message of Pius XII, Christmas Eve, 1942, *A.A.S.* XXXV, 1943, pp. 9-24; and Discourse of John XXIII, Jan. 4, 1963, *A.A.S.* LV, 1963, pp. 89-91.

8 Cf. Encycl. *Divini Redemptoris* Pius XI, *A.A.S.* XXIX, 1937, p. 78; and Radio Message of Pius XII, Pentecost, June 1, 1941, *A.A.S.* XXXIII, 1941, pp. 195-205.

9 Cf. Radio Message of Pius XII, Christmas Eve, 1942, *A.A.S.* XXXV, 1943, pp. 9-24.

10 *Divinae Institutioners,* Book IV, ch. 28, 2; Patrologia Latina, 6, 535.

11 Encycl. *Libertas Praestantissimum, Acta Leonis* XIII, VIII, 1888, pp. 237-238.

12 Cf. Radio Message of Pius XII, Christmas Eve, 1942, *A.A.S.* XXXV, 1943, pp. 9-24.

13 Cf. Encycl. *Casti Connubii* of Pius XI, *A.A.S.* XXII, 1930, pp. 539-592; and Radio Message of Pius XII, Christmas Eve, 1942, *A.A.S.* XXXV, 1943, pp. 9-24.

14 Cf. Radio Message of Pius XII, Pentecost, June 1, 1941, *A.A.S.* XXXIII, 1941, p. 201.

15 Cf. Encycl. *Rerum Novarum* of Leo XIII, *Acta Leonis* XIII, XI, 1891, pp. 128-129.

16 Cf. Encycl. *Mater et Magistra* of John XXIII, *A.A.S.* LIII, 1961, p. 422.

17 Cf. Radio Message, Pentecost, June 1, 1941, *A.A.S.* XXXIII, 1941, p.201.

18 Encycl. *Mater et Magistra, A.A.S.* LIII, 1961, p. 428.

19 Cf. *Ibid.,* p. 430.

20 Cf. Encycl. *Rerum Novarum* of Leo XIII, *Acta Leonis* XIII, XI, 1891, pp. 134-142; Encycl. *Quadragesimo Anno* of Pius XI, *A.A.S.* XXIII, 1931, pp. 199-200: Encycl. *Sertum Laetitiue* Pius XII, *A.A.S.* XXXI, 1939, pp. 635-644.

21 Ct. *A.A.S.* LIII, 1961, p. 430.

22 Cf. Radio Message of Pius XII, Christmas Eve, 1952, *A.A.S.* XLV, 1953, pp. 33-46.

23 Cf. Radio Message, Christmas Eve, 1944, *A.A.S.* XXXVII, 1945, p.12.

24 Cf. Radio Message, Christmas Eve, 1942, *A.A.S.* XXXV, 1943, p. 21.

25 *Eph.* 4, 25.

26 Radio Message of Pius XII, Christmas Eve, 1942, *A.A.S.*. XXXV, 1943, p. 14.

27 *Summa Theal.,* Ia-IIae, q. 19, a. 4; cf. a. 9.

28 *Rom.* 13, 1-6.

29 *In Epist, ad Rom.* c. 13, vv. 1-2 homil. XXIII: Patrologia Graeca, 60, 615.

30 Encycl. *Immortale Dei* of Leo XIII, *Acta Leonis* XIII, V, 1885, p. 120.

31 Cf. Radio Message, Christmas Eve, 1944, *A.A.S.* XXXVII, 1945, p. 15.

32 Cf. Encycl. *Diuturnum ilud* of Leo XIII, *Acta Leonis* XIII, II 1881, p. 274.

33 Cf. *Ibid.*, p. 278; Encycl. *Immortale Dei* of Leo XIII, *Acta Leonis* XIII, V, 1885, p. 130.

34 *Act.* 5, 29.

35 *Summa Theol.*, Ia-IIae, q. 93, a. 3 and 2um; Cf. Radio Message of Pius XII, Christmas Eve, 1944, *A.A.S.* XXXVII, 1945, pp. 5-23.

36 Cf. Encycl. *Diuturnum illud* of Leo XIII, *Acta Leonis* XIII, II, 1881, pp. 271-272; and Radio Message of Pius XII, Christmas Eve, 1944, *A.A.S.* XXXVII, 1945, pp. 5-23.

37 Cf. Radio Message of Pius XII, Christmas Eve, 1942, *A.A.S.* XXXV, 1943, p. 13; and Encycl. *Immortale Dei* of Leo XIII, *Acta Leonis* XIII, V, 1885, p. 120.

38 Cf. Encycl *Summi Pontificatus* XII, *A.A.S.* XXXI, 1939, pp. 412-453.

39 Cf. Encycl. *Mit brennender Sorge* of Pius XI, *A.A.S.* XXIX, 1937, p. 159; and Encycl. *Divini Redemptoris, A.A.S.* XXIX, 1937, pp. 65-106.

40 Encycl. *Immotale Dei, Acta Leonis* XIII, V, 1885, p. 121.

41 Cf. Encycl. *Rerum Novarum* of Leo XIII, *Acta Leonis* XIII, XI, 1891, pp. 133-134.

42 Cf. Encycl. *Summi Pontificatus* of Pius XII, *A.A.S.* XXXI, 1939, p. 433.

43 *A.A.S.* LIII, 1961, p. 19.

44 Cf. Encycl. *Quadragesimo Anno* of Pius XI, *A.A.S.* XXIII, 1931, p. 215.

45 Cf. Radio Message of Pius XII, Pentecost, June 1, 1941, *A.A.S.* XXXIII, 1941, p. 200.

46 Cf. Encycl. *Mit brennender Sorge* of Pius XI, *A.A.S.* XXIX, 1937, p. 159; and Encycl. *Divini Redemptoris*, *A.A.S.* XXIX, 1937, p. 79; and Radio Message of Pius XII, Christmas Eve, 1942, *A.A.S.* XXXV, 1943, pp. 9-24.

47 Cf. Encycl. *Divini Redemptoris* of Pius XI, *A.A.S.* XXIX, 1937, p. 81; and Radio Message of Pius XII, Christmas Eve, 1942, *A.A.S.* XXXV, 1943, pp. 9-24.

48 Encycl. *Mater et Magistra* of John XXIII, *A.A.S.* LIII, 1961, p.415.

49 Cf. Radio Message of Pius XII, Christmas Eve, 1942, *A.A.S.* XXXV, 1943, p. 21.

50 Cf. Radio Message of Pius XII, Christmas Eve, 1944, *A.A.S.* XXXVII, 1945, pp. 15-16.

51 Cf. Radio Message of Pius XII, Christmas Eve, 1942, *A.A.S.* XXXV, 1943, p. 12.

52 Cf. Apostolic letter *Annum ingressi* of Leo XIII, *Acta Leonis* XIII, XXII, 1902-1903, pp. 52-80.

53 *Wis.*, 6, 1-4.

54 Cf. Radio Message of Pius XII, Christmas Eve, 1941, *A.A.S.* XXIV, 1942, p. 16.

55 Cf. Radio Message of Pius XII, Christmas Eve, 1940, *A.A.S.* XXXIII, 1941, pp. 5-14.

56 *De civitate Dei*, Book IV, ch. 4; Patrologia Latina, 41, 115; cf. Radio Message of Pius XII, Christmas Eve, 1939, *A.A.S.* XXXII, 1940, pp. 5-13.

57 Cf. Radio Message of Pius XII, Christmas Eve, 1941, *A.A.S.* XXXIV, 1942, pp. 10-21.

58 Cf. Encycl *Mater et Magistra* of John XXIII, *A.A.S.*LIII, 1961. p.439.

59 Cf. Radio Message, Christmas Eve. 1941, *A.A.S.* XXXIV, 1942, p. 17; and Exhortation of Benedict XV to the rulers of peoples at war, Aug. 1, 1917, *A.A.S.* IX, 1917, p. 418.

60 Cf. Radio Message, Aug. 24, 1939, *A.A.S.* XXXI, 1939, p.334.

61 *A.A.S.* LIII, 1961, pp. 440-441.

62 Cf. Radio Message, Christmas Eve, 1941, *A.A.S.* XXXIV, 1942, pp. 16-17.

63 Encycl. *Mater et Magstra* of John XXIII, *A.A.S.* LIII, 1961, 443.

64 Cf. Address of Pius XII to youths of Catholic Action from the dioceses of Italy gathered in Rome, Sept. 12, 1948, *A.A.S.*XL, p. 412.

65 Cf. Encycl. *Mater et Magistra* of John XXIII, *A.A.S.* LIII, 1961, p. 454.

66 *Ibid.*, p. 456.

67 *Ibid.*, p. 456; of Encycl. *Immortale Dei* of Leo XIII, *Acta Lenois* XIII, V, 1885, p. 128; Encycl. *Ubi Arcano* of Pius XI, *A.A.S.* XIV, 1922, p. 698; and Address of Pius XII to Delegates of the International Union of Catholic Women's Leagues gathered in Rome for a joint convention, Sept. 11, 1947, *A.A.S.* XXXIX, 1947 p. 486.

68 Cf. Address to workers from the dioceses of Italy gathered in Rome, Pentecost, June 13, 1943, *A.A.S.* XXXV, 1943, p. 175.

69 *Miscellanea Augustiniana. . .Sermones post Maurinos reperti* of St. Augustine, Rome, 1930, p. 633.

70 Cf. *Is.* 9, 5.

71 *Eph.* 2, 14-17.

72 Responsory at Matins on the Friday after Easter.

73 *Jn.* 14, 17.

GAUDIUM ET SPES, Pastoral Constitution on the Church in the Modern World, December 7, 1965.

1 Cf. *John* 18:37; *Matt.* 20:28; *Mark* 10:45.

2 Cf. *Rom.* 7:14 ff.

3 Cf. 2 *Cor.* 5:15.

4 Cf. *Acts* 4:12.

5 Cf. *Heb.* 13:8.

6 Cf. *Col.* 1:15.

7 Cf. *Gen.* 1:26; *Wis.* 2:23.

8 Cf. *Sir.* 17:3-10.

9 Cf. *Rom.* 1:21-25.

10 Cf. *John* 8:34.

11 Cf. *Dan.* 3:57-90.

12 Cf. 1 *Cor.* 6:13-20.

13 Cf. 1 *Kings* 16:7; *Jer.* 17:10.

14 Cf. *Sir.* 17:7-8.

15 Cf. *Rom.* 2:14-16.

16 Cf. Pius XII, radio address on the correct formation of a Christian conscience in the young, March 23, 1952: *AAS* (1952), p. 271.

17 Cf. *Matt.* 22:37-40; *Gal.* 5:14.

18 Cf. *Sir.* 15:14.

19 Cf. 2 *Cor.* 5:10.

20 Cf. *Wis.* 1:13; 2:23-24; *Rom.* 5:21; 6:23; *Jas.* 1:15.

21 Cf. 1 *Cor.* 15:56-67.

22 Cf. Pius XI, Encyclical Letter *Divini Redemptoris*, March 19, 1937: *AAS* 29 (1937), pp. 65-106; Pius XII, Encyclical Letter *Ad Apostolorum Principis*, June 29, 1958: *AAS* 50 (1958), pp. 601-614; John XXIII, Encyclical Letter *Mater et Magistra*, May 15, 1961: *AAS* 53 (1961), pp. 451-453; Paul VI, Encyclical Letter *Ecclesiam Suam*, Aug. 6, 1964: *AAS* 56 (1964), pp. 651-653.

23 Cf. Second Vatican Council, *Dogmatic Constitution on the Church*, Chapter I, n. 8: *AAS* 57 (1965), p. 12.

24 Cf. *Phil.* 1:27.

25 St. Augustine, *Confessions* I, 1: *PL* 32, 661.

26 Cf. *Rom.* 5:14. Cf. Tertullian, *De carnis resurrectione* 6: "The shape that the slime of the earth was given was intended with a view to Christ, the future man.": P. 2, 282; *CSEL* 47, p. 33, 1. 12-13.

27 Cf. 2 *Cor.* 4:4.

28 Cf. Second Council of Constantinople, canon 7: "The divine Word was not changed into a human nature, nor was a human nature absorbed by the Word." Denzinger 219 (428).—Cf. also Third Council of Constantinople: "For just as His most holy and immaculate human nature, though deified, was not destroyed (theotheisa ouk anerethe), but rather remained in its proper state and mode of being": Denzinger 291 (556).—Cf. Council of Chalcedon: "to be acknowledged in two natures, without confusion, change, division, or separation." Denzinger 148 (302).

29 Cf. Third Council of Constantinople: "and so His human will, though deified, is not destroyed": Denzinger 291 (556).

30 Cf. *Heb.* 4:15.

31 Cf. 2 *Cor.* 5:18-19; *Col.* 1:20-22.

32 Cf. 1 *Pet.* 2:21; *Matt.* 16:24; *Luke* 14:27.

33 Cf. *Rom.* 8:29; *Col.* 1:18.

34 Cf. *Rom.* 8:1-11.

35 Cf. 2 *Cor.* 4:14.

36 Cf. *Phil.* 3:10; *Rom.* 8:17.

37 Cf. SecondVatican Council, *Dogmatic Constitution on the Church*, Chapter 2, n. 16: *AAS* 57 (1965), p. 20.

38 Cf. *Rom.* 8:32.

39 Cf. The Byzantine Easter Liturgy.

40 Cf. *Rom.* 8:15 and *Gal.* 4:6; cf. also *John* 1:12 and *John* 3:1-2.

41 Cf. John XXIII, Encyclical Letter *Mater et Magistra*, May 15, 1961: *AAS* 53 (1961), pp. 401-464, and Encyclical Letter *Pacem in Terris*, April 11, 1963: *AAS* 55 (1963), pp. 257-304; Paul VI, Encyclical Letter *Ecclesiam Suam*, Aug. 6, 1964: *AAS* 54 (1964), pp. 609-659.

42 Cf. *Luke* 17:33.

43 Cf. St. Thomas, 1 *Ethica Lect.* 1.

44 Cf. John XXIII, Encyclical Letter *Mater et Magistra: AAS* 53 (1961), p. 418. Cf. also Pius XI, Encyclical Letter *Quadragesimo Anno: AAS* 23, (1931), p. 222 ff.

45 Cf. John XXIII, Encyclical Letter *Mater et Magistra:AAS* 53 (1961).

46 Cf. *Mark* 2:27.

47 Cf. John XXIII, Encyclical Letter *Pacem in Terris: AAS* 55 (1963), p. 266.

48 Cf. *Jas.* 2:15-16.

49 Cf. *Luke* 16:19-31.

50 Cf. John XXIII, Encyclical Letter *Pacem in Terris: AAS* 55 (1963), p. 299 and 300.

51 Cf. *Luke* 6:37-38; *Matt.* 7:1-2; *Rom.* 2:1-11; 14:10; 14:10-12.

52 Cf. *Matt.* 5:43-47.

53 Cf. *Dogmatic Constitution on the Church*, Chapter II, n. 9: *AAS* 57 (1965), pp. 12-13.

54 Cf. *Exodus* 24:1-8.

55 Cf. *Gen.* 1:26-27; 9:2-3; *Wis.* 9:3.

56 Cf. *Ps.* 8:7 and 10.

57 Cf. John XXIII, Encyclical Letter *Pacem in Terris: AAS* 55 (1963), p. 297.

58 Cf. message to all mankind sent by the Fathers at the beginning of the Second Vatican Council, Oct. 20, 1962: *AAS* 54 (1962), p. 823.

59 Cf. Paul VI, address to the diplomatic corps, Jan. 7, 1965: *AAS* 57 (1965), p. 232.

60 Cf. First Vatican Council, *Dogmatic Constitution on the Catholic Faith*, Chapter III; Denz. 1785-1786 (3004-3005).

61 Cf. Msgr. Pio Paschini, *Vita e opere di Galileo Galilei*, 2 volumes, Vatican Press (1964).

62 Cf. *Matt.* 24:13; 13:24-30 and 36-43.

63 Cf. 2 *Cor.* 6:10.

64 Cf. *John* 1:3 and 14.

65 Cf. *Eph.* 1:10.

66 Cf. *John* 3:6; *Rom.* 5:8-10.

67 Cf. *Acts* 2: 36; *Matt.* 28:18.

68 Cf. *Rom.* 15:16.

69 Cf. *Acts* 1:7.

70 Cf. 1 *Cor.* 7:31; St. Irenaeus, *Adversus haereses*, V. 36, *PG*, VIII, 1221.

71 Cf. 2 *Cor.* 5:2; 2 *Pet.* 3:13.

72 Cf. 1 *Cor.* 2:9; *Apoc.* 21:4-5.

73 Cf. 1 *Cor.* 15:42 and 53.

74 Cf. 1 *Cor.* 13:8; 3:14.

75 Cf. *Rom.* 8:19-21.

76 Cf. *Luke* 9:25.

77 Cf. Pius XI, Encyclical Letter *Quadragesimo Anno:AAS*, 23 (1931), p. 207.

78 Preface of the Feast of Christ the King.

79 Cf. Paul VI, Encyclical Letter *Ecclesiam suam*, III: *AAS* 56 (1964), pp. 637-659.

80 Cf. Titus 3:4: "love of mankind."

81 Cf. *Eph.* 1:3; 5-6; 13-14, 23.

82 Second Vatican Council, *Dogmatic Constitution on the Church*, Chapter I, n. 8: *AAS* 57 (1965), p. 12.

83 *Ibid.*, Chapter II, no. 9: *AAS* 57 (1965), p. 14: Cf. n. 8: *AAS loc. cit.*, p. 11.

84 *Ibid.*, Chapter I, n. 8: *AAS* 57 (1965), pp. 11.

85 Cf. *ibid.*, Chapter IV, n. 38: *AAS* 57 (1965), p. 43, with note 120.

86 Cf. *Rom.* 8:14-17.

87 Cf. *Matt.* 22:39.

88 *Dogmatic Constitution on the Church*, Chapter II, n. 9: *AAS* 57 (1956), pp. 12-14.

89 Cf. Pius XII, Address to the International Union of Institutes of Archeology, History and History of Art, March 9, 1956: *AAS* 48 (1956), p. 212: "Its divine Founder, Jesus Christ, has not given it any mandate or fixed any end of the cultural order. The goal which Christ assigns to it is strictly religious . . . The Church must lead men to God, in order that they may be given over to him without reserve. . . . The Church can never lose sight of the strictly religious, supernatural goal. The meaning of all its activities, down to the last canon of its Code, can only cooperate directly or indirectly in this goal."

90 *Dogmatic Constitution on the Church*, Chapter I, n. 1: *AAS* 57 (1965), p. 5.

91 Cf. *Heb.* 13:14.

92 Cf. 2 *Thes.* 3:6-13; *Eph.* 4:28.

93 Cf. *Is.* 58:1-12.

94 Cf. *Matt.* 23:3-23; *Mark* 7:10-13.

95 Cf. John XXIII, Encyclical Letter *Mater et Magistra,* IV: *AAS* 53 (1961), pp. 456-457; cf. I: *AAS loc. cit.*, pp. 407, 410-411.

96 Cf. *Dogmatic Constitution on the Church*, Chapter III, n. 28: *AAS* 57 (1965), p. 35.

97 *Ibid.*, n. 28: *AAS loc. cit.*, pp. 35-36.

98 Cf. St. Ambrose, *De virginitate,* Chapter VIII, n. 48: *ML* 16, 278.

99 Cf. *Dogmatic Constitution on the Church*, Chapter II, n. 15: *AAS* 57 (1965), p. 20.

100 Cf. *Dogmatic Constitution on the Church*, Chapter III, n. 13: *AAS* 57 (1965), p. 17.

101 Cf. Justin, *Dialogus cum Tryphene*, Chapter 100; *MG* 6, 729 (ed Otto), 1897, pp. 391-393: ". . . but the greater the number of persecutions which are inflicted upon us, so much the greater the number of other men who become devout believers through the name of Jesus." Cf. Tertullian, *Apologeticus*, Chapter L, 13: "Every time you mow us down like grass, we increase in number: the blood of Christians is a seed!" Cf. *Dogmatic Constitution on the Church*, Chapter II, n. 9: *AAS* 57 (1965), p. 14.

102 Cf. *Dogmatic Constitution on the Church*, Chapter II, n. 15: *AAS* 57 (1965), p. 20.

103 Cf. Paul VI, address given on Feb. 3, 1965.

104 Cf. St. Augustine, *De Bene coniugali PL* 40, 375-376 and 394; St. Thomas, *Summa Theologica*, Suppl. Quaest. 49, art. 3 ad 1; *Decretum pro Armenis:* Denz.-Schoen. 1327; Pius XI, Encyclical Letter *Casti Connubii: AAS* 22 (1930), pp. 547-548; Denz.-Schoen. 3703-3714.

105 Cf. Pius XI, Encyclical Letter *Casti Connubii: AAS* 22 (1930), pp. 546-547; Denz.-Schoen. 3706.

106 Cf. Osee 2; *Jer.* 3:6-13; *Ezech.* 16 and 23; *Is.* 54.

107 Cf. *Matt.* 9:15; *Mark* 2:19-20; *Luke* 5:34-35; *John* 3:29; cf. also 2 *Cor.* 11:2; *Eph.* 5:25.

108 Cf. *Eph.* 5:25.

109 Cf. Second Vatican Council, *Dogmatic Constitution on the Church: AAS* 57 (1965), pp. 15-16; 40-41; 47.

110 Pius XI, Encyclical Letter *Casti Connubii: AAS* 22 (1930), p. 583.

111 Cf. 1 *Tim.* 5:3.

112 Cf. *Eph.* 5:32.

113 Cf. *Gen.* 2:22-24; *Prov.* 5:18-20; 31: 10-31; *Tob.* 8:4-8; *Cant.* 1:2-3; 2:16; 4:16-5: 1; 7:8-11; 1 *Cor.* 7:3-6; *Eph.* 5:25-33.

114 Cf. Pius XI, Encyclical Letter *Casti Connubii: AAS* 22 (1930), p. 547 and 548; Denz.-Schoen. 3707.

115 Cf. 1 *Cor.* 7:5.

116 Cf. Pius XII, Address, *Tra le visite*, Jan. 20, 1958: *AAS* 50 (1958), p. 91.

117 Cf. Pius XI, Encyclical Letter *Casti Connubii: AAS* (1930): Denz-Schoen. 3716-3718; Pius XII, *Allocutio Conventui Unionis Italicae inter Obstetrices*, Oct. 29, 1951: *AAS* 43 (1951), pp. 835-854; Paul VI, address to a group of cardinals, June 23, 1964: *AAS* 56 (1964), pp. 581-589. Certain questions which need further and more careful investigation have been handed over, at the command of the Supreme Pontiff, to a commission for the study of population, family, and births, in order that, after it fulfills its function, the Supreme Pontiff may pass judgment. Since the doctrine of the magisterium is such, this holy Synod does not intend to propose immediately concrete solutions.

118 Cf. *Eph.* 5:16; *Col.* 4:5.

119 Cf. *Sacramentarium Gregorianum: PL* 78, 262.

120 Cf. *Rom.* 5:15 and 18; 6:5-11; *Gal.* 2:20.

121 Cf. *Eph.* 5:25-27.

122 Cf. Introductory statement of this constitution, n. 4 ff.

123 Cf. *Col.* 3:1-2.

124 Cf. *Gen.* 1:28.

125 Cf. *Prov.* 8:30-31.

126 Cf. St. Irenaeus, *Adversus haereses*, III, 11, 8 (ed. Sagnard, p. 200; cf. *ibid.*, 16, 6: pp. 290-291; 21, 10-22: pp. 370-372; 22, 3: p. 378; etc.).

127 Cf. *Eph.* 1:10.

128 Cf. the words of Pius XI to Father M.D. Roland-Gosselin: "It is necessary never to lose sight of the fact that the objective of the Church is to evangelize, not to civilize. If it civilizes, it is for the sake of evangelization." (Semaines sociales de France, Versailles, 1936, pp. 461-462).

129 First Vatican Council, *Constitution on the Catholic Faith:* Denzinger 1795, 1799 (3015, 3019). Cf. Pius XI, Encyclical Letter *Quadragesimo Anno: AAS* 23 (1931), p. 190.

130 Cf. John XXIII, Encyclical Letter *Pacem in Terris: AAS* 55 (1963), p. 260.

131 Cf. John XXIII, Encyclical Letter *Pacem in Terris: AAS* 55 (1963), p. 283; Pius XII, radio address, Dec. 24, 1941: *AAS* 34 (1942), pp. 16-17.

132 John XXIII, Encyclical Letter *Pacem in Terris: AAS* 55 (1963), p. 260.

133 Cf. John XXIII, prayer delivered on Oct. 11, 1962, at the beginning of the Council: *AAS* 54 (1962), p. 792.

134 Cf. *Constitution on the Sacred Liturgy*, n. 123: *AAS* 56 (1964), p. 131; Paul VI, discourse to the artists of Rome: *AAS* 56 (1964), pp. 439-442.

135 Cf. Second Vatican Council, *Decree on Priestly Training and Declaration on Christian Education.*

136 Cf. *Dogmatic Constitution on the Church*, Chapter IV, n. 37: *AAS* 57 (1965), pp. 42-43.

137 Cf. Pius XII, address on March 23, 1952: *AAS* 44 (1953), p. 273; John XXIII, allocution to the Catholic Association of Italian Workers, May 1, 1959: *AAS* 51 (1959), p. 358.

138 Cf. Pius XI, Encyclical Letter *Quadragesimo Anno: AAS* 23 (1931), p. 190 ff. Pius XII, address of March 23, 1952: *AAS* 44 (1952),

p. 276 ff; John XXIII, Encyclical Letter *Mater et Magistra: AAS* 53 (1961), p. 450; Vatican Council II, *Decree on the Media of Social Communication*, Chapter I, n. 6: *AAS* 56 (1964), p. 147.

139 Cf. *Matt.* 16:26; *Luke* 16:1-31; *Col.* 3:17.

140 Cf. Leo XIII, Encyclical Letter *Libertas*, in *Acta Leonis* XIII, t. VIII, p. 220 ff; Pius XI, Encyclical Letter *Quadragesimo Anno: AAS* 23 (1931), p. 191 ff; Pius XI, Encyclical Letter *Divini Redemptoris: AAS* 39 (1937), p. 65 ff; Pius XII, *Nuntius natalicius* 1941: *AAS* 34 (1942), p. 10 ff; John XXIII, Encyclical Letter *Mater et Magistra: AAS* 53 (1961), pp. 401-464.

141 In reference to agricultural problems cf. especially John XXIII, Encyclical Letter *Mater et Magistra: AAS* 53 (1961), p. 341 ff.

142 Cf. Leo XIII, Encyclical Letter *Rerum Novarum: AAS* 23 (1890-91), p. 649, p. 662; Pius XI, Encyclical Letter *Quadragesimo Anno: AAS* 23 (1931), pp. 200-201; Pius XI, Encyclical Letter *Divini Redemptoris: AAS* 29 (1937), p. 92; Pius XII, radio address on Christmas Eve, 1942: *AAS* 35 (1943), p. 20; Pius XII, allocution of June 13, 1943: *AAS* 35 (1943), p. 172; Pius XII, radio address to the workers of Spain, March 11, 1951: *AAS* 43 (1951), p. 215; John XXIII, Encyclical Letter *Mater et Magistra: AAS* 53 (1961), p. 419.

143 Cf. John XXIII, Encyclical Letter *Mater et Magistra: AAS* 53 (1961), pp. 408, 424, 427; however, the word "curatione" has been taken from the Latin text of the Encyclical Letter *Quadragesimo Anno: AAS* 23 (1931), p. 199. Under the aspect of the evolution of the question cf. also: Pius XII, allocution of June 3, 1950: *AAS* 42 (1950), pp. 485-488: Paul VI, allocution of June 8, 1964: *AAS* 56 (1964), pp. 574-579.

144 Cf. Pius XII, Encyclical *Sertum Laetitiae: AAS* 31 (1939), p. 642; John XXIII, consistorial allocution: *AAS* 52 (1960), pp. 5-11; John XXIII, Encyclical Letter *Mater et Magistra: AAS* 53 (1961), p. 411.

145 Cf. St. Thomas, *Summa Theologica*: II-II, 1. 32, a. 5 ad 2; *Ibid.* q. 66, a. 2: cf. explanation in Leo XIII, Encyclical Letter *Rerum Novarum: AAS* 23 (1890-91) p. 651; cf. Also Pius XII, allocution of June 1, 1941: *AAS* 33 (1941), p. 199; Pius XII, birthday radio address 1954: *AAS* 47 (1955), p. 27.

146 Cf. St. Basil, *Hom. in illud Lucae "Destruam horrea mea,"* n. 2 (*PG* 31, 263); Lactantius, *Divinarum institutionum*, lib. V. on justice (*PL* 6, 565 B); St. Augustine, *In Ioann. Ev.* tr. 50, n. 6 (*PL* 35, 1760); St. Augustine, *Enarratio in Ps.* CXLVII, 12 (*PL* 37, 192); St. Gregory the Great, *Homiliae in Ev.*, hom. 20 (*PL* 76, 1165); St. Gregory the Great, *Regulae Pastoralis liber*, pars III, c. 21 (*PL* 77, 87); St. Bonaventure, *IN III Sent.* d. 33, dub. 1 (ed Quaracchi, III, 728); St.

Bonaventure, *In IV Sent.* d. 15, p. II, a.2 q.1 (ed. cit. IV, 371 b); q. de superfluo (ms. Assisi, Bibl. Comun. 186, ff. 112-aa3); St. Albert the Great, *In III Sent.*, d. 33, a.3, sol. 1 (ed. Borgnet XXVIII, 611); Id. *In IV Sent.* d. 15, a. 16 (ed. cit. XXIX, 494-497). As for the determination of what is superfluous in our day and age, cf. John XXIII, radio-television message of Sept. 11, 1962: *AAS* 54 (1962) p. 682: "The obligation of every man, the urgent obligation of the Christian man, is to reckon what is superfluous by the measure of the needs of others, and to see to it that the administration and the distribution of created goods serve the common good."

147 In that case, the old principle holds true: "In extreme necessity all goods are common, that is, all goods are to be shared." On the other hand, for the order, extension, and manner by which the principle is applied in the proposed text, besides the modern authors: cf. St. Thomas, *Summa Theologica* II-II, q. 66, 1. 7. Obviously, for the correct application of the principle, all the conditions that are morally required must be met.

148 Cf. Gratian, *Decretum*, C. 21, dist. LXXXVI (ed. Friedberg I, 302). This axiom is also found already in *PL* 54, 591 A (cf. in Antonianum 27 (1952) 349-366).

149 Cf. Leo XIII, Encyclical Letter *Rerum Novarum: AAS* 23 (1890-91), pp. 643-646; Pius XI, Encyclical Letter *Quadragesimo Anno: AAS* 23 (1931), p. 191; Pius XII, radio message of June 1, 1941: *AAS* 33 (1941), p. 199; Pius XII, radio message on Christmas Eve 1942: *AAS* 35 (1943), p. 17; Pius XII, radio message of Sept. 1, 1944: *AAS* 36 (1944), p. 253; John XXIII, Encyclical Letter *Mater et Magistra: AAS* 53 (1961), pp. 428-429.

150 Cf. Pius XI, Encyclical Letter *Quadragesimo Anno: AAS* 23 (1931), p. 214; John XXIII, Encyclical Letter *Mater et Magistra: AAS* 53 (1961), p. 429.

151 Cf. Pius XII, radio message of Pentecost 1941: *AAS* 44 (1941), p. 199; John XXIII, Encyclical Letter *Mater et Magistra: AAS* 53 (1961), p. 430.

152 For the right use of goods according to the doctrine of the New Testament, cf. *Luke* 3:11; 10:30 ff; 11:41; 1 *Pet.* 4:3; *Mark* 8:36; 12: 39-41; *Jas.* 5:1-6; 1 *Tim.* 6:8; *Eph.* 4:28; 2 *Cor.* 8:13; 1 *John* 3:17 ff.

153 Cf. John XXIII, Encyclical Letter *Mater et Magistra: AAS* 53 (1961), p. 417.

154 Cf. John XXIII, *ibid.*

155 Cf. *Rom.* 13:1-5.

156 Cf. *Rom.* 13:5.

157 Cf. Pius XII, radio message, Dec. 24,1942: *AAS* 35 (1943), pp. 9-24; Dec. 24, 1944: *AAS* 37 (1945), pp. 11-17; John XXIII, Encyclical Letter *Pacem in Terris: AAS* 55 (1963), pp. 263, 271, 277 and 278.

158 Cf. Pius XII, radio message of June 7, 1941: *AAS* 33 (1941), p. 200; John XXIII, Encyclical Letter *Pacem in Terris*: 1.c., p. 273 and 274.

159 Cf. John XXIII, Encyclical Letter *Mater et Magistra: AAS* 53 (1961), p. 416.

160 Pius XI, allocution "Ai dirigenti della Federazione Universitaria Cattolica". *Discorsi di Pio XI* (ed. Bertetto), Turin, vol. 1 (1960), p. 743.

161 Cf. Second Vatican Council, *Dogmatic Constitution on the Church*, n. 13: *AAS* 57 (1965), p. 17.

162 Cf. *Luke* 2:14.

163 *Eph.* 2:16; *Col.* 1:20-22.

164 Cf. John XIII, Encyclical Letter *Pacem in Terris*, April 11, 1963: *AAS* 55 (1963), p. 291: "Therefore in this age of ours which prides itself on its atomic power, it is irrational to believe that war is still an apt means of vindicating violated rights."

165 Cf. Pius XII, allocution of Sept. 30, 1954: *AAS* 46 (1954), p. 589; radio message of Dec. 24, 1954: *AAS* 47 (1955), pp. 15 ff; John XXIII, Encyclical Letter *Pacem in Terris: AAS* 55 (1963), pp. 286-291; Paul VI, allocution to the United Nations, Oct. 4, 1965.

166 Cf. John XXIII, Encyclical Letter *Pacem in Terris*, where reduction of arms is mentioned: *AAS* (1963), p. 287.

167 Cf. 2 *Cor.* 2:6.

168 Cf. *Matt.* 7:21.

Address of Pope Paul VI to the United Nations General Assembly, October 4, 1965.

1 *Is.* 2, 4.

2 *Eph.* 4, 23.

POPULORUM PROGRESSIO, Encyclical Letter of Pope Paul VI on the Development of Peoples, March 26, 1967.

1 Cf. *Acta Leonis* XIII, t, XI (1892), pp. 97-148.

2 Cf. *AAS* 23 (1931), pp. 177-228.

3 Cf. *AAS* 53 (1961), pp. 401-64.

4 Cf. *AAS* 55 (1963), pp. 257-304.

5 Cf. in particular the Radio Message of June 1, 1941, for the 50th anniversary of *Rerum Novarum,* in *AAS* 33 (1941), pp. 195-205; Christmas Radio Message of 1942, in *AAS* 35 (1943), pp. 9-24; Address to a group of workers on the anniversary of *Rerum Novarum,* May 14, 1953, in *AAS* 45 (1953), pp. 402-8.

6 Cf. Encyclical *Mater et Magistra,* May 15, 1961: *AAS* 53 (1961), p. 440.

7 *Gaudium et Spes,* nn. 63-72: *AAS* 58 (1966), pp. 1084-94.

8 Mout Proprio *Catholicam Christi Ecclesiam,* Jan. 6, 1967, *AAS* 59 (1967), p. 27.

9 Encyclical *Rerum Novarum,* May 15, 1891: *Acta Leonis* XIII, t. XI (1892), p. 98.

10 *Gaudium et Spes,* n. 63, § 3.

11 Cf. *Lk* 7: 22.

12 *Gaudium et Spes,* n. 3, § 2.

13 Cf. Encyclical *Immortale Dei,* Nov. 1, 1885: *Acta Leonis* XIII, t. V (1885), p. 127.

14 *Gaudium et Spes,* n. 4, § 1.

15 L.-J. Lebret, O. P., *Dynamique concrète du développement* Paris: Economie et Humanisme, Les Editions Ouvrières, 1961, p. 28.

16 2 *Thes* 3: 10.

17 Cf., for example, J. Maritain, *Les conditions spirituelles du progrès et de la paix,* in *Rencontre des ccultures à l'UNESCO sous le signe du Concile oecumenique Vatican* II, Paris: Mame, 1966, p. 66.

18 Cf. *Mt* 5: 3.

19 *Gen* 1: 28.

20 *Gaudium et Spes,* n. 69, § 1.

21 1 *Jn* 3: 17.

22 *De Nabuthe,* c. 12, n. 53; (P. L. 14, 747), Cf. J.-R. Palanque, *Saint Ambroise et l'empire romain,* Paris: de Boccard, 1933, pp. 336 f.

23 Letter to the 52nd Session of the French Social Weeks (Brest, 1965), in *L'homme et la revolution urbaine,* Lyons, Chronique sociale, 1965, pp. 8 and 9. Cf. *L'Osservatore Romano,* July 10, 1965; *Documentation catholique,* t. 62, Paris, 1965, col. 1365.

24 *Gaudium et Spes,* n. 71, § 6.

25 Cf., *ibid.,* n. 65, § 3.

26 Encyclical *Quadragesimo Anno,* May 15, 1931, *AAS* 23 (1931), p. 212.

27 Cf., for example, Colin Clark, *The Conditions of Economic Progress,* 3rd ed., London: Macmillan and Co., and New York: St. Martin's Press. 1960, pp. 3-6.

28 Letter to the 51st Session of the French Social Weeks (Lyons, 1964), in *Le travail et les travailleurs dans la societè contemporaine,* Lyons, Chronique sociale, 1965, p. 6. Cf. *L'Osservatore Romano,* July 10, 1964; *Documentation catholique,* t. 61, Paris, 1964, col. 931.

29 Cf., for example, M.-D. Chenu, O. P., *Pour une theologie ud travail,* Paris: Editions due Seuil, 1955. Eng. tr.: *The Theology of Work: An Exploration,* Dublin: Gill and Son, 1963.

30 *Mater et Magistra, AAS* 53 (1961), n. 423.

31 Cf., for example, O. von Nell-Breuning, S. J., *Wirtschaft und Gesellschaft,* t. 1: *Grundfragen,* Freiburg: Herder, 1956, pp. 183-84.

32 *Eph* 4: 13.

33 Cf., for example, Bishop Manuel Larrain Errazuriz of Talca, Chile, President of CELAM, *Lettre pastorale sur le developpement et la paix.* Paris: Pax Christi, 1965.

34 *Gaudium et Spes,* n. 26, § 4.

35 *Mater et Magistra, AAS* 53 (1961), p. 414.

36 *L'Osservatore Romano,* Sept. 11, 1965; *Documentation catholique,* t. 62, Paris, 1965, col. 1674-75.

37 *Mt* 19: 16.

38 *Gaudium et Spes,* n. 52, § 2.

39 Cf. *ibid.,* n. 50-51 and note 14; and n. 87, §§ 2 and 3.

40 *Ibid.,* n. 15, § 3.

41 *Mt* 16: 26.

42 *Gaudium et Spes,* n. 57, § 4.

43 *Ibid..* n. 19, § 2.

44 Cf., for example, J. Maritain, *L'humanisme intégral,* Paris: Aubier, 1936. Eng. tr.: *True Humanism,* London: Geoffrey Bles, and New York: Charles Scribner's Sons, 1938.

45 H. de Lubac, S. J., *Le drame de l'humanisme athée,* 3rd ed., Paris, Spes, 1945, p. 10. Eng. tr. *The Drama of Atheistic Humanism,* London: Sheed and Ward, 1949, p. VII.

46 *Pensées,* éd. Brunschivicg, n. 434. Cf. M. Zundel, *L'homme passe l'homme,* Le Caire, Editions du lien, 1944.

47 Address to the Representatives of non-Christian Religions, Dec. 3, 1964, *AAS* 57 (1965), p. 132.

48 *Ja* 2: 15-16.

49 Cf. *Mater et Magistra, AAS* 53 (1961), pp. 440 f.

50 Cf. *AAS* 56 (1964), pp. 57-58.

51 Cf. *Encicliche e Discorsi di Paolo* VI, vol. IX, Roma, ed. Paoline, 1966, pp. 132-36, *Documentation catholique,* t. 43, Paris, 1966 col. 403-6.

52 Cf. *Lk* 16: 19-31.

53 *Faudium et Spes,* n. 86, § 3.

54 *Lk* 12: 20.

55 Message to the world, entrusted to Journalists on Dec. 4, 1964. Cf. *AAS* 57 (1965), p. 135.

56 Cf. *AAS* 56 (1964), pp. 639 f.

57 Cf. *Acta Leonis* XIII, t. XI (1892), p. 131.

58 Cf. *ibid.,* p. 98.

59 *Gaudium et Spes,* n. 85, § 2.

60 Cf. Encyclical *Fidei Donum,* Apr. 21, 1957, *AAS* 49 (1957), p. 246.

61 *Mt* 25: 35-36.

62 *Mk* 8: 2.

63 Address of John XXIII upon Reception of the Balzan Prize for Peace, May 10, 1963, *AAS* 55 (1963), p. 455.

64 *AAS* 57 (1965), p. 896.

65 Cf. Encyclical *Pacem in terris,* Apr. 11, 1963, *AAS* 55 (1963), p. 301.

66 *AAS* 57 (1965), p. 880.

67 Cf. *Eph.* 4: 12; *Lumen Gentium,* n. 13.

68 Cf. *Apostolicam Actuositatem,* nn. 7, 13 and 24.

HUMANAE VITAE, Encyclical Letter of Pope Paul VI on the Regulation of Birth, July 25, 1968.

1 Cf. Pius IX, encyclical *Qui Pluribus,* Nov. 9, 1946; in PII IX P. M. Acta, l, pp. 9-10; St. Pius X, encyc. *Singulari Quadam,* Sept. 24, 1912; in *AAS* IV (1912), p. 658; Pius XI, encyc. *Casti Connubii,* Dec. 31, 1930; in *AAS* XXII (1930), pp. 579-581; Pius XII, allocution *Magnificate Dominum* to the episcopate of the Catholic world, Nov. 2, 1954; in *AAS* XLVI (1954), pp. 671-672; John XXIII, encyc. *Mater et Magistra,* May 15, 1961; in *AAS* LIII (1961), p. 457.

2 Cf. *Matt.* 28: 18-19.

3 Cf. *Matt.* 7: 21.

4 Cf. *Catechismus Romanus Concilii Tridentini,* part II, ch. VIII; Leo XIII, encyc. *Arcanum,* Feb. 19, 1880; in *Acta Leonis* XIII, II (1881), pp. 26-29, Pius XI, encyc. *Divini Illius Magistri,* Dec. 31, 1929, in *AAS* XXII (1930), pp. 58-61; encyc. *Casti Connubii,* in *AAS* XXII (1930), pp. 545-546; Pius XII, alloc. to the Italian medico-biological union of St. Luke, Nov. 12, 1944, in *Discorsi e Radiomessaggi,* VI, pp. 191-192; to the Italian Catholic union of midwives, Oct. 29, 1951, in *AAS* XLIII (1951), pp. 857-859; to the seventh Congress of the International Society of Haematology, Sept. 12, 1958 in *AAS* I. (1958), pp. 734-735; John XXIII, encyc. *Mater et Magistra,* in *AAS* LIII (1961), pp. 446-447; *Codex Iuris Canonici,* Canon 1067; Can. 1968, S 1, Can. 1066 S 1-2; Second Vatican Council, Pastoral constitution *Gaudium et Spes,* nos. 47-52.

5 Cf. Paul VI, allocution to the Sacred College, June 23, 1964, in *AAS* LVI (1964), p. 588; to the Commission for Study of Problems of Population, Family and Birth, March 27, 1965, in *AAS* LVII (1965), p. 388, to the National Congress of the Italian Society of Obstetrics and Gynaecology, Oct. 29, 1966, in *AAS* LVIII (1966), p. 1168.

6 Cf. *I John* 4: 8.

7 Cf. *Eph.* 3: 15.

8 Cf. II Vat. Council, Pastoral const. *Gaudium et Spes,* No. 50.

9 Cf. St. Thomas, *Summa Theologica,* I-II, q. 94, art. 2.

10 Cf. Pastoral Const. *Gaudium et Spes,* nos. 50, 51.

11 *Ibid.,* no. 49.

12 Cf. Pius XI, encyc. *Casti Connubii,* in *AAS* XXII (1930), p. 560; Pius XII, in *AAS* XLIII (1951), p. 843.

13 Cf. John XXIII, encyc. *Mater et Magistra,* in *AAS* LIII (1961), p. 447.

14 Cf. *Catechismus Romanus Concilii Tridentini,* part. II, Ch. VIII; Pius XI, encyc. *Casti Connubii,* in *AAS* XXII(1930), pp. 562-564; Pius XII, *Discorsi e Radiomessaggi,* VI (1944), pp. 191-192; *AAS* XLIII (1951), pp. 842-843; pp. 857-859; John XXIII, encyc. *Pacem in Terris,* Apr. 11, 1963, in *AAS* LV (1963), pp. 259-260; *Gaudium et Spes,* no. 51.

15 Cf. Pius XI, encyc. *Casti Connubii,* in *AAS* (1930) p. 565; decree of the Holy Office, Feb. 22, 1940, in *AAS* L (1958), pp. 734-735.

16 Cf. *Catechismus Romanus Concilii Tridentini,* part. II, Ch. VIII; Pius XI, encyc. *Casti Connubii,* in *AAS* XXII (1930), pp. 559-561; Pius XII, *AAS* XLIII (1951), p. 843; *AAS* L (1958), pp. 734-735; John XXIII, encyc. *Mater et Magistra,* in *AAS* LIII (1961), p. 447.

17 Cf. Pius XII, alloc. to the National Congress of the Union of Catholic Jurists, Dec. 6, 1953, in *AAS* XLV (1953), pp. 798-799.

18 Cf. *Rom.* 3: 8.

19 Cf. Pius XII, alloc. to Congress of the Italian Association of Urology, Oct. 8, 1953, in *AAS* XLV (1953), pp. 674-675; *AAS* L (1958) pp. 734-735.

20 Cf. Pius XII, *AAS* XLIII (1951), p. 846.

21 Cf. *AAS* XLV (1953), pp. 674-675; *AAS* XLVIII (1956), pp. 461-462.

22 Cf. *Luke* 2: 34.

23 Cf. Paul VI, encyc. *Populorum Progressio,* March 26, 1967, No. 21.

24 Cf. *Rom.* 8.

25 Cf. II Vatican Council, decree *Inter Mirifica,* On the Media of Social Communication, nos. 6-7.

26 Cf. encyc. *Mater et Magistra,* in *AAS* LIII (1961), p. 447.

27 Cf. encyc. *Populorum Progressio,* nos. 48-55.

28 Cf. Pastoral Const. *Gaudium et Spes,* no. 52.

29 Cf. *AAS* XLIII (1951), p. 859.

30 Cf. Pastoral Const. *Gaudium of Spes,* no. 51.

31 Cf. *Matt.* 11: 30.

32 Cf. Pastoral Const. *Gaudium et Spes,* no. 48; II Vatican Council, Dogmatic Const. *Lumen Gentium,* no. 35.

33 *Matt.* 7: 14; cf. *Heb.* 11-12.

34 Cf. *Tit.* 2: 12.

35 Cf. *I Cor.* 7: 31.

36 Cf. *Rom.* 5: 5.

37 *Eph.* 5: 25, 28-29, 32-33.

38 Cf. Dogmatic Const. *Lumen Gentium,* nos. 35 and 41; Pastoral Const. *Gaudium et Spes,* nos. 48-49; II Vatican Council, Decree *Apostolicam Actuositatem,* no. 11.

39 Cf. Dogmatic Const. *Lumen Gentium,* no. 25.

40 Cf. *I Cor.* 1: 10.

41 Cf. *John* 3: 17.

The Church and Human Rights, Pontifical Commission, December 10, 1974.

1 Paul VI, "Message to the UN on the 25th Anniversary of the Universal Declaration of Human Rights," 10 December 1973, *L'Osservatore Romano,* English edition, 20 December 1973, no. 51, p. 10; *AAS,* LXV (1973), 677.

2 Cf. *PT* 18. Even on the plane of fundamental human rights the case of anyone who enjoys a right but abuses it must be regarded as unlawful.

3 *PT* 12.

4 *PT* 13.

5 *PT* 18.

6 *Pacem in Terris* teaches: "Political communities are reciprocally subjects of rights and duties. The same moral law, which governs relations between individual human beings, serves also to regulate the relations of political communities with one another." *PT* 30.

7 Paul VI, Message to the UN on the 25th Anniversary of the Universal Declaration of Human Rights, *op. cit.,* p.3.

8 *Ibid.*

9 *Pacem in Terris,* 47; *AAS,* LV (1963), 295.

10 Cf. *GS* 43.

11 Cf. Pius VI, Letter *Quod Aliquantum* (10 March 1791); Encyclical *Adeo Nota* (23 April 1791); Pius VII, Apostolic Letter *Post Tam Diuturnas* (29 April 1814); Gregory XVI, Encyclical *Mirari Vos* (15

August 1832); Piux IX, Encyclicals *Nostis et Nobiscum* (8 December 1849) and *Quanta Cura* (8 December 1864).

12 Encyclical *Libertas,* 2; *Acta Leonis* XIII, VIII (1889), 213; *Acta Sanctae Sedis* V, XX (1887-8), 593-4.

13 *MM* 3; cf. Pius XI, *Quadragesimo Anno; AAS* XXIII (1931),189.

14 Paul VI, *OA* 1.

15 John XXIII, *Ai Coltivatori Diretti* (20 April 1961), *Discorsi, Messaggi, Colloqui del Santo Padre Giovanni XXIII* (Vatican City: Typis Polyglottis Vaticanis, 1962), III, 218.

16 In *Mater et Magistra MM* 3.

17 Cf. Pius Xi, *Divini Redemptoris,* 27-8; *AAS,* XXIX (1937), 78-79;

18 Pius XII, Christmas Broadcast 1942, no. 13, *AAS,* XXX (1943),19;

19 Cf. *AAS,* XXXVII (1945), 13 ff.

20 Cf. *AAS,* XXXIII (1941), 202-203.

21 Cf. Pius XII, Christmas Broadcast, 1944, no. 15; *AAS,* XXXVII (1945), 19 ff.; and Pius XII, Christmas Broadcast, 1941, no. 17; *AAS,* XXXIV (1942), 16-19.

22 Discourse to commemorate the 50th Anniversary of the Encyclical *Rerum Novarum,* 1 June 1941, *AAS,* XXXIII (1941), 200;

23 Cf. *Reflections by Cardinal Maurice Roy on the Occasion of the Tenth Anniversary of the Encylcial "Pacem in Terris" of Pope John XXIII, 11 April 1963-11 April 1973,* (Vatican City: Typis Poliglottis Vaticanis, 1973), *passim.*

24 Cf. *GS* 3.

25 *JW,* p. 6. Notice is drawn especially to the eight proposals at the end of the document which foster those initiatives and institutions which are working for peace, international justice, and the development of man, *op. cit.,* pp. 22-24.

26 "Human Rights and Reconciliation," Message of the 1974 Synod of Bishops, approved by show of hands on 23 October. Cf *L'Osservatore Romano,* English edition, 7 November 1974, no. 45, p. 2.

27 *Ibid.*

28 *Ibid.*

29 *GS* 44.

30 *Ibid.,* 43.

31 Cf. Pius XII, *passim;* Common Catholic doctrine; *GS* 26.

32 Cf. *PT* 3.

33 Cf. *OA* 14; *GS* 25; *MM* 58.

34 Cf. *PT* 31; *OA* 16; *GS* 29.

35 Cf. *PT* 18; *OA* 16; *GS* 29; *PP* 63.

36 Cf. *GS* 29; *OA* 16; "Council's Message to Women," 8 December 1965.

37 Cf. *GS* 29; Paul Vi, "Message to the UN on the 25th Anniversary of the Universal Declaration of Human Rights," *op. cit.*, p. 10; Declaration *Nostra Aetate*, 5.

38 Cf. *OA* 16; *GS* 26; *PT* 3.

39 Cf. *PT* 3; *GS* 26.

40 Cf. *PT* 4; *MM* 8, 10, 50; *GS* 26; "Message of 1974 Synod," *op. cit.*, p.2.

41 Cf. *GS* 26; *PT* 5.

42 Cf. *GS* 26.

43 Cf. Paul VI, "Address to Officers of the Italian National Press Federation," 23 June 1966, *Insegnamenti di Paolo VI* (Vatican City: Typis Polyglottis Vaticanis, 1966), IV, 312.

44 Cf. *PT* 6; *GS* 26; *DH* 2,3.

45 Cf. *PT* 5; *DH* 3.

46 Cf. *GS* 78, 79; cf. also *JW*, p. 22: "Let conscientious objection be recognized and regulated by law in each nation."

47 Cf. *PT* 5; *GS* 59, 73; *JW*, p. 18.

48 Cf. *PT* 5, 31; "Message of 1974 Synod," *op, cit.*, p. 2.

49 Cf. *PT* 6; *GS* 26, 73; *JW*, p. 11; "Message of 1974 Synod," *op, cit.* p. 2.

50 Cf. *PT* 11; Pius XII, Christmas Broadcast, 1942, *op. cit.*, no. 16.

51 Cf. *OA* 16.

52 Cf. *JW*, p. 18; *ibid.*, p. 11.

53 Cf. *PT* 12, 13; *OA* 24.

54 Cf. *PT* 9; *GS* 73; *CIC* nos. 682-725.

55 Cf. *PT* 9; *MM* 3.

56 Cf. *PT* 10; *OA* 17; *MM* 5.

57 Cf. Decree *Christus Dominus*, 18; *GS* 84.

58 Cf. *PT* 7; *GS* 26.

59 Cf. *OA* 18; *PT* 7.

60 Cf. *GS* 52; *MM* 50; "Message of 1974 Synod," *op. cit.*, p.2.

61 Cf. *JW*, p. 11; *GS* 26.

62 Cf. *OA* 13; *GS* 29; *JW*, p. 17

63 Cf. *JW*, p. 12.

64 Cf. *PT* 11; "Message of 1974 Synod," *op. cit.*, p.2.

65 Cf. *GS* 75, 68: *JW*, p. 18; *OA* 47; *MM* 16.

66 Cf. *OA* 14; *GS* 26, 67; *MM* 10.

67 Cf. *PT* 8.

68 Cf. *PT* 8.

69 Cf. *MM* 10, 66; *GS* 67.

70 Cf. *OA* 14; *GS* 67; Paul Vi, "Address of 1 May 1968," *AAS*, LX (1968), 330-331; *L'osservatore Romano*, English edition, 9 May 1968, no. 6, pp. 1,8; *MM* 11; *PT* 8; *Quadragesimo Anno*, *AAS*, XXIII (1931), 201-202.

71 Cf. *OA* 14; *GS* 68.

72 Cf. *GS* 69-71; *PP* 22-23; *PT* 8; *OA* 43; *MM* 3, 4, 18, 19, 20, 22.

73 Cf. *JW*, pp. 9,24; cf. also *PP* 43 *passim; GS* 9.

74 Cf. *OA* 16; "Message of 1974 Synod," *op. cit.*, p. 2.

75 Cf. *GS* 60; *PT* 5; *MM* 10.

76 Cf. Paul VI, "Message to the UN on the 25th Anniversary of the Universal Declaration of Human Rights," *op. cit.*, p. 3; *GS* 68; *MM* 11.

77 Cf. *PT* 33; *GS* 73.

78 Cf. Paul VI, "Address to the Uganda Parliament," *AAS*, LXI (1969), 582; *L'Osservatore Romano*, English edition, 7 August 1969, no. 32, pp. 1, 12; cf. *JW*, p. 10.

79 Paul VI, "Address to the General Audience on Wednesday, 4 September 1968," *Insegnamenti di Paolo VI*, (Vatican City: Typis Polyglottis Vaticanis, 1968), VI, 886-887; *L'Osservatore Romano*, English edition, 12 September, 1968, no. 24, p. 1.

80 *GS* 22.

81 *PT* 3.

82 *AAS*, XXXVII (1945), 15.

83 *GS* 41. The 1974 Synod in its Message on Human Rights says: "While the truths about human dignity and rights are accessible to all, it is in the Gospel that we find their fullest expression and our strongest

motive for commitment to their preservation and promotion," *op. cit.*, p. 2.

84 Paul VI, "Message to UN Secretary General," *AAS*, LXIV (1972), 215; *L'Osservatore Romano*, English edition, 17 February, 1972, no. 7, p. 5.

85 Paul VI, "Message to the UN on the 25th Anniversary of the Universal Declaration of Human Rights," *op. cit.*, p. 3.

86 *GS* 26.

87 *GS* 38.

88 *GS* 27; cf. also *GS* 47, 51, note 14.

89 *GS* 29.

90 *Ibid.*

91 *Ibid.*

92 Paul VI, "Message to the International Conference at Teheran on the 20th Anniversary of the Declaration on Human Rights: 15 April 1968," *AAS*, LX (1968), 284; *L'Osservatore Romano*, English edition, 2 May 1968, no. 5, p. 4.

93 *JW*, p. 15.

94 *GS* 76.

95 Cf. *Ep* 4: 23-24; *Jn* 3:5ff; *Tt* 3:5ff; cf. also *LG* 7; *GS* 37; Decree *Ad Gentes* 7, 15.

96 Cf. Declaration *Nostra Aetate*, 1; *GS* 92, 24, 45; cf. also "Message of 1974 Synod," *op. cit.*, p.2.

97 Cf. *GS* 15.

98 Cf. St. Thomas, I *Ethic*, Lect. 1; cf. also *GS* 24.

99 *"Creasti nos ad te, Domine, et inquietum est cor nostrum donec requiescat in te."* St. Augustine, *Confessiones* I, 1.

100 "In the design of God every man is called upon to develop and fulfil himself, for every life is a vocation." *PP* 15.

101 Cf. *GS* 26.

102 Paul VI, "Address to the Members of the International Congress on Canon Law," *L'Osservatore Romano*, English edition, 4 October 1973, no. 40, p. 2.

103 Cf. *GS* 38.

104 Cf. *Lk* 6:20-23.

105 *AA* 8.

106 *GS* 38.

107 *JW*, p. 14.

108 *GS* 42.

109 *PP* 47.

110 *JW*, p. 14.

111 Cf. *2P* 3:13.

112 *GS* 39.

113 Cf. Decree *Ad Gentes,* 5.

114 *JW*, pp. 17, 18.

115 "Message of 1974 Synod," *op. cit.*, p. 2.

116 Cf. *OA* 46.

117 Cf. *OA* 4.

118 "Letter of Cardinal J. Villot to the LX Session of the *Semaines sociales de France*" held at Lyons, 5-10 July 1973, *La Documentation Catholique,* 5-19 August 1973, no. 1637, p. 716; *L'Osservatore Romano,* English edition, 19 July 1973, no. 29, p. 4.

119 *OA* 4.

120 "Letter of Cardinal J. Villot," *op. cit.*, p. 4.

121 *OA* 46.

122 "Letter of Cardinal J. Villot," *op. cit.*, p. 4.

123 Cf. *OA* 50; cf. also *LG* 31; *AA* 5; *GS* 75.

124 *OA* 51.

125 Cf. *OA* 47; *GS* 68, 75; *MM* 16.

126 "Letter of Cardinal J. Villot," *op. cit.*, p. 4.

127 *GS* 76.

128 *OA* 4.

129 Decree *Ad Gentes,* 8.

130 Pontifical Commission Justice and Peace and the World Council of Churches, "Joint Statement on the 25th Anniversary of the Universal Declaration of Human Rights," *L'Osservatore Romano,* English edition, 20 December 1973, no. 51, p. 10.

131 *AA* 7; also cf. *GS* 43; *LG* 31-33; *AA* 29; *GS* 43.

132 1971 Synod of Bishops, *The Ministerial Priesthood* (Vatican City: Typis Polyglottis Vaticanis, 1971), p. 18.

133 Paul VI, "Address to the Diplomatic Corps, 10 January 1972," *AAS,* LXIV (1972), 55; *The Pope Speaks,* (1972), vol. 16, no. 4, p. 311.

134 Cf. *JW*, pp. 14-15.

135 "Address to the Diplomatic Corps," *op. cit.*, p. 309.

136 Paul VI, "Message to the UN on the 25th Anniversary of the Universal Declaration of Human Rights," *op. cit.*, p.3.

137 Cf. *JW*, p. 20.

138 Cf. *OA* 4; *JW*, p. 21.

139 "Message to the UN on the 25th Anniversary of Universal Declaration of Human Rights," *op. cit.*, p. 3.

140 *OA* 48.

141 Cf. *OA* 32-34; *MM* 13; also the "Message of the 1974 Synod," *op. cit.*, p. 2.

142 Paul VI, "Message to the UN on the 25th Anniversary of Universal Declaration of Human Rights," *op. cit.*, p. 3.

143 *JW*, p. 19.

144 *OA* 24.

145 Cf. *DH* 8.

146 Declaration on Christian Education, *Gravissimum Educationis*, 1.

147 Cf. *ibid.*, *passim.*

148 *GS* 82.

149 Cf. *GS* 89.

150 *OA* 24.

151 *PP* 15.

152 *Mater et Magistra; MM* 60.

153 *PP* 15; *GS* 35; cf. also *PP* 6.

154 *PP* 16.

155 *JW*, p. 21.

156 *Peace - The Desperate Imperative;* The Consultation on Christian Concern for Peace held at Baden, Austria, 3-9 April 1970 (Geneva, 1970), no 68, p. 67.

157 Cf. The Kyoto Conference, *Disarmament, Development, Human Rights*, (New Delhi, India, 1970), pp. 33-35.

158 Cf. *GS* 57.

159 Cf. Paul VI, "Message to the UN on the 25th Anniversary of the Universal Declaration of Human Rights," *op. cit.*, p. 10; also the "Joint Statement of the Pontifical Commission Justice and Peace and the World Council of Churches," *op. cit.*, p. 10.

160 "Message to the UN on its 25th Anniversary," *AAS*, LXII (1970), p. 686; *The Pope Speaks*, (1970), vol. 15, no. 3, p. 206.

161 Cf. *Acta of the General Assembly of Brazilian Bishops,* published 15 March 1973, Item 14. Cf. also the "Baden Consultation," *op. cit.*, n. 78, p. 69.

162 "Baden Consultation," *op. cit.*, no. 86, p. 72.

163 The Baden Consultation, *op. cit.*, no. 65, p. 65-66.

164 *Ibid*, no. 83, p. 71.

165 *OA* 37.

EVANGELII NUNTIANDI, Apostolic Exhortation of Pope Paul VI on Evangelization in the Modern World, December 8, 1975.

1 Cf. *Lk* 22:32.

2 2 *Cor* 11:28.

3 Cf. Second Vatican Ecumenical Council, Decree on the Church's Missionary Activity *Ad Gentes*, 1: *AAS* 58 (1966), p. 947.

4 Cf. *Eph* 4:24; 2:15; *Col* 3:10; *Gal* 3:27; *Rom* 13:14; 2 *Cor* 5:17.

5 2 *Cor* 5:20.

6 Cf. Paul VI, Address for the closing of the Third General Assembly of the Synod of Bishops (October 26, 1974): *AAS* 66 (1974), pp. 634-635; 637.

7 Paul VI, Address to the College of Cardinals (June 22, 1973): *AAS* 65 (1973), p. 383.

8 2 *Cor* 11:28.

9 1 *Tim* 5:17.

10 2 *Tim* 2:15.

11 Cf. 1 *Cor* 2:5.

12 *Lk* 4:43.

13 *Ibid.*

14 *Lk* 4:18; cf. *Is* 61;1.

15 Cf. *Mk* 1:1; *Rom* 1:1-3.

16 Cf. *Mt* 6:33.

17 Cf. *Mt* 5:3-12.

18 Cf. *Mt* 5-7.

19 Cf. *Mt* 10.

20 Cf. *Mt* 13.

21 Cf. *Mt* 18.

22 Cf. *Mt* 24-25.

23 Cf. *Mt* 24:36; *Acts* 1:7; 1 *Thess* 5:1-2.

24 Cf. *Mt* 11:12; *Lk* 16;16.

25 Cf. *Mt* 4:17.

26 *Mk* 1:27.

27 *Lk* 4:22.

28 *Jn* 7:46.

29 *Lk* 4:43.

30 *Jn* 11:52.

31 Cf. Second Vatican Ecumenical Council, Dogmatic Constitution on Divine Revelation *Dei Verbum*, 4: *AAS* 58 (1966), pp. 818-819.

32 1 *Pt* 2:9.

33 Cf. *Acts* 2:11.

34 *Lk* 4:43.

35 1 *Cor* 9:16.

36 "Declaration of the Synod Fathers," 4: *L'Osservatore Romano* (October 27, 1974), p. 6.

37 *Mt* 28:19.

38 *Acts* 2:41, 47.

39 Cf. Second Vatican Ecumenical Council, Dogmatic Constitution on the Church *Lumen Gentium*, 8: *AAS* 57 (1965), p. 11; Decree on the Church's Missionary Activity *Ad Gentes*, 5: *AAS* 58 (1966), pp. 951-952.

40 Cf. *Acts* 2:42-46; 4:32-35; 5:12-16.

41 Cf. *Acts* 2:11; 1 *Pt* 2:9.

42 Cf. Decree on the Church's Missionary Activity *Ad Gentes*, 5, 11-12: *AAS* 58 (1966), pp. 951-952, 959-961.

43 Cf. 2 *Cor* 4:5; Saint Augustine, *Sermo XLVI, De Pastoribus: CCL XLI*, pp. 529-530.

44 *Lk* 10:16; cf. Saint Cyprian, *De Unitate Ecclesiae*, 14: *PL* 4, 527; Saint Augustine, *Enarrat.* 88, *Sermo*, 2, 14: *PL* 37, 1140: Saint John Chrysostom, Hom. *de capto Eutropio*, 6: *PG* 52, 402.

45 *Eph* 5:25.

46 *Rev* 21:5, cf. 2 *Cor* 5:17; *Gal* 6:15.

47 Cf. *Rom* 6:4.

48 Cf. *Eph* 4:23-24; *Col* 3:9-10.

49 Cf. *Rom* 1:16; 1 *Cor* 1:18, 2:4.

50 Cf. 53: *AAS* 58 (1966), p. 1075.

51 Cf. Tertullian *Apologeticum,* 39: *CCL,* 1, pp. 150-153; Minucius *Felix, Octavius* 9 and 31: *CSLP,* Turin 1963[2], pp. 11-13, 47-48.

52 1 *Pt* 3:15.

53 Cf. Second Vatican Ecumenical Council, Dogmatic Constitution on the Church *Lumen Gentium,* 1, 9. 48: *AAS* 57 (1965), pp. 5, 12-14, 53-54; Pastoral Constitution on the Church in the Modern World *Gaudium et Spes,* 42, 45: *AAS* 58 (1966), pp. 1060-1061, 1065-1066; Decree on the Church's Missionary Activity *Ad Gentes,* 1, 5: *AAS* 58 (1966), pp. 947, 951-952.

54 Cf. *Rom* 1:16; 1 *Cor* 1:18.

55 Cf. *Acts* 17:22-23.

56 1 *Jn* 3:1; cf. *Rom* 8:14-17.

57 Cf. *Eph* 2:8; *Rom* 1:16. Cf. Sacred Congreagtion for the Doctrine of the Faith, *Declaratio ad fidem tuendam in mysteria Incarnationis et SS. Trinitatis e quibusdam recentibus erroribus* (February 21, 1972): *AAS* 64 (1972), pp. 237-241.

58 Cf. 1 *Jn* 3:2; *Rom* 8:29; *Phil* 3:20-21. Cf. Second Vatican Ecumenical Council, Dogmatic Constitution on the Church *Lumen Gentium,* 48-51: *AAS* 57 (1965), pp. 53-58.

59 Cf. Sacred Congregation for the Doctrine of the Faith, *Declaratio circa Catholicam Doctrinam de Ecclesia contra non-nullos errores hodiernos tuendam* (June 24, 1973): *AAS* 65 (1973), pp. 396-408.

60 Cf. Second Vatican Ecumenical Council, Pastoral Constitution on the Church in the Modern World *Gaudium et Spes,* 47-52: *AAS* 58 (1966), pp. 1067-1074; Paul VI, Encylcical Letter (Humanae Vitae: *AAS* 60 (1968), pp. 481-503.

61 Paul VI, Address for the opening of the Third General Assembly of the Synod of Bishops (September 27, 1974): *AAS* 66 (1974), p. 562.

62 *Ibid.*

63 Paul VI, Address to the *Campesinos* of Columbia (August 23, 1968): *AAS* 60 (1968), p. 623.

64 Paul VI, Address for the "Day of Development" at Bogotá (August 23, 1968): *AAS* 60 (1968), p. 627; cf. Saint Augustine, *Epistola* 229, 2: *PL* 33, 1020.

65 Paul VI, Address for the closing of the Third General Assembly of the Synod of Bishops (October 26, 1974): *AAS* 66 (1974), p. 637.

66 Address given on October 15, 1975: *L'Osservatore Romano* (October 17, 1975).

67 Pope Paul VI, Address to the Members of the *Consilium de Laicis* (October 2, 1974): *AAS* 66 (1974), p. 568.

68 Cf. 1 *Pt* 3:1.

69 *Rom* 10:14, 17.

70 Cf. 1 *Cor* 2:1-5.

71 *Rom* 10:17.

72 Cf. *Mt* 10:27; *Lk* 12:3.

73 *Mk* 16:15.

74 Cf. Saint Justin, 1 *Apol.* 46, 1-4: *PG* 6, 11 *Apol.* 7 (8) 1-4; 10, 1-3; 13, 3-4; *Florilegium Patristicum* II, Bonn 1911[2], pp. 81, 125, 129, 133; Clement of Alexandria, *Stromata* 1, 19, 91;94: *S. Ch.* pp. 117-118; 119-120; Second Vatican Ecumenical Council, Decree on the Church's Missionary Activity *Ad Gentes,* 11: *AAS* 58 (1966), p. 960; cf. Dogmatic Constitution on the Church *Lumen Gentium,* 17: *AAS* 57 (1965), p. 20.

75 Eusebius of Caesarea, *Praeparatio Evangelica* I, 1: *PG* 21, 26-28; cf. Second Vatican Ecumenical Council, Dogmatic Constitution on the Church *Lumen Gentium,* 16: *AAS* 57 (1965), p. 21.

76 Cf. *Eph* 3:8.

77 Cf. Henri de Lubac, *Le drame de l'humanisme athee,* ed. *Spes, Paris,* 1945.

78 Cf. Pastoral Constitution on the Church in the Modern World *Gaudium et Spes,* 59: *AAS* 58 (1966), p. 1080.

79 1 *Tim* 2:4.

80 *Mt* 9:36; 15:32.

81 *Rom* 10:15.

82 Declaration on Religious Liberty *Dignitatis Humanae,* 13: *AAS* 58 (1966), p. 939; cf. Dogmatic Constitution on the Church *Lumen Gentium,* 5: *AAS* 57 (1965), pp. 7-8; Decree on the Church's Missionary Activity *Ad Gentes,* 1: *AAS* 58 (1966), p. 947.

83 Decree on the Church's Missionary Activity *Ad Gentes,* 35: *AAS* 58 (1966), p. 983.

84 Saint Augustine, *Enarratio in Ps* 44:23 *CCL* XXXVIII, p. 510; cf. Decree on the Church's Missionary Activity *Ad Gentes,* 1: *AAS* 58 (1966), p. 947.

85 Saint Gregory the Great, *Homil. in Evangelia* 19, 1: *PL* 76, 1154.

86 *Acta* 1:8; cf. *Didache* 9, 1: Funk, *Patres Apostolici,* 1, 22.

87 *Mt* 28:20.

88 Cf. *Mt* 13:32.

89 Cf. *Mt* 13:47.

90 Cf. *Jn* 21:11.

91 Cf. *Jn* 10:1-16.

92 Cf. Second Vatican Ecumenical Council. Constitution on the Sacred Liturgy *Sacrosanctum Concilium,* 37-38: *AAS* 56 (1964), p. 110; cf. also the liturgical books and other documents subsequently issued by the Holy See for the putting into practice of the liturgical reform desired by the same Council.

93 Paul VI, Address for the closing of the Third General Assembly of the Synod of Bishops (October 26, 1974); *AAS* 66 (1974), p. 636.

94 Cf. *Jn* 15:16; *Mk* 3:13-19; *Lk* 6:13-16.

95 Cf. *Acts* 1:21-22.

96 Cf. *Mk* 3:14.

97 Cf. *Mk* 3:14-15; *Lk* 9:2.

98 *Acts* 4:8; cf. 2–14; 3:12.

99 Cf. St Leo the Great, *Sermo* 69, 3; *Sermo* 70, 1-3; *Sermo* 94, 3; *Sermo* 95, 2: *S.C.* 200, pp. 50-52; 58-66; 258-260; 268.

100 Cf. First Ecumenical Council of Lyons, Constitution *Ad apostolicae dignitatis: Concioliorum Oecumenicorum Decreta, ed. Istituto per le Scienze Religiose,* Bologna 1973[3], p. 278; Ecumenical Council of Vienne, Constitution *Ad providam Christi, ed. cit.,* p. 343; Fifth Lateran Ecumenical Council, Constitution *In apostolici culminis, ed. cit.,* p. 608; Constitution *Postquam ad universalis, ed. cit.,* p. 609; Constitution *Supernae dispositionis, ed. cit.,* p. 614; Constitution *Divina disponente clementia, ed. cit.,* p. 638.

101 Decree on the Church's Missionary Activity *Ad Gentes,* 38: *AAS* 58 (1966), p. 985.

102 Cf. Second Vatican Ecumenical Council, Dogmatic Constitution on the Church *Lumen Gentium,* 22: *AAS* 57 (1965), p. 26.

103 Cf. Second Vatican Ecumenical Council, Dogmatic Constitution on the Church *Lumen Gentium,* 10, 37: *AAS* 57 (1965), pp. 14-43; Decree on the Church's Missionary Activity *Ad Gentes,* 39: *AAS* 58 (1966), p. 986; Decree on the Ministry and Life of Priests *Presbyterorum Ordinis,* 2, 12, 13: *AAS* 58 (1966), pp. 992, 1010, 1011.

104 Cf. 1 *Thess* 2:9.

105 Cf. 1 *Pt* 5:4.

106 Dogmatic Constitution on the Church *Lumen Gentium*, 11: *AAS* 57 (1965), p. 16; Decree on the Apostolate of the Laith *Apostolicam Actuositatem*, 11: *AAS* 58 (1966), p. 848; Saint John Chrysostom, *In Genesim Serm.* VI, 2; VII, 1: *PG* 54, 607-68.

107 *Mt* 3:17.

108 *Mt* 4:1.

109 *Lk* 4:14.

110 *Lk* 4:18, 21; cf. *Is* 61:1.

111 *Jn* 20:22.

112 *Acts* 2:17.

113 Cf. *Acts* 4:8.

114 Cf. *Acts* 9:17.

115 Cf. *Acts* 6:5, 10; 7:55.

116 *Acts* 10:44.

117 *Acts* 9:31.

118 Cf. Second Vatican Ecumenical Council, Decree on the Church's Missionary Activity *Ad Gentes*, 4: *AAS* 58 (1966), pp. 950-951.

119 *Jn* 17:21.

120 Cf. *Acts* 20:28.

121 Cf. Decree on the Ministry and Life of Priests *Presbyterorum Ordinis*, 13: *AAS* 58 (1966), p. 1011.

122 Cf. *Heb.* 11:27.

123 Decree on the Church's Missionary Activity *Ad Gentes*, 6: *AAS* 58 (1966), pp. 954-955; cf. Decree on Ecumenism *Unitatis Redintegratio*, 1: *AAS* 57 (1965), pp. 90-91.

124 Bull *Apostolorum Limina*, VII: *AAS* 66 (1974), p. 305.

125 *Rom* 5:5.

126 Cf. *Jn* 8:32.

127 1 *Thess* 2:8; cf. *Phil* 1:8.

128 Cf. 1 *Thess* 2:7-11; 1 *Cor* 4:15; *Gal* 4:19.

129 Cf. 1 *Cor* 8:9-13; *Rom* 14:15.

130 Cf. *Rom* 12:11.

131 Cf. Second Vatican Ecumenical Council, Declaration on Religious Liberty *Dignitatis Humanae*, 4: *AAS* 58 (1966), p. 933.

132 Cf. *Ibid.*, 9-14: *loc. cit.*, pp. 935-940.

133 Cf. Second Vatican Ecumenical Council, Decree on the Church's Missionary Activity *Ad Gentes,* 7: *AAS* 58 (1966), p. 955.

134 Cf. *Rom* 1:16.

135 *Phil* 1:3-4, 7-8.

Address of Pope Paul VI to the Congregation of the Italian Women's Center, December 6, 1976.

1 *Pastoral Constitution on the Church in the World of Today,* no. 9.

2 *Acts* 1, 14.

3 See *Lk.* 8, 2-3.

4 *Mt.* 28, 1-10; *Mk.* 16, 1-8; *Lk.* 24, 1-11. 22-23; *Jn.* 20, 1-2. 11-18.

5 *Acts* 1, 14.

6 *Rom.* 16. 1-2. 12; *Phil.* 4, 2-3; *Col.* 4, 15; see *1 Cor* 11, 5a; *1 Tim.* 5, 16.

7 *Eph.* 5, 25.

8 *Pastoral Constitution on the Church in the World of Today,* no. 60.

9 See *Gn.* 1, 26-27.

Message of Pope Paul VI for World Peace Day, 1977, December 8, 1976.

1 See *Apoc.* 3, 20.

2 Encyclical Letter *Pacem in Terris* (April 11, 1963): *AAS* 55 (1963) 266 [*TPS* IX, 201].

3 *Vita Agricolae*, 30.

4 See *Lk.* 14, 31.

5 *Phil.* 4, 9.

6 *Jn.* 12, 25.

7 See *Mt.* 19, 29.

8 See *Mt.* 19, 11.

9 *Eph.* 2, 14.

3 1543 50000 1971